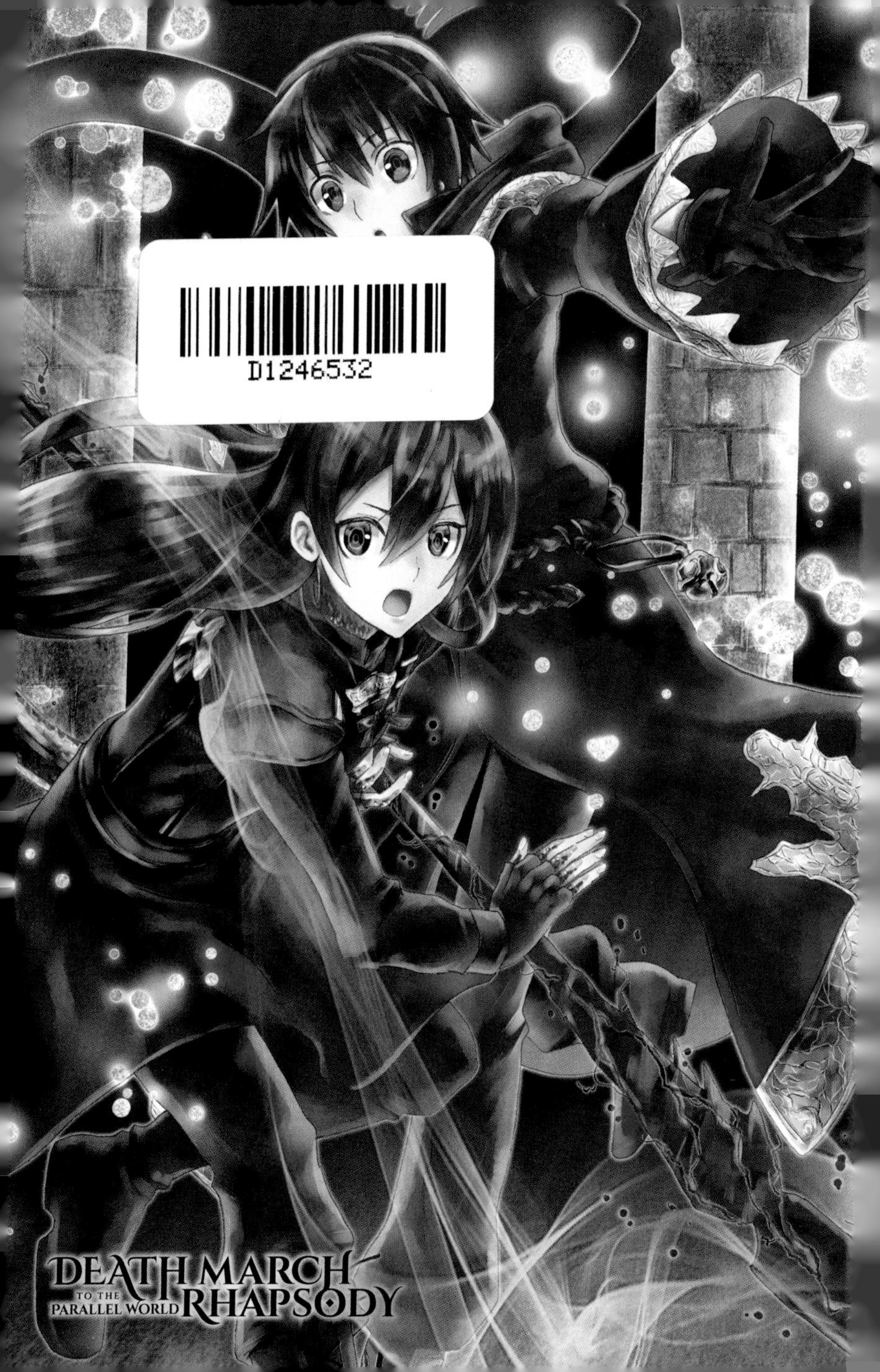
DEATH MARCH
TO THE PARALLEL WORLD
RHAPSODY

CONTENTS

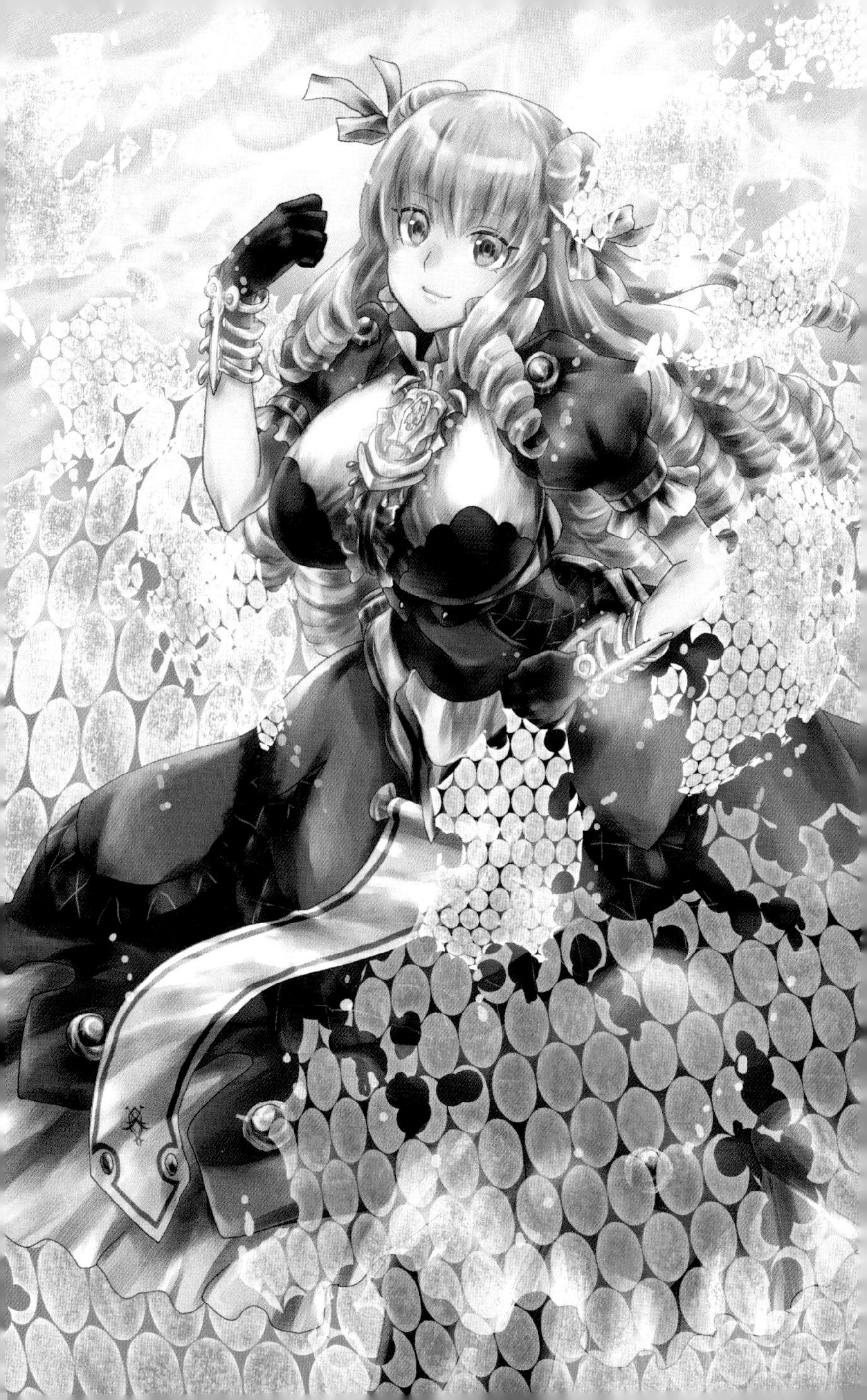

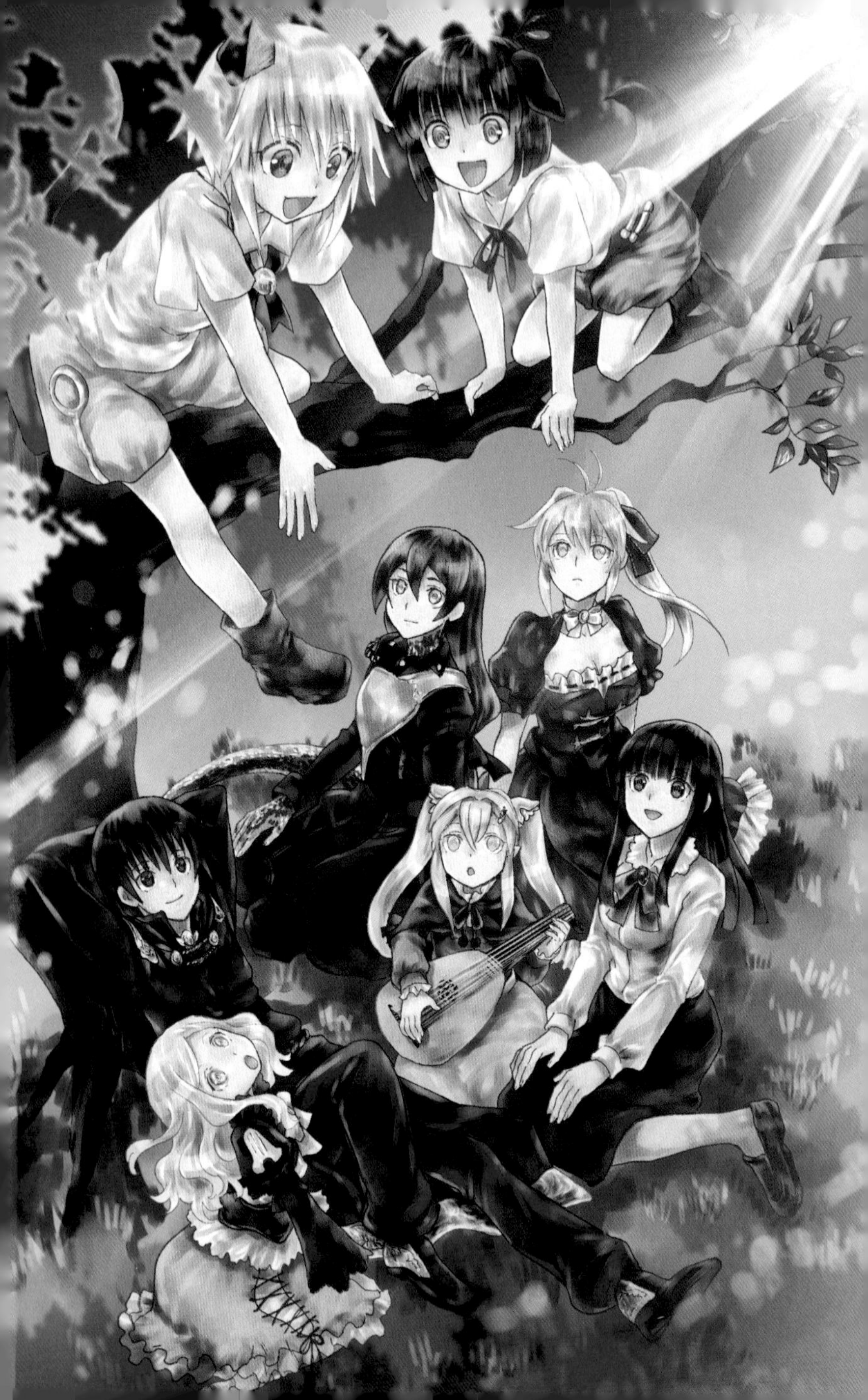

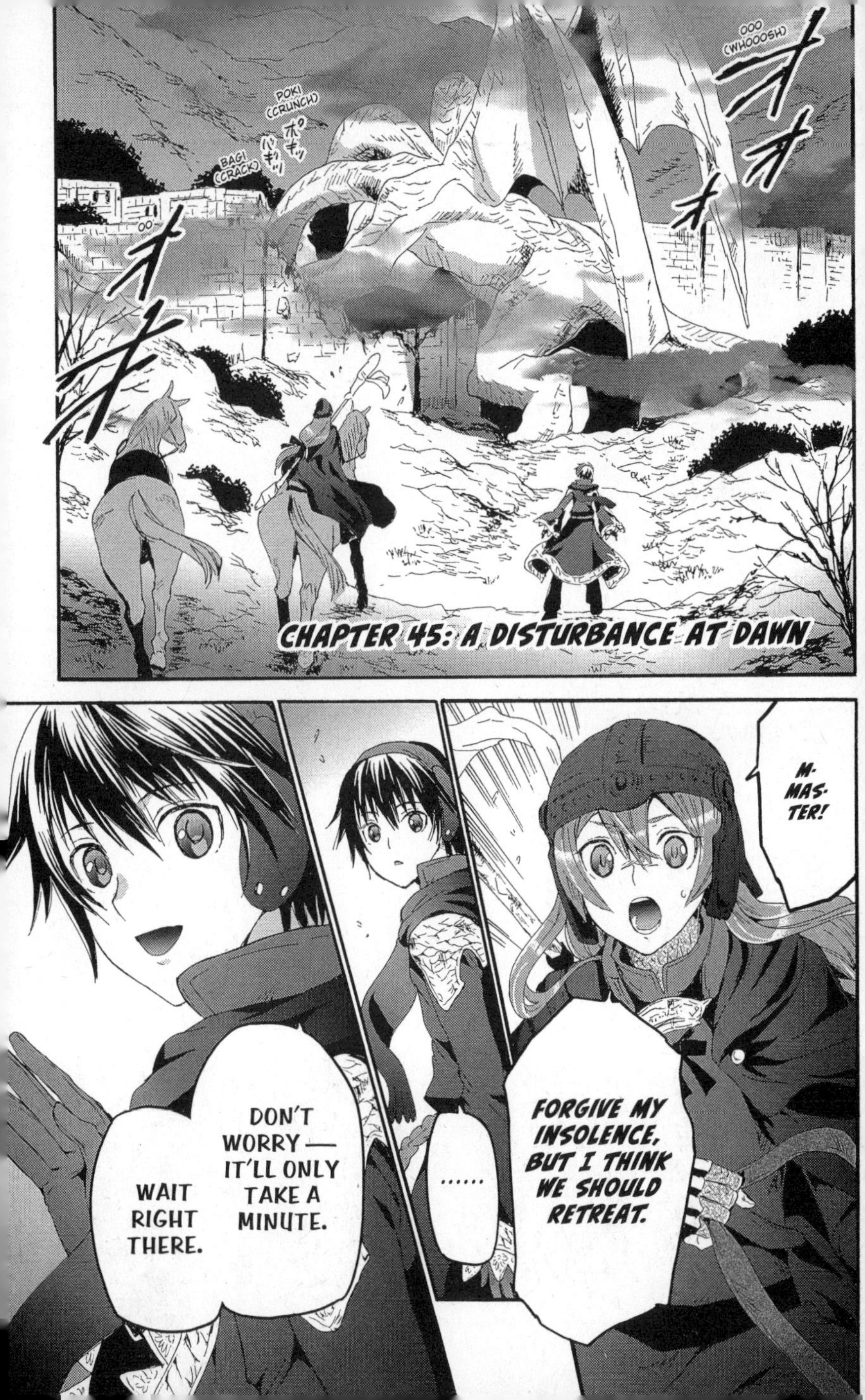
OOO (WHOOOSH)
POKI (CRUNCH)
BAGI (CRACK)
OO
CHAPTER 45: A DISTURBANCE AT DAWN
M-MAS-TER!
FORGIVE MY INSOLENCE, BUT I THINK WE SHOULD RETREAT.
......
DON'T WORRY— IT'LL ONLY TAKE A MINUTE.
WAIT RIGHT THERE.

DA
(DASH)

I'LL SHOW LIZA A BIT OF MY REAL STRENGTH TO EASE HER WORRIES.

SHE'S NOT THE TYPE TO SPILL A SECRET...

...SO IT SHOULDN'T BE A PROBLEM TO LET HER SEE.

Magic Arrow

AMOUNT 120

I'LL CHOOSE MAGIC ARROW—

SINCE IT'S FASTER THAN FIRE SHOT.

THE MAX AMOUNT, JUST IN CASE.

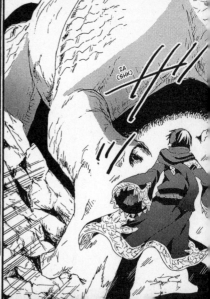

ZA
(SHK)

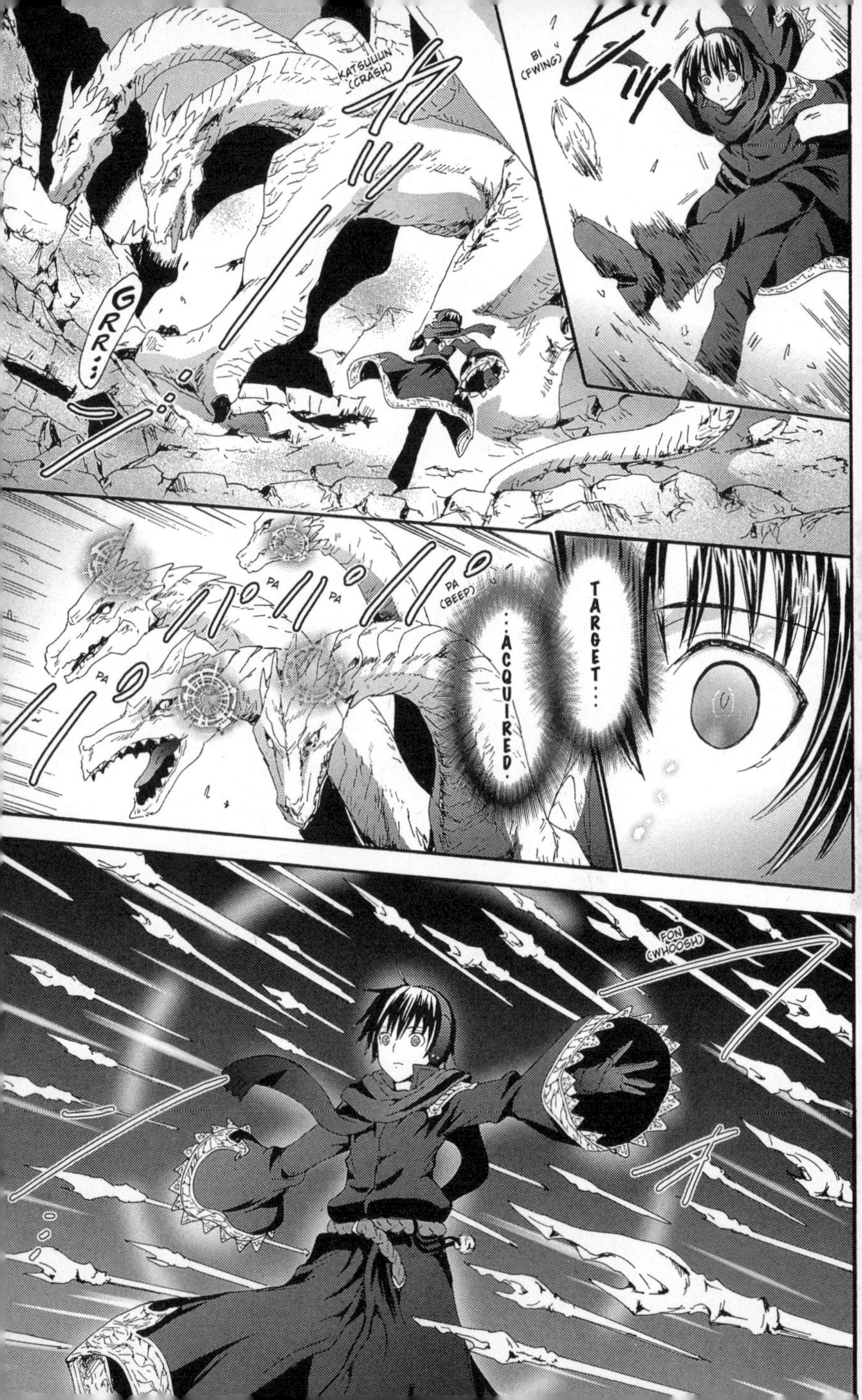
BI (FWING)
KATSUUUN (CRASH)
GRR...
TARGET...
...ACQUIRED.
PA
PA
PA
PA (BEEP)
FON (WHOOSH)

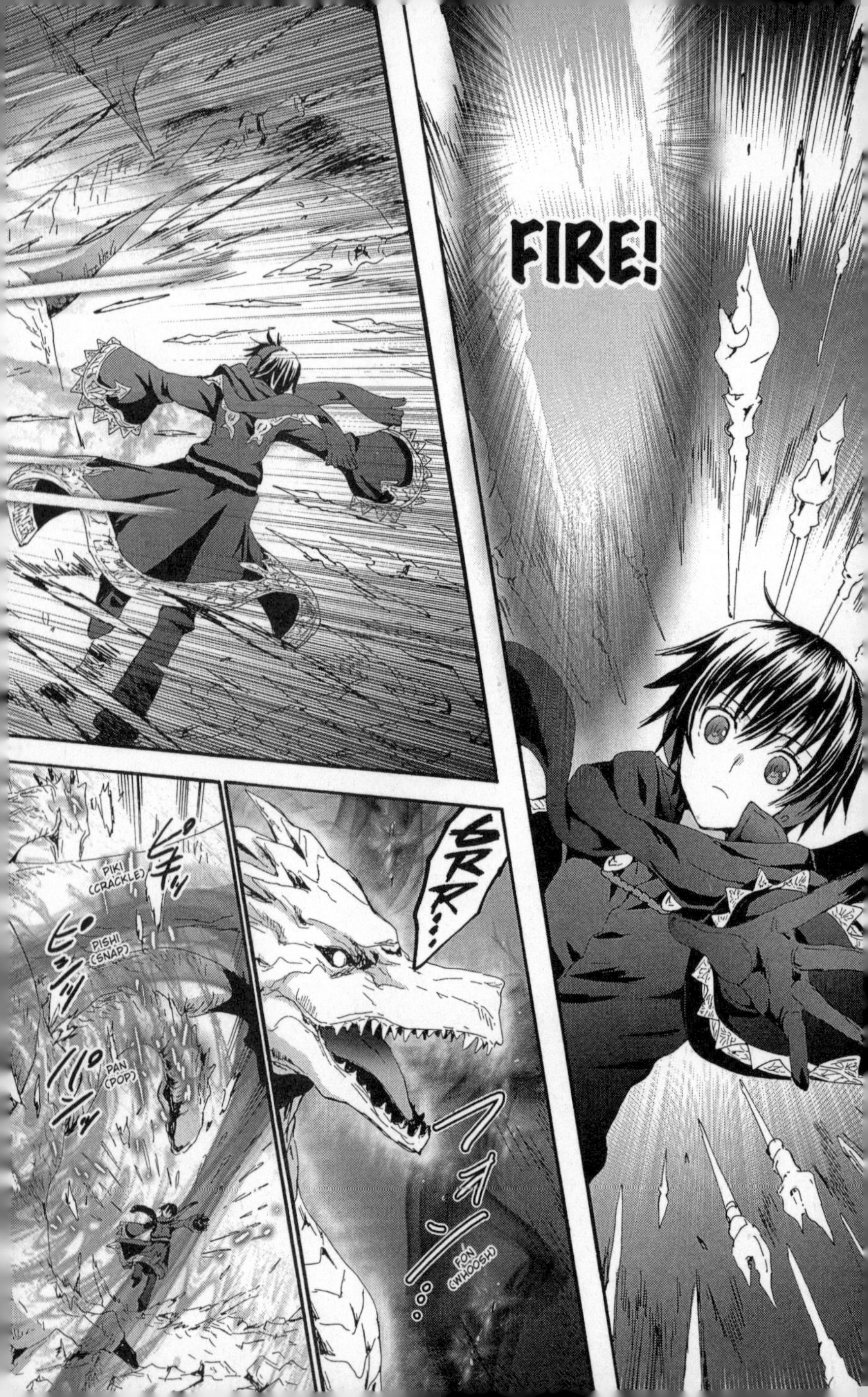
FIRE!
GRR...
PON (WHOOSH)
PIKI (CRACKLE)
PISHI (SNAP)
PAN (POP)

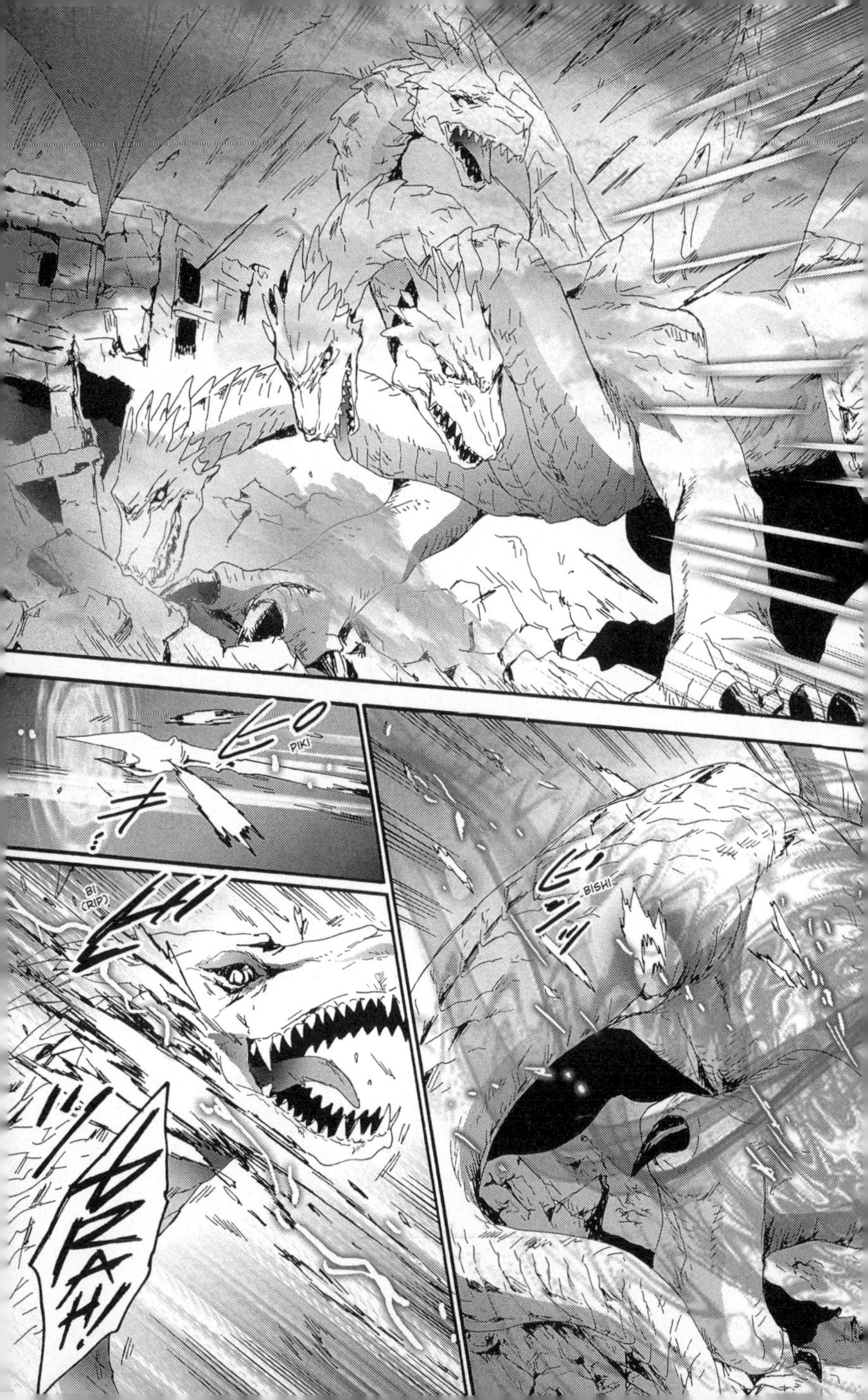
BISHI
PIKI
BI (RIP)
WRAAH!

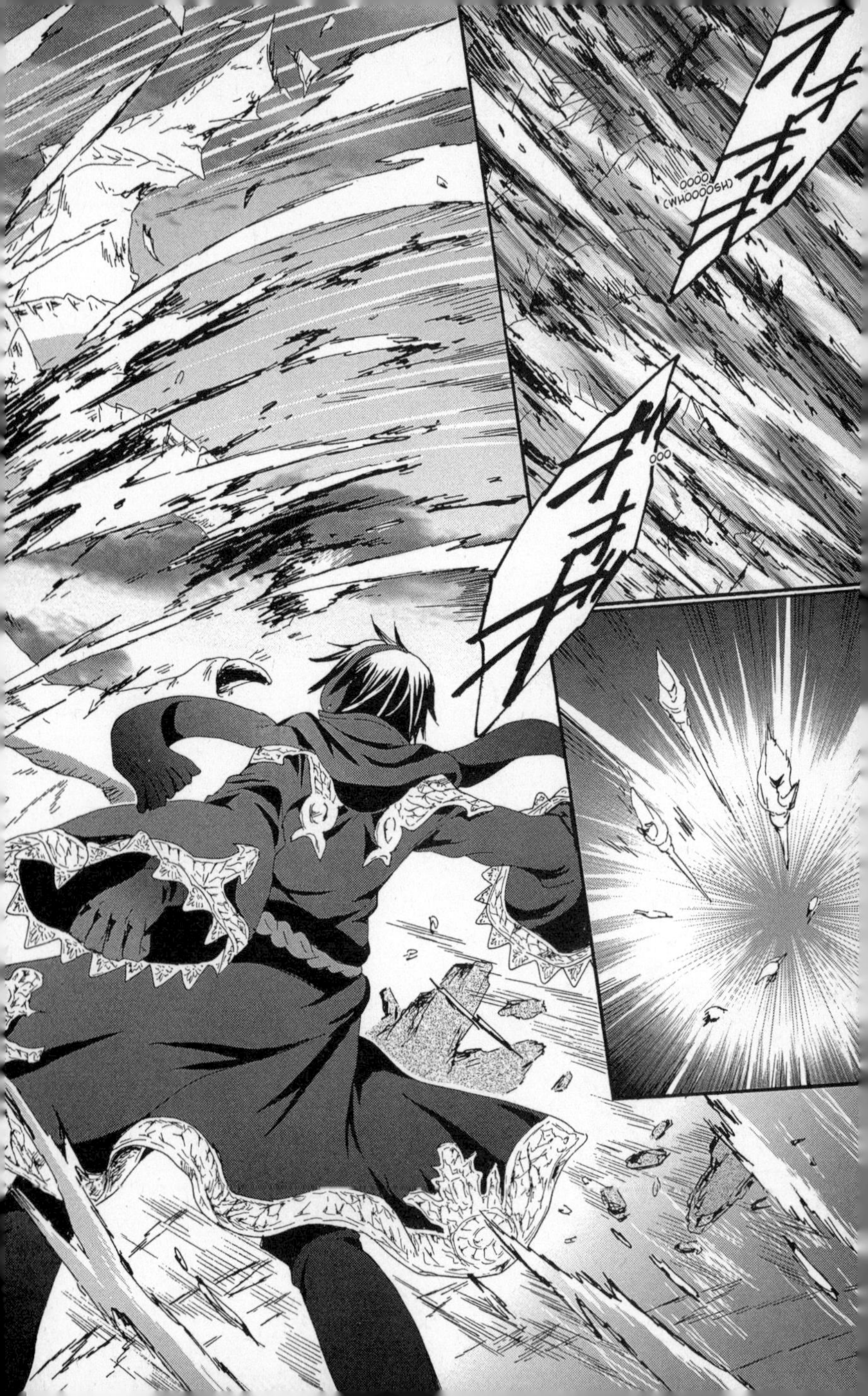
(WHOOOOSH
OOOO
OOO

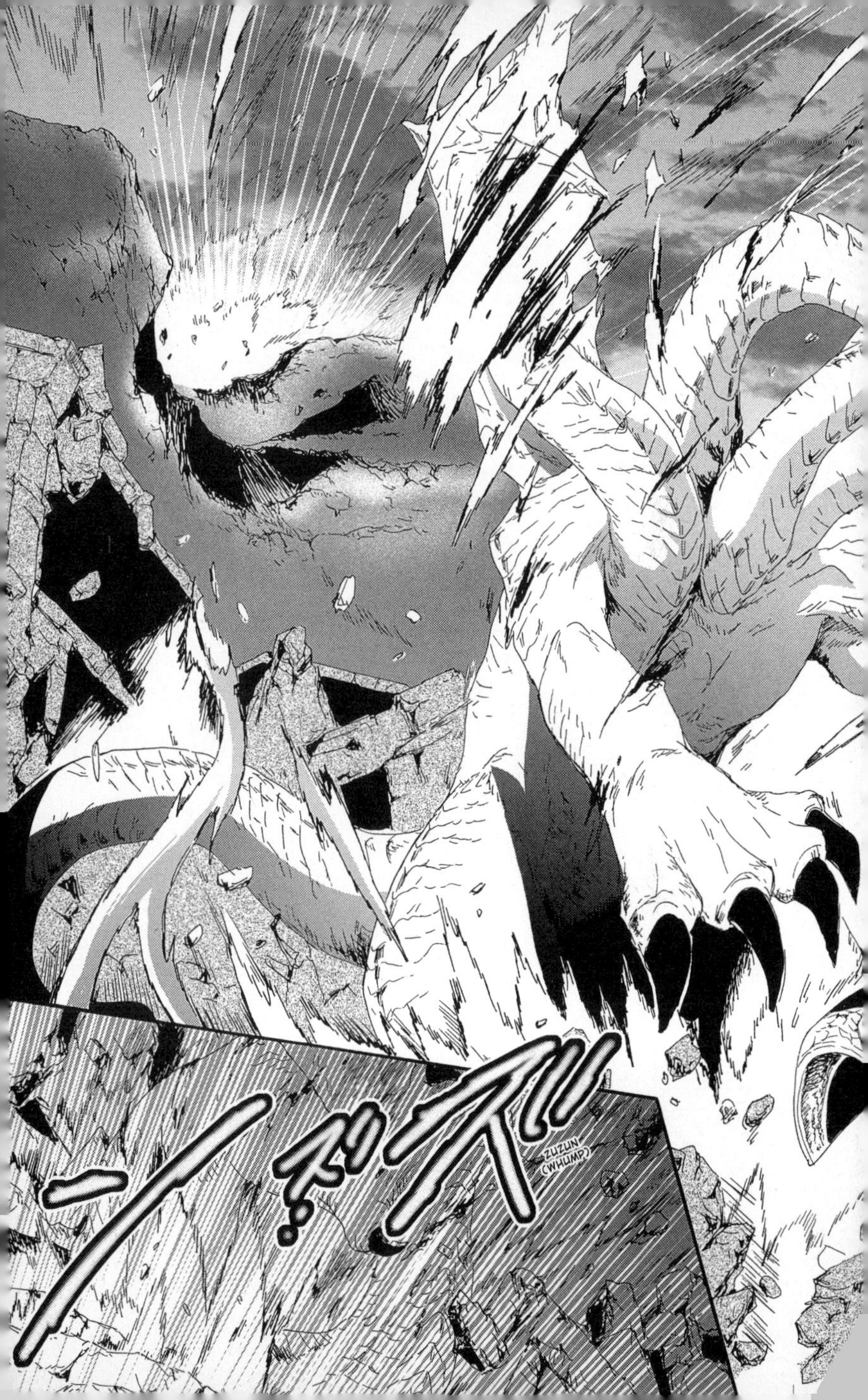
ZUZUN (WHUMP)

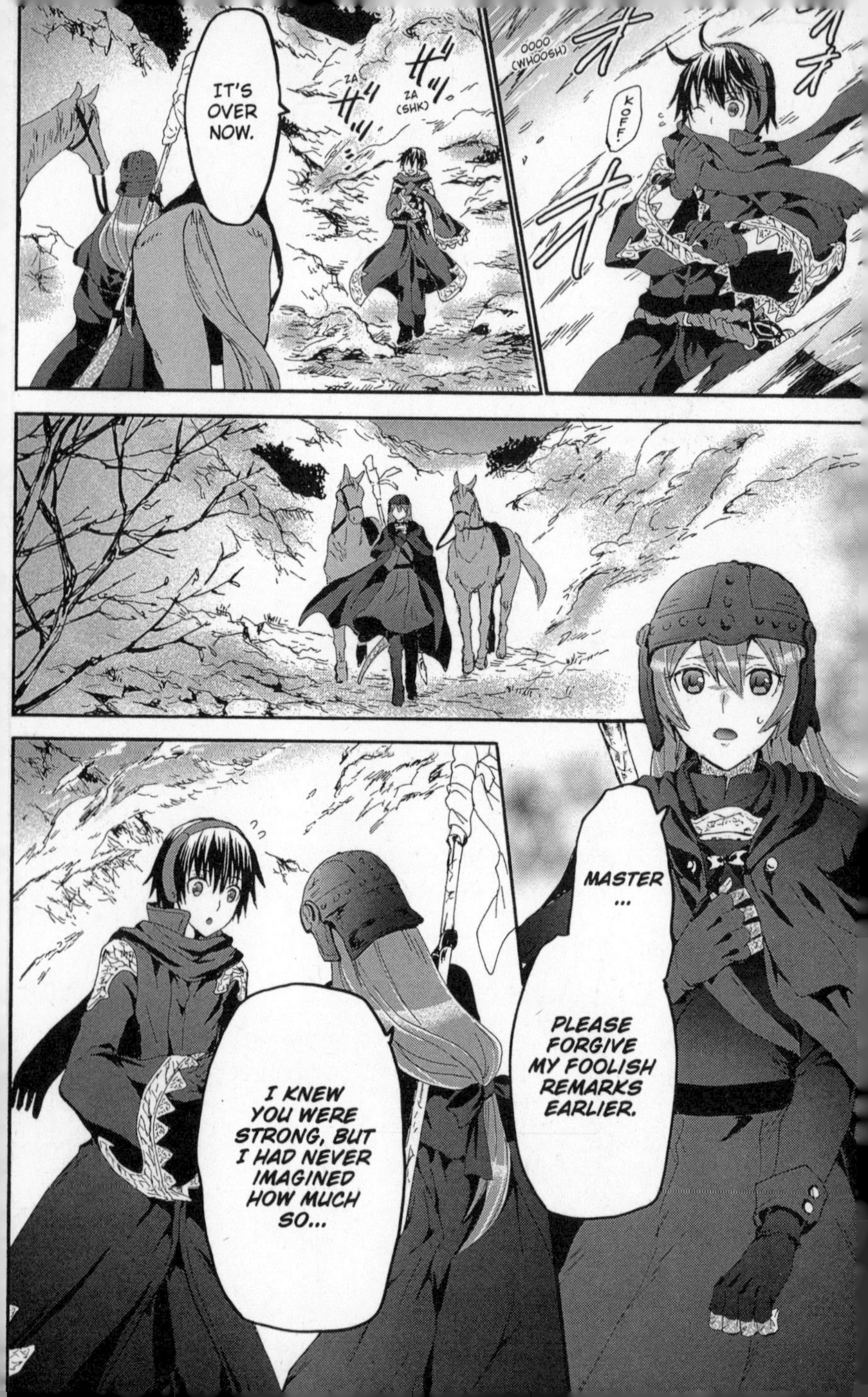
OOOO (WHOOSH)
KOFF.
ZA ZA (SHK)
IT'S OVER NOW.
MASTER ...
PLEASE FORGIVE MY FOOLISH REMARKS EARLIER.
I KNEW YOU WERE STRONG, BUT I HAD NEVER IMAGINED HOW MUCH SO...

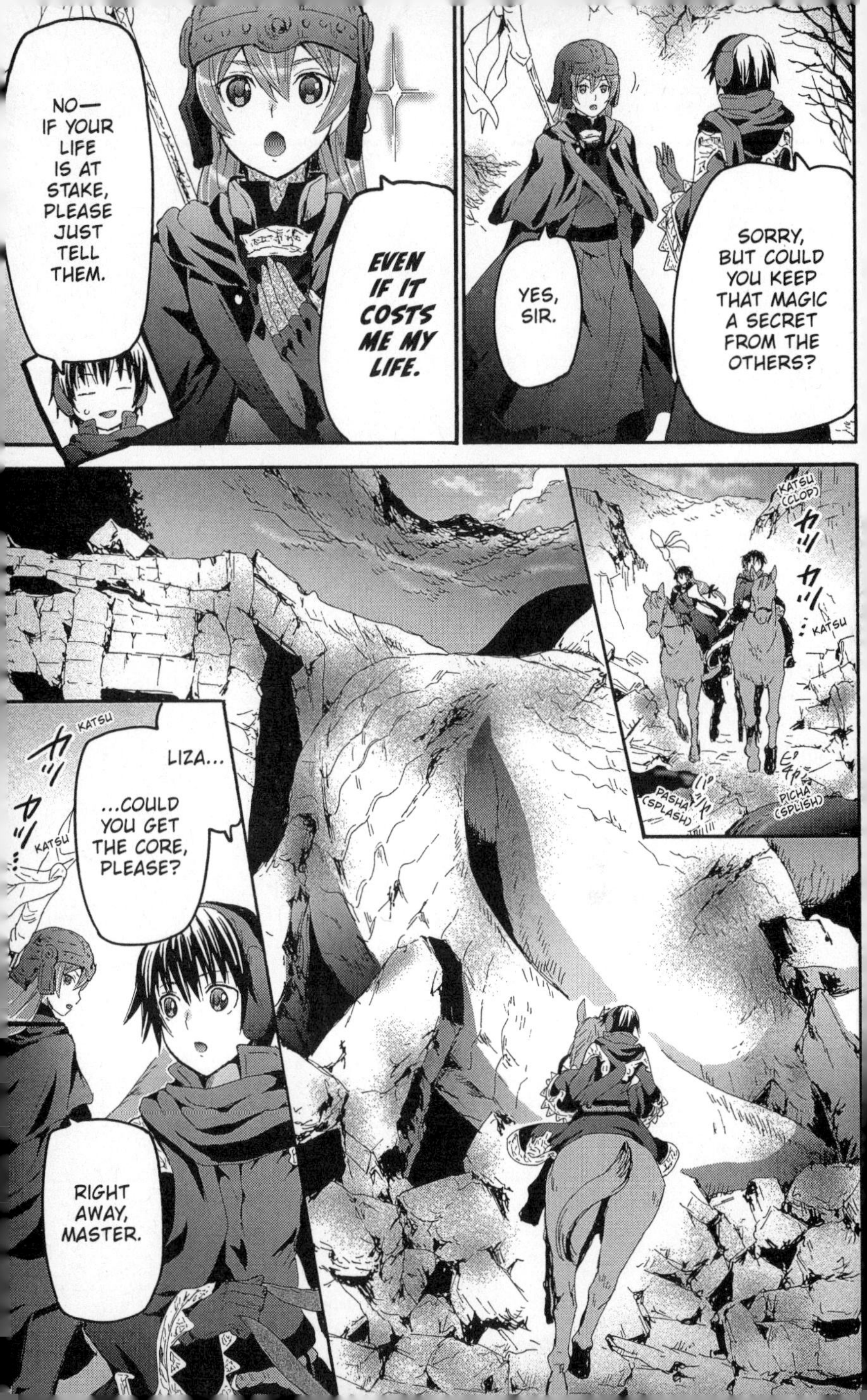
SORRY, BUT COULD YOU KEEP THAT MAGIC A SECRET FROM THE OTHERS?
YES, SIR.
EVEN IF IT COSTS ME MY LIFE.
NO— IF YOUR LIFE IS AT STAKE, PLEASE JUST TELL THEM.
KATSU (CLOP)
KATSU
PICHA (SPLISH)
PASHA (SPLASH)
KATSU
KATSU
LIZA...
...COULD YOU GET THE CORE, PLEASE?
RIGHT AWAY, MASTER.

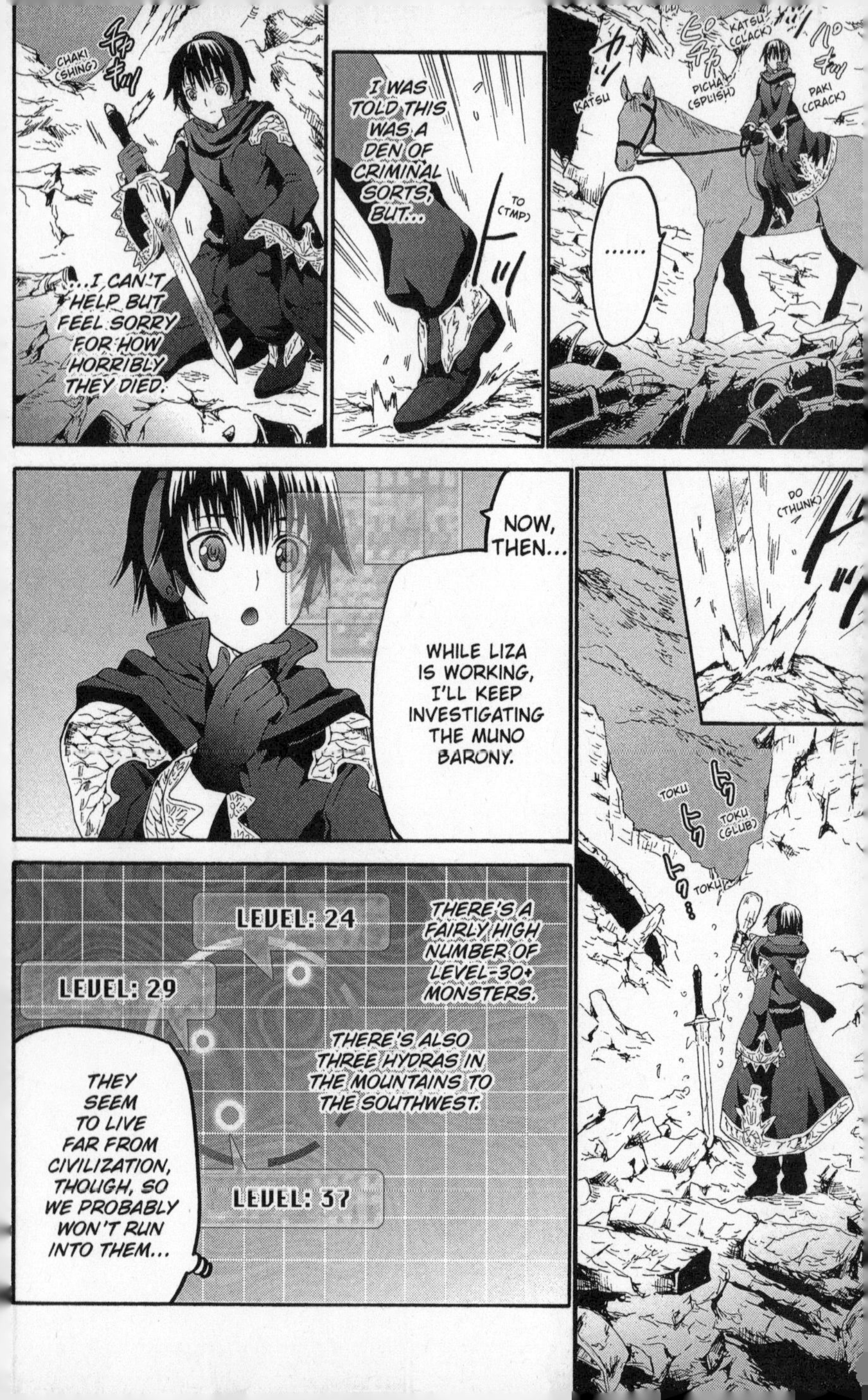
KATSU (CLACK)
PICHA (SPLISH)
PAKI (CRACK)
KATSU
......
I WAS TOLD THIS WAS A DEN OF CRIMINAL SORTS, BUT...
TO (TMP)
CHAKI (SHING)
...I CAN'T HELP BUT FEEL SORRY FOR HOW HORRIBLY THEY DIED.
DO (THUNK)
TOKU
TOKU (GLUB)
TOKU
NOW, THEN...
WHILE LIZA IS WORKING, I'LL KEEP INVESTIGATING THE MUNO BARONY.
THERE'S A FAIRLY HIGH NUMBER OF LEVEL-30+ MONSTERS.
LEVEL: 24
LEVEL: 29
THERE'S ALSO THREE HYDRAS IN THE MOUNTAINS TO THE SOUTHWEST.
THEY SEEM TO LIVE FAR FROM CIVILIZATION, THOUGH, SO WE PROBABLY WON'T RUN INTO THEM...
LEVEL: 37

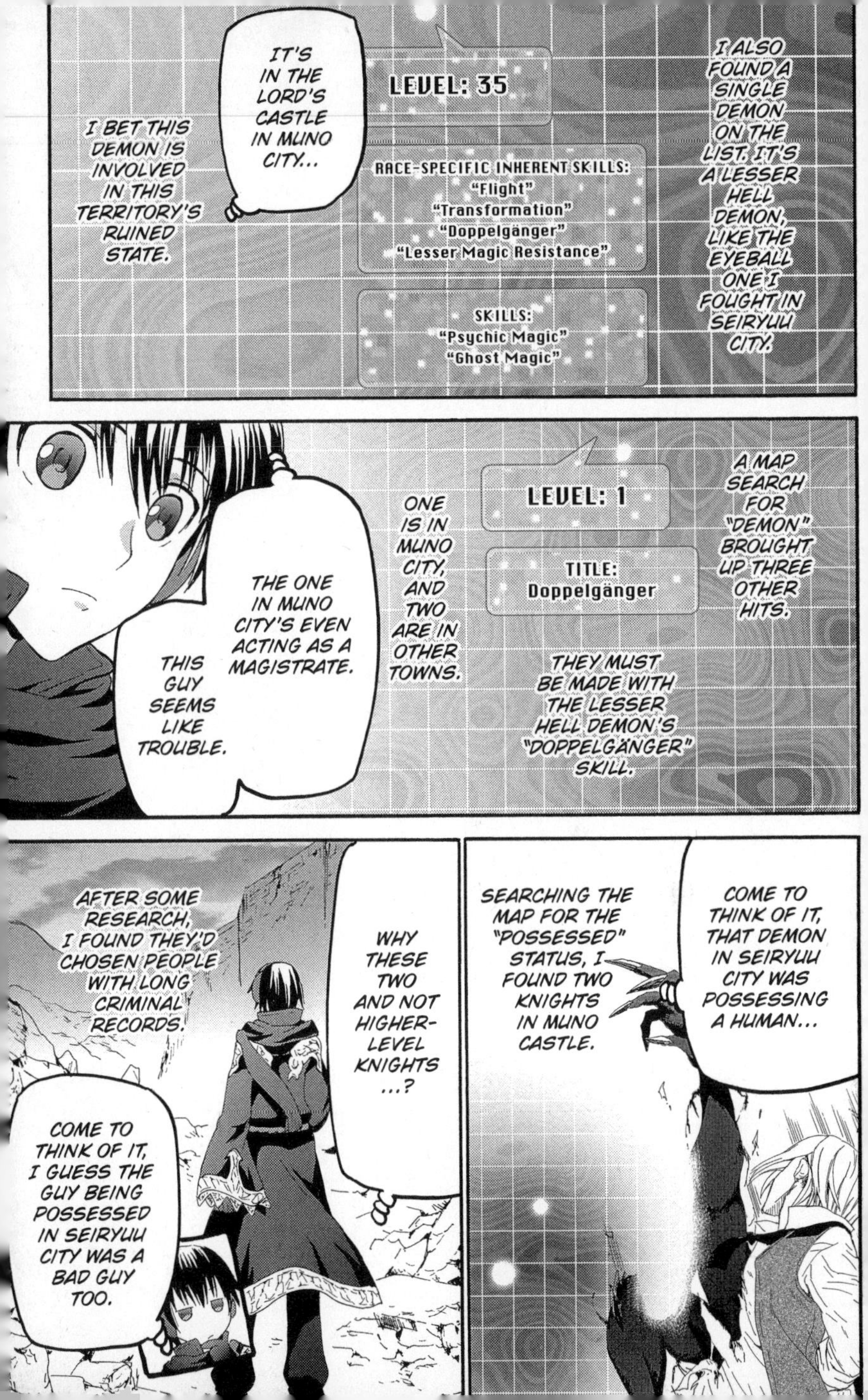
I ALSO FOUND A SINGLE DEMON ON THE LIST. IT'S A LESSER HELL DEMON, LIKE THE EYEBALL ONE I FOUGHT IN SEIRYUU CITY.
LEVEL: 35
RACE-SPECIFIC INHERENT SKILLS:
"Flight"
"Transformation"
"Doppelgänger"
"Lesser Magic Resistance"
SKILLS:
"Psychic Magic"
"Ghost Magic"
IT'S IN THE LORD'S CASTLE IN MUNO CITY...
I BET THIS DEMON IS INVOLVED IN THIS TERRITORY'S RUINED STATE.
A MAP SEARCH FOR "DEMON" BROUGHT UP THREE OTHER HITS.
LEVEL: 1
TITLE:
Doppelgänger
ONE IS IN MUNO CITY, AND TWO ARE IN OTHER TOWNS.
THEY MUST BE MADE WITH THE LESSER HELL DEMON'S "DOPPELGÄNGER" SKILL.
THE ONE IN MUNO CITY'S EVEN ACTING AS A MAGISTRATE.
THIS GUY SEEMS LIKE TROUBLE.
COME TO THINK OF IT, THAT DEMON IN SEIRYUU CITY WAS POSSESSING A HUMAN...
SEARCHING THE MAP FOR THE "POSSESSED" STATUS, I FOUND TWO KNIGHTS IN MUNO CASTLE.
WHY THESE TWO AND NOT HIGHER-LEVEL KNIGHTS ...?
AFTER SOME RESEARCH, I FOUND THEY'D CHOSEN PEOPLE WITH LONG CRIMINAL RECORDS.
COME TO THINK OF IT, I GUESS THE GUY BEING POSSESSED IN SEIRYUU CITY WAS A BAD GUY TOO.

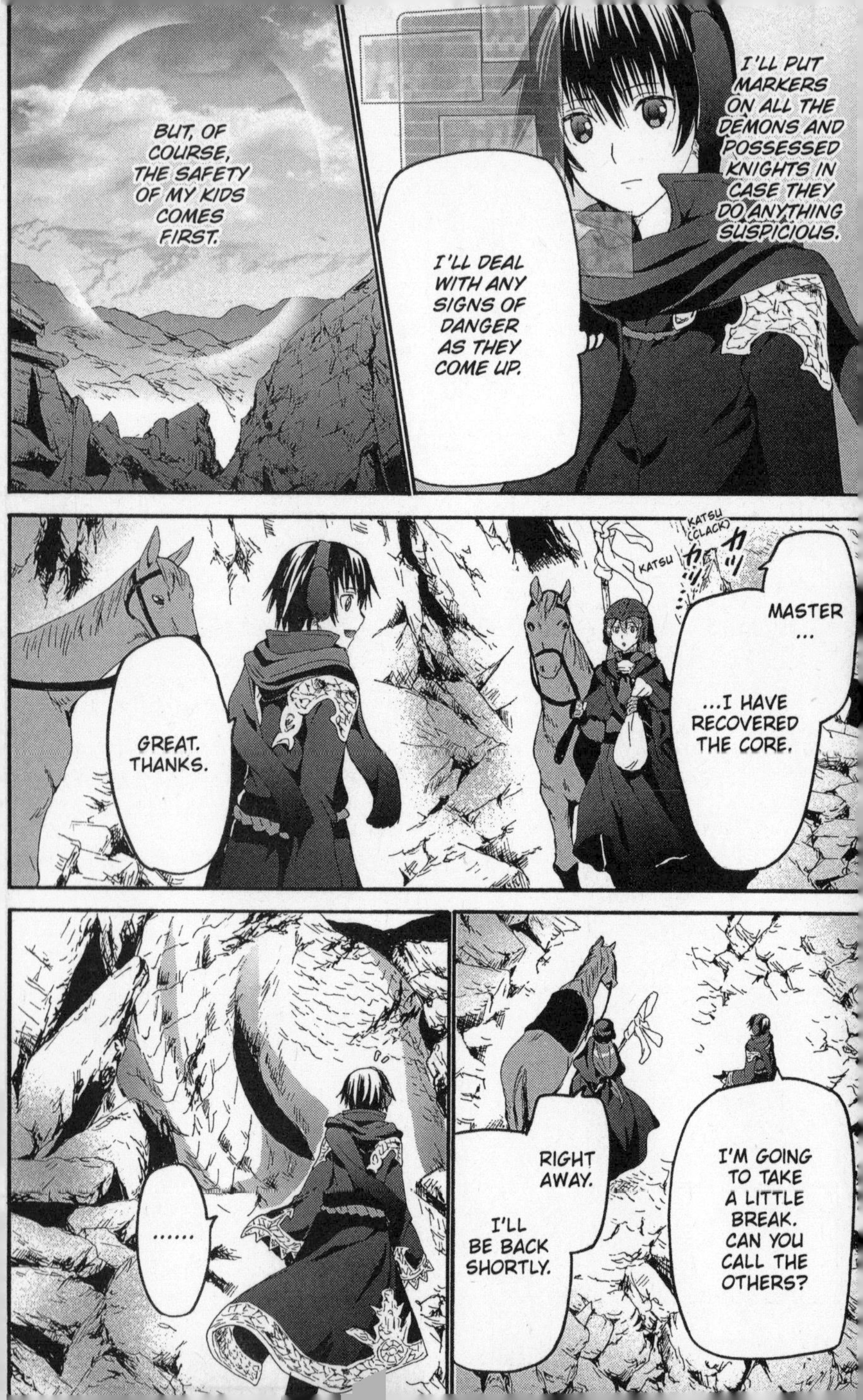
I'LL PUT MARKERS ON ALL THE DEMONS AND POSSESSED KNIGHTS IN CASE THEY DO ANYTHING SUSPICIOUS.
I'LL DEAL WITH ANY SIGNS OF DANGER AS THEY COME UP.
BUT, OF COURSE, THE SAFETY OF MY KIDS COMES FIRST.
KATSU (CLACK)
KATSU
MASTER...
...I HAVE RECOVERED THE CORE.
GREAT. THANKS.
I'M GOING TO TAKE A LITTLE BREAK. CAN YOU CALL THE OTHERS?
RIGHT AWAY.
I'LL BE BACK SHORTLY.
......

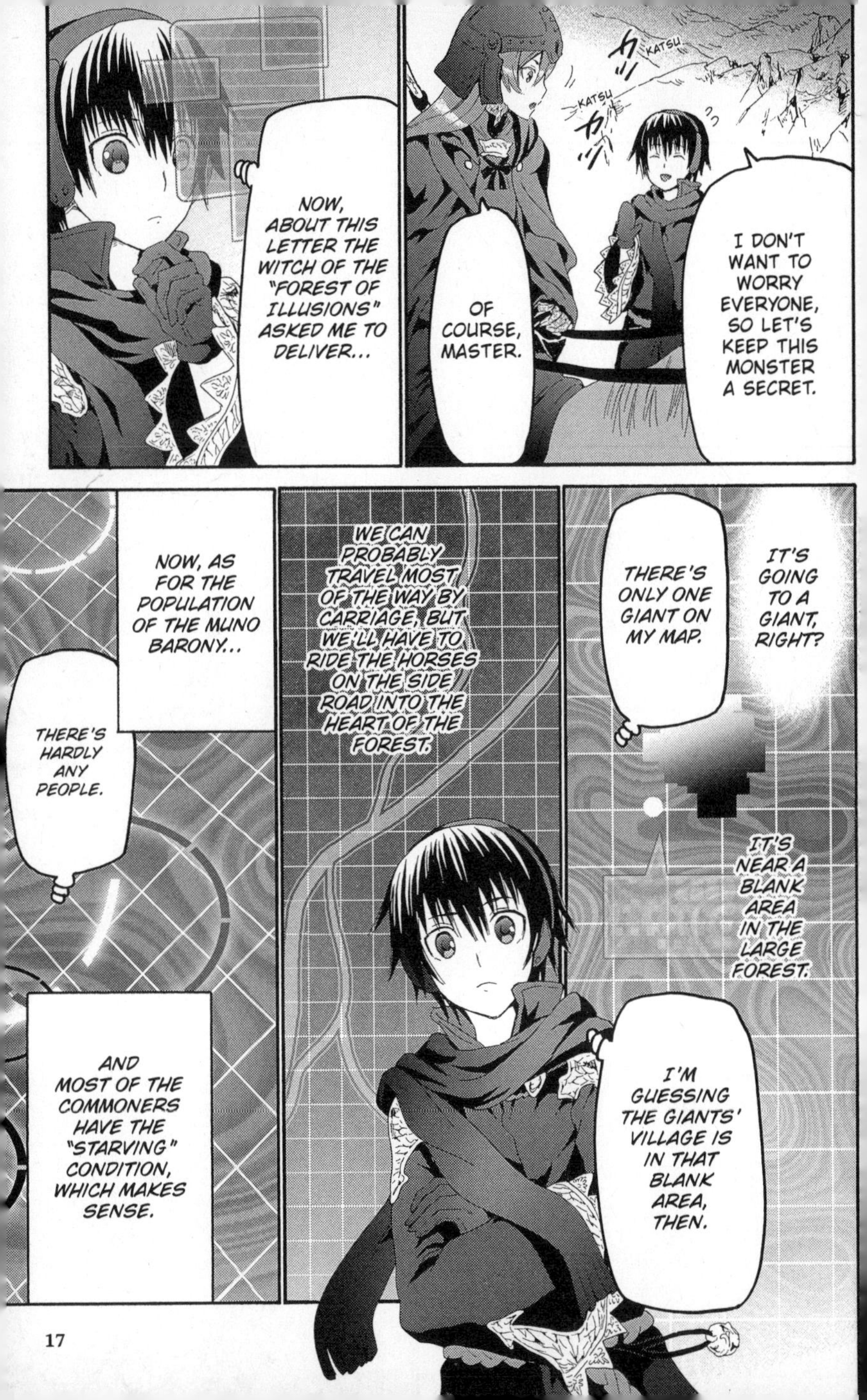
KATSU
KATSU
I DON'T WANT TO WORRY EVERYONE, SO LET'S KEEP THIS MONSTER A SECRET.
OF COURSE, MASTER.
NOW, ABOUT THIS LETTER THE WITCH OF THE "FOREST OF ILLUSIONS" ASKED ME TO DELIVER...
IT'S GOING TO A GIANT, RIGHT?
THERE'S ONLY ONE GIANT ON MY MAP.
IT'S NEAR A BLANK AREA IN THE LARGE FOREST.
I'M GUESSING THE GIANTS' VILLAGE IS IN THAT BLANK AREA, THEN.
WE CAN PROBABLY TRAVEL MOST OF THE WAY BY CARRIAGE, BUT WE'LL HAVE TO RIDE THE HORSES ON THE SIDE ROAD INTO THE HEART OF THE FOREST.
NOW, AS FOR THE POPULATION OF THE MUNO BARONY...
THERE'S HARDLY ANY PEOPLE.
AND MOST OF THE COMMONERS HAVE THE "STARVING" CONDITION, WHICH MAKES SENSE.

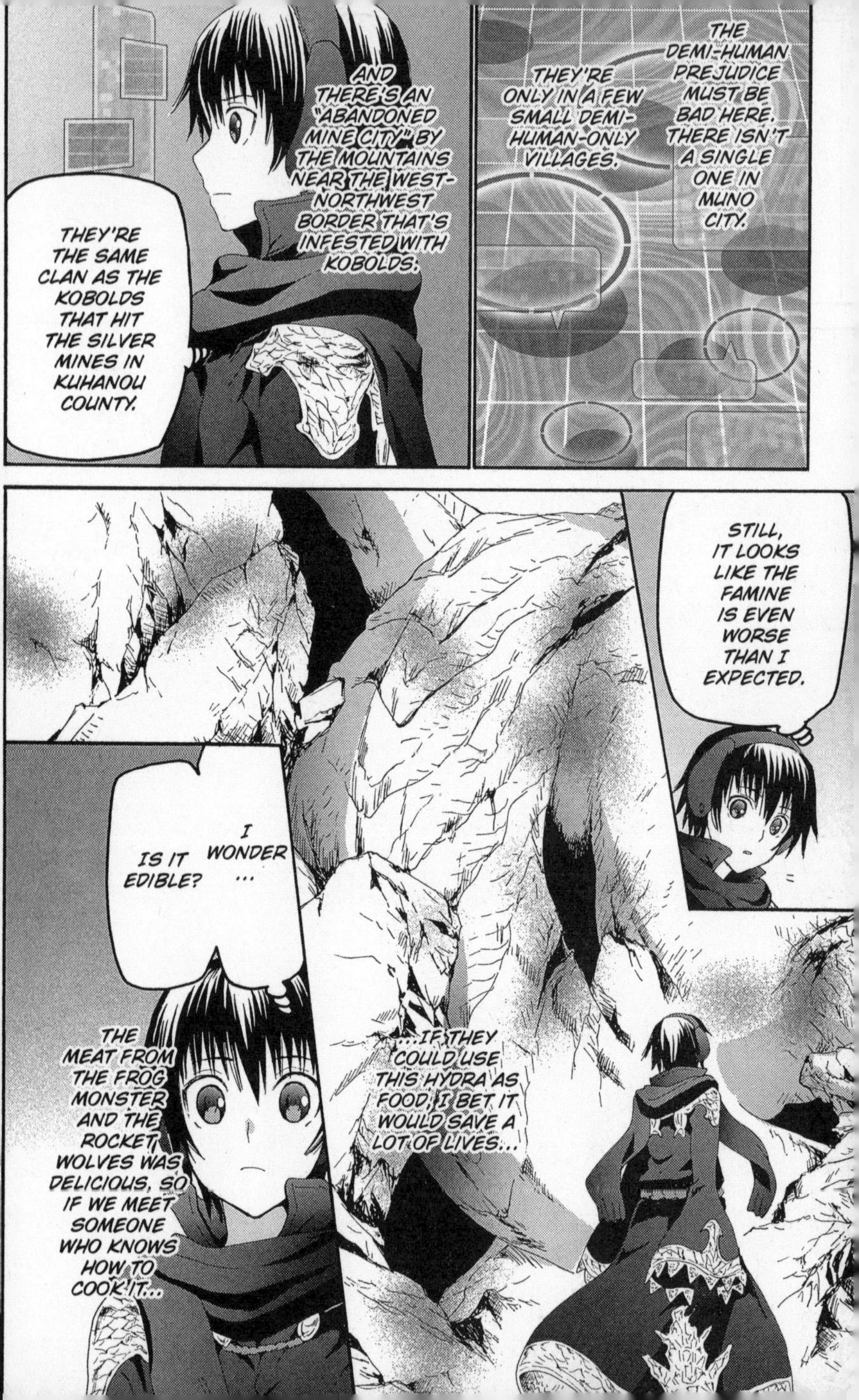
THE DEMI-HUMAN PREJUDICE MUST BE BAD HERE. THERE ISN'T A SINGLE ONE IN MUNO CITY.
THEY'RE ONLY IN A FEW SMALL DEMI-HUMAN-ONLY VILLAGES.
AND THERE'S AN "ABANDONED MINE CITY" BY THE MOUNTAINS NEAR THE WEST-NORTHWEST BORDER THAT'S INFESTED WITH KOBOLDS.
THEY'RE THE SAME CLAN AS THE KOBOLDS THAT HIT THE SILVER MINES IN KUHANOU COUNTY.
STILL, IT LOOKS LIKE THE FAMINE IS EVEN WORSE THAN I EXPECTED.
I WONDER...
IS IT EDIBLE?
...IF THEY COULD USE THIS HYDRA AS FOOD, I BET IT WOULD SAVE A LOT OF LIVES...
THE MEAT FROM THE FROG MONSTER AND THE ROCKET WOLVES WAS DELICIOUS, SO IF WE MEET SOMEONE WHO KNOWS HOW TO COOK IT...

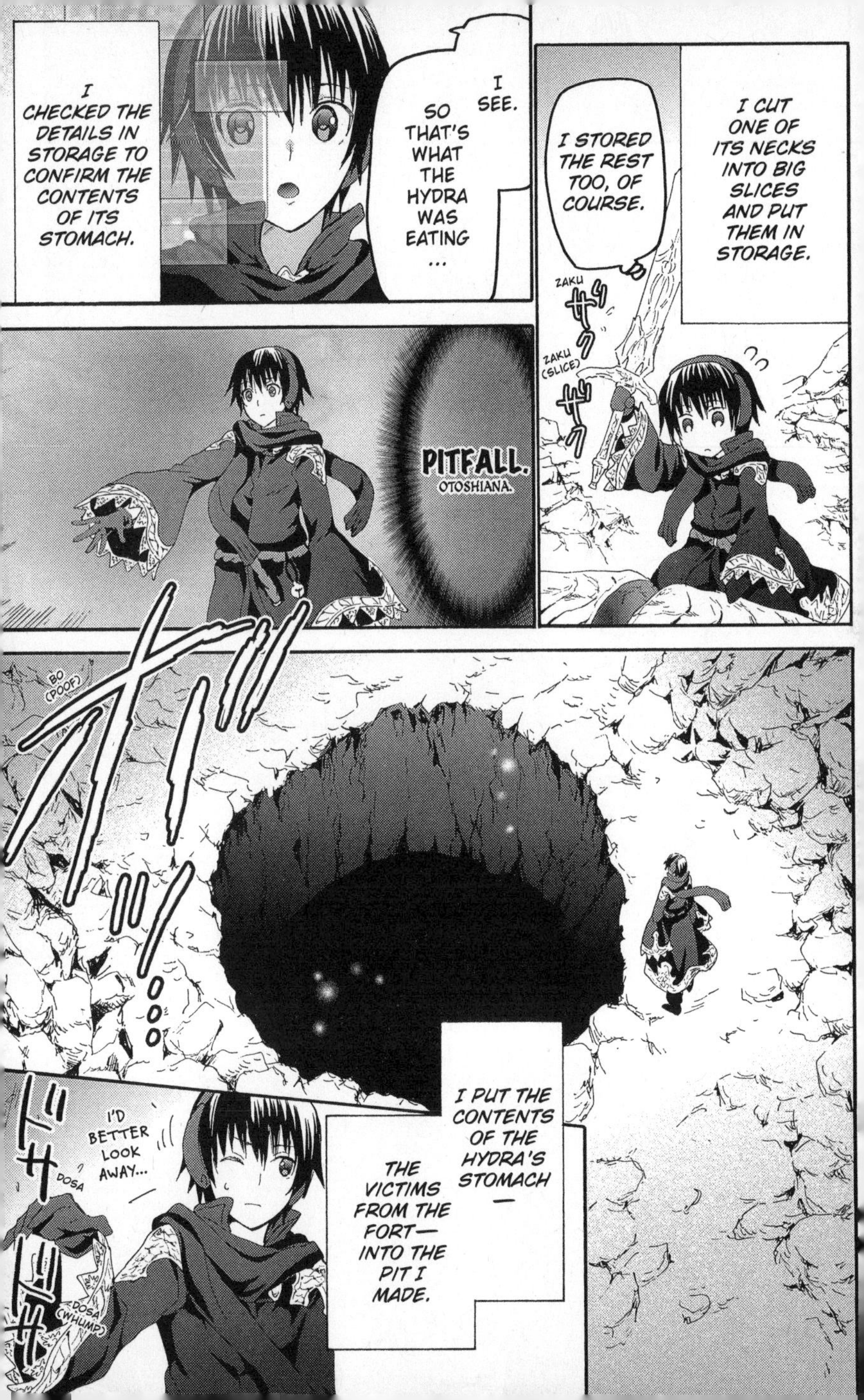
I CUT ONE OF ITS NECKS INTO BIG SLICES AND PUT THEM IN STORAGE.
I STORED THE REST TOO, OF COURSE.
ZAKU
ZAKU (SLICE)
I SEE.
SO THAT'S WHAT THE HYDRA WAS EATING...
I CHECKED THE DETAILS IN STORAGE TO CONFIRM THE CONTENTS OF ITS STOMACH.
PITFALL.
OTOSHIANA.
BO (POOF)
I PUT THE CONTENTS OF THE HYDRA'S STOMACH—
THE VICTIMS FROM THE FORT—INTO THE PIT I MADE.
I'D BETTER LOOK AWAY...
DOSA
DOSA (WHUMP)

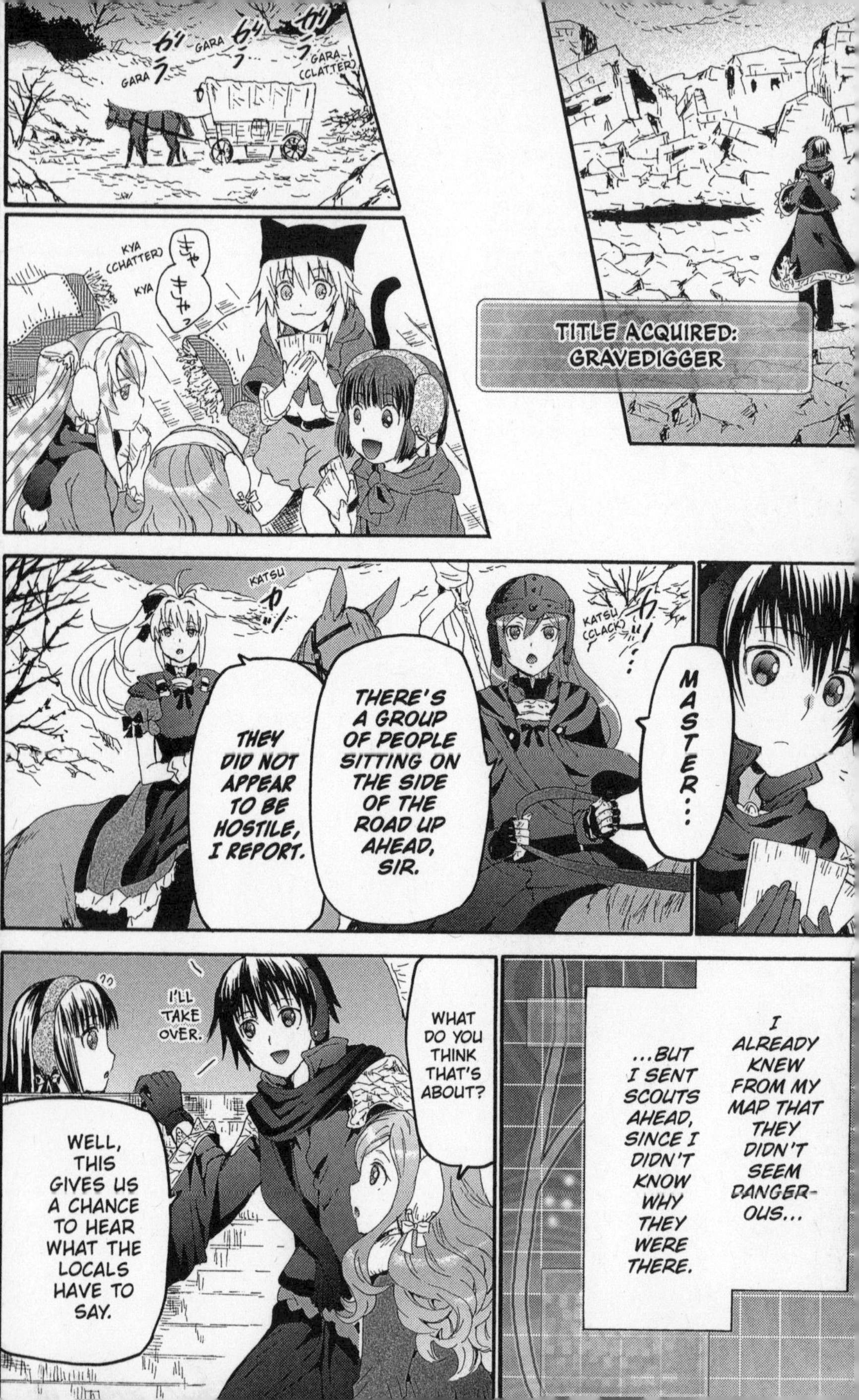
TITLE ACQUIRED: GRAVEDIGGER
GARA
GARA
GARA (CLATTER)
GARA
KYA (CHATTER)
KYA
MASTER...
KATSU (CLACK)
THERE'S A GROUP OF PEOPLE SITTING ON THE SIDE OF THE ROAD UP AHEAD, SIR.
THEY DID NOT APPEAR TO BE HOSTILE, I REPORT.
KATSU
I ALREADY KNEW FROM MY MAP THAT THEY DIDN'T SEEM DANGEROUS...
...BUT I SENT SCOUTS AHEAD, SINCE I DIDN'T KNOW WHY THEY WERE THERE.
WHAT DO YOU THINK THAT'S ABOUT?
I'LL TAKE OVER.
WELL, THIS GIVES US A CHANCE TO HEAR WHAT THE LOCALS HAVE TO SAY.

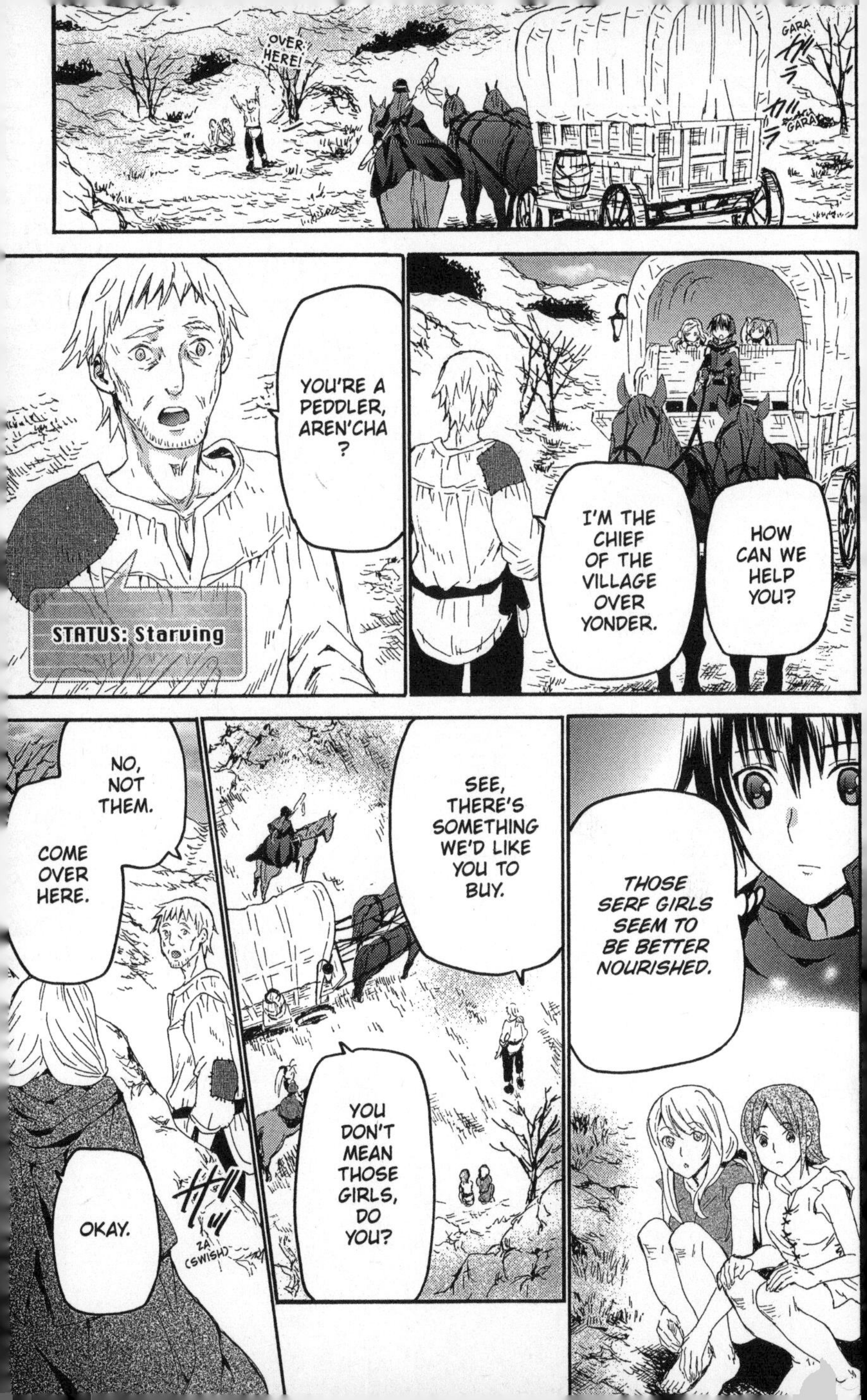
GARA
GARA
OVER HERE!
HOW CAN WE HELP YOU?
I'M THE CHIEF OF THE VILLAGE OVER YONDER.
YOU'RE A PEDDLER, AREN'CHA?
STATUS: Starving
THOSE SERF GIRLS SEEM TO BE BETTER NOURISHED.
SEE, THERE'S SOMETHING WE'D LIKE YOU TO BUY.
YOU DON'T MEAN THOSE GIRLS, DO YOU?
NO, NOT THEM.
COME OVER HERE.
OKAY.
ZA (SWISH)

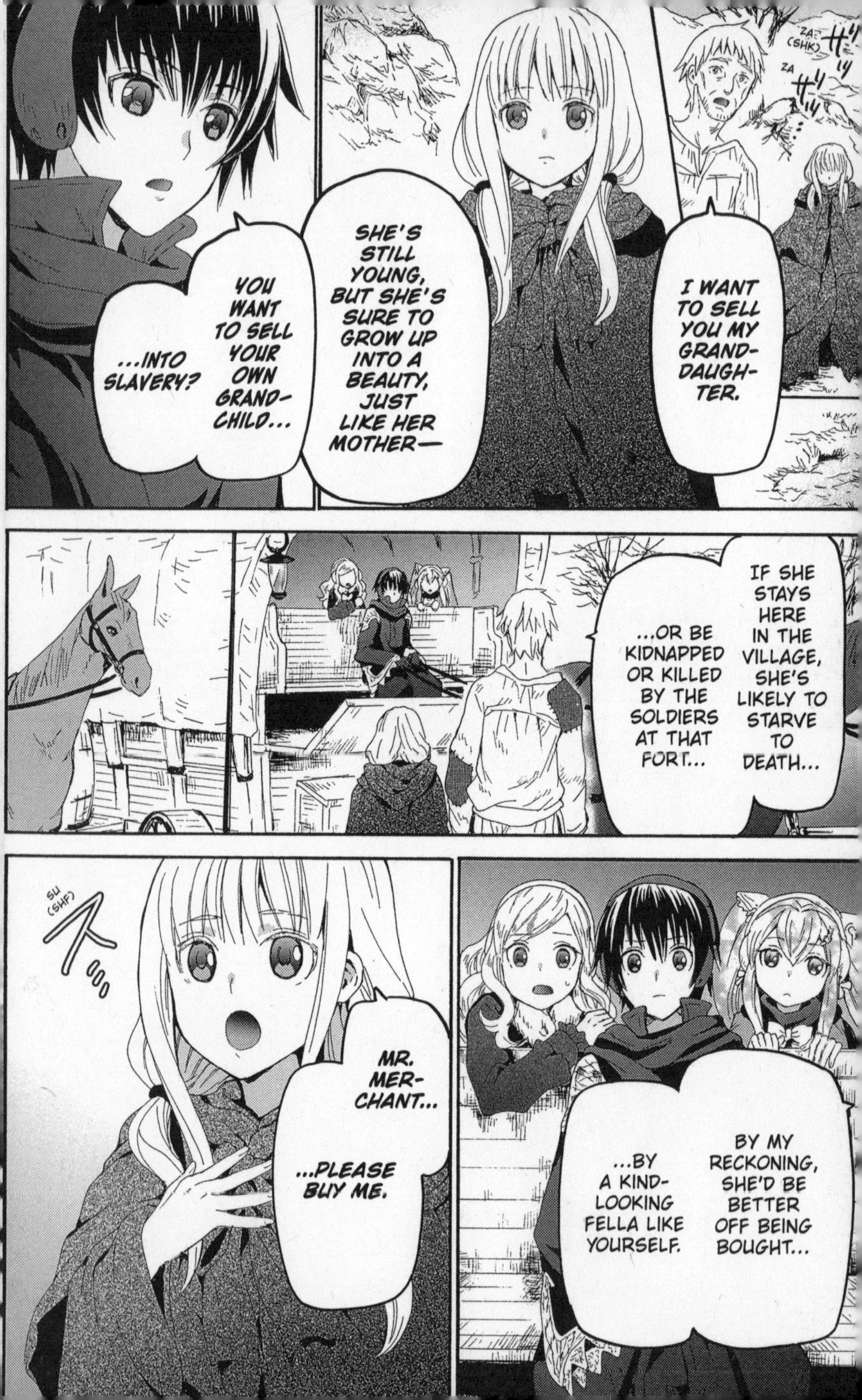
ZA (SHK)
ZA
I WANT TO SELL YOU MY GRANDDAUGHTER.
SHE'S STILL YOUNG, BUT SHE'S SURE TO GROW UP INTO A BEAUTY, JUST LIKE HER MOTHER—
YOU WANT TO SELL YOUR OWN GRANDCHILD...
...INTO SLAVERY?
IF SHE STAYS HERE IN THE VILLAGE, SHE'S LIKELY TO STARVE TO DEATH...
...OR BE KIDNAPPED OR KILLED BY THE SOLDIERS AT THAT FORT...
BY MY RECKONING, SHE'D BE BETTER OFF BEING BOUGHT...
...BY A KIND-LOOKING FELLA LIKE YOURSELF.
SU (SHF)
MR. MERCHANT...
...PLEASE BUY ME.

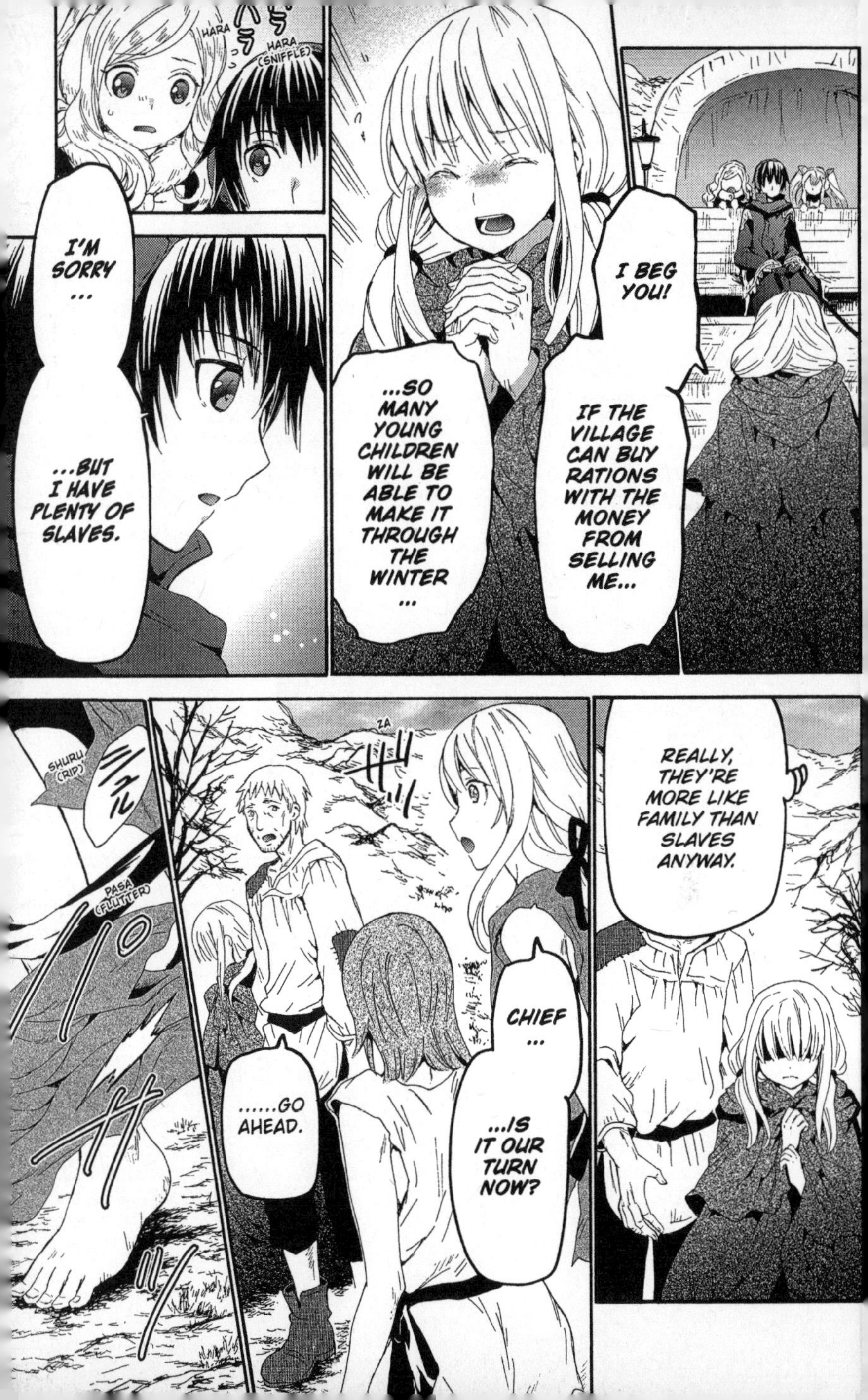
I BEG YOU!
IF THE VILLAGE CAN BUY RATIONS WITH THE MONEY FROM SELLING ME...
...SO MANY YOUNG CHILDREN WILL BE ABLE TO MAKE IT THROUGH THE WINTER ...
HARA
HARA (SNIFFLE)
I'M SORRY ...
...BUT I HAVE PLENTY OF SLAVES.
REALLY, THEY'RE MORE LIKE FAMILY THAN SLAVES ANYWAY.
ZA
CHIEF ...
...IS IT OUR TURN NOW?
......GO AHEAD.
SHURU (RIP)
PASA (FLUTTER)

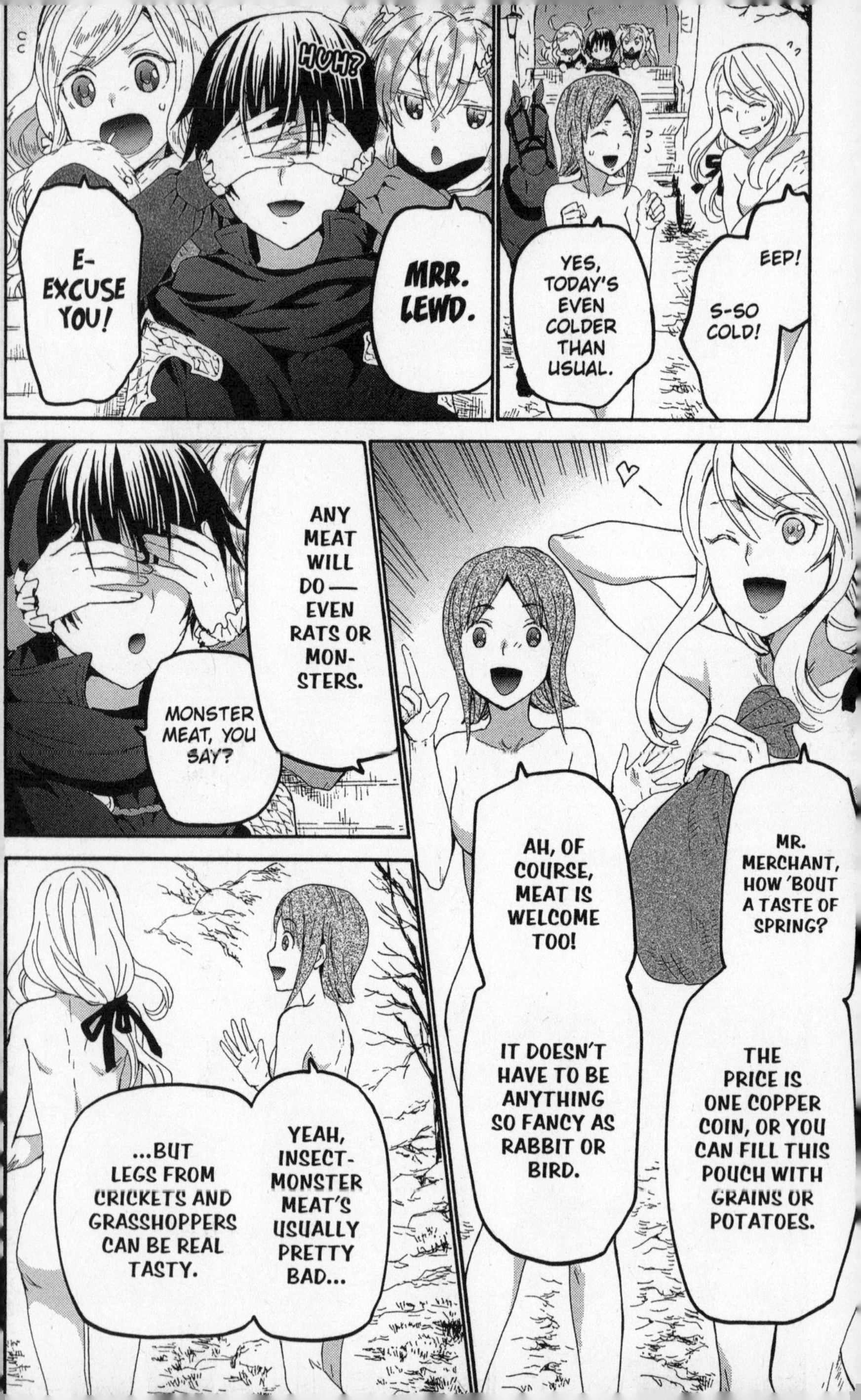
EEP!
S-SO COLD!
YES, TODAY'S EVEN COLDER THAN USUAL.
HUH?
MRR. LEWD.
E-EXCUSE YOU!
MR. MERCHANT, HOW 'BOUT A TASTE OF SPRING?
THE PRICE IS ONE COPPER COIN, OR YOU CAN FILL THIS POUCH WITH GRAINS OR POTATOES.
AH, OF COURSE, MEAT IS WELCOME TOO!
IT DOESN'T HAVE TO BE ANYTHING SO FANCY AS RABBIT OR BIRD.
ANY MEAT WILL DO—EVEN RATS OR MONSTERS.
MONSTER MEAT, YOU SAY?
YEAH, INSECT-MONSTER MEAT'S USUALLY PRETTY BAD...
...BUT LEGS FROM CRICKETS AND GRASSHOPPERS CAN BE REAL TASTY.

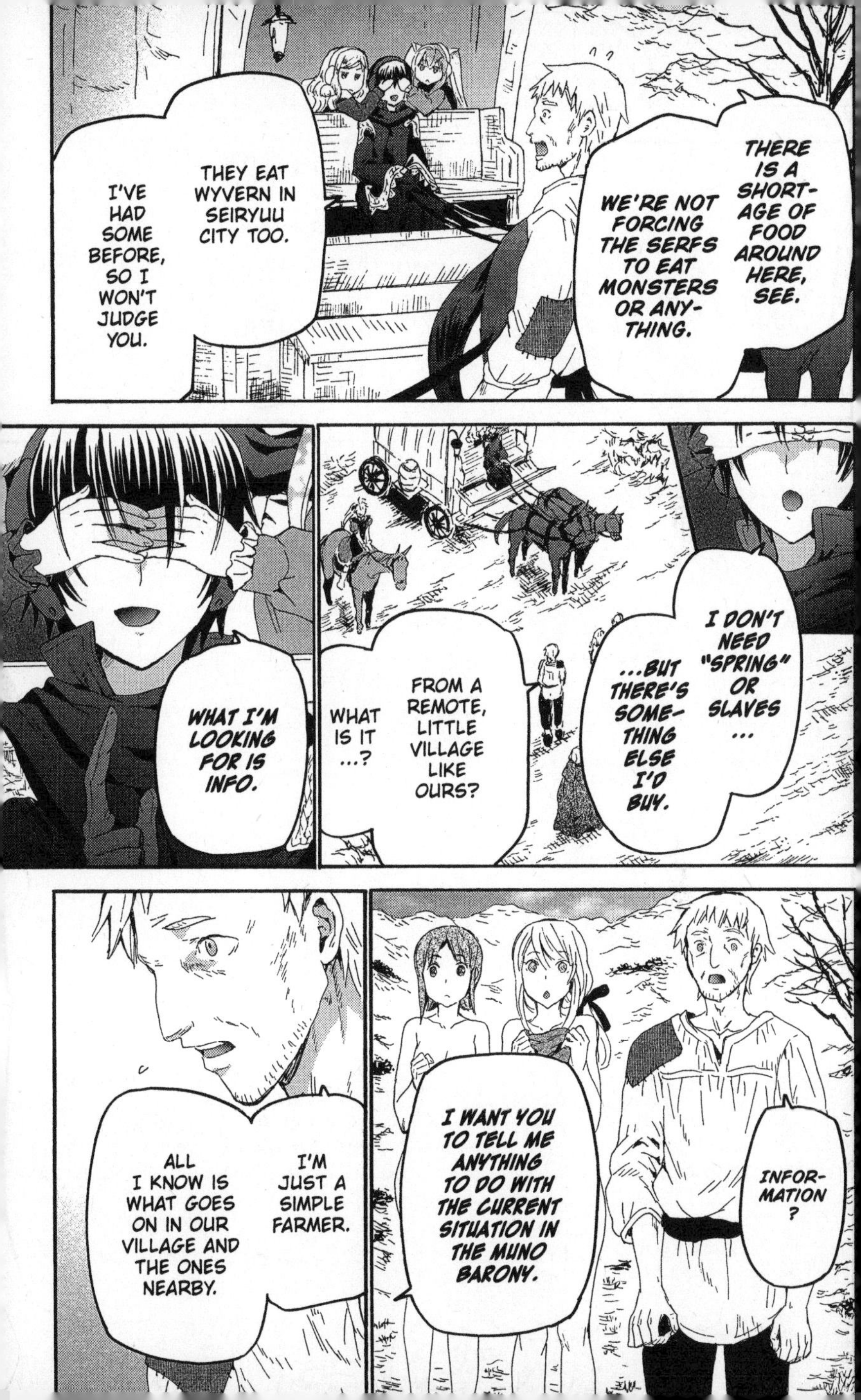
THERE IS A SHORTAGE OF FOOD AROUND HERE, SEE.
WE'RE NOT FORCING THE SERFS TO EAT MONSTERS OR ANYTHING.
THEY EAT WYVERN IN SEIRYUU CITY TOO.
I'VE HAD SOME BEFORE, SO I WON'T JUDGE YOU.
I DON'T NEED "SPRING" OR SLAVES...
...BUT THERE'S SOMETHING ELSE I'D BUY.
FROM A REMOTE, LITTLE VILLAGE LIKE OURS?
WHAT IS IT...?
WHAT I'M LOOKING FOR IS INFO.
INFORMATION?
I WANT YOU TO TELL ME ANYTHING TO DO WITH THE CURRENT SITUATION IN THE MUNO BARONY.
I'M JUST A SIMPLE FARMER.
ALL I KNOW IS WHAT GOES ON IN OUR VILLAGE AND THE ONES NEARBY.

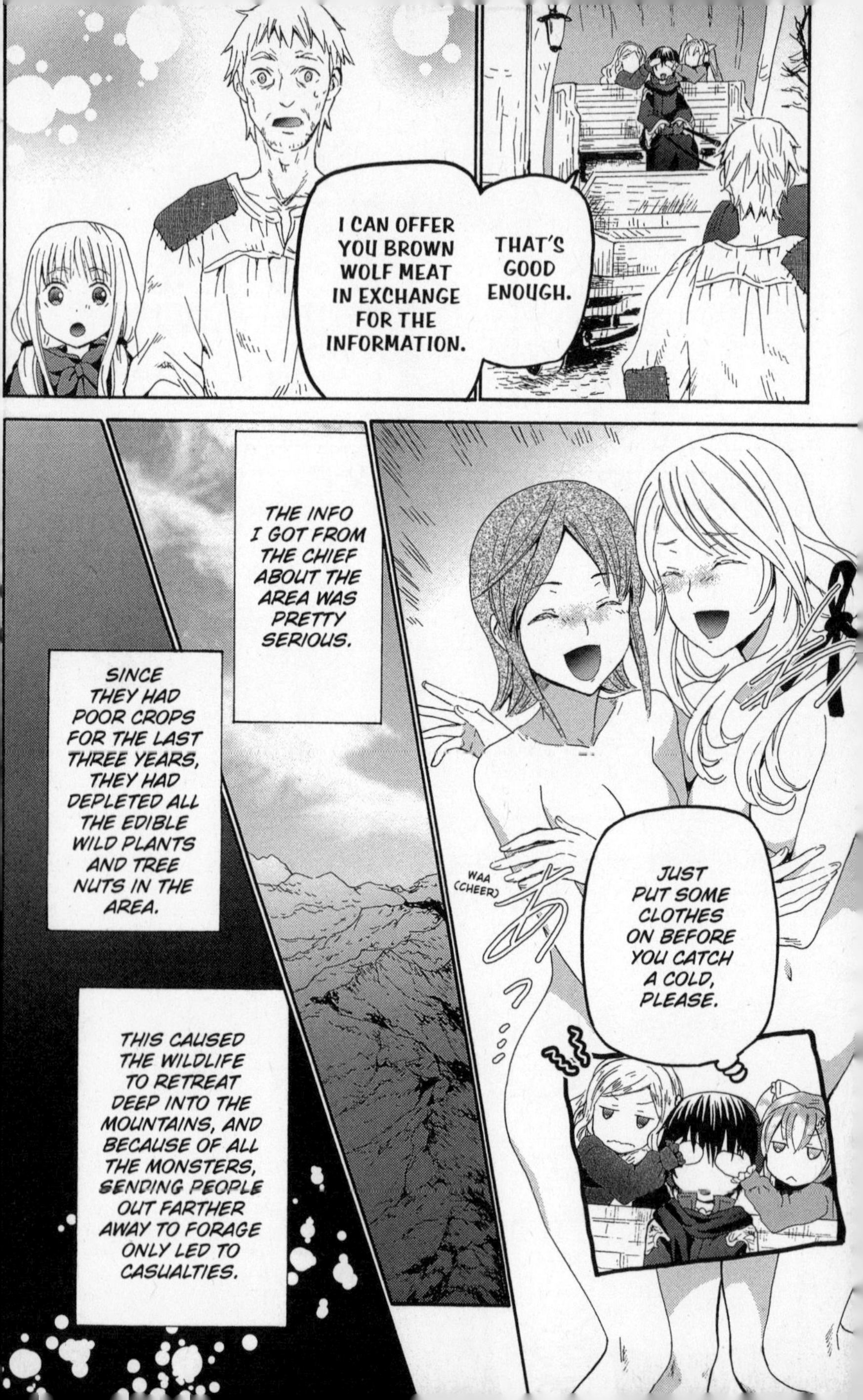
I CAN OFFER YOU BROWN WOLF MEAT IN EXCHANGE FOR THE INFORMATION.
THAT'S GOOD ENOUGH.
WAA (CHEER)
JUST PUT SOME CLOTHES ON BEFORE YOU CATCH A COLD, PLEASE.
THE INFO I GOT FROM THE CHIEF ABOUT THE AREA WAS PRETTY SERIOUS.
SINCE THEY HAD POOR CROPS FOR THE LAST THREE YEARS, THEY HAD DEPLETED ALL THE EDIBLE WILD PLANTS AND TREE NUTS IN THE AREA.
THIS CAUSED THE WILDLIFE TO RETREAT DEEP INTO THE MOUNTAINS, AND BECAUSE OF ALL THE MONSTERS, SENDING PEOPLE OUT FARTHER AWAY TO FORAGE ONLY LED TO CASUALTIES.

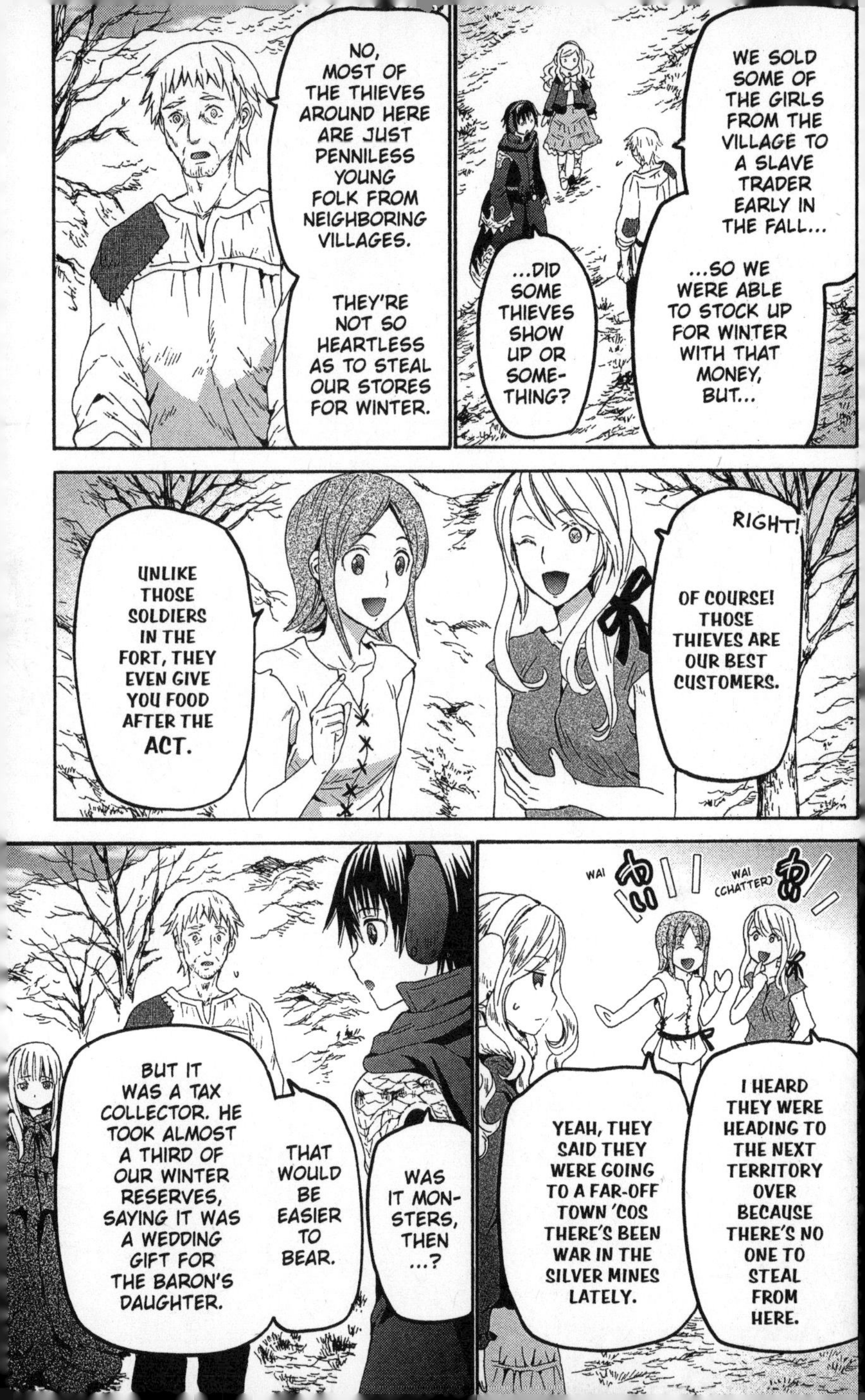

WE SOLD SOME OF THE GIRLS FROM THE VILLAGE TO A SLAVE TRADER EARLY IN THE FALL...
...SO WE WERE ABLE TO STOCK UP FOR WINTER WITH THAT MONEY, BUT...
...DID SOME THIEVES SHOW UP OR SOME-THING?
NO, MOST OF THE THIEVES AROUND HERE ARE JUST PENNILESS YOUNG FOLK FROM NEIGHBORING VILLAGES.
THEY'RE NOT SO HEARTLESS AS TO STEAL OUR STORES FOR WINTER.
RIGHT!
OF COURSE! THOSE THIEVES ARE OUR BEST CUSTOMERS.
UNLIKE THOSE SOLDIERS IN THE FORT, THEY EVEN GIVE YOU FOOD AFTER THE ACT.
WAI
WAI (CHATTER)
I HEARD THEY WERE HEADING TO THE NEXT TERRITORY OVER BECAUSE THERE'S NO ONE TO STEAL FROM HERE.
YEAH, THEY SAID THEY WERE GOING TO A FAR-OFF TOWN 'COS THERE'S BEEN WAR IN THE SILVER MINES LATELY.
WAS IT MON-STERS, THEN ...?
THAT WOULD BE EASIER TO BEAR.
BUT IT WAS A TAX COLLECTOR. HE TOOK ALMOST A THIRD OF OUR WINTER RESERVES, SAYING IT WAS A WEDDING GIFT FOR THE BARON'S DAUGHTER.

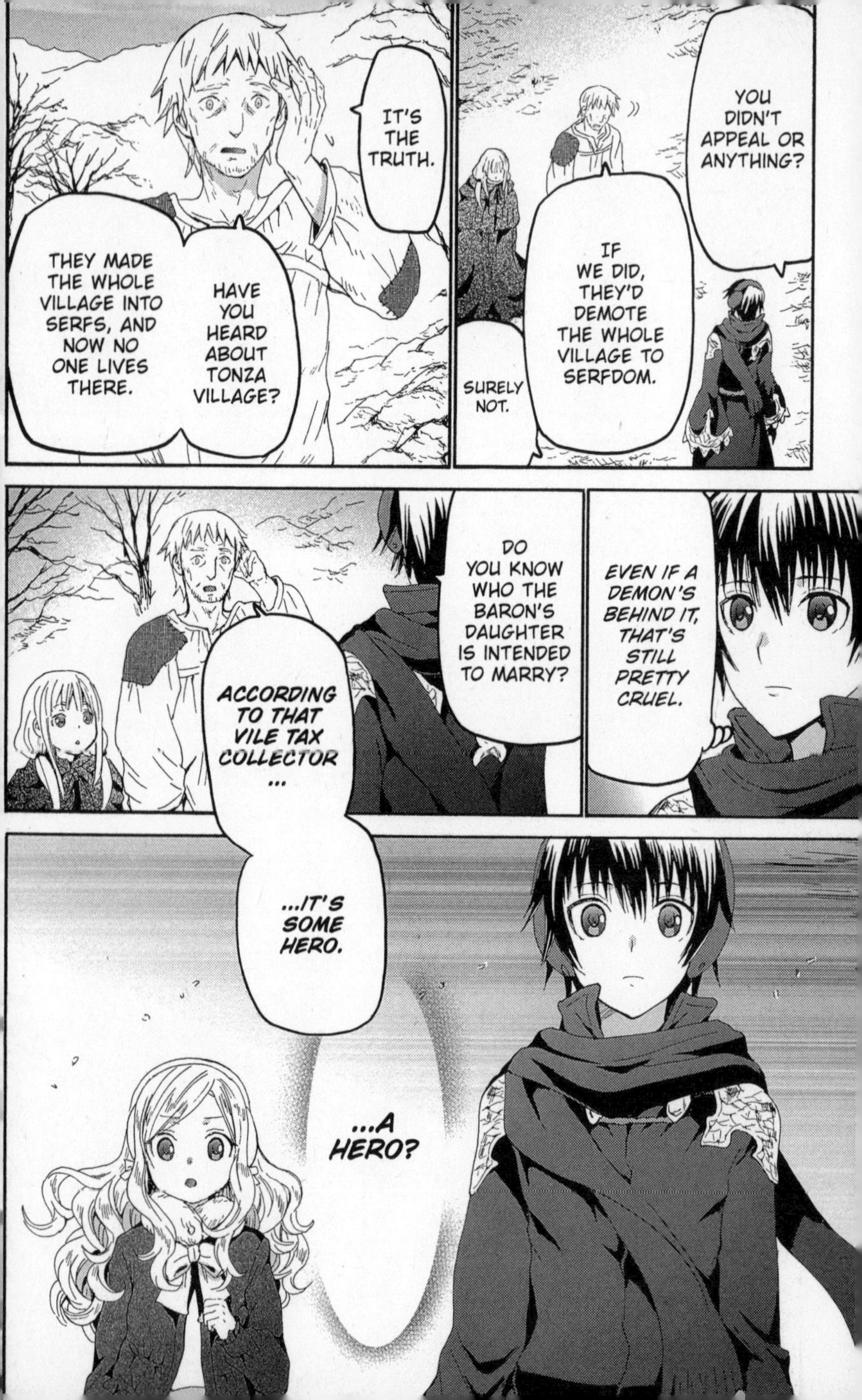
YOU DIDN'T APPEAL OR ANYTHING?
IF WE DID, THEY'D DEMOTE THE WHOLE VILLAGE TO SERFDOM.
SURELY NOT.
IT'S THE TRUTH.
HAVE YOU HEARD ABOUT TONZA VILLAGE?
THEY MADE THE WHOLE VILLAGE INTO SERFS, AND NOW NO ONE LIVES THERE.
EVEN IF A DEMON'S BEHIND IT, THAT'S STILL PRETTY CRUEL.
DO YOU KNOW WHO THE BARON'S DAUGHTER IS INTENDED TO MARRY?
ACCORDING TO THAT VILE TAX COLLECTOR...
...IT'S SOME HERO.
...A HERO?

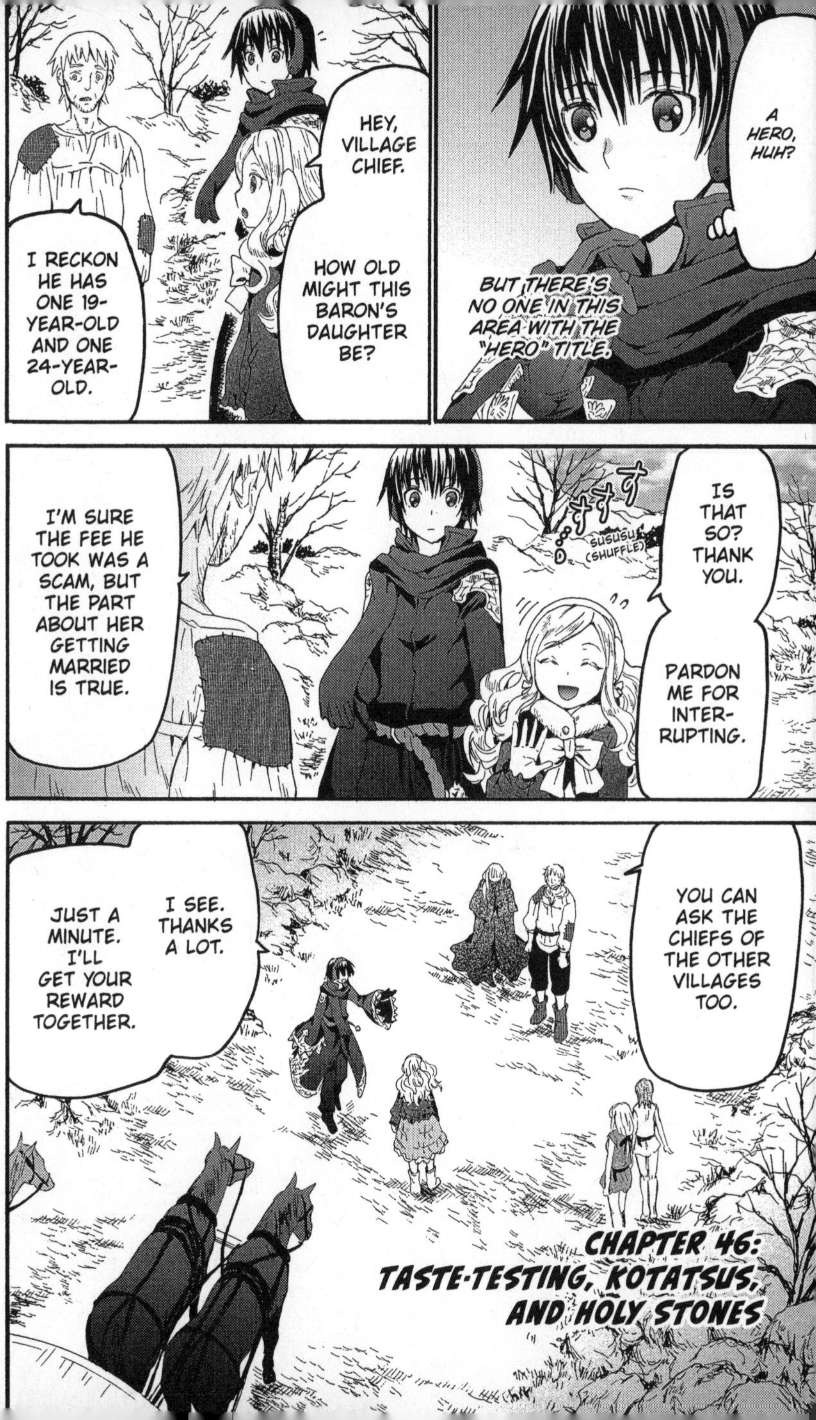
A HERO, HUH?
BUT THERE'S NO ONE IN THIS AREA WITH THE "HERO" TITLE.
HEY, VILLAGE CHIEF.
HOW OLD MIGHT THIS BARON'S DAUGHTER BE?
I RECKON HE HAS ONE 19-YEAR-OLD AND ONE 24-YEAR-OLD.
IS THAT SO? THANK YOU.
PARDON ME FOR INTERRUPTING.
すすす
SUSUSU (SHUFFLE)
I'M SURE THE FEE HE TOOK WAS A SCAM, BUT THE PART ABOUT HER GETTING MARRIED IS TRUE.
YOU CAN ASK THE CHIEFS OF THE OTHER VILLAGES TOO.
I SEE. THANKS A LOT.
JUST A MINUTE. I'LL GET YOUR REWARD TOGETHER.
CHAPTER 46: TASTE-TESTING, KOTATSUS, AND HOLY STONES

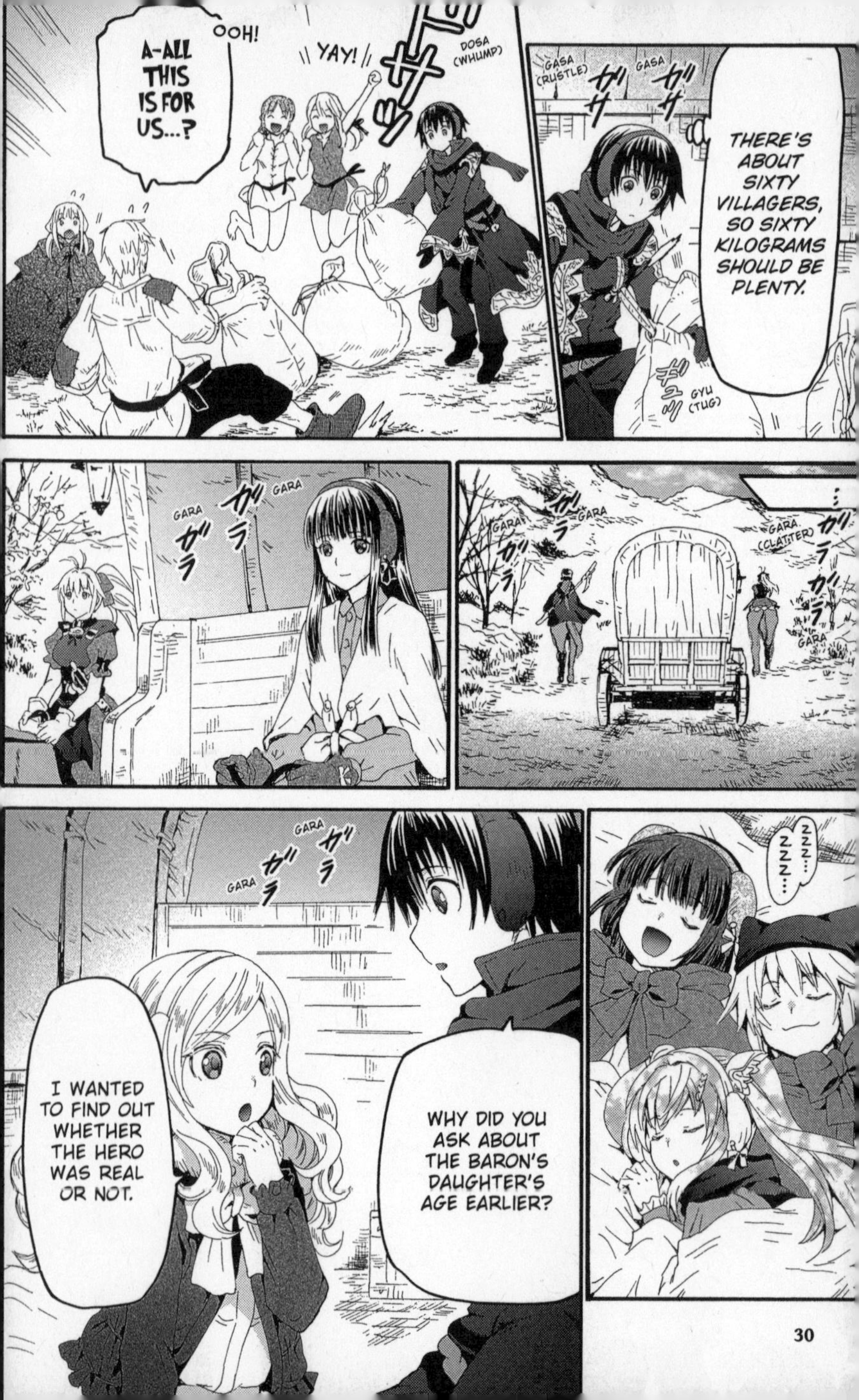
GASA (RUSTLE)
GASA
THERE'S ABOUT SIXTY VILLAGERS, SO SIXTY KILOGRAMS SHOULD BE PLENTY.
GYU (TUG)
DOSA (WHUMP)
YAY!
OOH!
A-ALL THIS IS FOR US...?
GARA (CLATTER)
GARA
GARA
GARA
GARA
GARA
GARA
ZZZ... ZZZ...
GARA
GARA
WHY DID YOU ASK ABOUT THE BARON'S DAUGHTER'S AGE EARLIER?
I WANTED TO FIND OUT WHETHER THE HERO WAS REAL OR NOT.

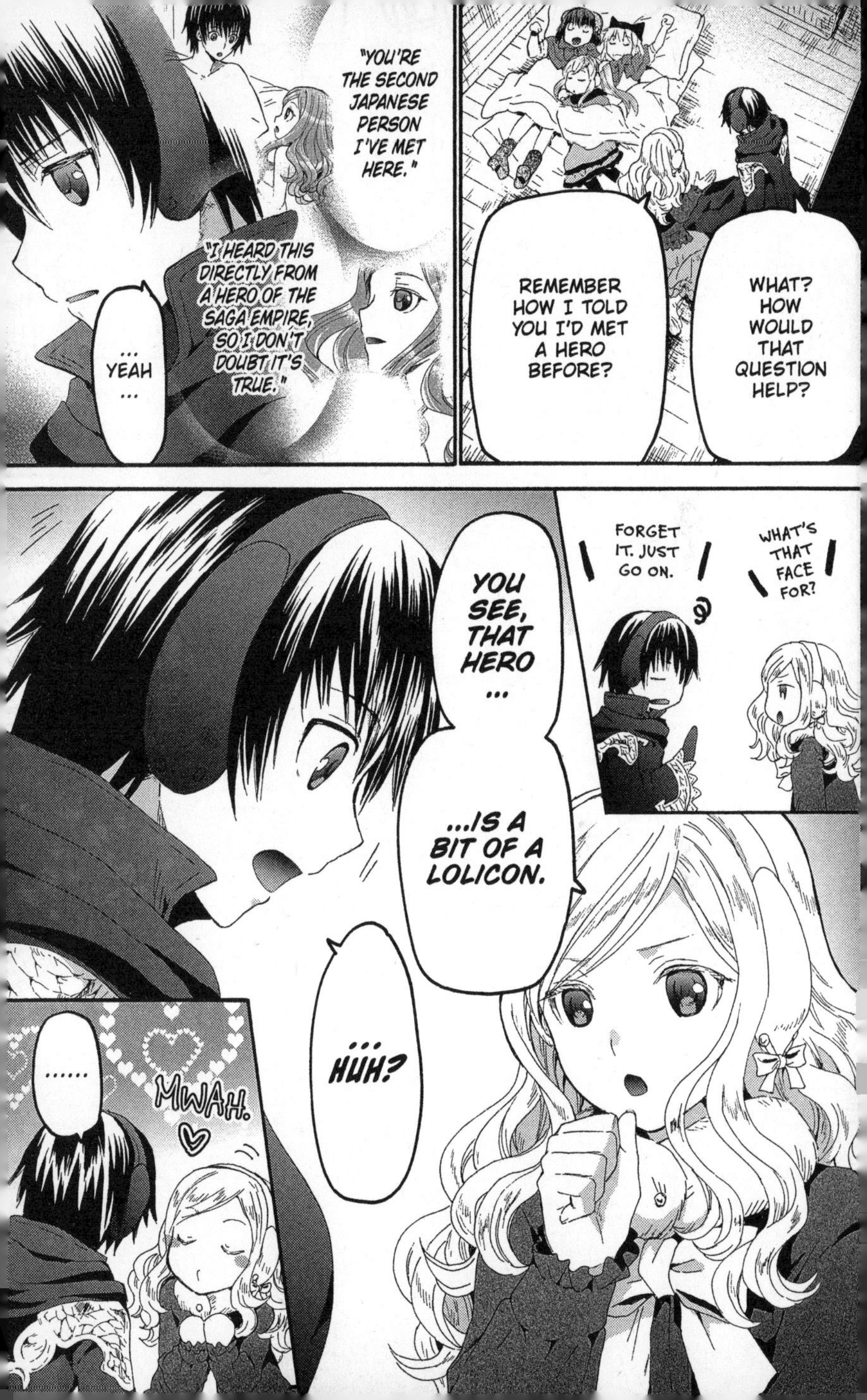
WHAT? HOW WOULD THAT QUESTION HELP?
REMEMBER HOW I TOLD YOU I'D MET A HERO BEFORE?
"YOU'RE THE SECOND JAPANESE PERSON I'VE MET HERE."
"I HEARD THIS DIRECTLY FROM A HERO OF THE SAGA EMPIRE, SO I DON'T DOUBT IT'S TRUE."
... YEAH ...
WHAT'S THAT FACE FOR?
FORGET IT. JUST GO ON.
YOU SEE, THAT HERO ...
...IS A BIT OF A LOLICON.
... HUH?
......
MWAH.

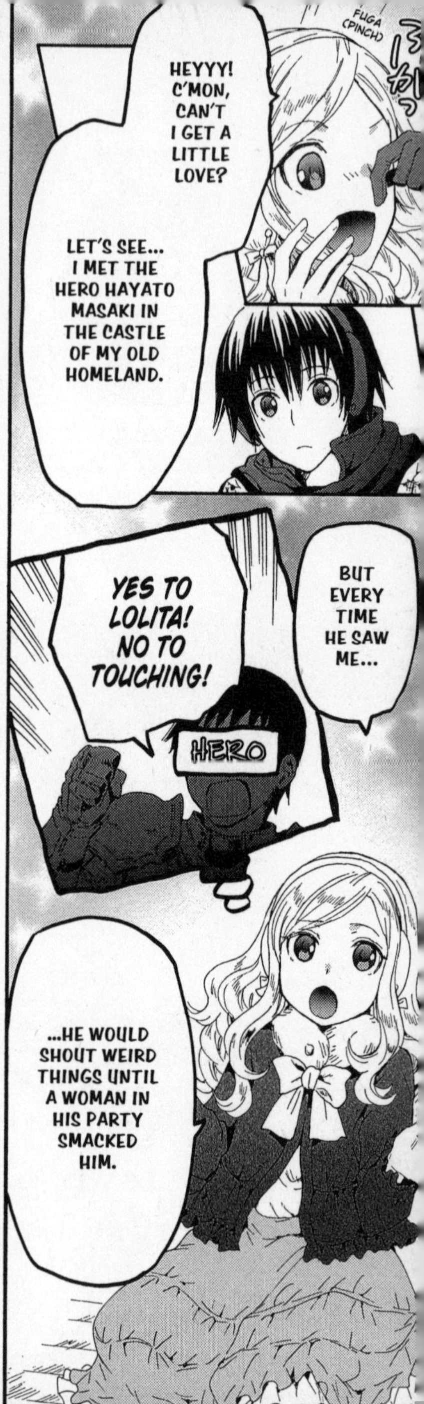
FUGA (PINCH)
HEYYY! C'MON, CAN'T I GET A LITTLE LOVE?
LET'S SEE... I MET THE HERO HAYATO MASAKI IN THE CASTLE OF MY OLD HOMELAND.
BUT EVERY TIME HE SAW ME...
YES TO LOLITA! NO TO TOUCHING!
HERO
...HE WOULD SHOUT WEIRD THINGS UNTIL A WOMAN IN HIS PARTY SMACKED HIM.
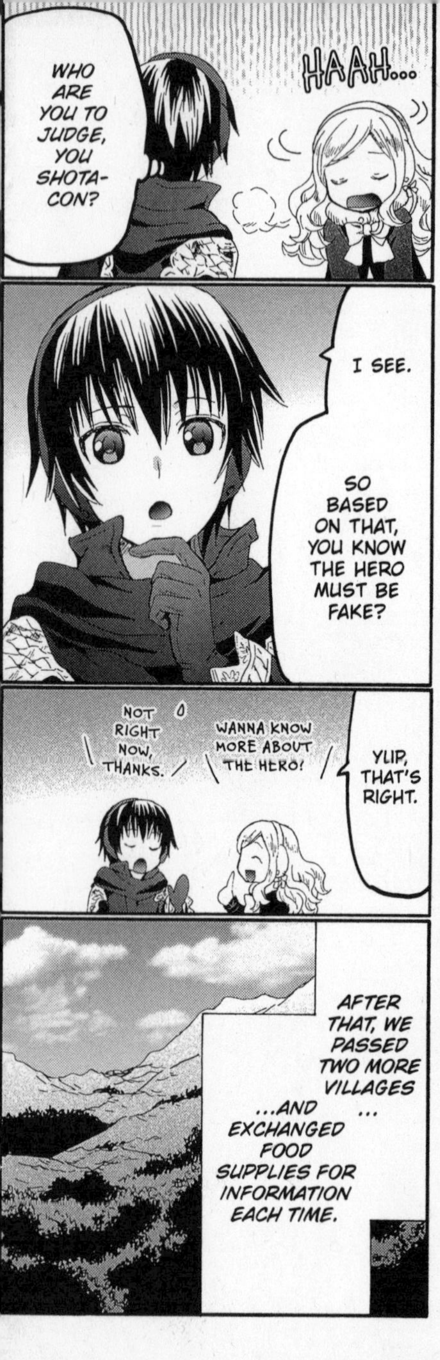
HAAAH...
WHO ARE YOU TO JUDGE, YOU SHOTA-CON?
I SEE.
SO BASED ON THAT, YOU KNOW THE HERO MUST BE FAKE?
YUP, THAT'S RIGHT.
WANNA KNOW MORE ABOUT THE HERO!
NOT RIGHT NOW, THANKS.
AFTER THAT, WE PASSED TWO MORE VILLAGES ...
...AND EXCHANGED FOOD SUPPLIES FOR INFORMATION EACH TIME.

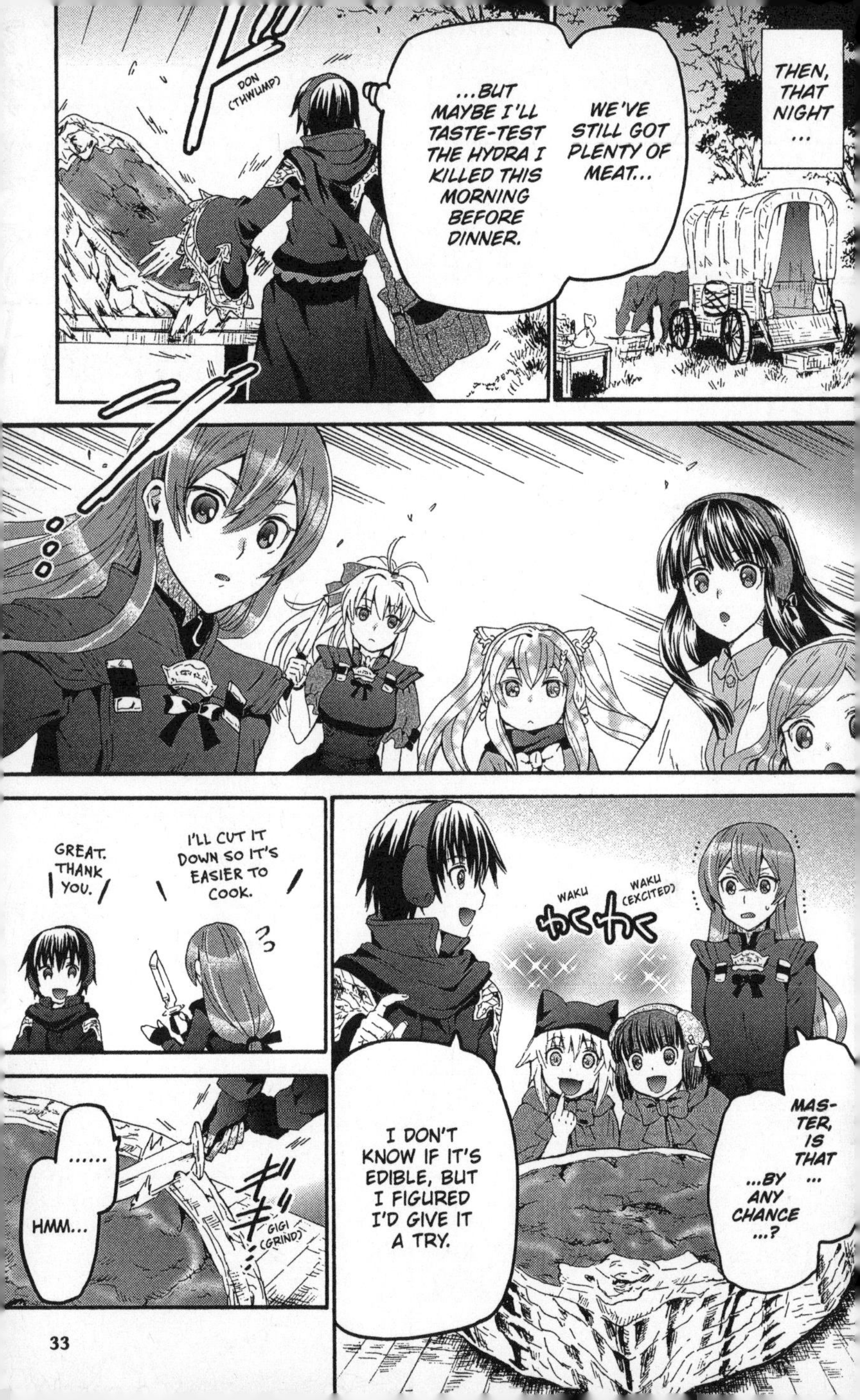
THEN, THAT NIGHT...
WE'VE STILL GOT PLENTY OF MEAT...
...BUT MAYBE I'LL TASTE-TEST THE HYDRA I KILLED THIS MORNING BEFORE DINNER.
DON (THWUMP)
WAKU WAKU (EXCITED)
MASTER, IS THAT ... ...BY ANY CHANCE ...?
I DON'T KNOW IF IT'S EDIBLE, BUT I FIGURED I'D GIVE IT A TRY.
I'LL CUT IT DOWN SO IT'S EASIER TO COOK.
GREAT. THANK YOU.
......
HMM...
GIGI (GRIND)

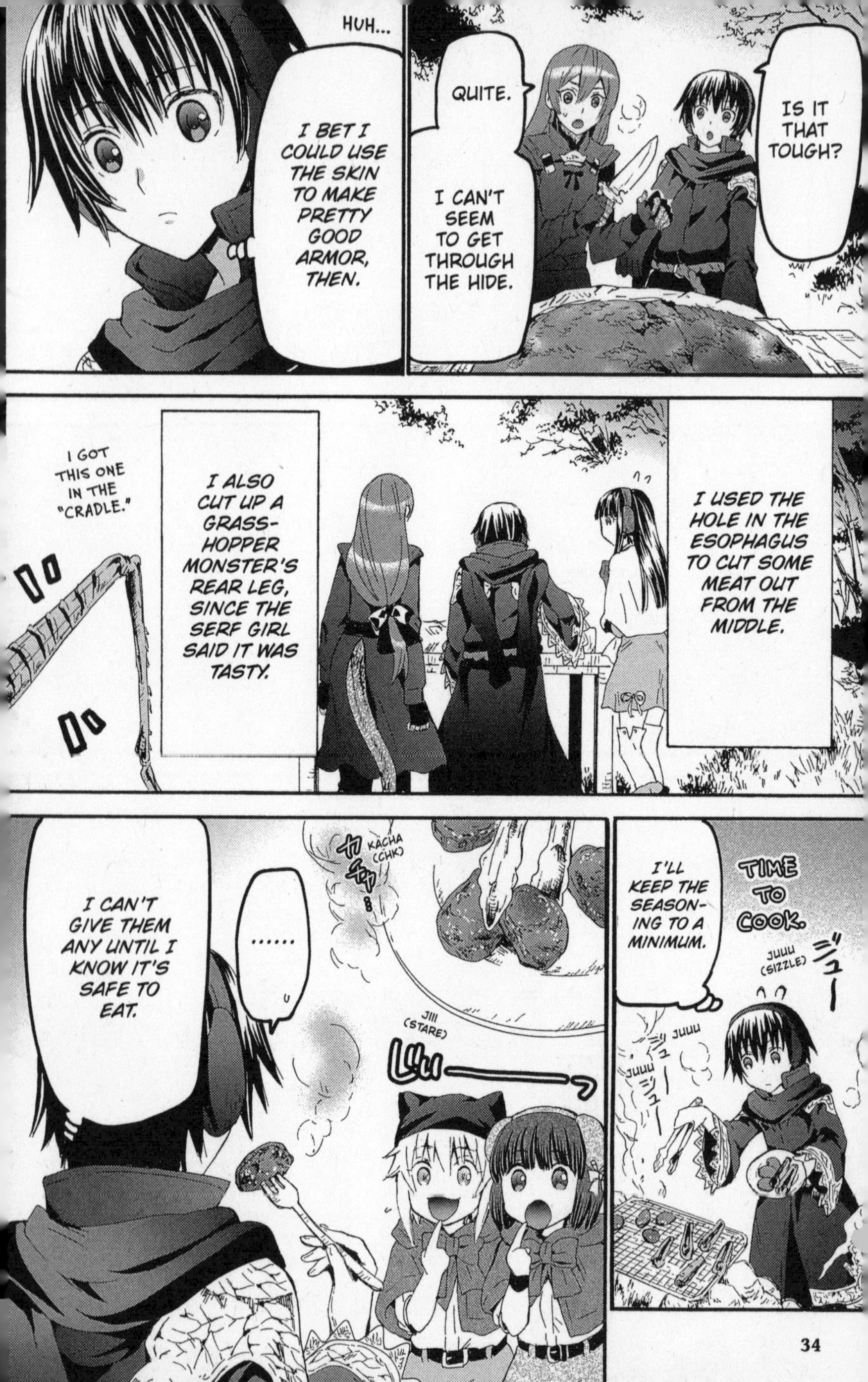
IS IT THAT TOUGH?
QUITE.
I CAN'T SEEM TO GET THROUGH THE HIDE.
HUH...
I BET I COULD USE THE SKIN TO MAKE PRETTY GOOD ARMOR, THEN.
I USED THE HOLE IN THE ESOPHAGUS TO CUT SOME MEAT OUT FROM THE MIDDLE.
I ALSO CUT UP A GRASS-HOPPER MONSTER'S REAR LEG, SINCE THE SERF GIRL SAID IT WAS TASTY.
I GOT THIS ONE IN THE "CRADLE."
TIME TO COOK.
I'LL KEEP THE SEASON-ING TO A MINIMUM.
JUUU (SIZZLE)
JUUU
JUUU
KACHA (CHK)
......
I CAN'T GIVE THEM ANY UNTIL I KNOW IT'S SAFE TO EAT.
JIII (STARE)

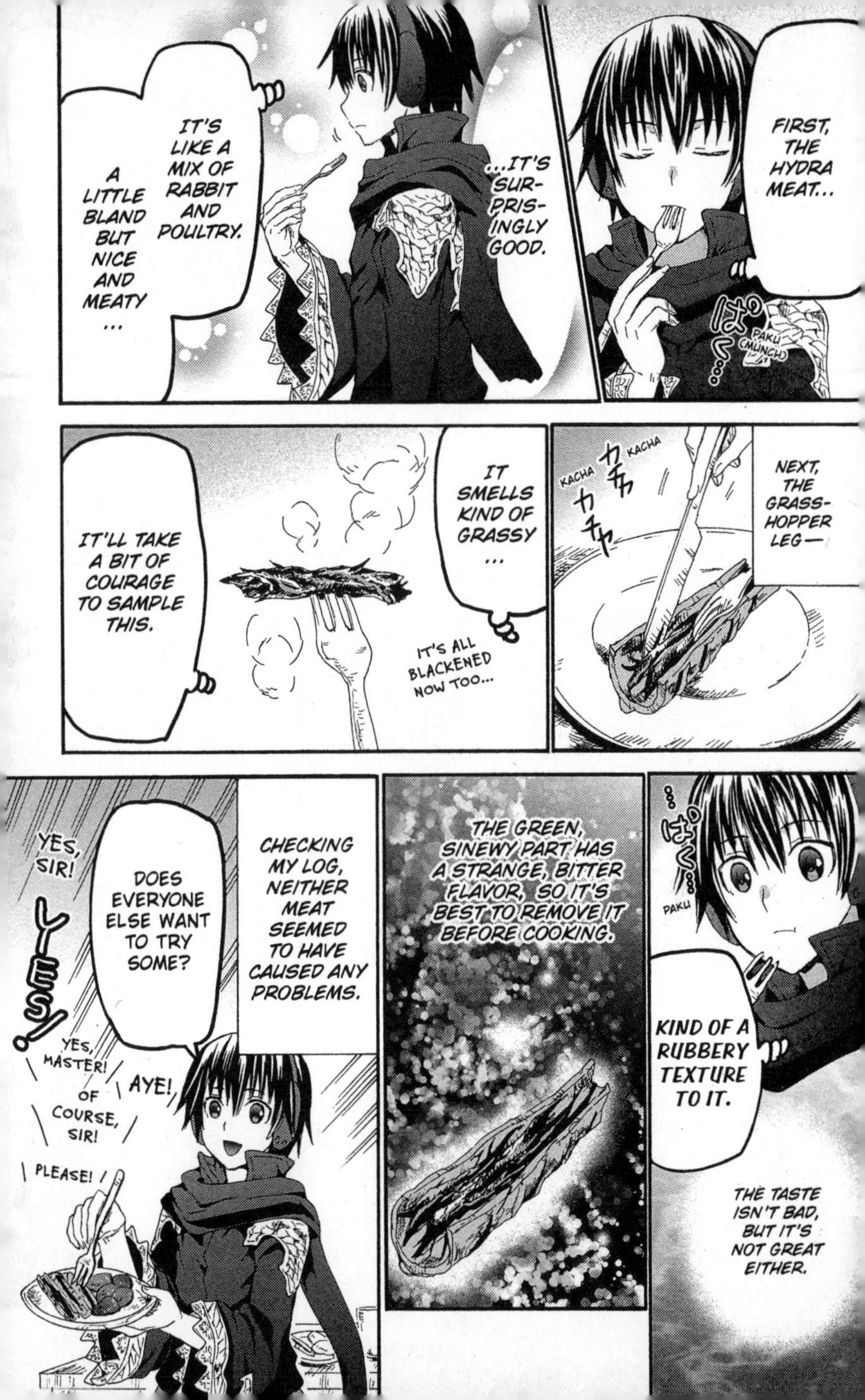
FIRST, THE HYDRA MEAT...
ぱく...
PAKU (MUNCH)
...IT'S SUR-PRIS-INGLY GOOD.
IT'S LIKE A MIX OF RABBIT AND POULTRY.
A LITTLE BLAND BUT NICE AND MEATY...
NEXT, THE GRASS-HOPPER LEG—
カチャ
KACHA
カチャ
KACHA
IT SMELLS KIND OF GRASSY...
IT'S ALL BLACKENED NOW TOO...
IT'LL TAKE A BIT OF COURAGE TO SAMPLE THIS.
...ぱく...
PAKU
KIND OF A RUBBERY TEXTURE TO IT.
THE TASTE ISN'T BAD, BUT IT'S NOT GREAT EITHER.
THE GREEN, SINEWY PART HAS A STRANGE, BITTER FLAVOR, SO IT'S BEST TO REMOVE IT BEFORE COOKING.
CHECKING MY LOG, NEITHER MEAT SEEMED TO HAVE CAUSED ANY PROBLEMS.
DOES EVERYONE ELSE WANT TO TRY SOME?
YES, SIR!
YES!
YES, MASTER!
AYE!
OF COURSE, SIR!
PLEASE!

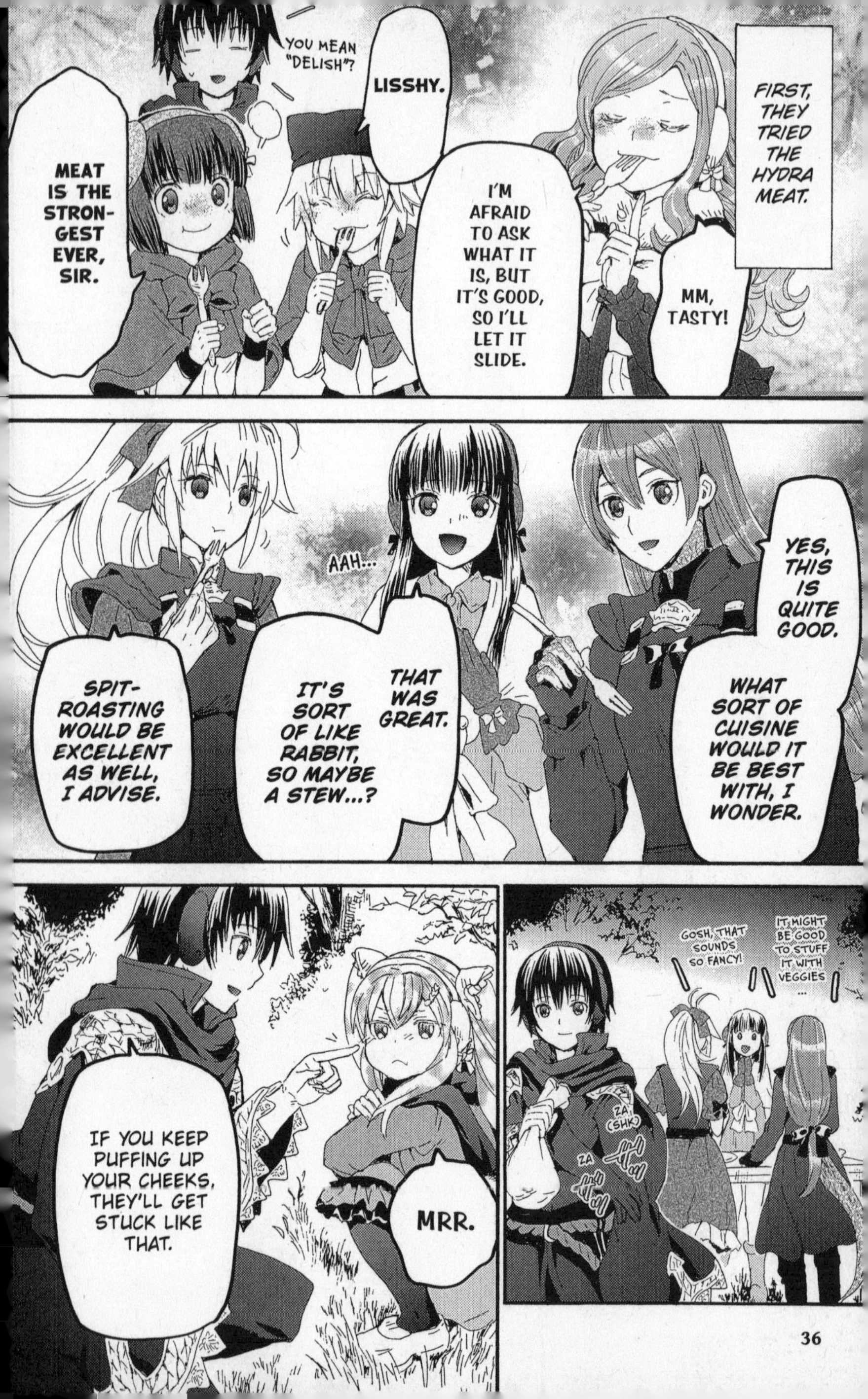
FIRST, THEY TRIED THE HYDRA MEAT.
MM, TASTY!
I'M AFRAID TO ASK WHAT IT IS, BUT IT'S GOOD, SO I'LL LET IT SLIDE.
LISSHY.
YOU MEAN "DELISH"?
MEAT IS THE STRONGEST EVER, SIR.
YES, THIS IS QUITE GOOD.
WHAT SORT OF CUISINE WOULD IT BE BEST WITH, I WONDER.
THAT WAS GREAT.
IT'S SORT OF LIKE RABBIT, SO MAYBE A STEW...?
AAH...
SPIT-ROASTING WOULD BE EXCELLENT AS WELL, I ADVISE.
IT MIGHT BE GOOD TO STUFF IT WITH VEGGIES...
GOSH, THAT SOUNDS SO FANCY!
ZA (SHK)
ZA
MRR.
IF YOU KEEP PUFFING UP YOUR CHEEKS, THEY'LL GET STUCK LIKE THAT.

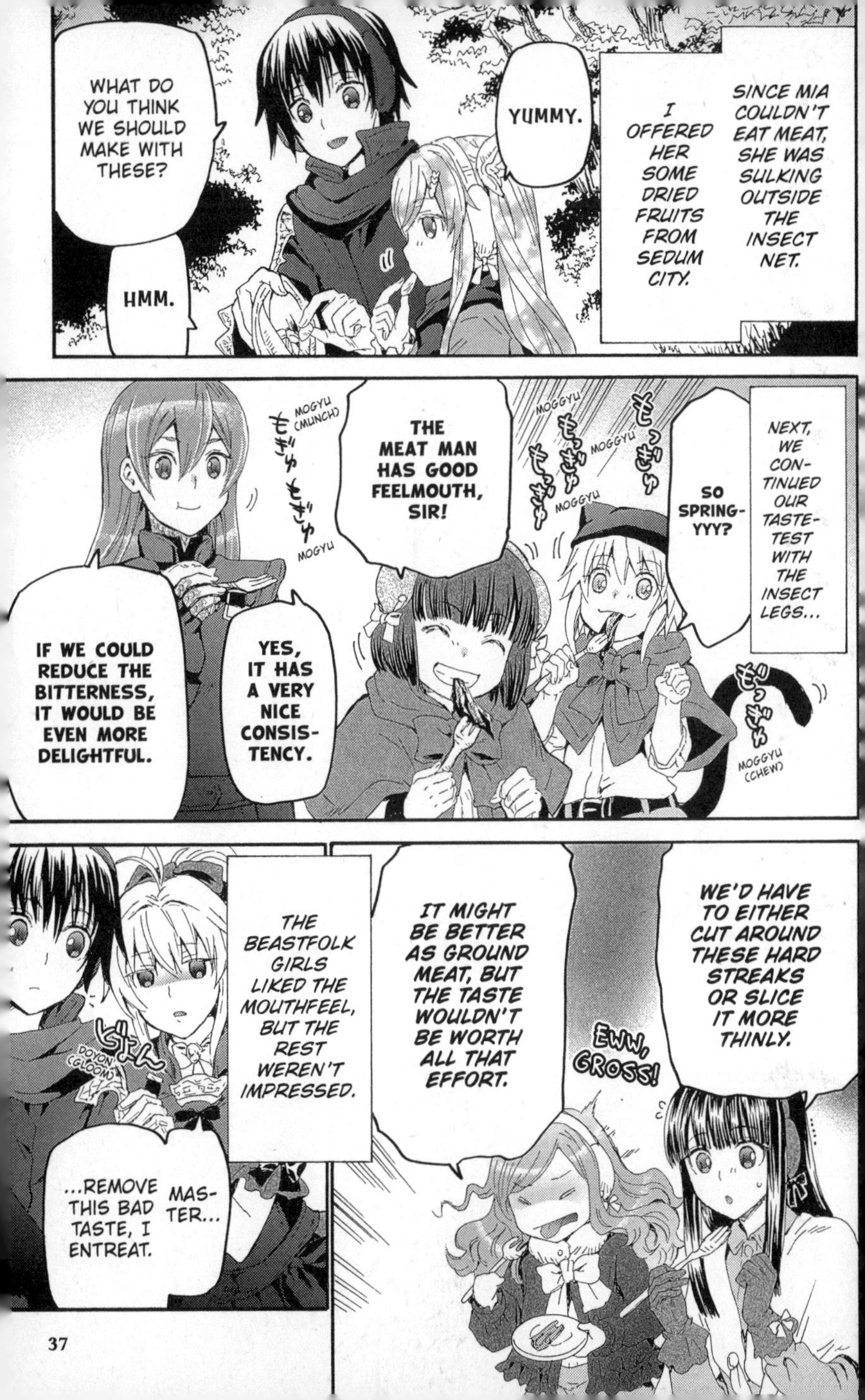
SINCE MIA COULDN'T EAT MEAT, SHE WAS SULKING OUTSIDE THE INSECT NET.
I OFFERED HER SOME DRIED FRUITS FROM SEDUM CITY.
YUMMY.
WHAT DO YOU THINK WE SHOULD MAKE WITH THESE?
HMM.
NEXT, WE CONTINUED OUR TASTE-TEST WITH THE INSECT LEGS...
SO SPRING-YYY?
MOGGYU
MOGGYU
MOGGYU
MOGGYU (CHEW)
THE MEAT MAN HAS GOOD FEELMOUTH, SIR!
MOGYU (MUNCH)
MOGYU
YES, IT HAS A VERY NICE CONSISTENCY.
IF WE COULD REDUCE THE BITTERNESS, IT WOULD BE EVEN MORE DELIGHTFUL.
WE'D HAVE TO EITHER CUT AROUND THESE HARD STREAKS OR SLICE IT MORE THINLY.
EWW, GROSS!
IT MIGHT BE BETTER AS GROUND MEAT, BUT THE TASTE WOULDN'T BE WORTH ALL THAT EFFORT.
THE BEASTFOLK GIRLS LIKED THE MOUTHFEEL, BUT THE REST WEREN'T IMPRESSED.
DOYON (GLOOM)
MASTER...
...REMOVE THIS BAD TASTE, I ENTREAT.

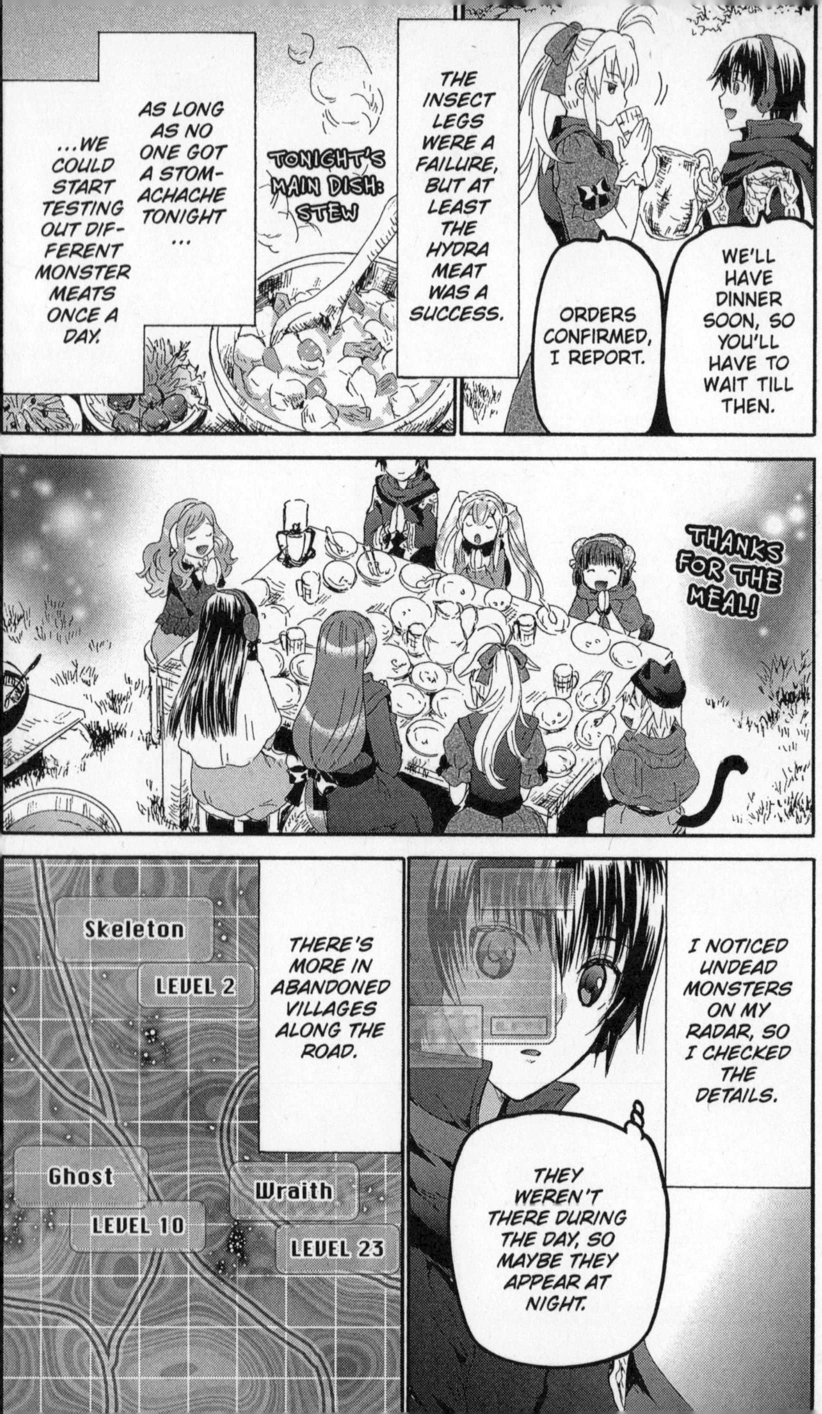
WE'LL HAVE DINNER SOON, SO YOU'LL HAVE TO WAIT TILL THEN.
ORDERS CONFIRMED, I REPORT.
THE INSECT LEGS WERE A FAILURE, BUT AT LEAST THE HYDRA MEAT WAS A SUCCESS.
TONIGHT'S MAIN DISH: STEW
AS LONG AS NO ONE GOT A STOM-ACHACHE TONIGHT...
...WE COULD START TESTING OUT DIF-FERENT MONSTER MEATS ONCE A DAY.
THANKS FOR THE MEAL!
I NOTICED UNDEAD MONSTERS ON MY RADAR, SO I CHECKED THE DETAILS.
THEY WEREN'T THERE DURING THE DAY, SO MAYBE THEY APPEAR AT NIGHT.
THERE'S MORE IN ABANDONED VILLAGES ALONG THE ROAD.
Skeleton
LEVEL 2
Ghost
LEVEL 10
Wraith
LEVEL 23

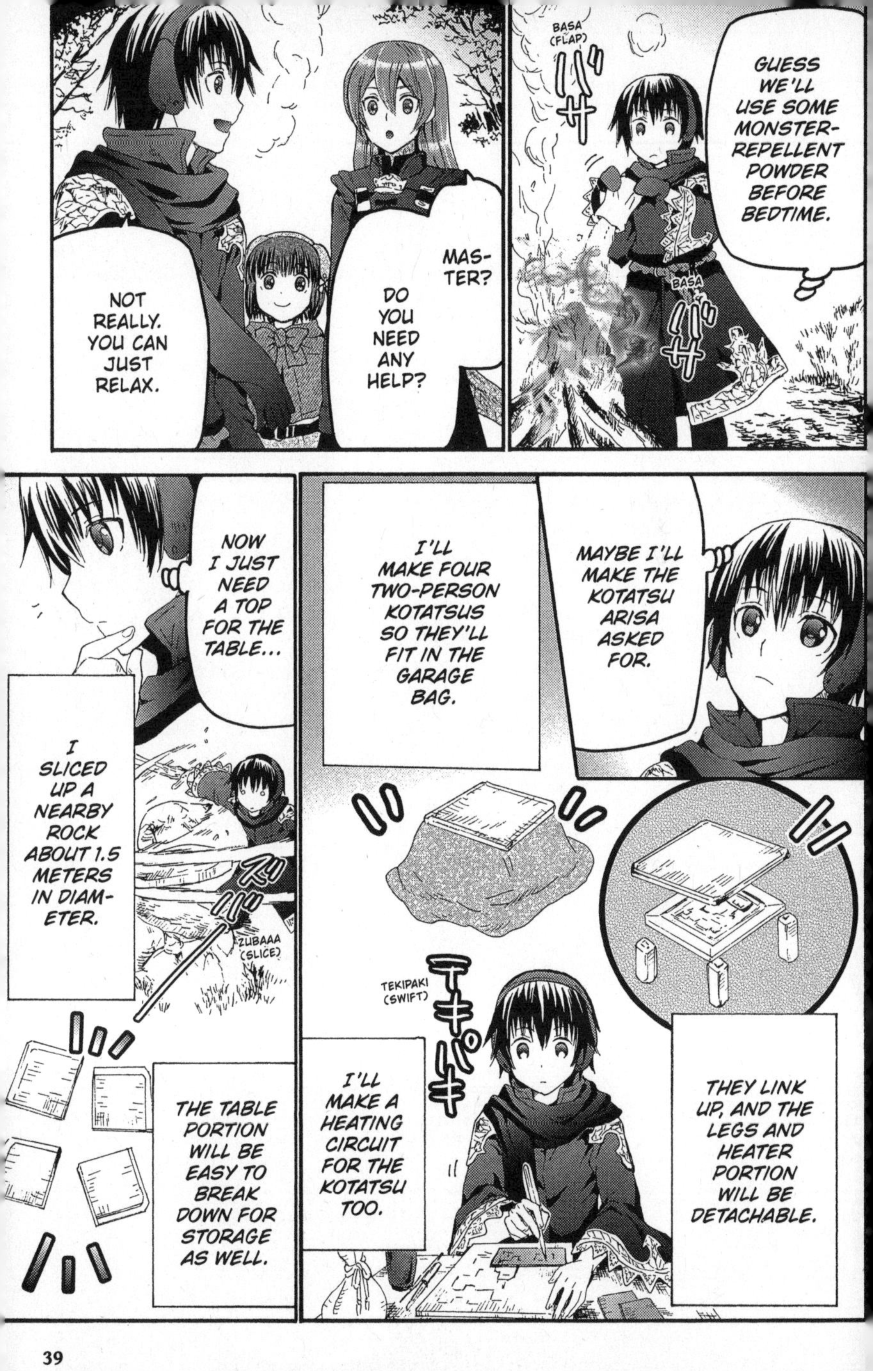
BASA (FLAP)
GUESS WE'LL USE SOME MONSTER-REPELLENT POWDER BEFORE BEDTIME.
BASA
MASTER?
DO YOU NEED ANY HELP?
NOT REALLY. YOU CAN JUST RELAX.
MAYBE I'LL MAKE THE KOTATSU ARISA ASKED FOR.
I'LL MAKE FOUR TWO-PERSON KOTATSUS SO THEY'LL FIT IN THE GARAGE BAG.
TEKIPAKI (SWIFT)
THEY LINK UP, AND THE LEGS AND HEATER PORTION WILL BE DETACHABLE.
I'LL MAKE A HEATING CIRCUIT FOR THE KOTATSU TOO.
NOW I JUST NEED A TOP FOR THE TABLE...
I SLICED UP A NEARBY ROCK ABOUT 1.5 METERS IN DIAMETER.
ZUBAAA (SLICE)
THE TABLE PORTION WILL BE EASY TO BREAK DOWN FOR STORAGE AS WELL.

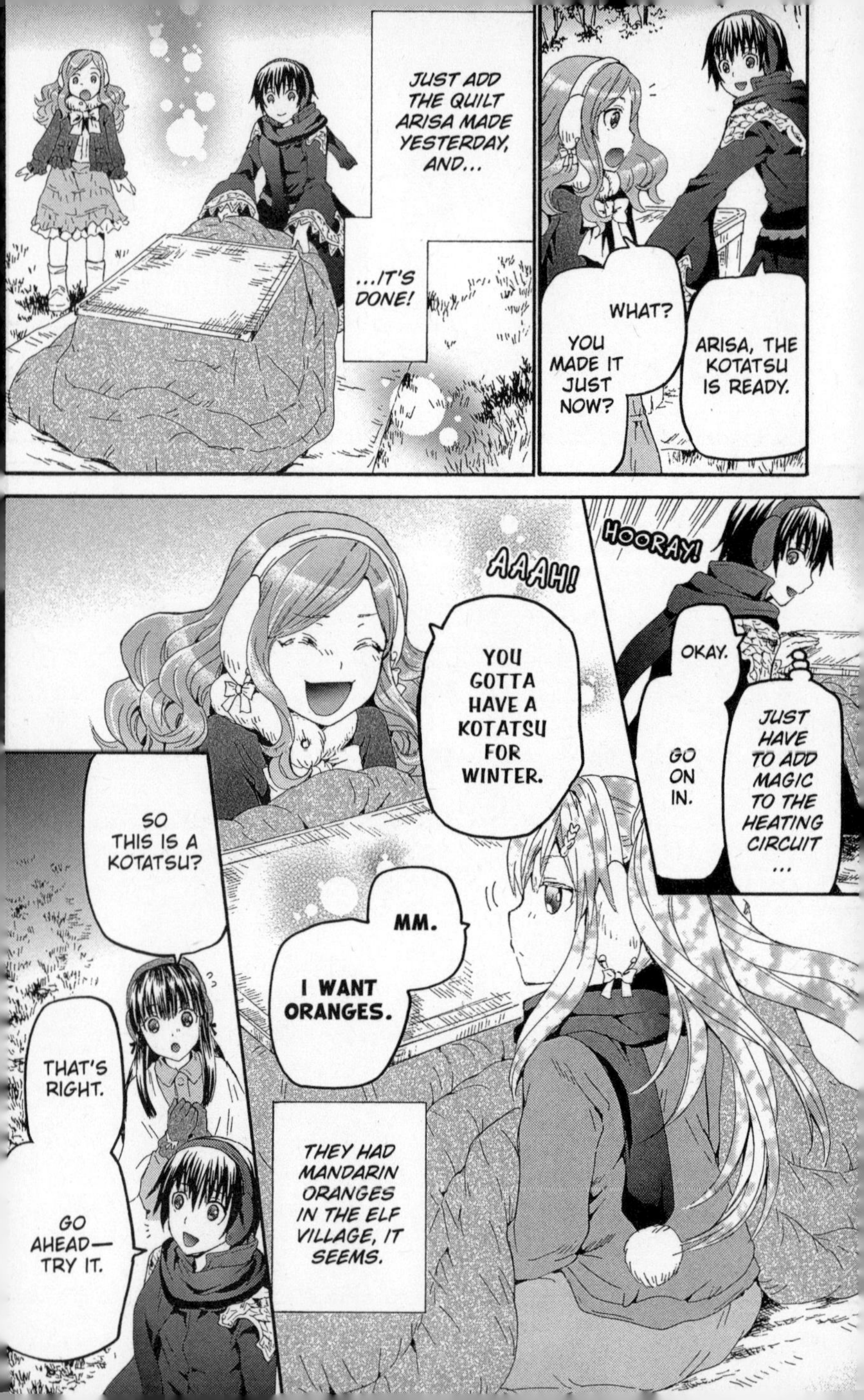
ARISA, THE KOTATSU IS READY.
WHAT? YOU MADE IT JUST NOW?
JUST ADD THE QUILT ARISA MADE YESTERDAY, AND...
...IT'S DONE!
HOORAY!
JUST HAVE TO ADD MAGIC TO THE HEATING CIRCUIT...
OKAY. GO ON IN.
AAAH!
YOU GOTTA HAVE A KOTATSU FOR WINTER.
MM. I WANT ORANGES.
THEY HAD MANDARIN ORANGES IN THE ELF VILLAGE, IT SEEMS.
SO THIS IS A KOTATSU?
THAT'S RIGHT. GO AHEAD— TRY IT.

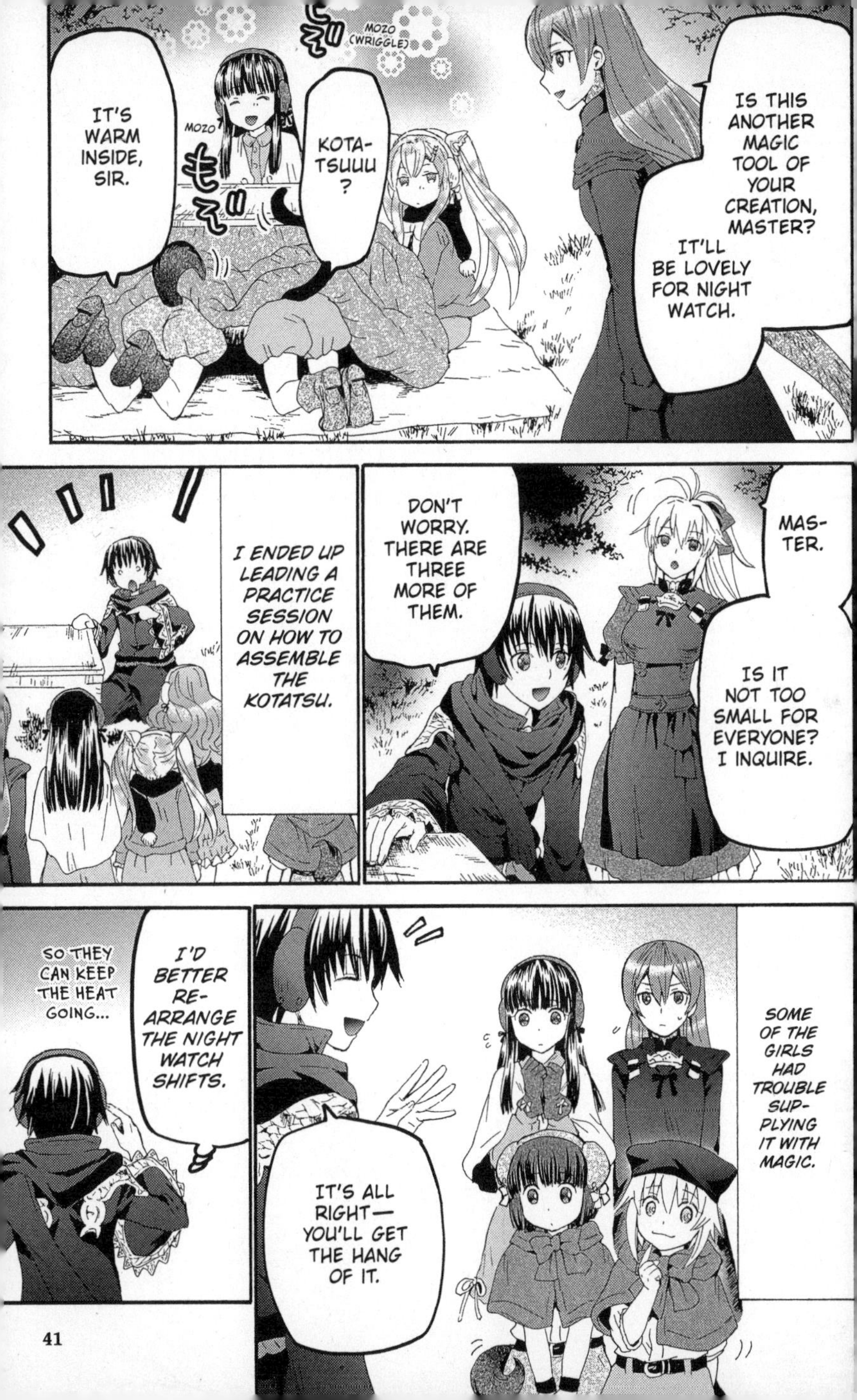
IS THIS ANOTHER MAGIC TOOL OF YOUR CREATION, MASTER?
IT'LL BE LOVELY FOR NIGHT WATCH.
MOZO (WRIGGLE)
KOTA-TSUUU?
MOZO
IT'S WARM INSIDE, SIR.
MAS-TER.
IS IT NOT TOO SMALL FOR EVERYONE? I INQUIRE.
DON'T WORRY. THERE ARE THREE MORE OF THEM.
I ENDED UP LEADING A PRACTICE SESSION ON HOW TO ASSEMBLE THE KOTATSU.
SOME OF THE GIRLS HAD TROUBLE SUP-PLYING IT WITH MAGIC.
IT'S ALL RIGHT—YOU'LL GET THE HANG OF IT.
I'D BETTER RE-ARRANGE THE NIGHT WATCH SHIFTS.
SO THEY CAN KEEP THE HEAT GOING...

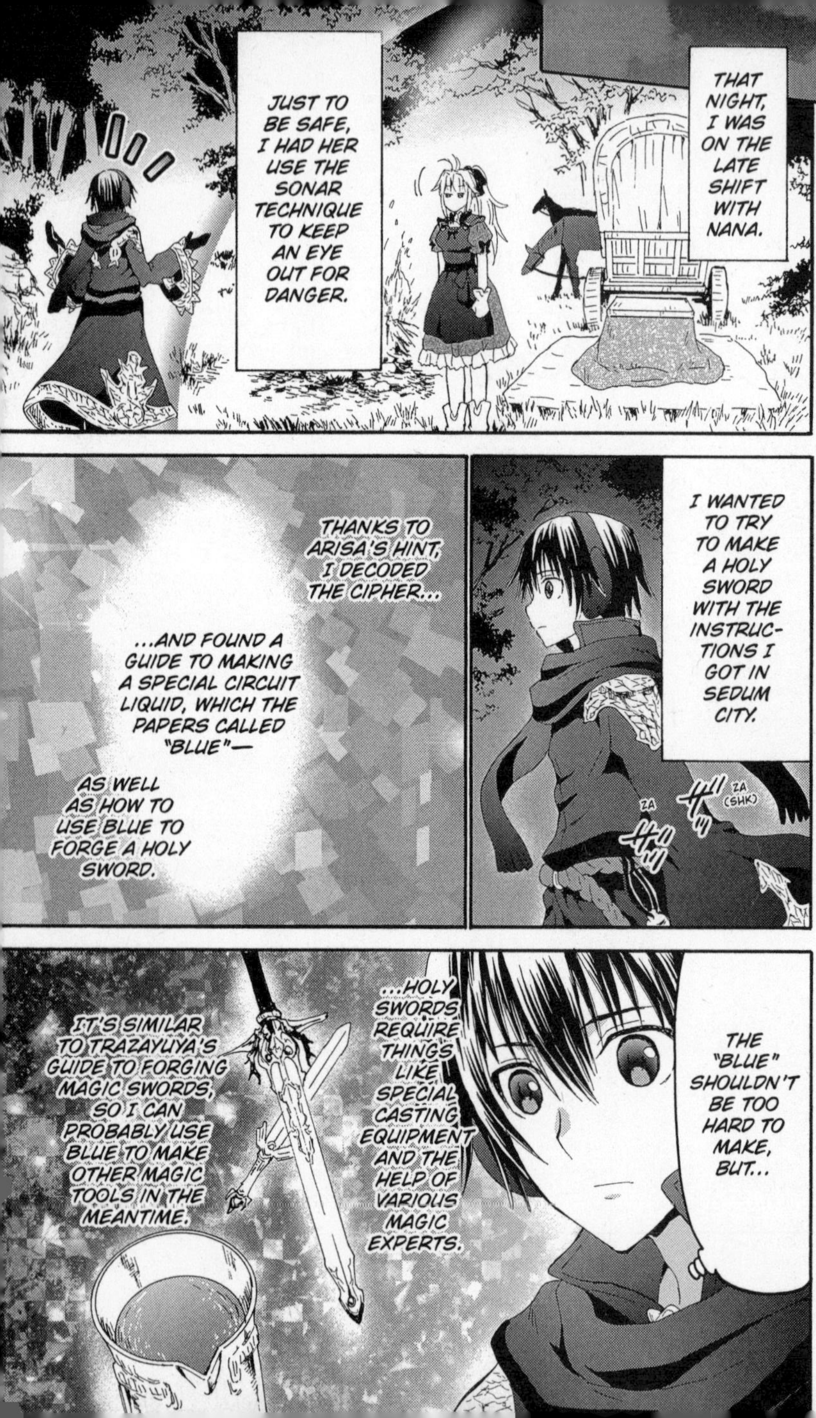
THAT NIGHT, I WAS ON THE LATE SHIFT WITH NANA.
JUST TO BE SAFE, I HAD HER USE THE SONAR TECHNIQUE TO KEEP AN EYE OUT FOR DANGER.
I WANTED TO TRY TO MAKE A HOLY SWORD WITH THE INSTRUC-TIONS I GOT IN SEDUM CITY.
ZA (SHK)
ZA
THANKS TO ARISA'S HINT, I DECODED THE CIPHER...
...AND FOUND A GUIDE TO MAKING A SPECIAL CIRCUIT LIQUID, WHICH THE PAPERS CALLED "BLUE"—
AS WELL AS HOW TO USE BLUE TO FORGE A HOLY SWORD.
THE "BLUE" SHOULDN'T BE TOO HARD TO MAKE, BUT...
...HOLY SWORDS REQUIRE THINGS LIKE SPECIAL CASTING EQUIPMENT AND THE HELP OF VARIOUS MAGIC EXPERTS.
IT'S SIMILAR TO TRAZAYUYA'S GUIDE TO FORGING MAGIC SWORDS, SO I CAN PROBABLY USE BLUE TO MAKE OTHER MAGIC TOOLS IN THE MEANTIME.

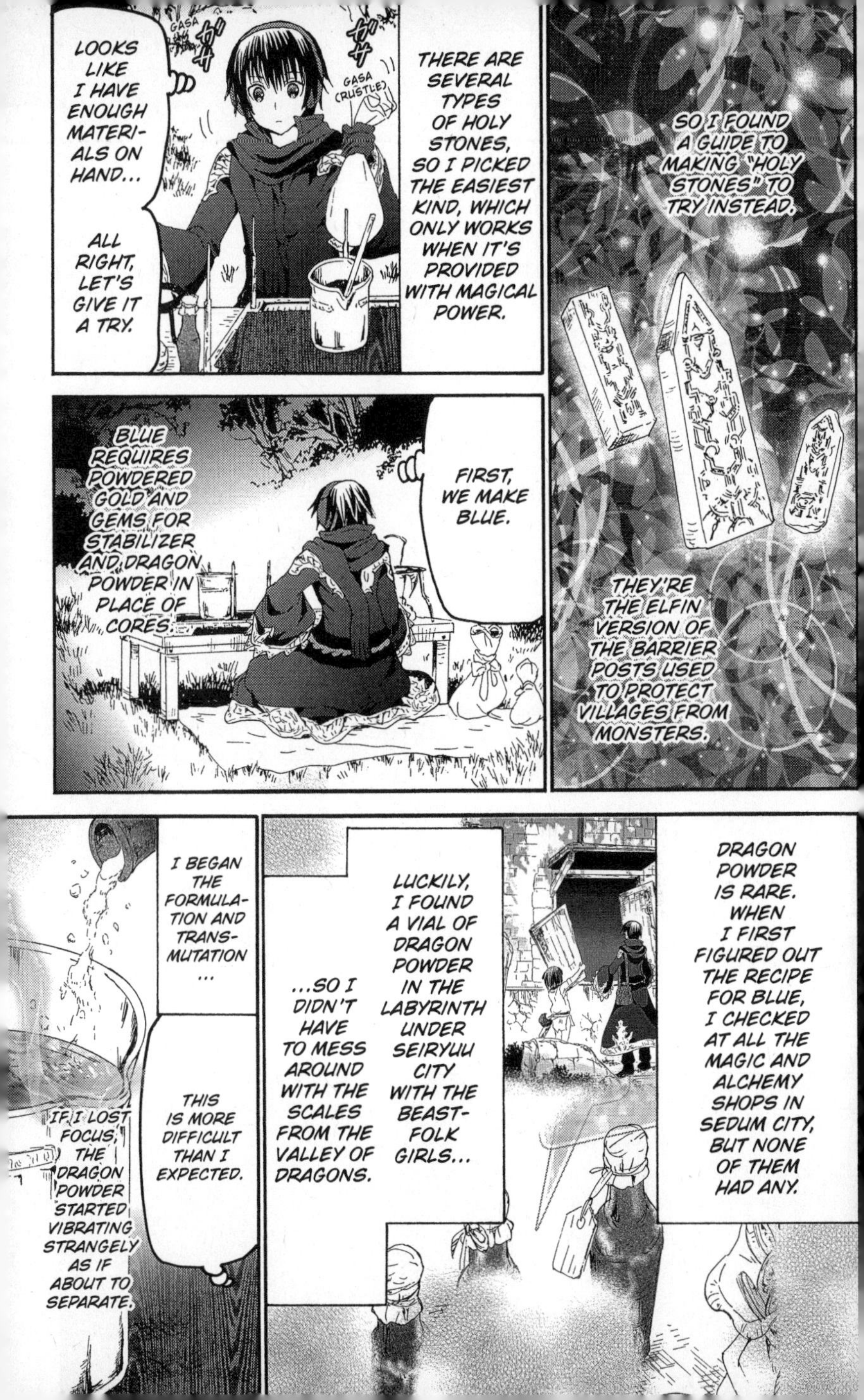
SO I FOUND A GUIDE TO MAKING "HOLY STONES" TO TRY INSTEAD.
THEY'RE THE ELFIN VERSION OF THE BARRIER POSTS USED TO PROTECT VILLAGES FROM MONSTERS.
THERE ARE SEVERAL TYPES OF HOLY STONES, SO I PICKED THE EASIEST KIND, WHICH ONLY WORKS WHEN IT'S PROVIDED WITH MAGICAL POWER.
GASA (RUSTLE)
GASA
LOOKS LIKE I HAVE ENOUGH MATERI-ALS ON HAND...
ALL RIGHT, LET'S GIVE IT A TRY.
FIRST, WE MAKE BLUE.
BLUE REQUIRES POWDERED GOLD AND GEMS FOR STABILIZER AND DRAGON POWDER IN PLACE OF CORES.
DRAGON POWDER IS RARE. WHEN I FIRST FIGURED OUT THE RECIPE FOR BLUE, I CHECKED AT ALL THE MAGIC AND ALCHEMY SHOPS IN SEDUM CITY, BUT NONE OF THEM HAD ANY.
LUCKILY, I FOUND A VIAL OF DRAGON POWDER IN THE LABYRINTH UNDER SEIRYUU CITY WITH THE BEAST-FOLK GIRLS...
...SO I DIDN'T HAVE TO MESS AROUND WITH THE SCALES FROM THE VALLEY OF DRAGONS.
I BEGAN THE FORMULA-TION AND TRANS-MUTATION...
THIS IS MORE DIFFICULT THAN I EXPECTED.
IF I LOST FOCUS, THE DRAGON POWDER STARTED VIBRATING STRANGELY AS IF ABOUT TO SEPARATE.

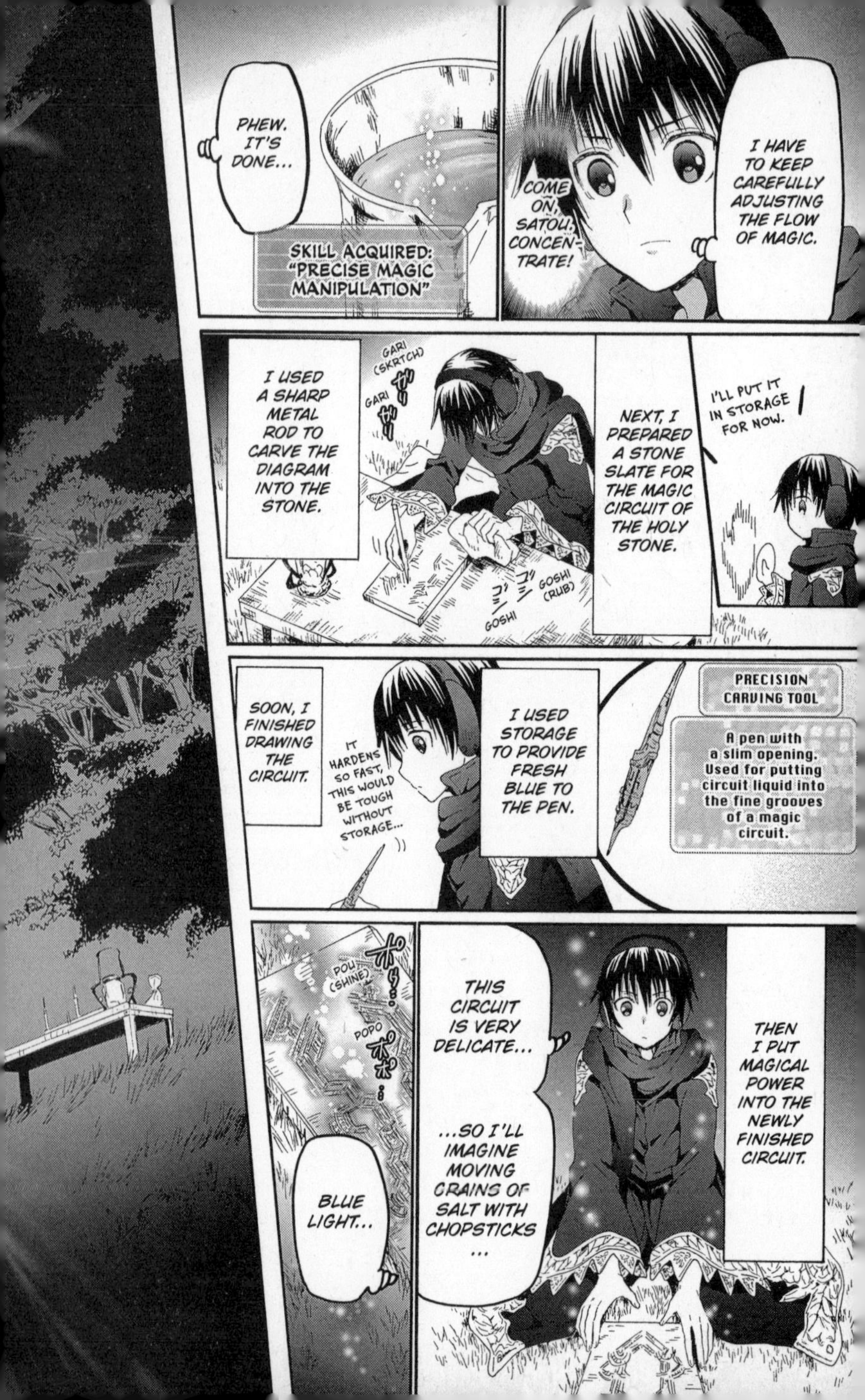
I HAVE TO KEEP CAREFULLY ADJUSTING THE FLOW OF MAGIC.
COME ON, SATOU. CONCENTRATE!
PHEW. IT'S DONE...
SKILL ACQUIRED: "PRECISE MAGIC MANIPULATION"
I'LL PUT IT IN STORAGE FOR NOW.
NEXT, I PREPARED A STONE SLATE FOR THE MAGIC CIRCUIT OF THE HOLY STONE.
GARI (SKRTCH)
GARI
GOSHI (RUB)
GOSHI
I USED A SHARP METAL ROD TO CARVE THE DIAGRAM INTO THE STONE.
PRECISION CARVING TOOL
A pen with a slim opening. Used for putting circuit liquid into the fine grooves of a magic circuit.
I USED STORAGE TO PROVIDE FRESH BLUE TO THE PEN.
IT HARDENS SO FAST, THIS WOULD BE TOUGH WITHOUT STORAGE...
SOON, I FINISHED DRAWING THE CIRCUIT.
THEN I PUT MAGICAL POWER INTO THE NEWLY FINISHED CIRCUIT.
THIS CIRCUIT IS VERY DELICATE...
...SO I'LL IMAGINE MOVING GRAINS OF SALT WITH CHOPSTICKS...
POU (SHINE)
POPO
BLUE LIGHT...

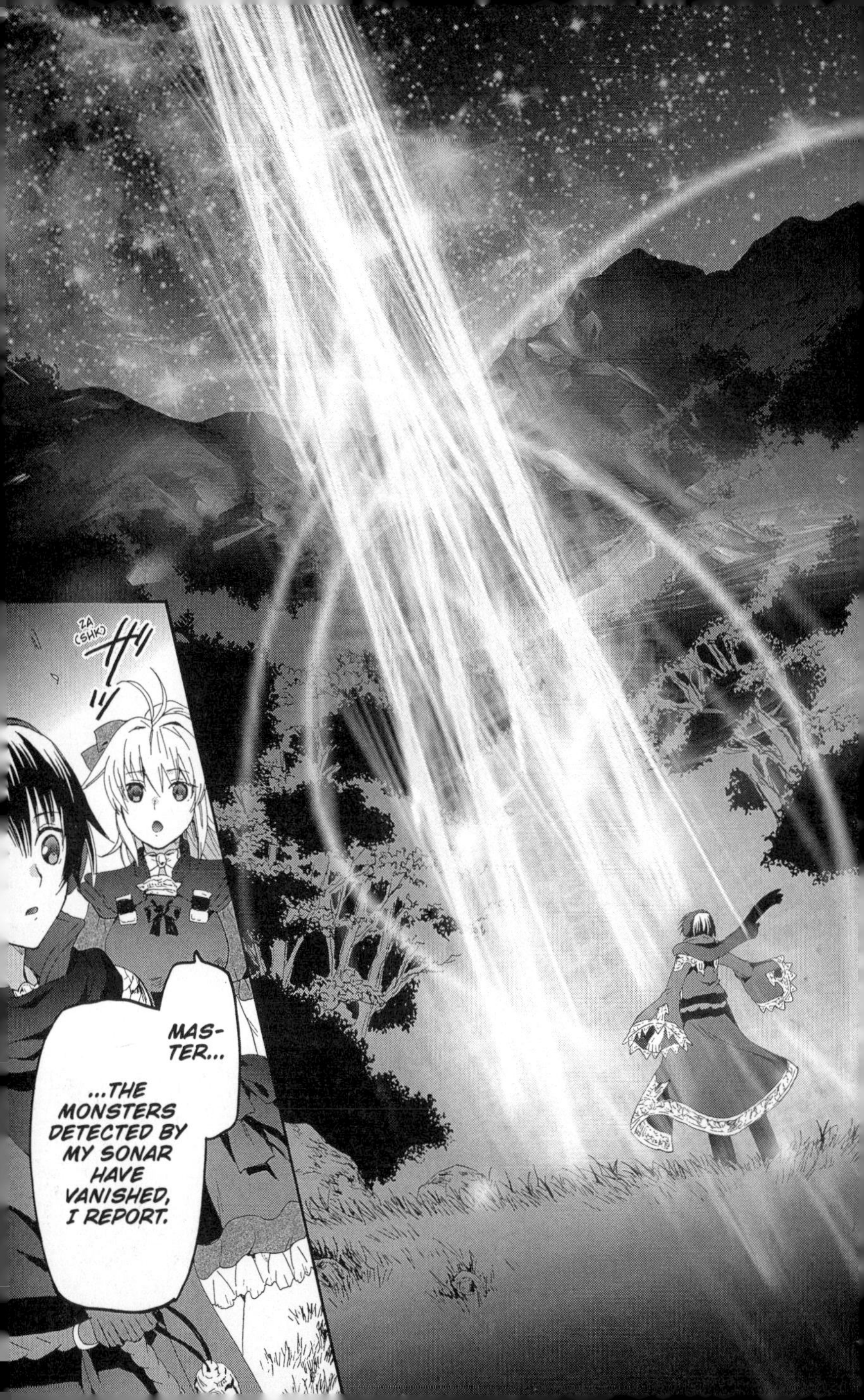
ZA (SHK)
MAS-TER... ...THE MONSTERS DETECTED BY MY SONAR HAVE VANISHED, I REPORT.

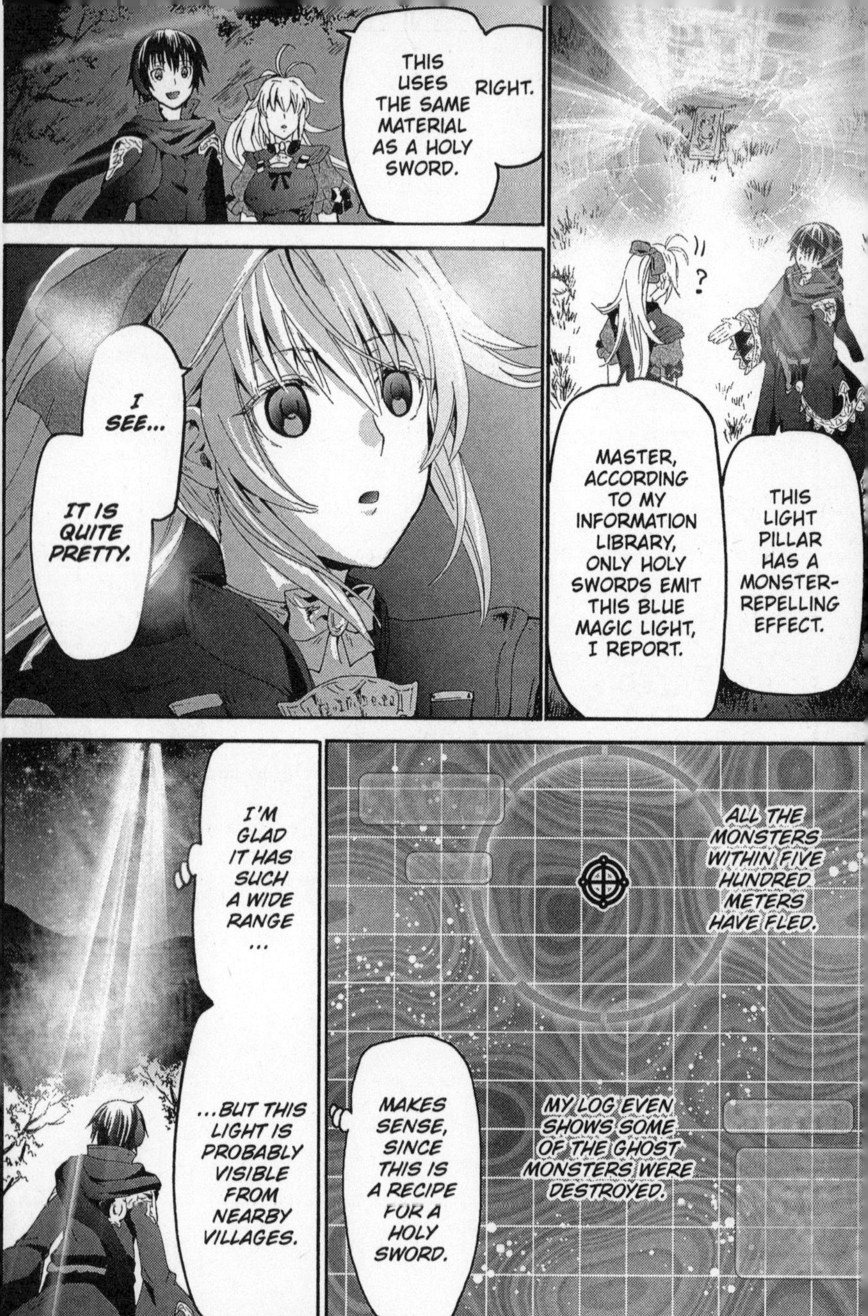
?
THIS LIGHT PILLAR HAS A MONSTER-REPELLING EFFECT.
MASTER, ACCORDING TO MY INFORMATION LIBRARY, ONLY HOLY SWORDS EMIT THIS BLUE MAGIC LIGHT, I REPORT.
RIGHT.
THIS USES THE SAME MATERIAL AS A HOLY SWORD.
I SEE...
IT IS QUITE PRETTY.
ALL THE MONSTERS WITHIN FIVE HUNDRED METERS HAVE FLED.
MY LOG EVEN SHOWS SOME OF THE GHOST MONSTERS WERE DESTROYED.
MAKES SENSE, SINCE THIS IS A RECIPE FOR A HOLY SWORD.
I'M GLAD IT HAS SUCH A WIDE RANGE...
...BUT THIS LIGHT IS PROBABLY VISIBLE FROM NEARBY VILLAGES.

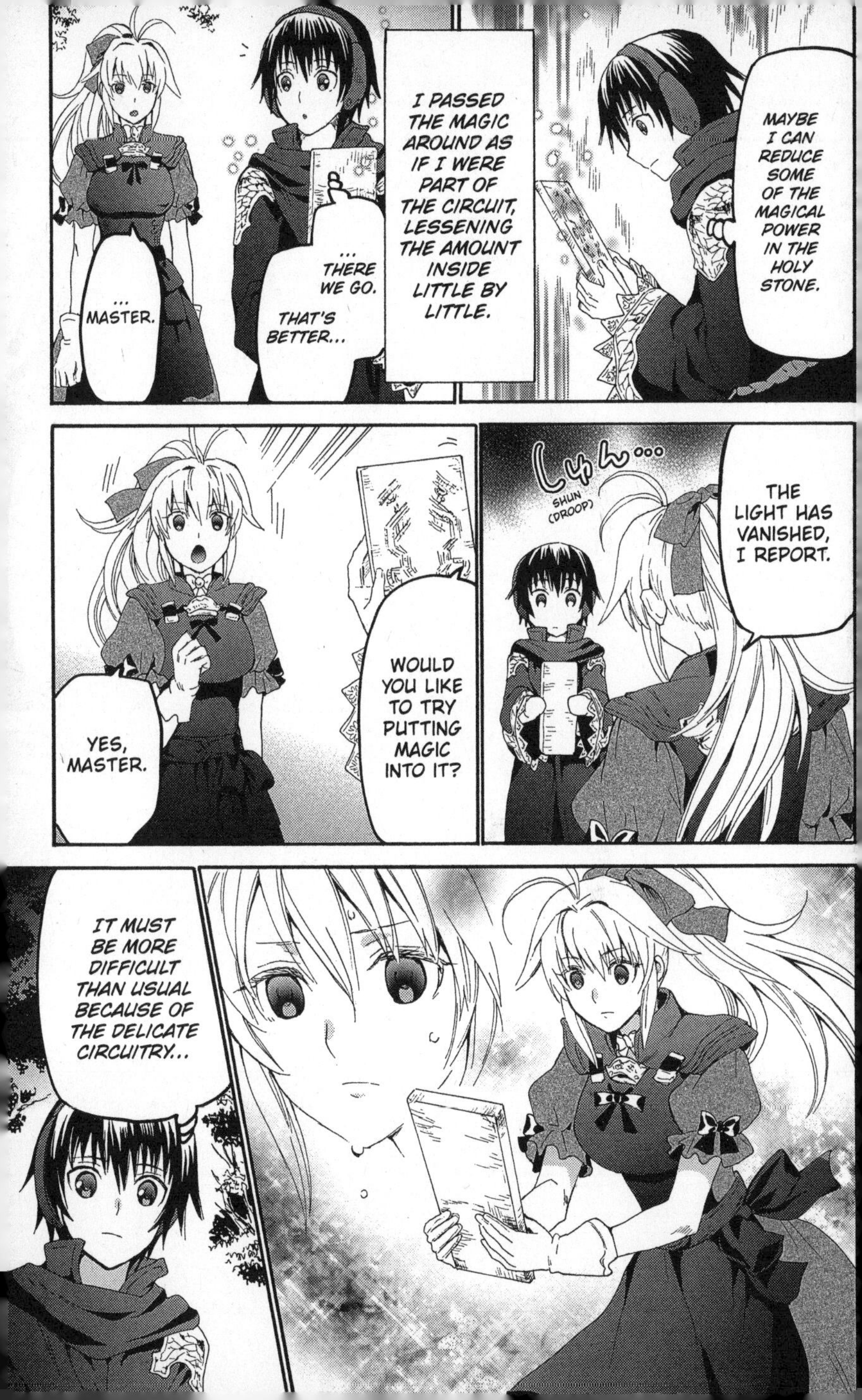
MAYBE I CAN REDUCE SOME OF THE MAGICAL POWER IN THE HOLY STONE.
I PASSED THE MAGIC AROUND AS IF I WERE PART OF THE CIRCUIT, LESSENING THE AMOUNT INSIDE LITTLE BY LITTLE.
... THERE WE GO.
THAT'S BETTER...
... MASTER.
THE LIGHT HAS VANISHED, I REPORT.
しゅん…
SHUN (DROOP)
WOULD YOU LIKE TO TRY PUTTING MAGIC INTO IT?
YES, MASTER.
IT MUST BE MORE DIFFICULT THAN USUAL BECAUSE OF THE DELICATE CIRCUITRY...

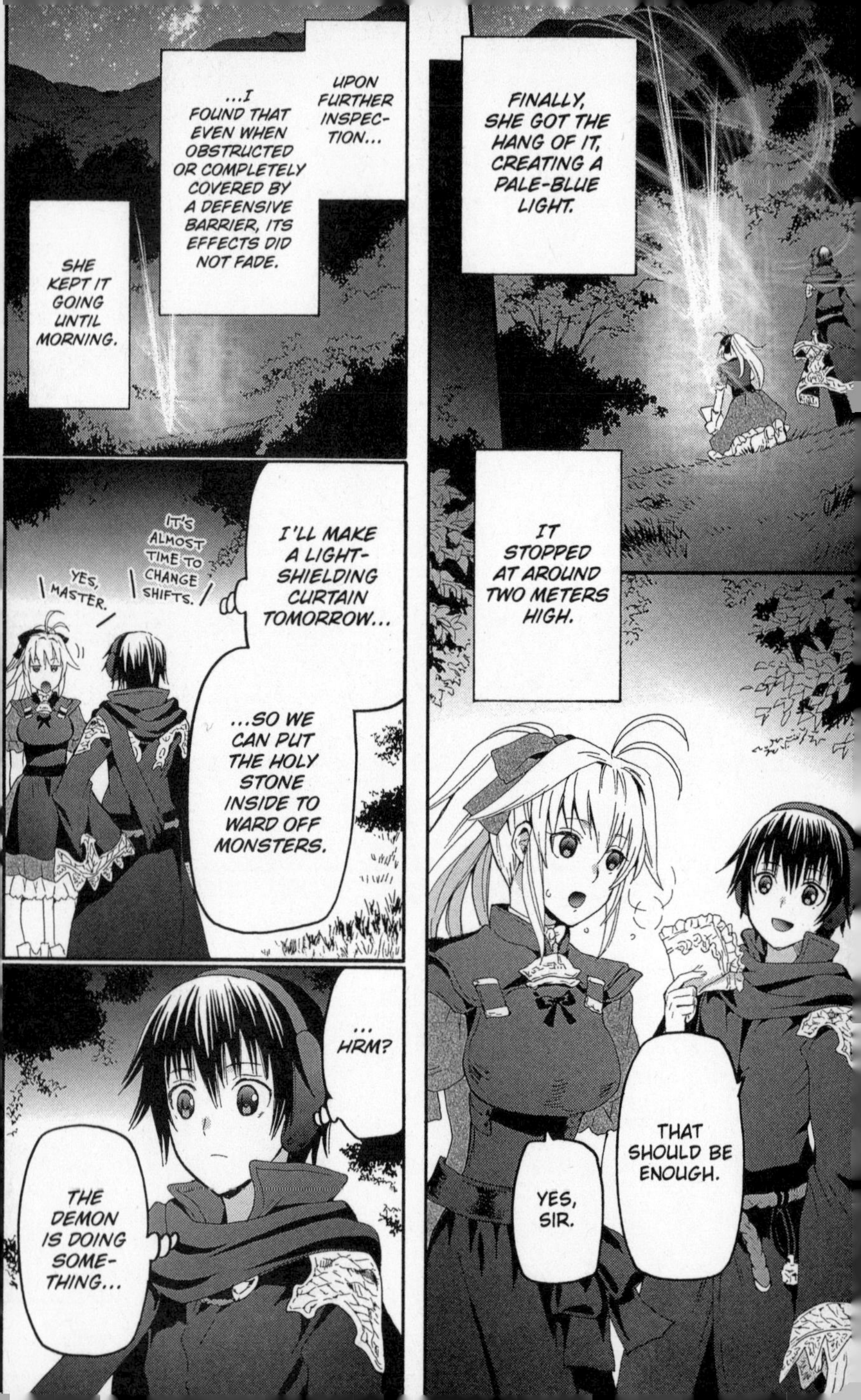
FINALLY, SHE GOT THE HANG OF IT, CREATING A PALE-BLUE LIGHT.
IT STOPPED AT AROUND TWO METERS HIGH.
THAT SHOULD BE ENOUGH.
YES, SIR.
UPON FURTHER INSPECTION...
...I FOUND THAT EVEN WHEN OBSTRUCTED OR COMPLETELY COVERED BY A DEFENSIVE BARRIER, ITS EFFECTS DID NOT FADE.
SHE KEPT IT GOING UNTIL MORNING.
I'LL MAKE A LIGHT-SHIELDING CURTAIN TOMORROW...
...SO WE CAN PUT THE HOLY STONE INSIDE TO WARD OFF MONSTERS.
IT'S ALMOST TIME TO CHANGE SHIFTS.
YES, MASTER.
... HRM?
THE DEMON IS DOING SOMETHING...

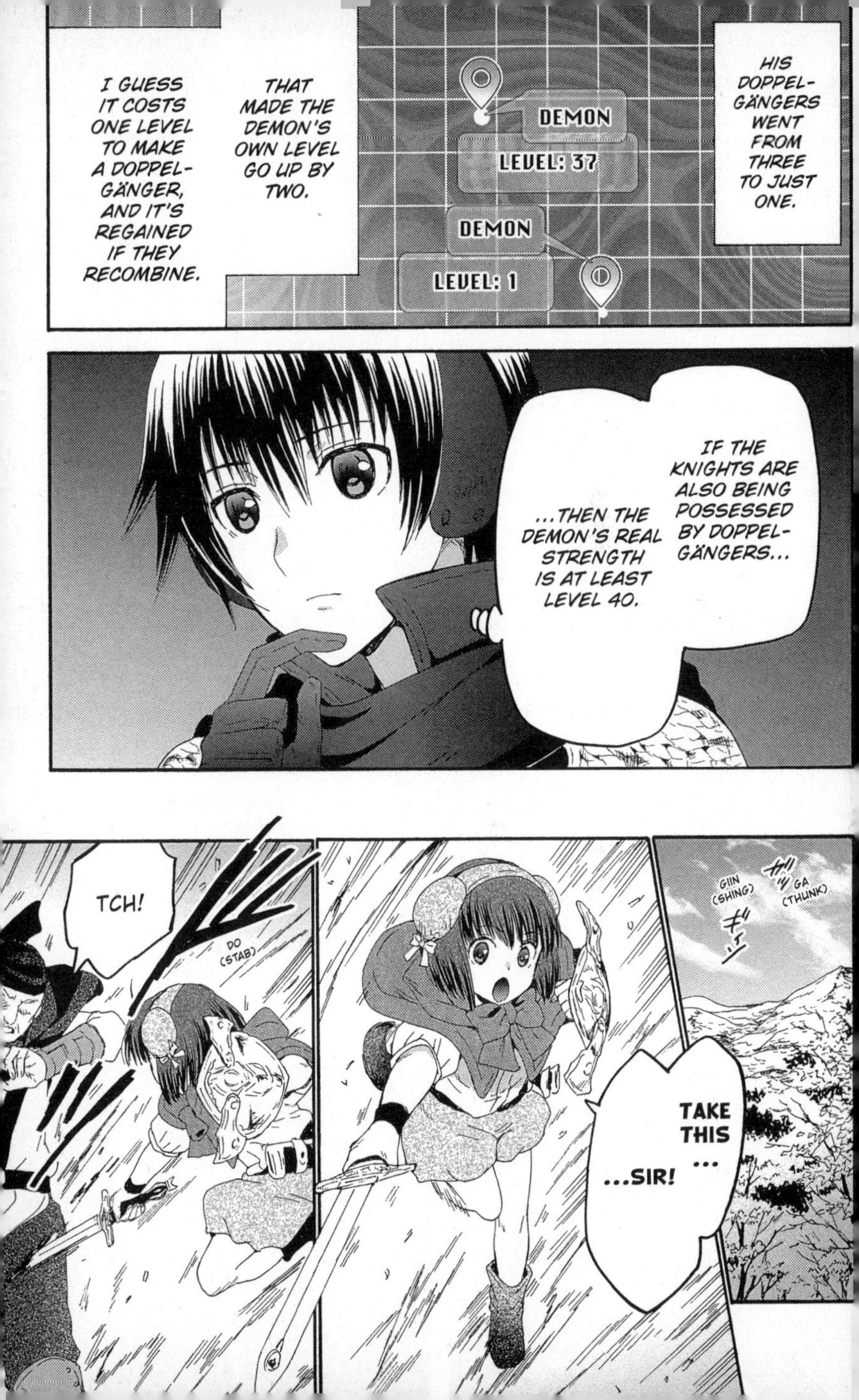
HIS DOPPEL-GÄNGERS WENT FROM THREE TO JUST ONE.
DEMON
LEVEL: 37
DEMON
LEVEL: 1
THAT MADE THE DEMON'S OWN LEVEL GO UP BY TWO.
I GUESS IT COSTS ONE LEVEL TO MAKE A DOPPEL-GÄNGER, AND IT'S REGAINED IF THEY RECOMBINE.
IF THE KNIGHTS ARE ALSO BEING POSSESSED BY DOPPEL-GÄNGERS...
...THEN THE DEMON'S REAL STRENGTH IS AT LEAST LEVEL 40.
GIIN (SHING)
GA (THUNK)
TAKE THIS...
...SIR!
DO (STAB)
TCH!

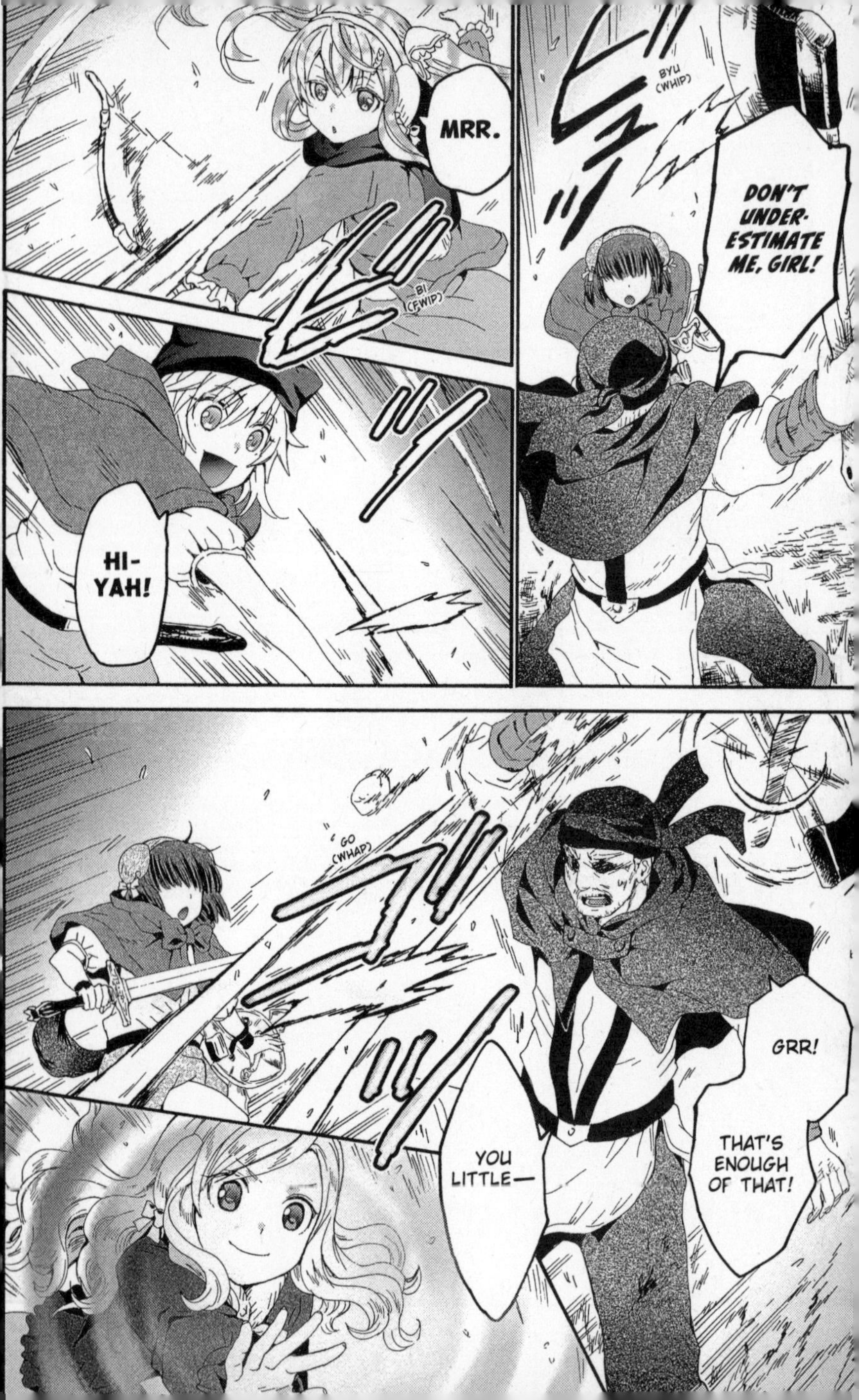
BYU (WHIP)
DON'T UNDER-ESTIMATE ME, GIRL!
MRR.
BI (FWIP)
HI-YAH!
GRR!
THAT'S ENOUGH OF THAT!
YOU LITTLE—
GO (WHAP)

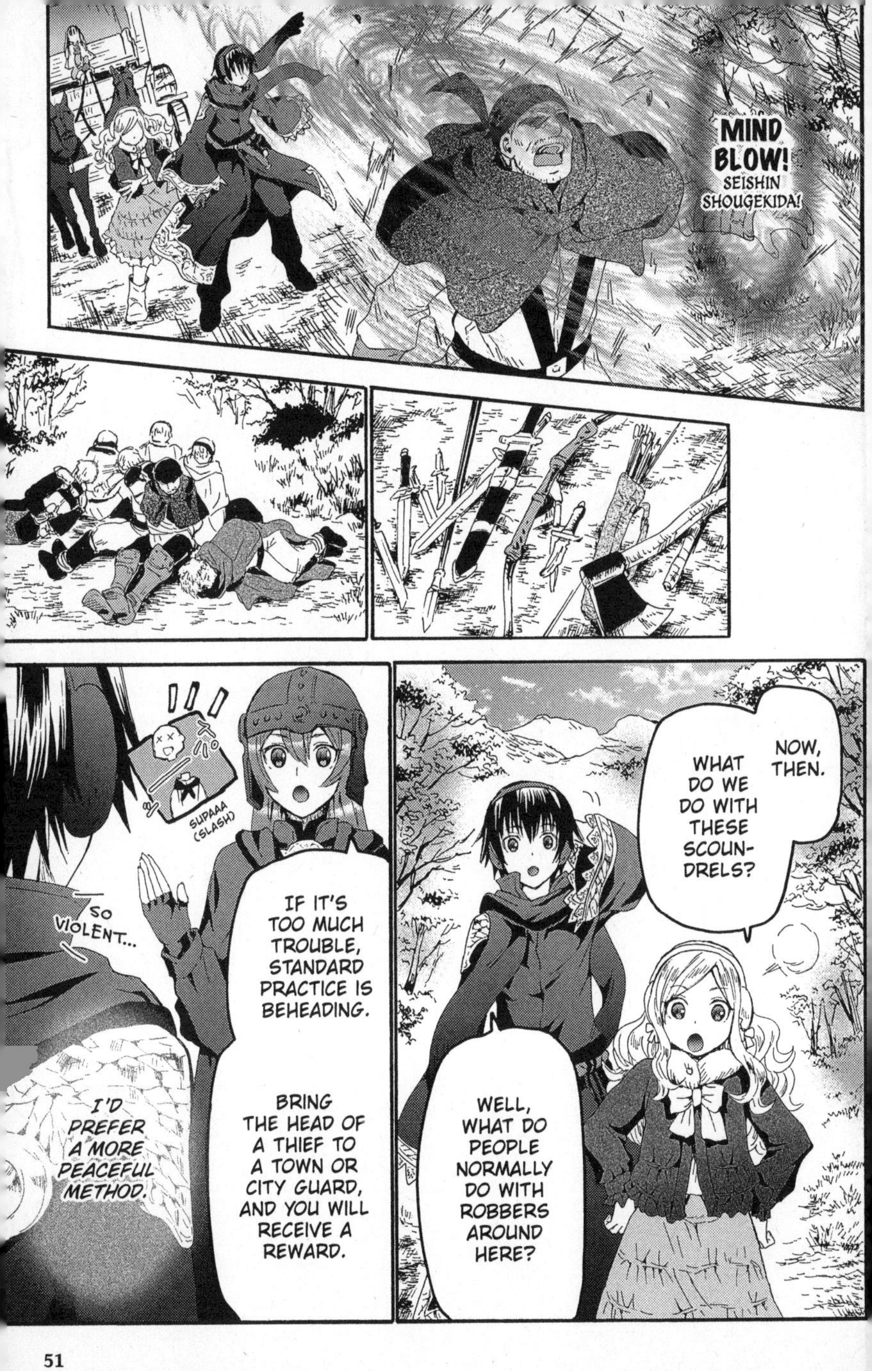
MIND BLOW!
SEISHIN SHOUGEKIDA!
NOW, THEN.
WHAT DO WE DO WITH THESE SCOUNDRELS?
WELL, WHAT DO PEOPLE NORMALLY DO WITH ROBBERS AROUND HERE?
IF IT'S TOO MUCH TROUBLE, STANDARD PRACTICE IS BEHEADING.
SUPAAA (SLASH)
BRING THE HEAD OF A THIEF TO A TOWN OR CITY GUARD, AND YOU WILL RECEIVE A REWARD.
SO VIOLENT...
I'D PREFER A MORE PEACEFUL METHOD.

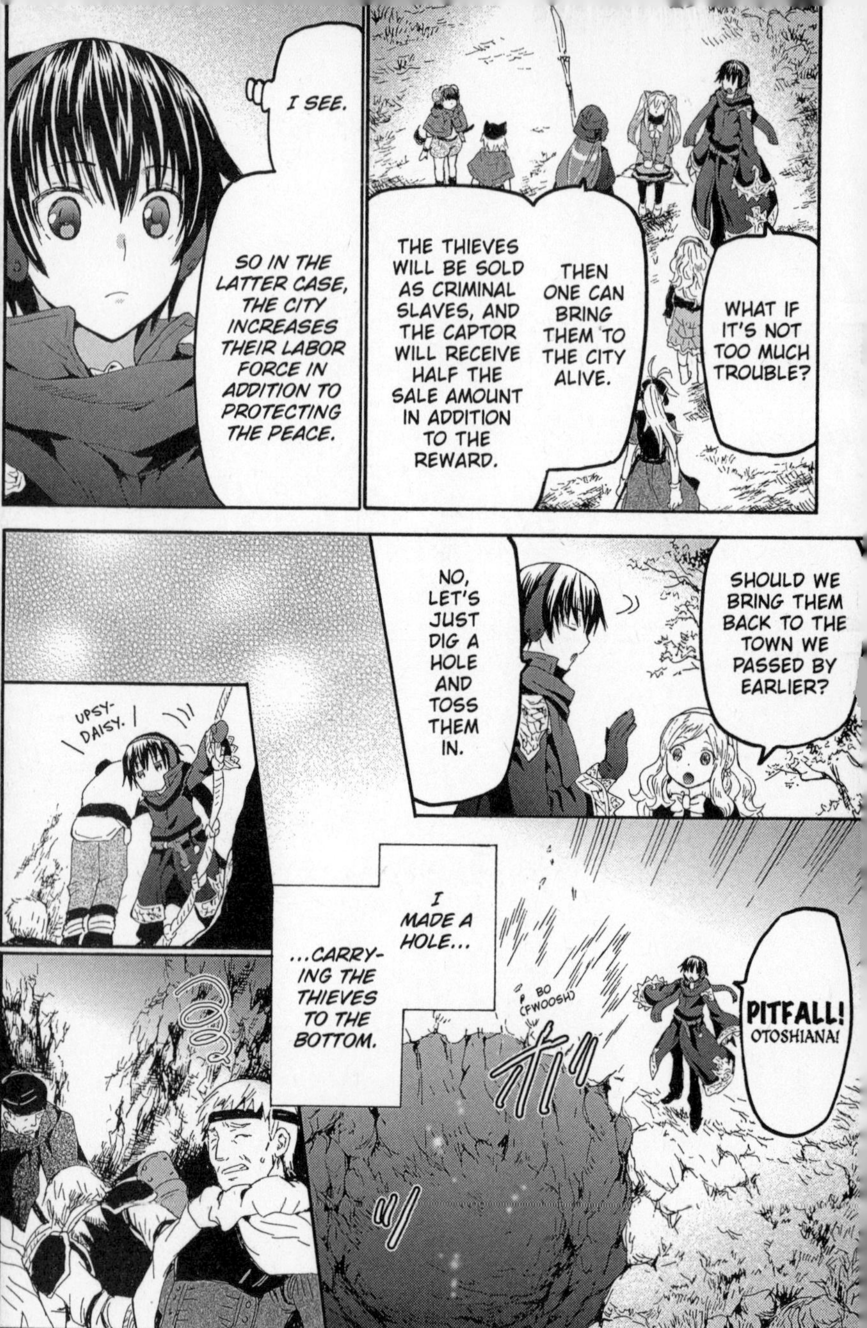
WHAT IF IT'S NOT TOO MUCH TROUBLE?
THEN ONE CAN BRING THEM TO THE CITY ALIVE.
THE THIEVES WILL BE SOLD AS CRIMINAL SLAVES, AND THE CAPTOR WILL RECEIVE HALF THE SALE AMOUNT IN ADDITION TO THE REWARD.
I SEE.
SO IN THE LATTER CASE, THE CITY INCREASES THEIR LABOR FORCE IN ADDITION TO PROTECTING THE PEACE.
SHOULD WE BRING THEM BACK TO THE TOWN WE PASSED BY EARLIER?
NO, LET'S JUST DIG A HOLE AND TOSS THEM IN.
PITFALL! OTOSHIANA!
BO (FWOOSH)
I MADE A HOLE...
...CARRYING THE THIEVES TO THE BOTTOM.
UPSY-DAISY.

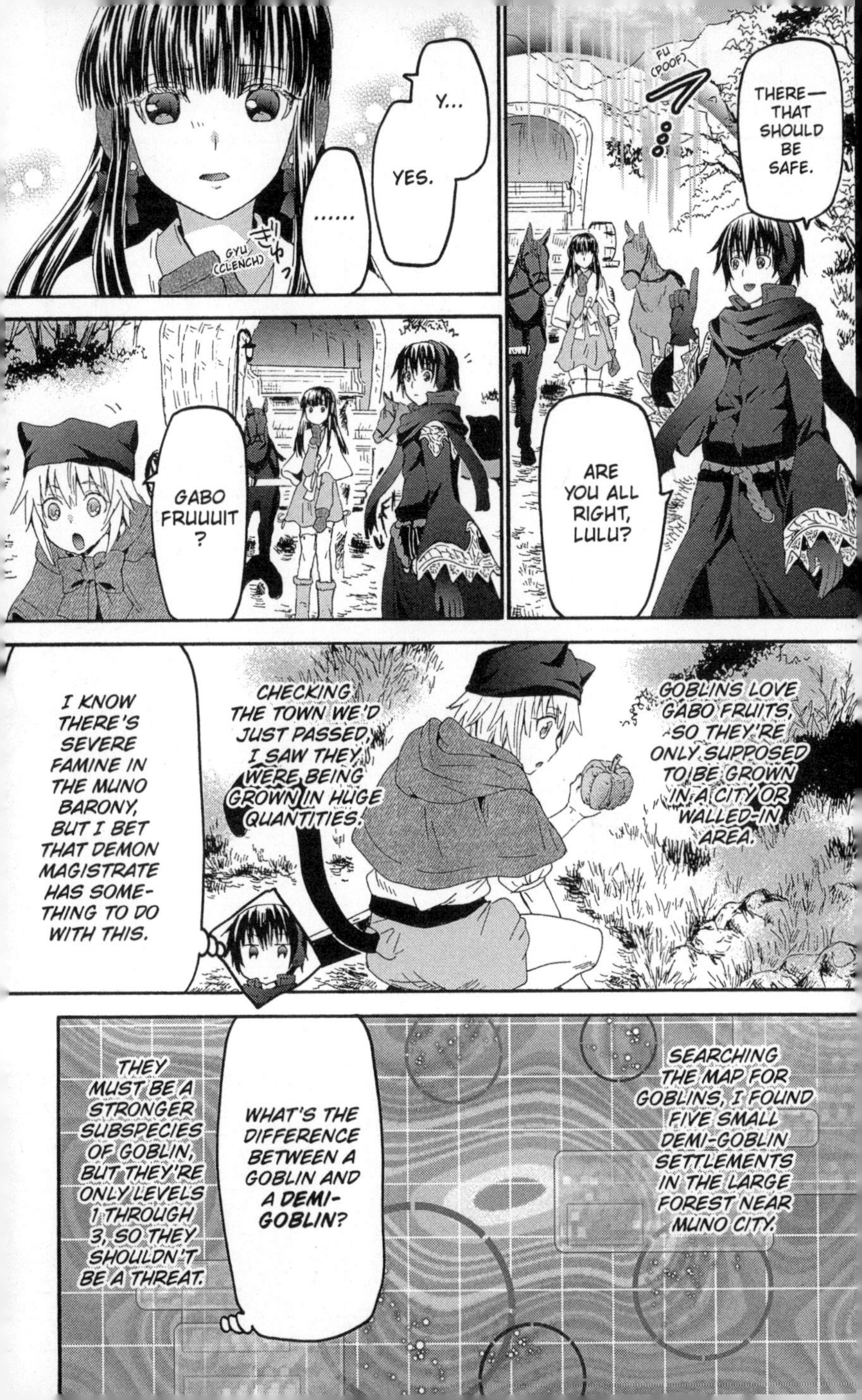
FU (POOF)
THERE— THAT SHOULD BE SAFE.
ARE YOU ALL RIGHT, LULU?
Y...
YES.
......
GYU (CLENCH)
GABO FRUUUIT?
GOBLINS LOVE GABO FRUITS, SO THEY'RE ONLY SUPPOSED TO BE GROWN IN A CITY OR WALLED-IN AREA.
CHECKING THE TOWN WE'D JUST PASSED, I SAW THEY WERE BEING GROWN IN HUGE QUANTITIES.
I KNOW THERE'S SEVERE FAMINE IN THE MUNO BARONY, BUT I BET THAT DEMON MAGISTRATE HAS SOMETHING TO DO WITH THIS.
SEARCHING THE MAP FOR GOBLINS, I FOUND FIVE SMALL DEMI-GOBLIN SETTLEMENTS IN THE LARGE FOREST NEAR MUNO CITY.
WHAT'S THE DIFFERENCE BETWEEN A GOBLIN AND A DEMI-GOBLIN?
THEY MUST BE A STRONGER SUBSPECIES OF GOBLIN, BUT THEY'RE ONLY LEVELS 1 THROUGH 3, SO THEY SHOULDN'T BE A THREAT.

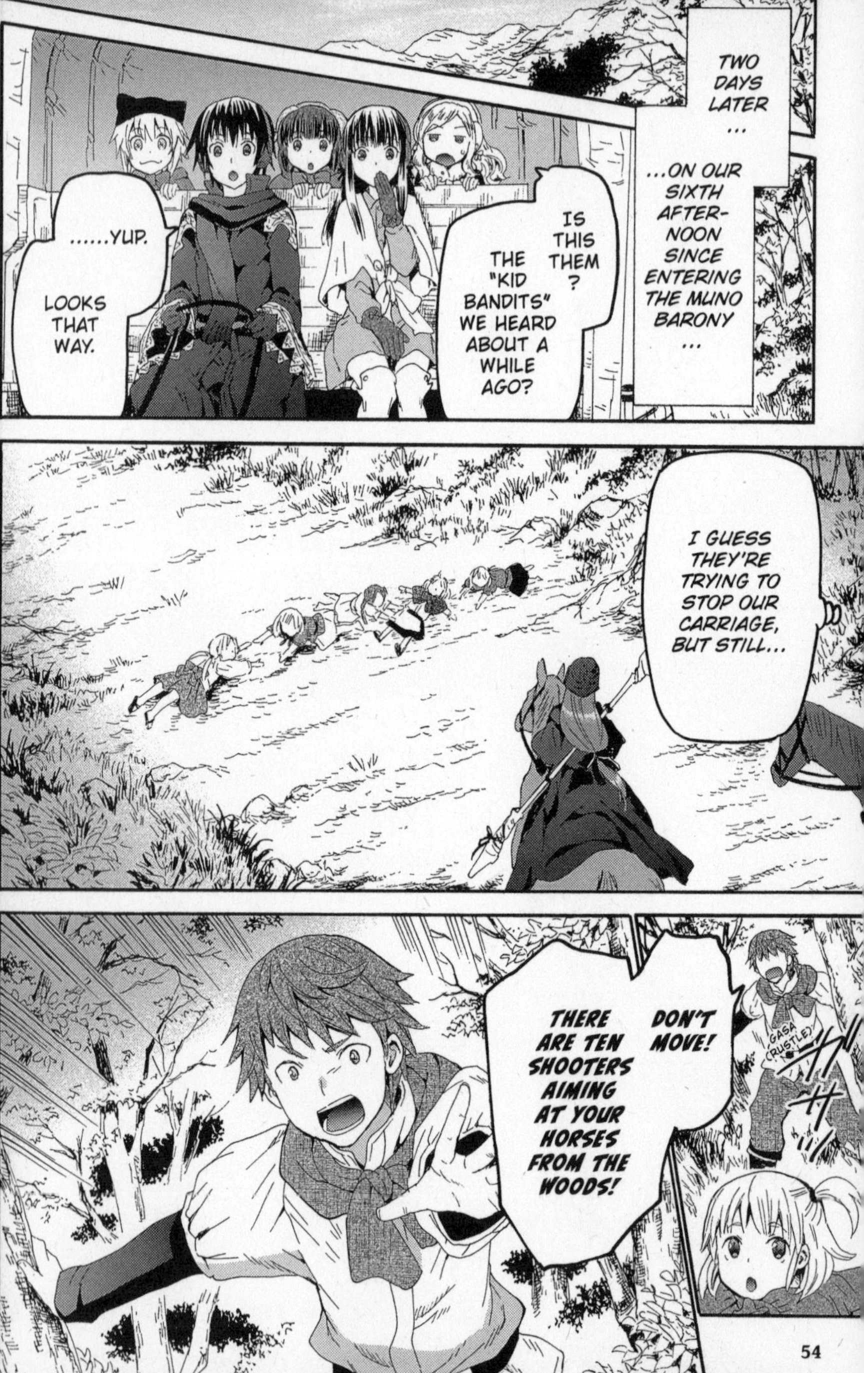
TWO DAYS LATER ...
...ON OUR SIXTH AFTER-NOON SINCE ENTERING THE MUNO BARONY ...
IS THIS THEM?
THE "KID BANDITS" WE HEARD ABOUT A WHILE AGO?
......YUP.
LOOKS THAT WAY.
I GUESS THEY'RE TRYING TO STOP OUR CARRIAGE, BUT STILL...
DON'T MOVE!
THERE ARE TEN SHOOTERS AIMING AT YOUR HORSES FROM THE WOODS!
GASA (RUSTLE)

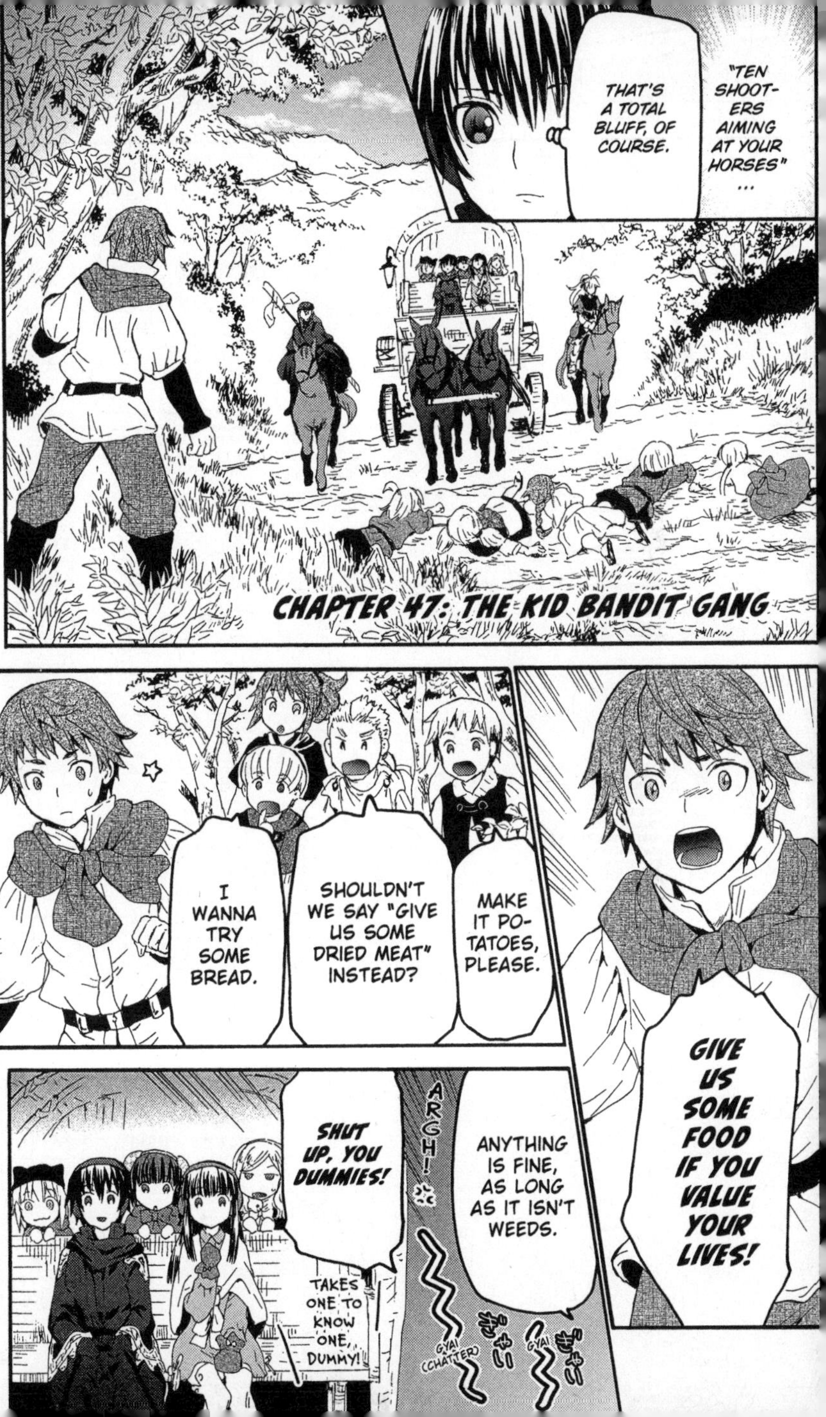
"TEN SHOOTERS AIMING AT YOUR HORSES"...
THAT'S A TOTAL BLUFF, OF COURSE.
CHAPTER 47: THE KID BANDIT GANG
GIVE US SOME FOOD IF YOU VALUE YOUR LIVES!
MAKE IT POTATOES, PLEASE.
SHOULDN'T WE SAY "GIVE US SOME DRIED MEAT" INSTEAD?
I WANNA TRY SOME BREAD.
ANYTHING IS FINE, AS LONG AS IT ISN'T WEEDS.
ARGH!
SHUT UP, YOU DUMMIES!
TAKES ONE TO KNOW ONE, DUMMY!
ぎゃい GYAI
ぎゃい GYAI (CHATTER)

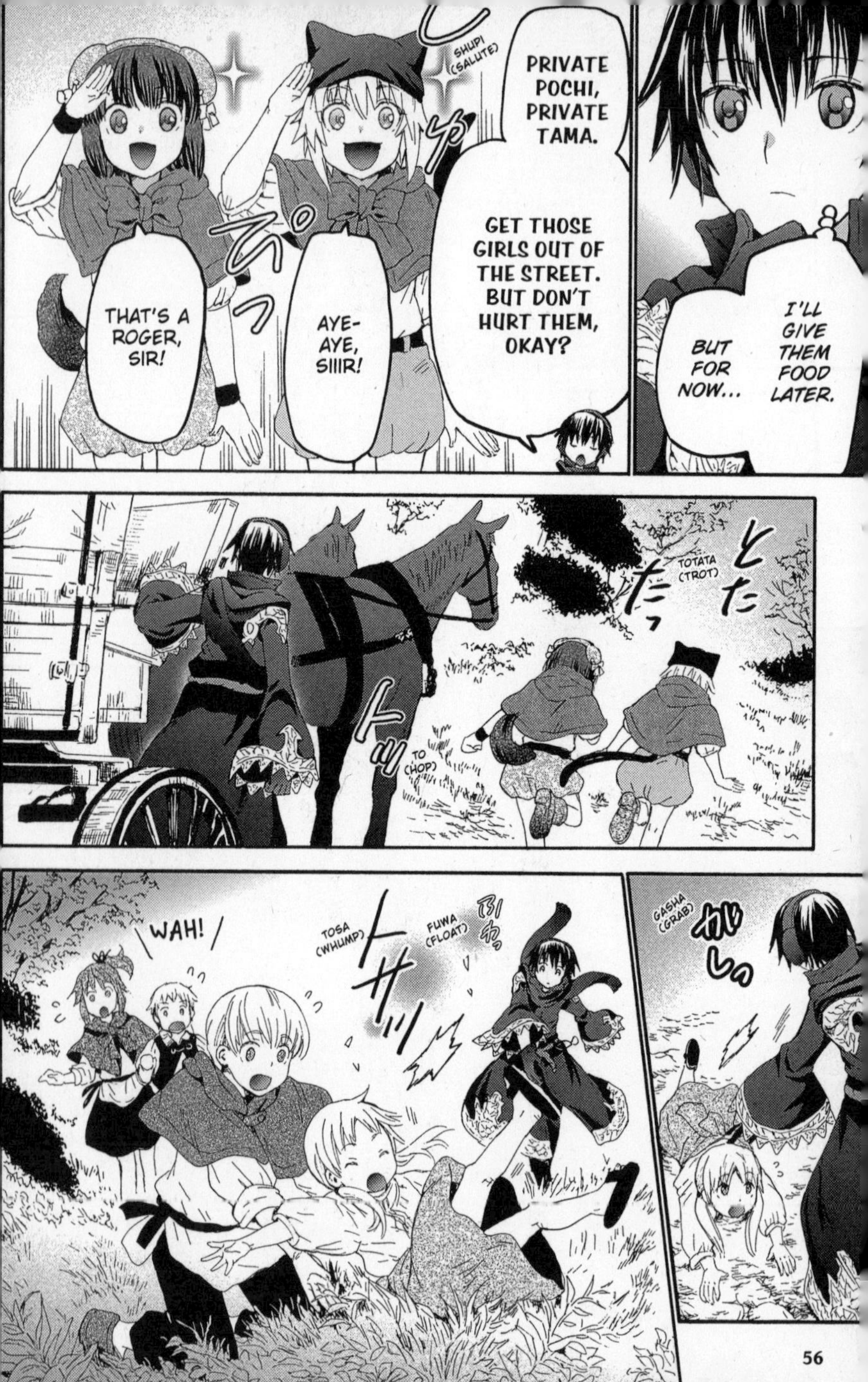
I'LL GIVE THEM FOOD LATER.
BUT FOR NOW...
PRIVATE POCHI, PRIVATE TAMA.
GET THOSE GIRLS OUT OF THE STREET. BUT DON'T HURT THEM, OKAY?
SHUPI (SALUTE)
AYE-AYE, SIIIR!
THAT'S A ROGER, SIR!
TOTATA (TROT)
TO (HOP)
GASHA (GRAB)
FUWA (FLOAT)
TOSA (WHUMP)
WAH!

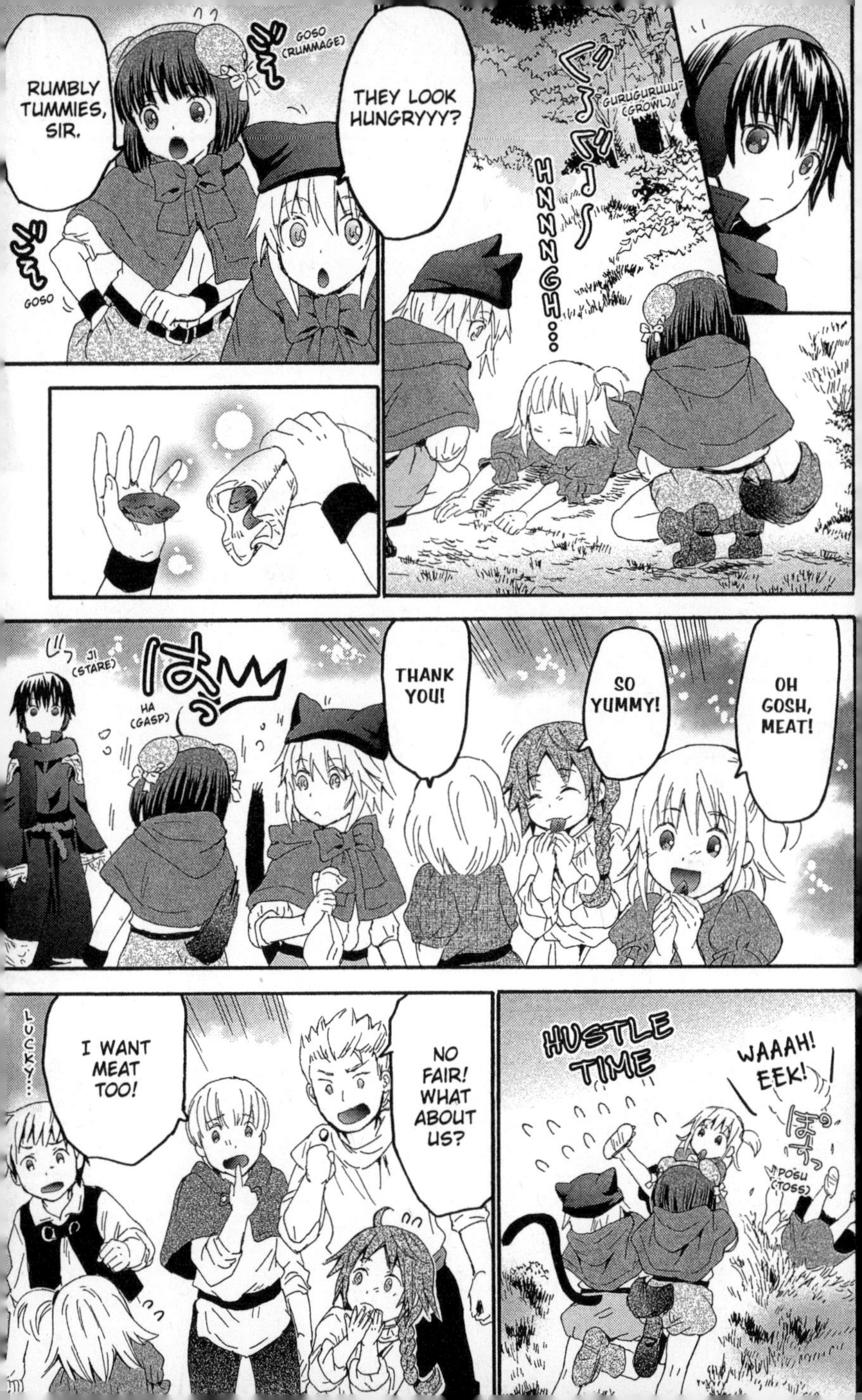
GURUGURUUU (GROWL)
HNNNNGH...
THEY LOOK HUNGRYYY?
GOSO (RUMMAGE)
RUMBLY TUMMIES, SIR.
GOSO
OH GOSH, MEAT!
SO YUMMY!
THANK YOU!
HA (GASP)
JI (STARE)
WAAAH! EEK!
POSU (TOSS)
HUSTLE TIME
NO FAIR! WHAT ABOUT US?
I WANT MEAT TOO!
LUCKY...

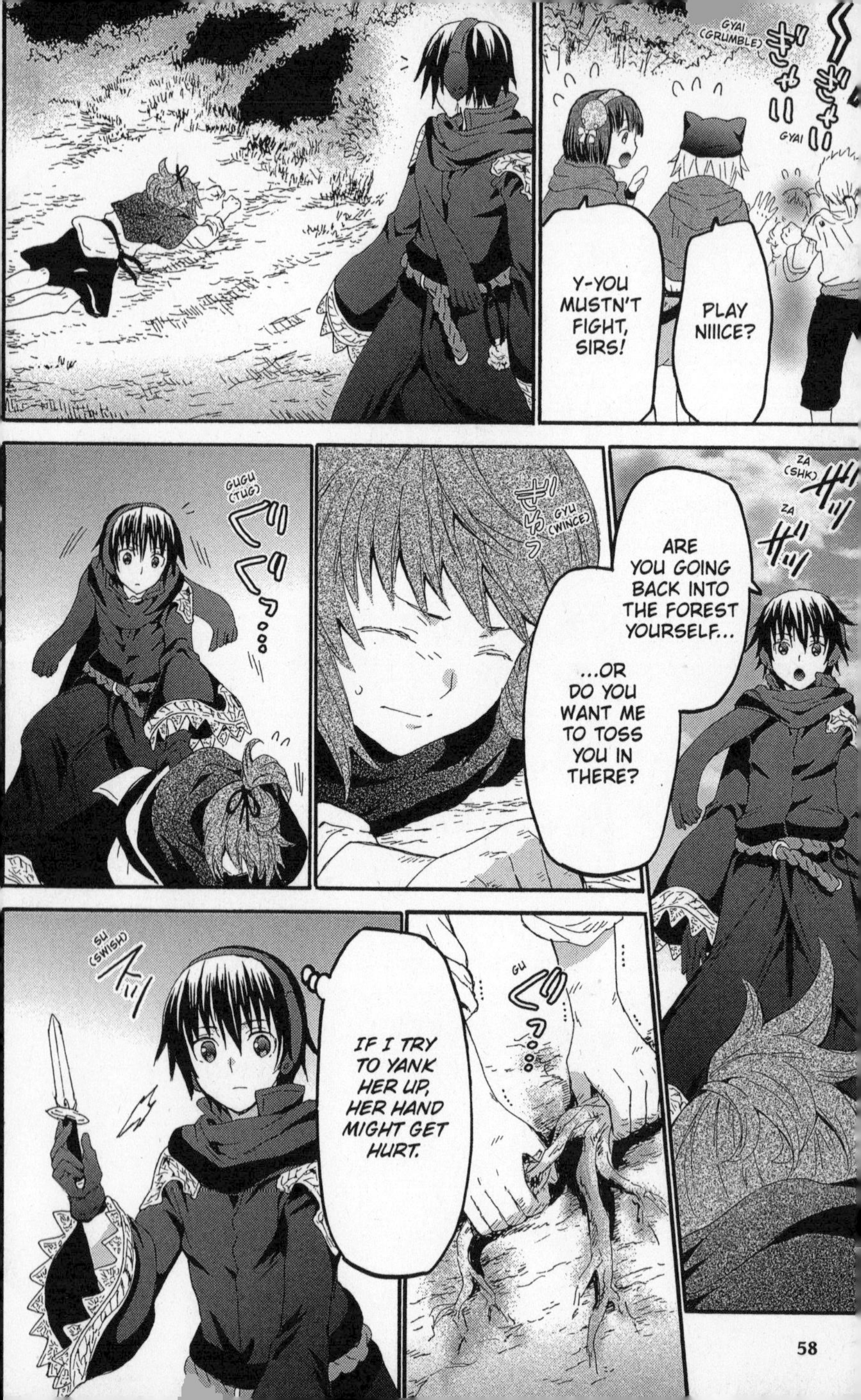
GYAI (GRUMBLE)
GYAI
PLAY NIIICE?
Y-YOU MUSTN'T FIGHT, SIRS!
ZA (SHK)
ZA
ARE YOU GOING BACK INTO THE FOREST YOURSELF...
...OR DO YOU WANT ME TO TOSS YOU IN THERE?
GYU (WINCE)
GUGU (TUG)
GU
IF I TRY TO YANK HER UP, HER HAND MIGHT GET HURT.
SU (SWISH)

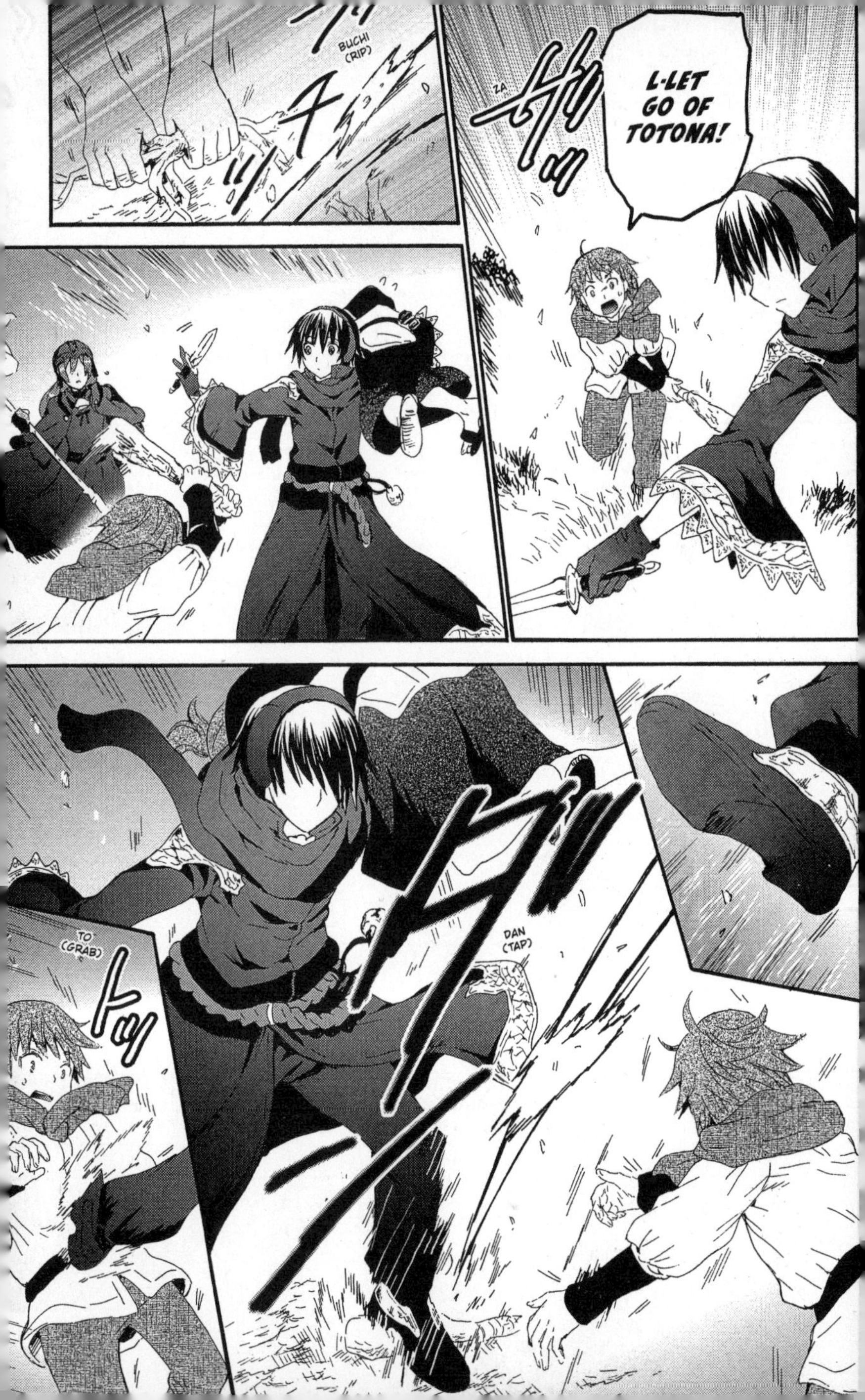
ZA
L-LET GO OF TOTONA!
BUCHI (RIP)
DAN (TAP)
TO (GRAB)

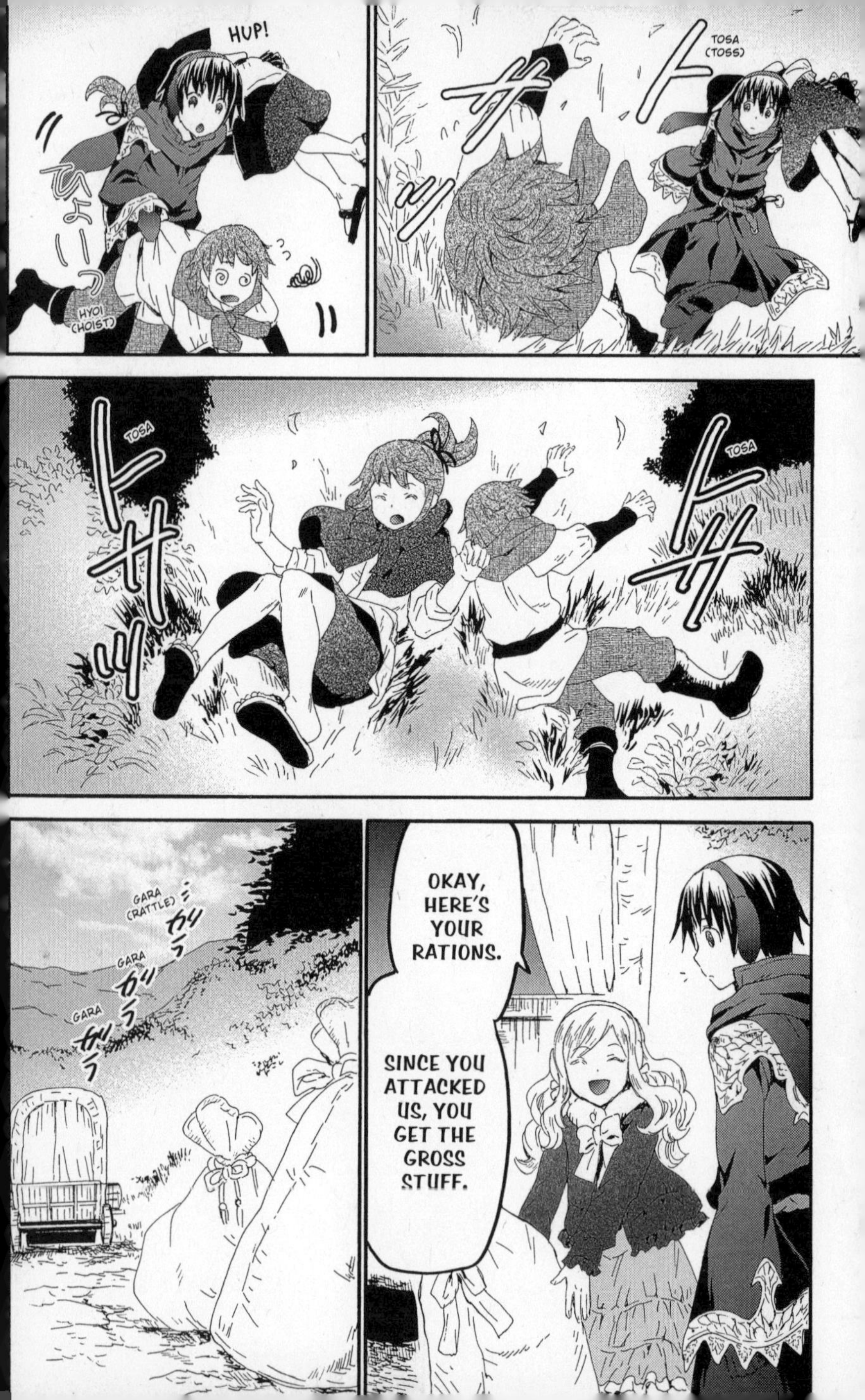
TOSA (TOSS)
HUP!
ひょいっ
HYOI (HOIST)
TOSA
TOSA
OKAY, HERE'S YOUR RATIONS.
SINCE YOU ATTACKED US, YOU GET THE GROSS STUFF.
GARA (RATTLE)
ガラ
GARA
ガラ
GARA
ガラ

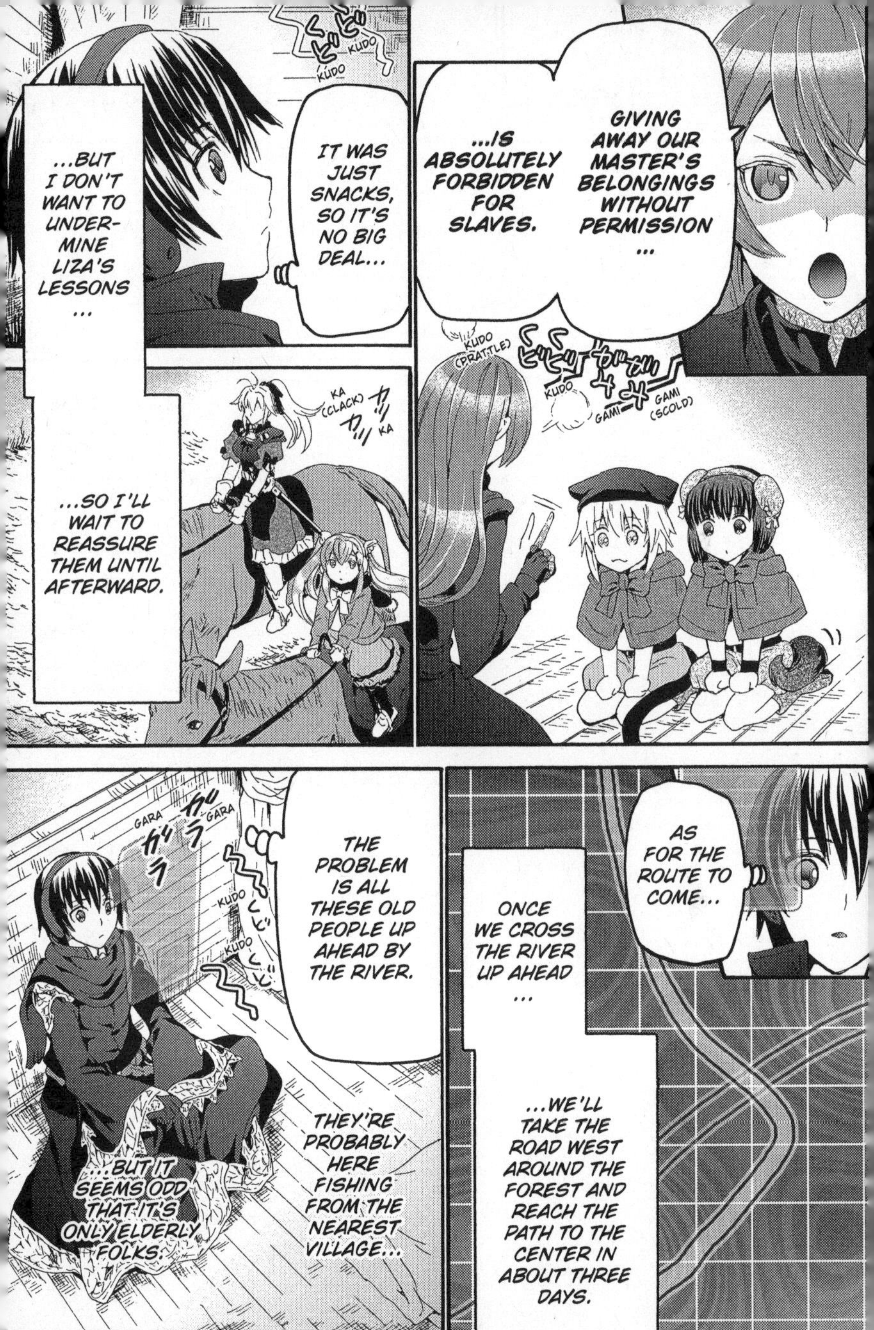
KUDO
KUDO
GIVING AWAY OUR MASTER'S BELONGINGS WITHOUT PERMISSION...
...IS ABSOLUTELY FORBIDDEN FOR SLAVES.
KUDO
IT WAS JUST SNACKS, SO IT'S NO BIG DEAL...
...BUT I DON'T WANT TO UNDER-MINE LIZA'S LESSONS...
KUDO (PRATTLE)
KUDO
GAMI
GAMI (SCOLD)
KA (CLACK)
KA
...SO I'LL WAIT TO REASSURE THEM UNTIL AFTERWARD.
AS FOR THE ROUTE TO COME...
ONCE WE CROSS THE RIVER UP AHEAD...
...WE'LL TAKE THE ROAD WEST AROUND THE FOREST AND REACH THE PATH TO THE CENTER IN ABOUT THREE DAYS.
GARA
GARA
KUDO
KUDO
THE PROBLEM IS ALL THESE OLD PEOPLE UP AHEAD BY THE RIVER.
THEY'RE PROBABLY HERE FISHING FROM THE NEAREST VILLAGE...
...BUT IT SEEMS ODD THAT IT'S ONLY ELDERLY FOLKS.

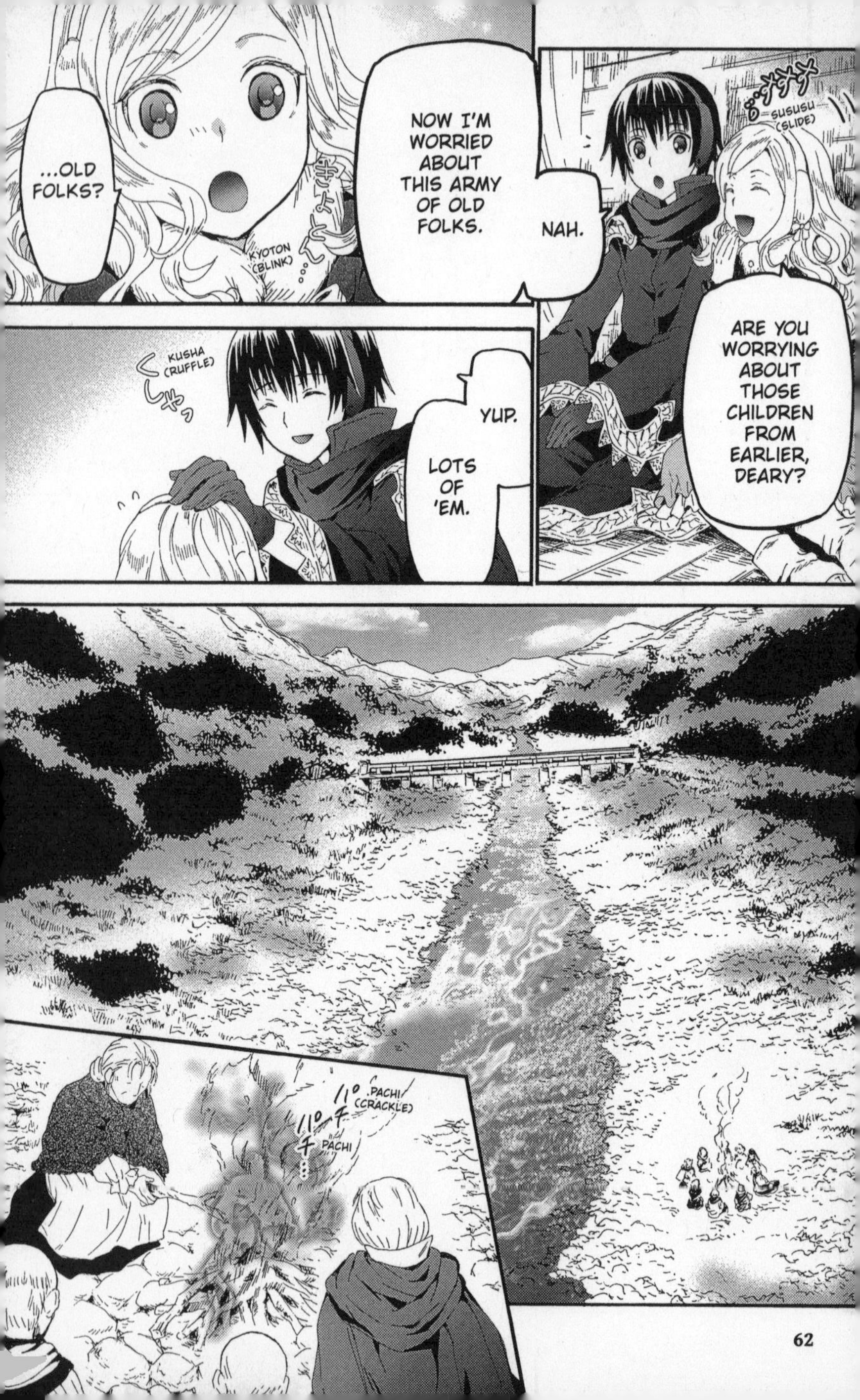
SUSUSU (SLIDE)
ARE YOU WORRYING ABOUT THOSE CHILDREN FROM EARLIER, DEARY?
NAH.
NOW I'M WORRIED ABOUT THIS ARMY OF OLD FOLKS.
KYOTON (BLINK)
...OLD FOLKS?
YUP.
LOTS OF 'EM.
KUSHA (RUFFLE)
PACHI (CRACKLE)
PACHI

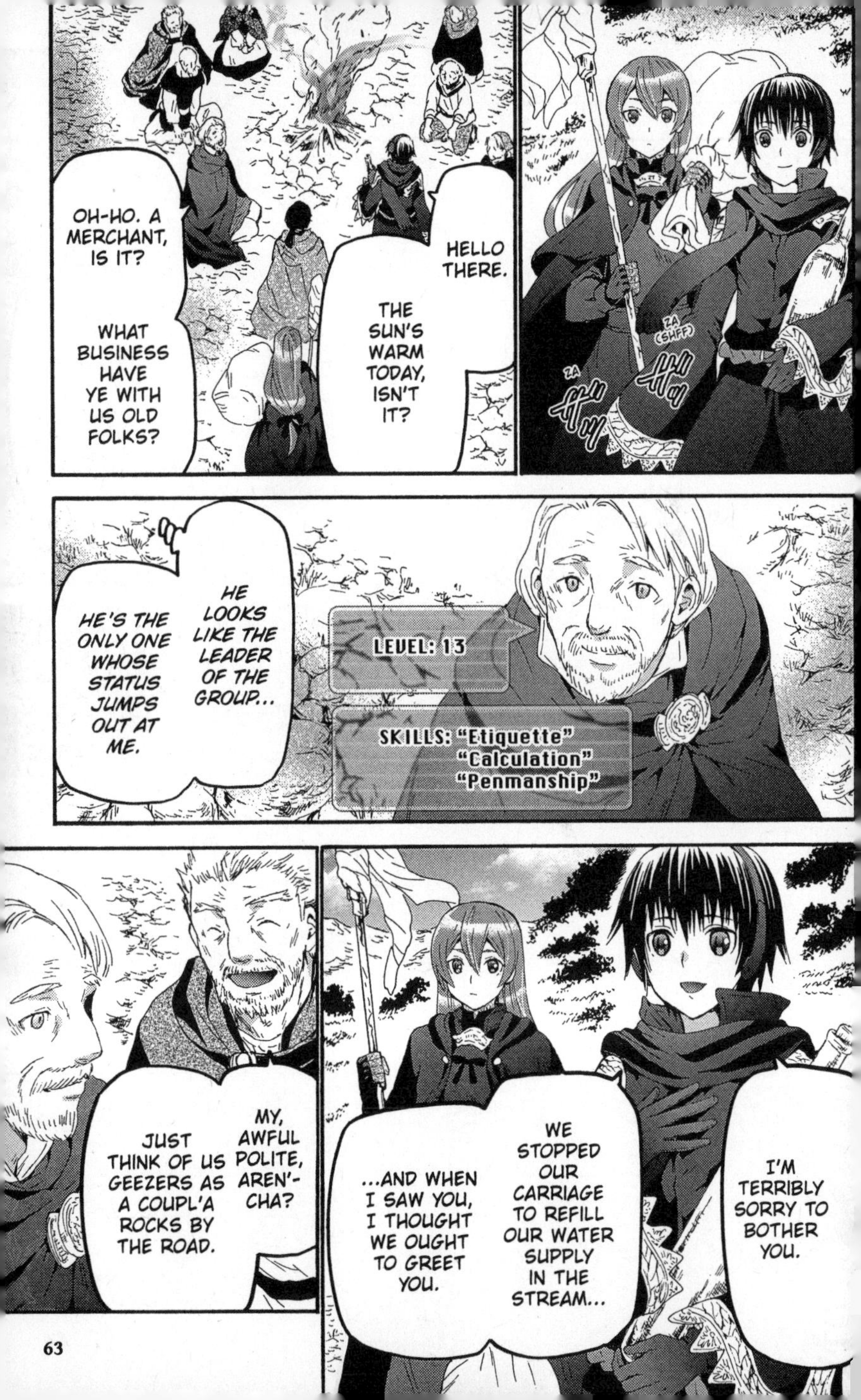
ZA
ZA (SHFF)
HELLO THERE.
THE SUN'S WARM TODAY, ISN'T IT?
OH-HO. A MERCHANT, IS IT?
WHAT BUSINESS HAVE YE WITH US OLD FOLKS?
LEVEL: 13
SKILLS: "Etiquette" "Calculation" "Penmanship"
HE LOOKS LIKE THE LEADER OF THE GROUP...
HE'S THE ONLY ONE WHOSE STATUS JUMPS OUT AT ME.
I'M TERRIBLY SORRY TO BOTHER YOU.
WE STOPPED OUR CARRIAGE TO REFILL OUR WATER SUPPLY IN THE STREAM...
...AND WHEN I SAW YOU, I THOUGHT WE OUGHT TO GREET YOU.
MY, AWFUL POLITE, AREN'-CHA?
JUST THINK OF US GEEZERS AS A COUPL'A ROCKS BY THE ROAD.

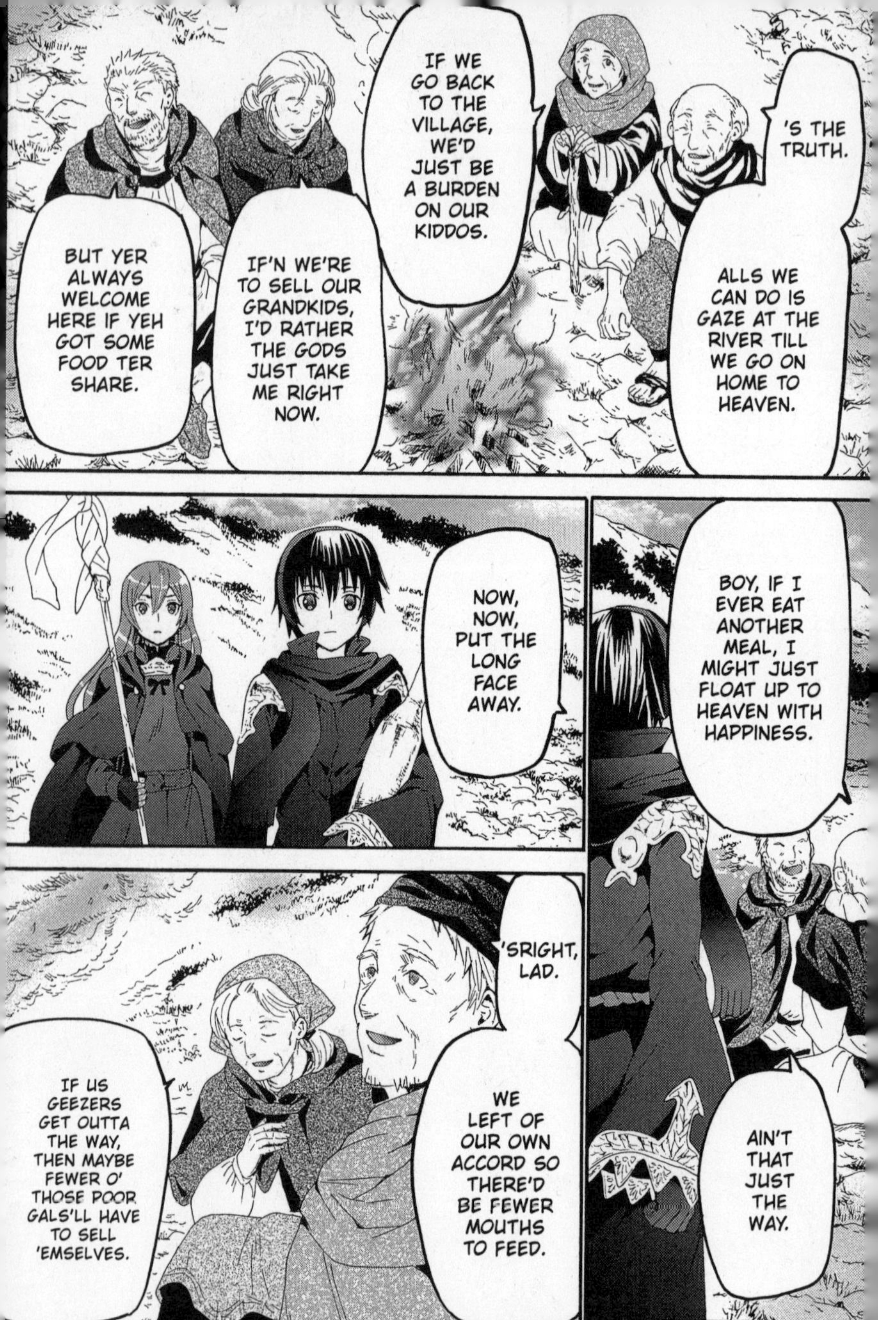
IF WE GO BACK TO THE VILLAGE, WE'D JUST BE A BURDEN ON OUR KIDDOS.
'S THE TRUTH.
ALLS WE CAN DO IS GAZE AT THE RIVER TILL WE GO ON HOME TO HEAVEN.
IF'N WE'RE TO SELL OUR GRANDKIDS, I'D RATHER THE GODS JUST TAKE ME RIGHT NOW.
BUT YER ALWAYS WELCOME HERE IF YEH GOT SOME FOOD TER SHARE.
BOY, IF I EVER EAT ANOTHER MEAL, I MIGHT JUST FLOAT UP TO HEAVEN WITH HAPPINESS.
AIN'T THAT JUST THE WAY.
NOW, NOW, PUT THE LONG FACE AWAY.
'SRIGHT, LAD.
WE LEFT OF OUR OWN ACCORD SO THERE'D BE FEWER MOUTHS TO FEED.
IF US GEEZERS GET OUTTA THE WAY, THEN MAYBE FEWER O' THOSE POOR GALS'LL HAVE TO SELL 'EMSELVES.

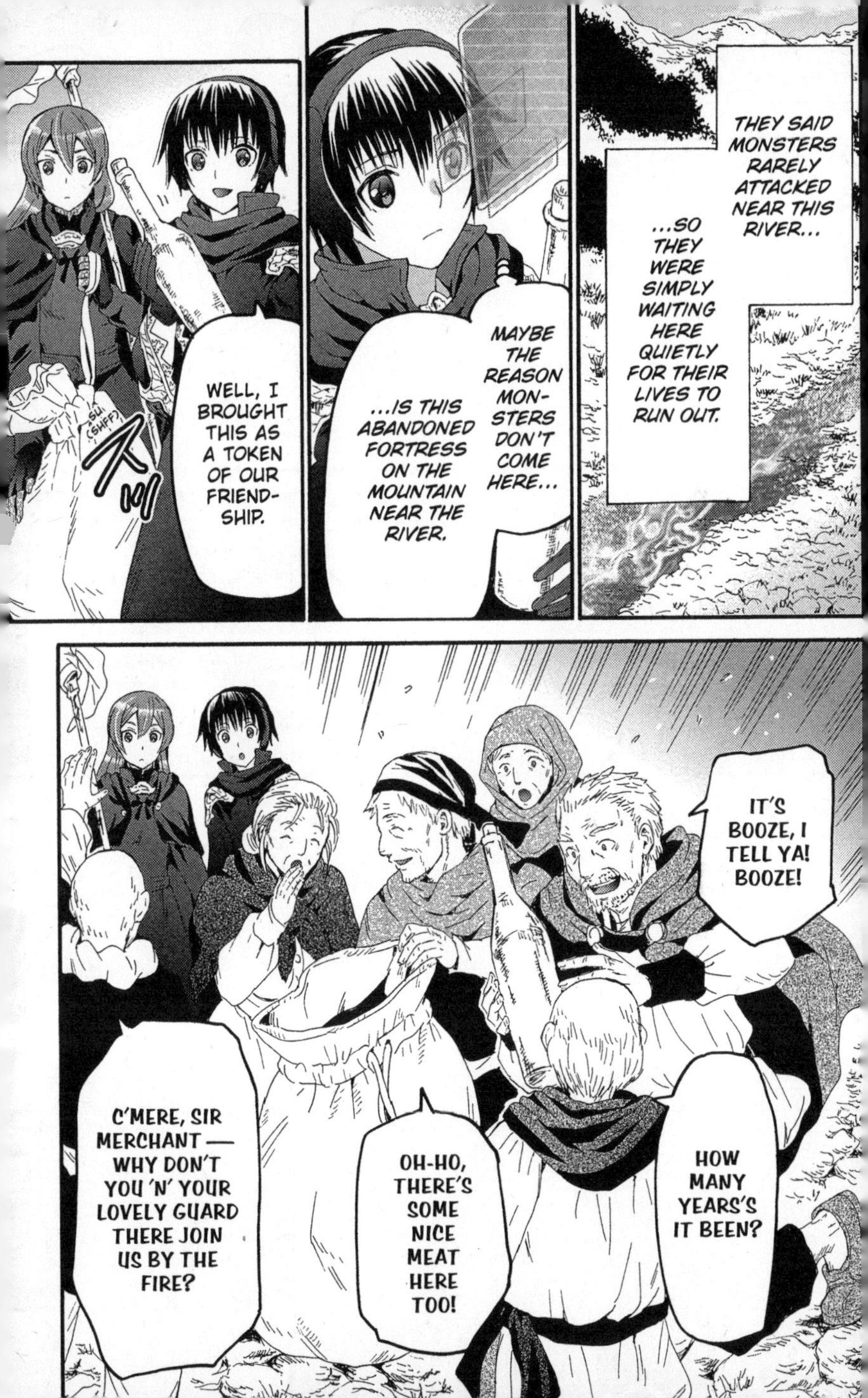
THEY SAID MONSTERS RARELY ATTACKED NEAR THIS RIVER...
...SO THEY WERE SIMPLY WAITING HERE QUIETLY FOR THEIR LIVES TO RUN OUT.
MAYBE THE REASON MON-STERS DON'T COME HERE...
...IS THIS ABANDONED FORTRESS ON THE MOUNTAIN NEAR THE RIVER.
WELL, I BROUGHT THIS AS A TOKEN OF OUR FRIEND-SHIP.
SU (SHFF)
IT'S BOOZE, I TELL YA! BOOZE!
HOW MANY YEARS'S IT BEEN?
OH-HO, THERE'S SOME NICE MEAT HERE TOO!
C'MERE, SIR MERCHANT — WHY DON'T YOU 'N' YOUR LOVELY GUARD THERE JOIN US BY THE FIRE?

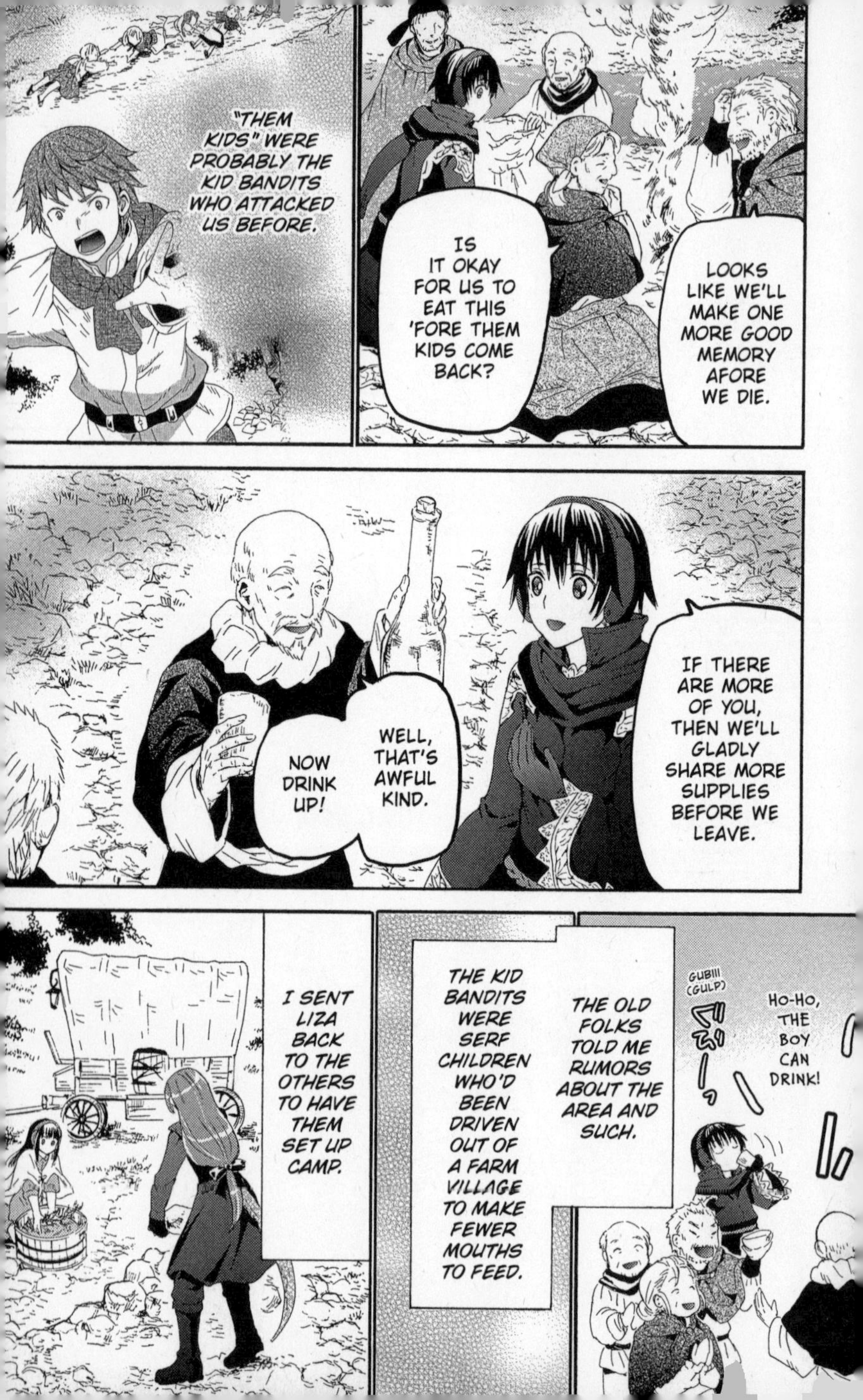
LOOKS LIKE WE'LL MAKE ONE MORE GOOD MEMORY AFORE WE DIE.
IS IT OKAY FOR US TO EAT THIS 'FORE THEM KIDS COME BACK?
"THEM KIDS" WERE PROBABLY THE KID BANDITS WHO ATTACKED US BEFORE.
IF THERE ARE MORE OF YOU, THEN WE'LL GLADLY SHARE MORE SUPPLIES BEFORE WE LEAVE.
WELL, THAT'S AWFUL KIND.
NOW DRINK UP!
GUBIII (GULP)
HO-HO, THE BOY CAN DRINK!
THE OLD FOLKS TOLD ME RUMORS ABOUT THE AREA AND SUCH.
THE KID BANDITS WERE SERF CHILDREN WHO'D BEEN DRIVEN OUT OF A FARM VILLAGE TO MAKE FEWER MOUTHS TO FEED.
I SENT LIZA BACK TO THE OTHERS TO HAVE THEM SET UP CAMP.

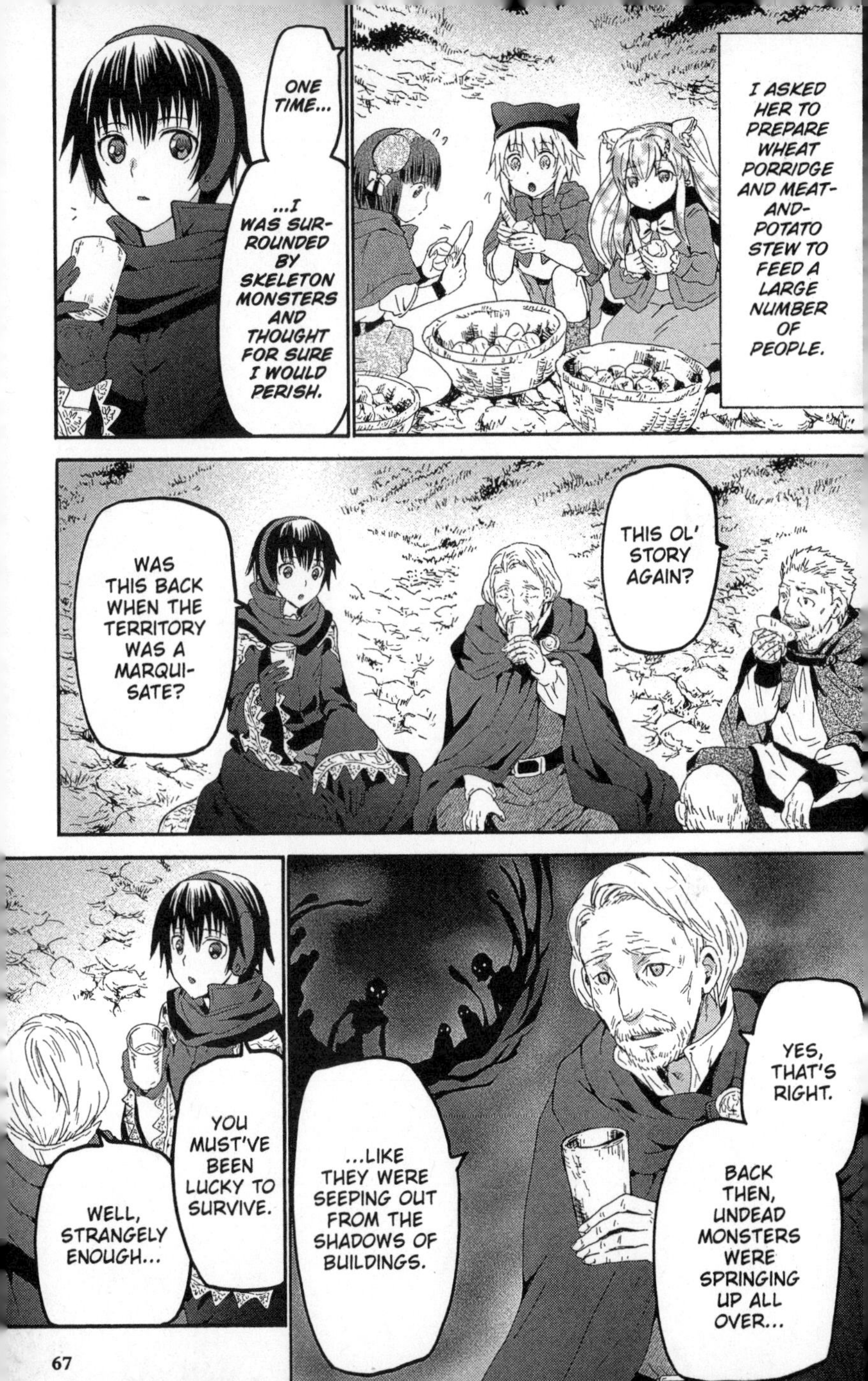

I ASKED HER TO PREPARE WHEAT PORRIDGE AND MEAT-AND-POTATO STEW TO FEED A LARGE NUMBER OF PEOPLE.
ONE TIME...
...I WAS SURROUNDED BY SKELETON MONSTERS AND THOUGHT FOR SURE I WOULD PERISH.
THIS OL' STORY AGAIN?
WAS THIS BACK WHEN THE TERRITORY WAS A MARQUISATE?
YES, THAT'S RIGHT.
BACK THEN, UNDEAD MONSTERS WERE SPRINGING UP ALL OVER...
...LIKE THEY WERE SEEPING OUT FROM THE SHADOWS OF BUILDINGS.
YOU MUST'VE BEEN LUCKY TO SURVIVE.
WELL, STRANGELY ENOUGH...

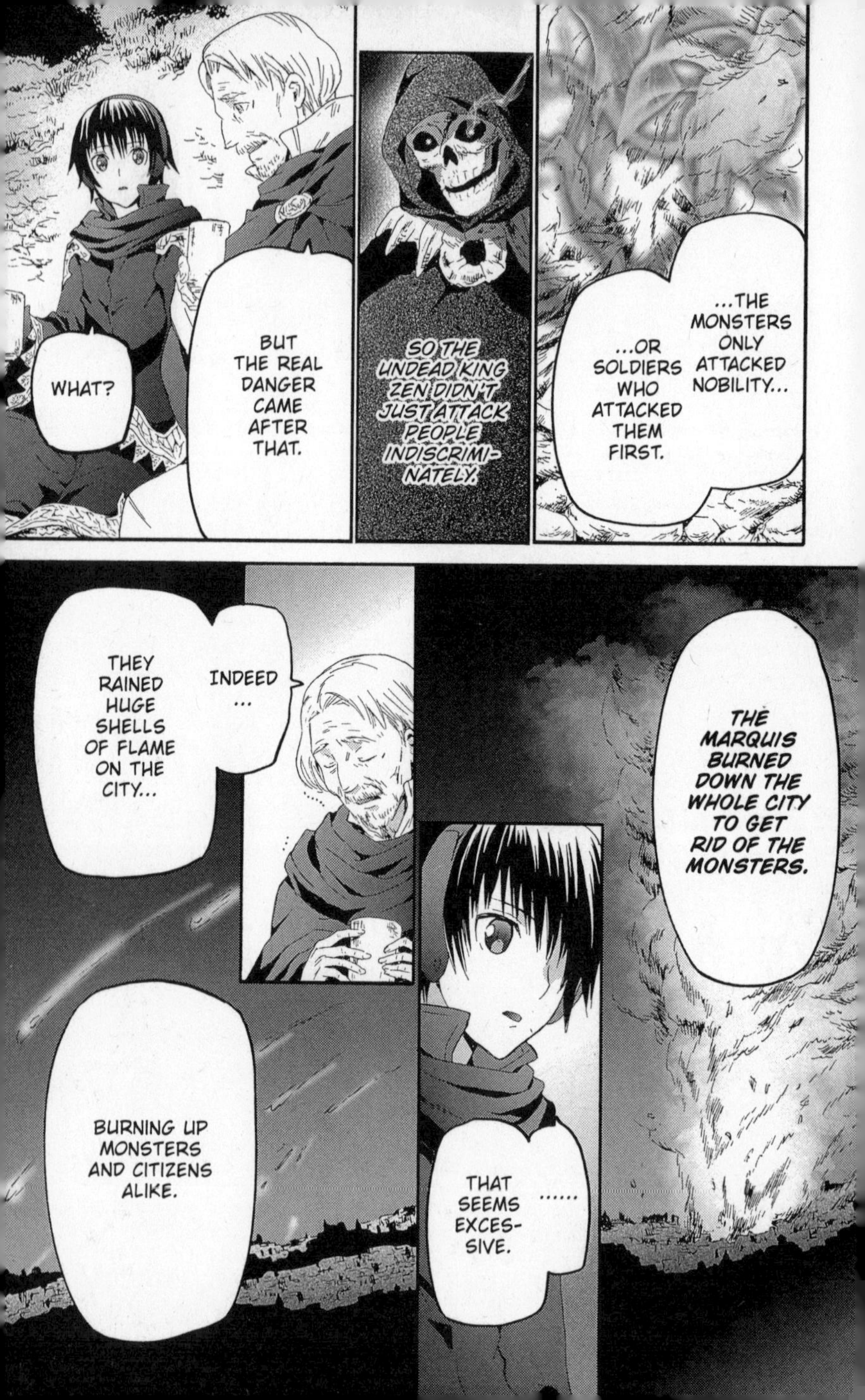
...THE MONSTERS ONLY ATTACKED NOBILITY...
...OR SOLDIERS WHO ATTACKED THEM FIRST.
SO THE UNDEAD KING ZEN DIDN'T JUST ATTACK PEOPLE INDISCRIMINATELY.
BUT THE REAL DANGER CAME AFTER THAT.
WHAT?
THE MARQUIS BURNED DOWN THE WHOLE CITY TO GET RID OF THE MONSTERS.
INDEED...
THEY RAINED HUGE SHELLS OF FLAME ON THE CITY...
BURNING UP MONSTERS AND CITIZENS ALIKE.
......
THAT SEEMS EXCESSIVE.

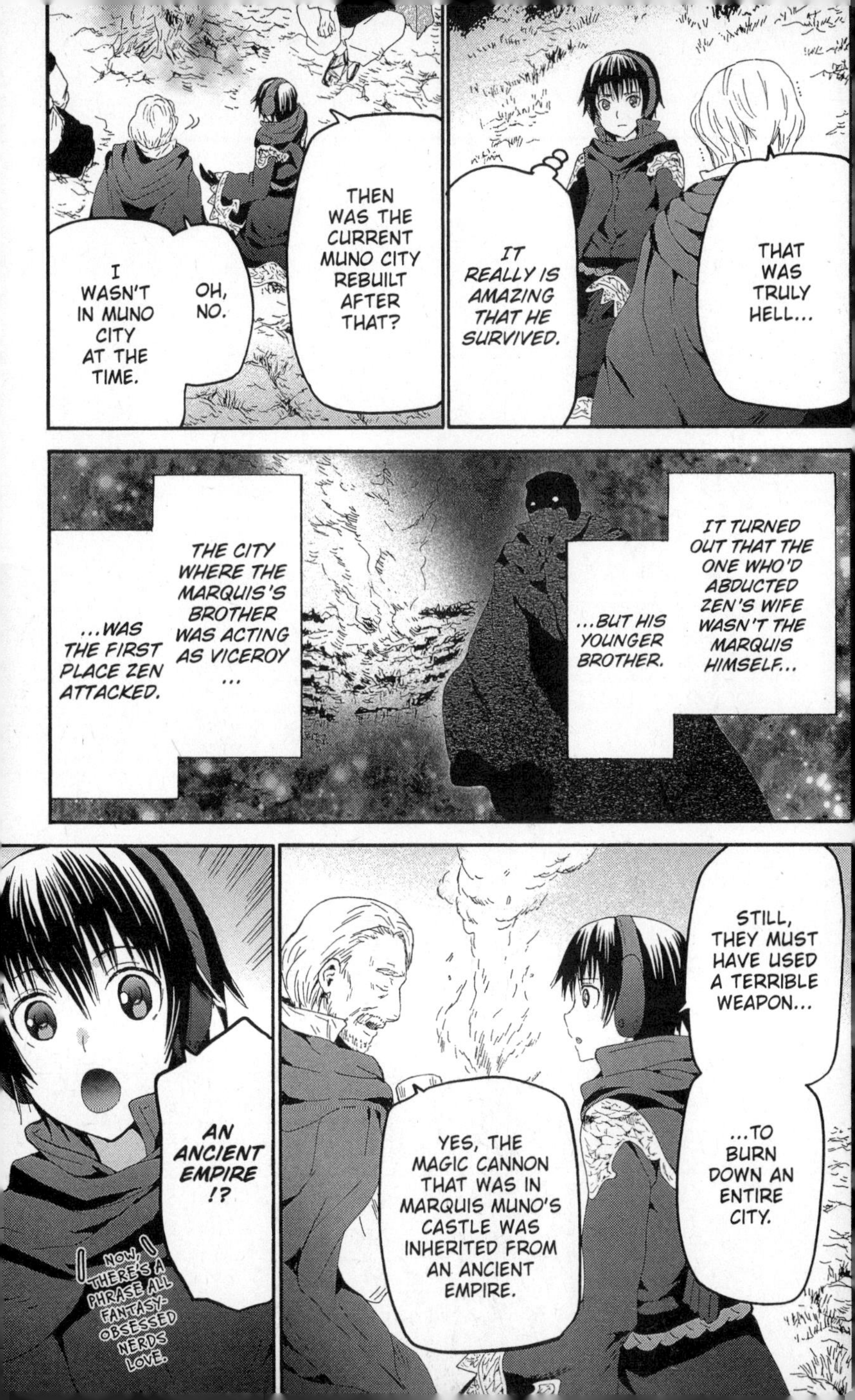
THAT WAS TRULY HELL...
IT REALLY IS AMAZING THAT HE SURVIVED.
THEN WAS THE CURRENT MUNO CITY REBUILT AFTER THAT?
OH, NO.
I WASN'T IN MUNO CITY AT THE TIME.
IT TURNED OUT THAT THE ONE WHO'D ABDUCTED ZEN'S WIFE WASN'T THE MARQUIS HIMSELF...
...BUT HIS YOUNGER BROTHER.
THE CITY WHERE THE MARQUIS'S BROTHER WAS ACTING AS VICEROY ...
...WAS THE FIRST PLACE ZEN ATTACKED.
STILL, THEY MUST HAVE USED A TERRIBLE WEAPON...
...TO BURN DOWN AN ENTIRE CITY.
YES, THE MAGIC CANNON THAT WAS IN MARQUIS MUNO'S CASTLE WAS INHERITED FROM AN ANCIENT EMPIRE.
AN ANCIENT EMPIRE !?
NOW, THERE'S A PHRASE ALL FANTASY-OBSESSED NERDS LOVE.

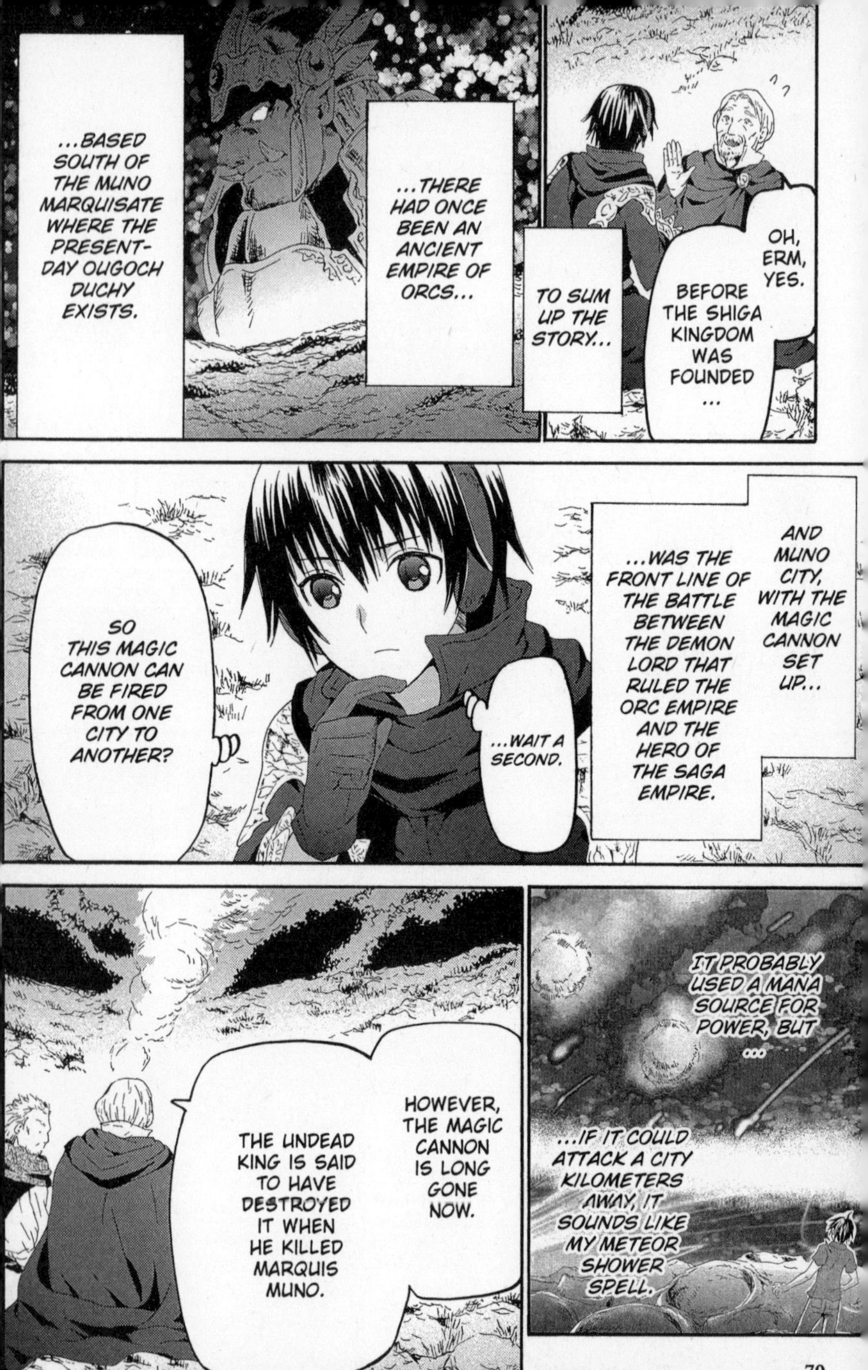
OH, ERM, YES.
BEFORE THE SHIGA KINGDOM WAS FOUNDED ...
TO SUM UP THE STORY...
...THERE HAD ONCE BEEN AN ANCIENT EMPIRE OF ORCS...
...BASED SOUTH OF THE MUNO MARQUISATE WHERE THE PRESENT-DAY OUGOCH DUCHY EXISTS.
AND MUNO CITY, WITH THE MAGIC CANNON SET UP...
...WAS THE FRONT LINE OF THE BATTLE BETWEEN THE DEMON LORD THAT RULED THE ORC EMPIRE AND THE HERO OF THE SAGA EMPIRE.
...WAIT A SECOND.
SO THIS MAGIC CANNON CAN BE FIRED FROM ONE CITY TO ANOTHER?
IT PROBABLY USED A MANA SOURCE FOR POWER, BUT ...
...IF IT COULD ATTACK A CITY KILOMETERS AWAY, IT SOUNDS LIKE MY METEOR SHOWER SPELL.
HOWEVER, THE MAGIC CANNON IS LONG GONE NOW.
THE UNDEAD KING IS SAID TO HAVE DESTROYED IT WHEN HE KILLED MARQUIS MUNO.

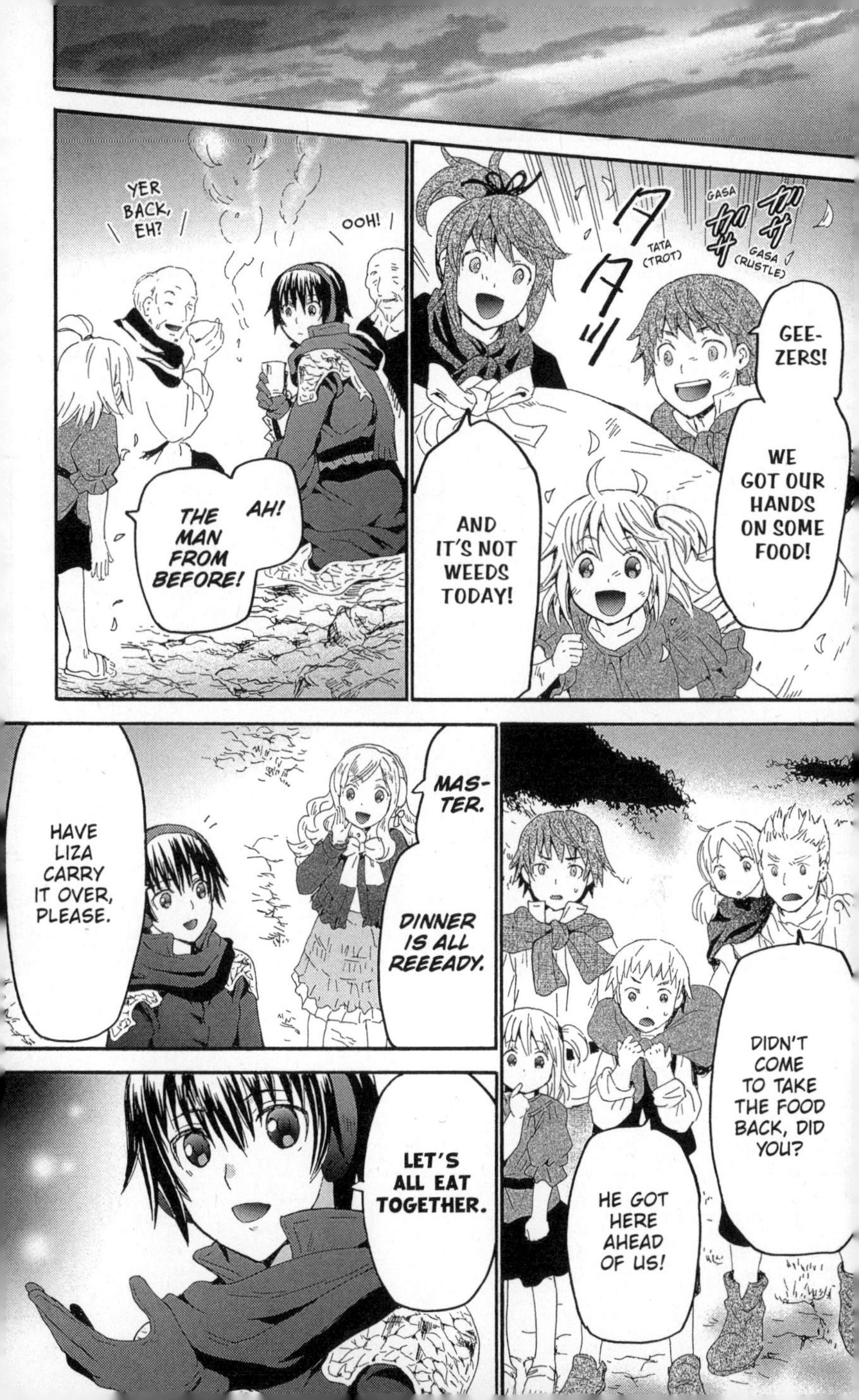
TATA (TROT)
GASA GASA (RUSTLE)
GEE-ZERS!
WE GOT OUR HANDS ON SOME FOOD!
AND IT'S NOT WEEDS TODAY!
OOH!
YER BACK, EH?
AH! THE MAN FROM BEFORE!
DIDN'T COME TO TAKE THE FOOD BACK, DID YOU?
HE GOT HERE AHEAD OF US!
MAS-TER.
DINNER IS ALL REEEADY.
HAVE LIZA CARRY IT OVER, PLEASE.
LET'S ALL EAT TOGETHER.

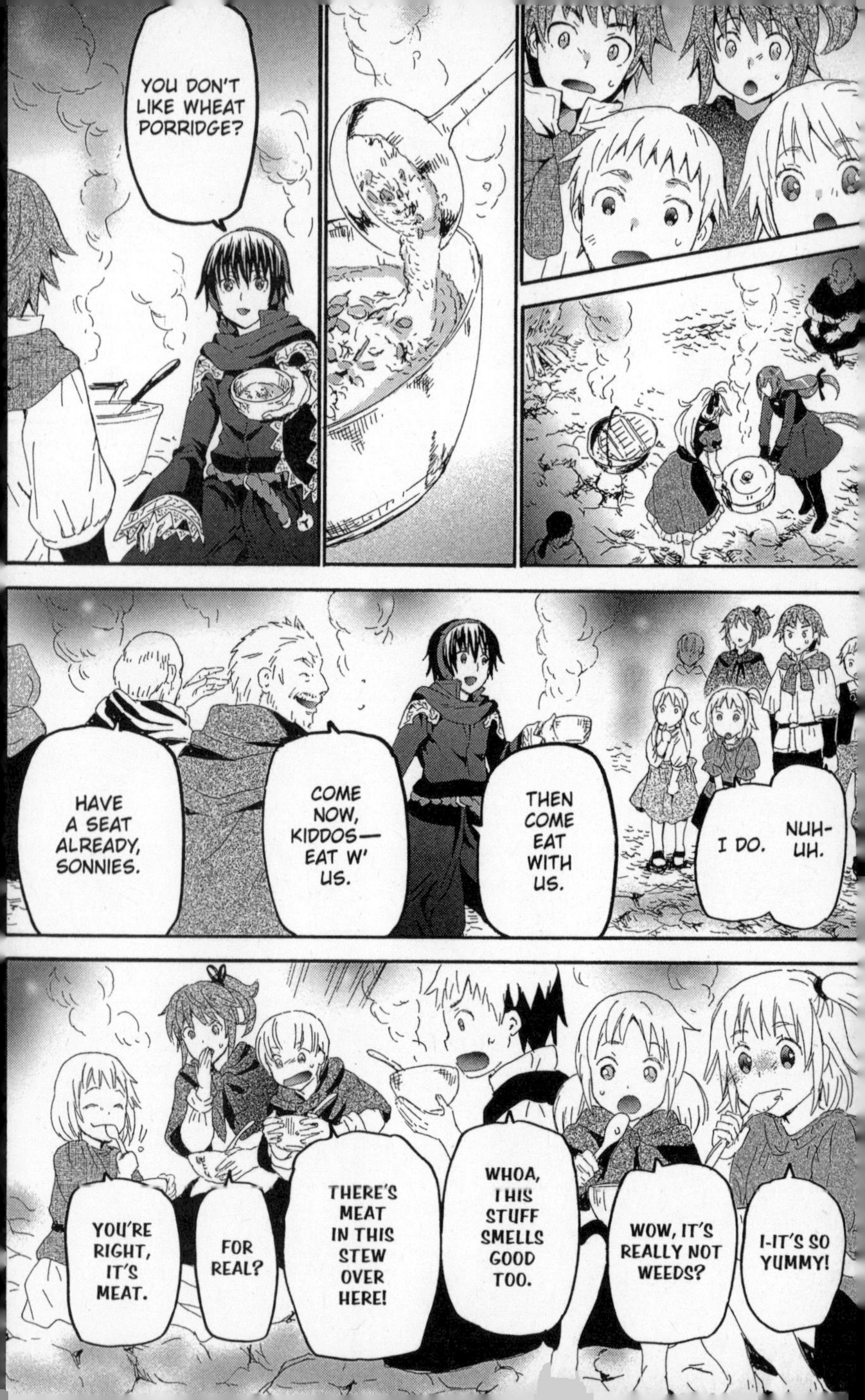
YOU DON'T LIKE WHEAT PORRIDGE?
NUH-UH.
I DO.
THEN COME EAT WITH US.
COME NOW, KIDDOS—EAT W' US.
HAVE A SEAT ALREADY, SONNIES.
I-IT'S SO YUMMY!
WOW, IT'S REALLY NOT WEEDS?
WHOA, THIS STUFF SMELLS GOOD TOO.
THERE'S MEAT IN THIS STEW OVER HERE!
FOR REAL?
YOU'RE RIGHT, IT'S MEAT.

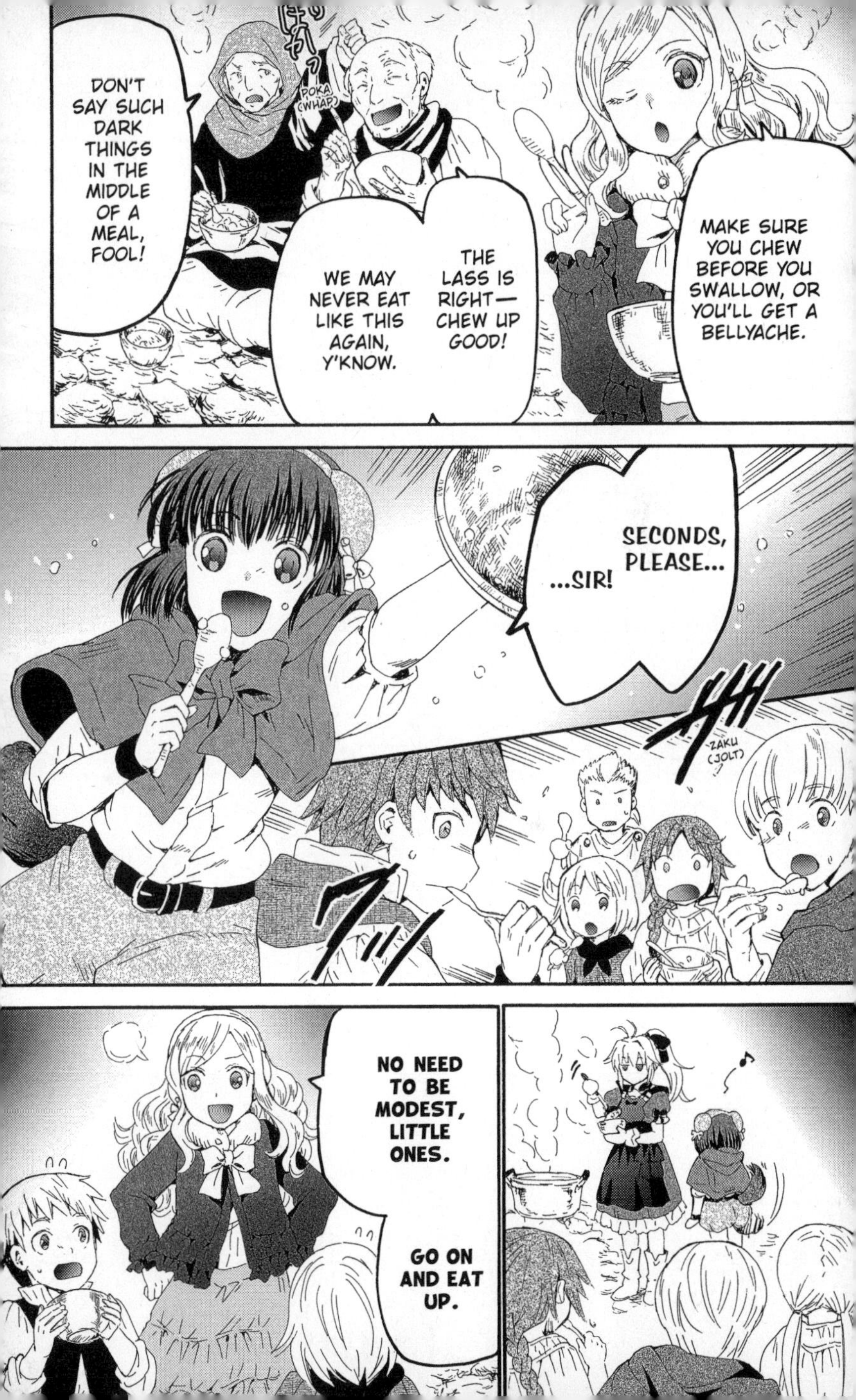
MAKE SURE YOU CHEW BEFORE YOU SWALLOW, OR YOU'LL GET A BELLYACHE.
THE LASS IS RIGHT— CHEW UP GOOD!
WE MAY NEVER EAT LIKE THIS AGAIN, Y'KNOW.
POKA (WHAP)
DON'T SAY SUCH DARK THINGS IN THE MIDDLE OF A MEAL, FOOL!
SECONDS, PLEASE...
...SIR!
ZAKU (JOLT)
NO NEED TO BE MODEST, LITTLE ONES.
GO ON AND EAT UP.

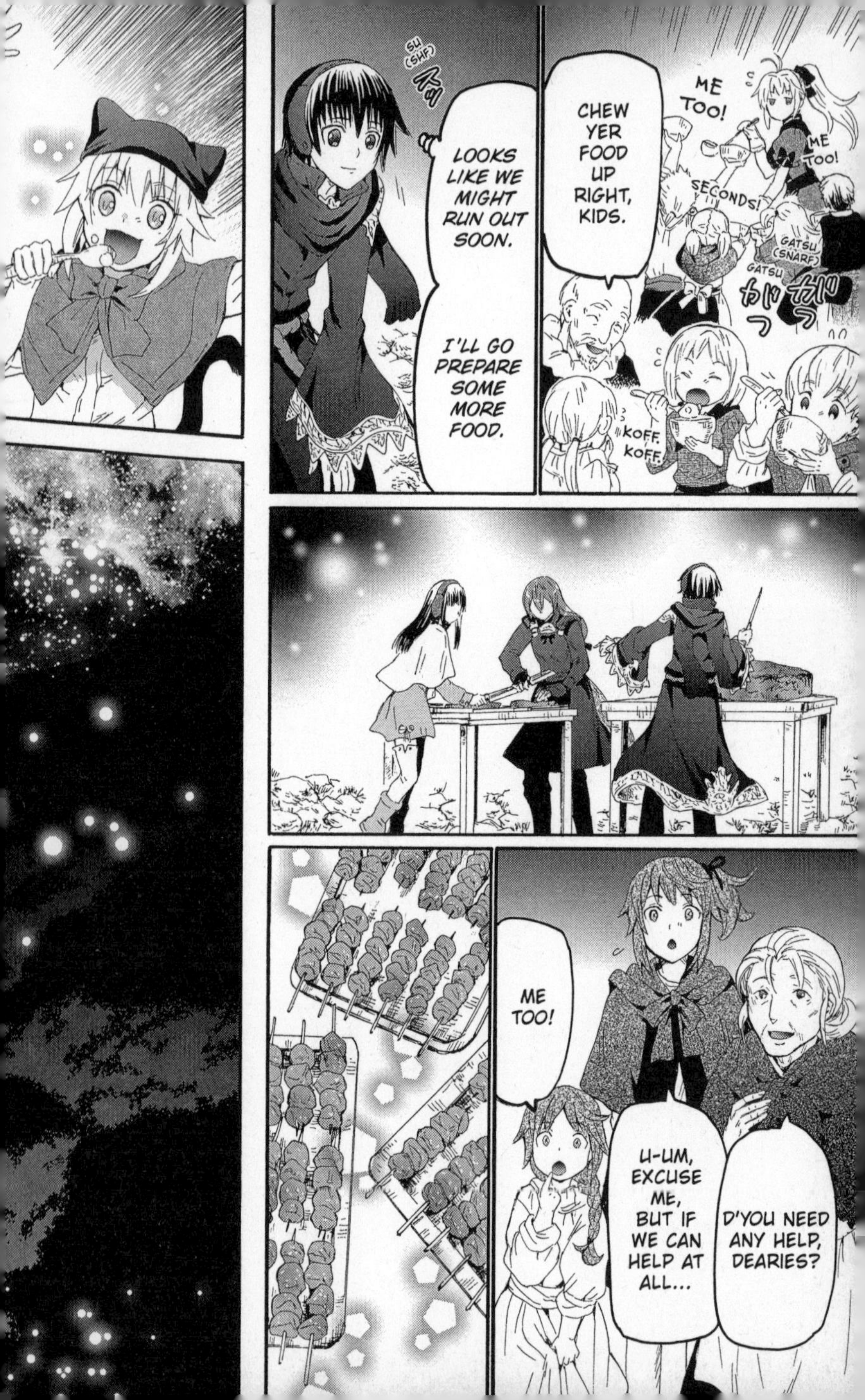
CHEW YER FOOD UP RIGHT, KIDS.
ME TOO!
ME TOO!
SECONDS!
GATSU (SNARF)
GATSU
KOFF. KOFF.
SU (SHF)
LOOKS LIKE WE MIGHT RUN OUT SOON.
I'LL GO PREPARE SOME MORE FOOD.
D'YOU NEED ANY HELP, DEARIES?
U-UM, EXCUSE ME, BUT IF WE CAN HELP AT ALL...
ME TOO!

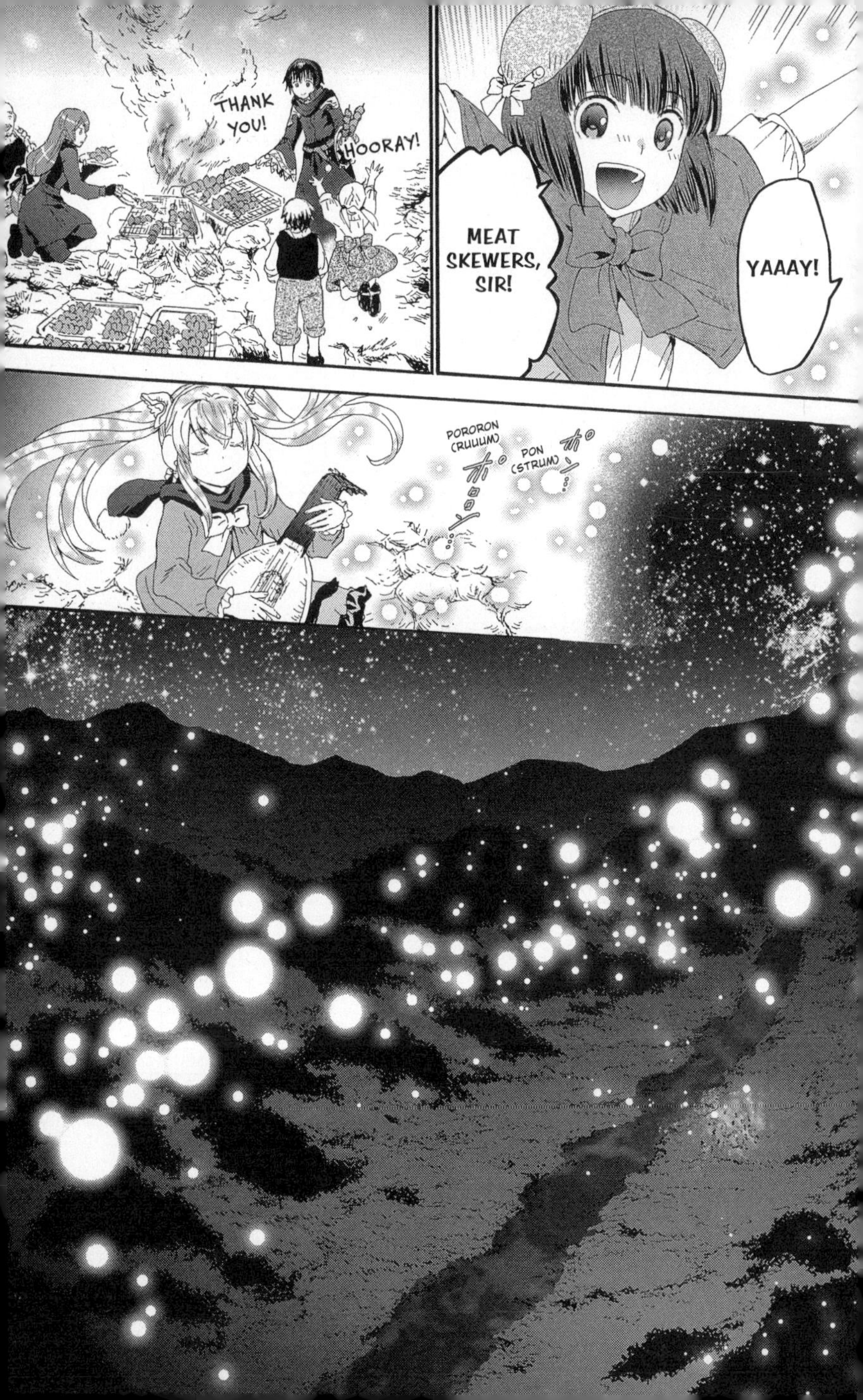
YAAAY!
MEAT SKEWERS, SIR!
THANK YOU!
HOORAY!
PON (STRUM)
PORORON (RUUUM)

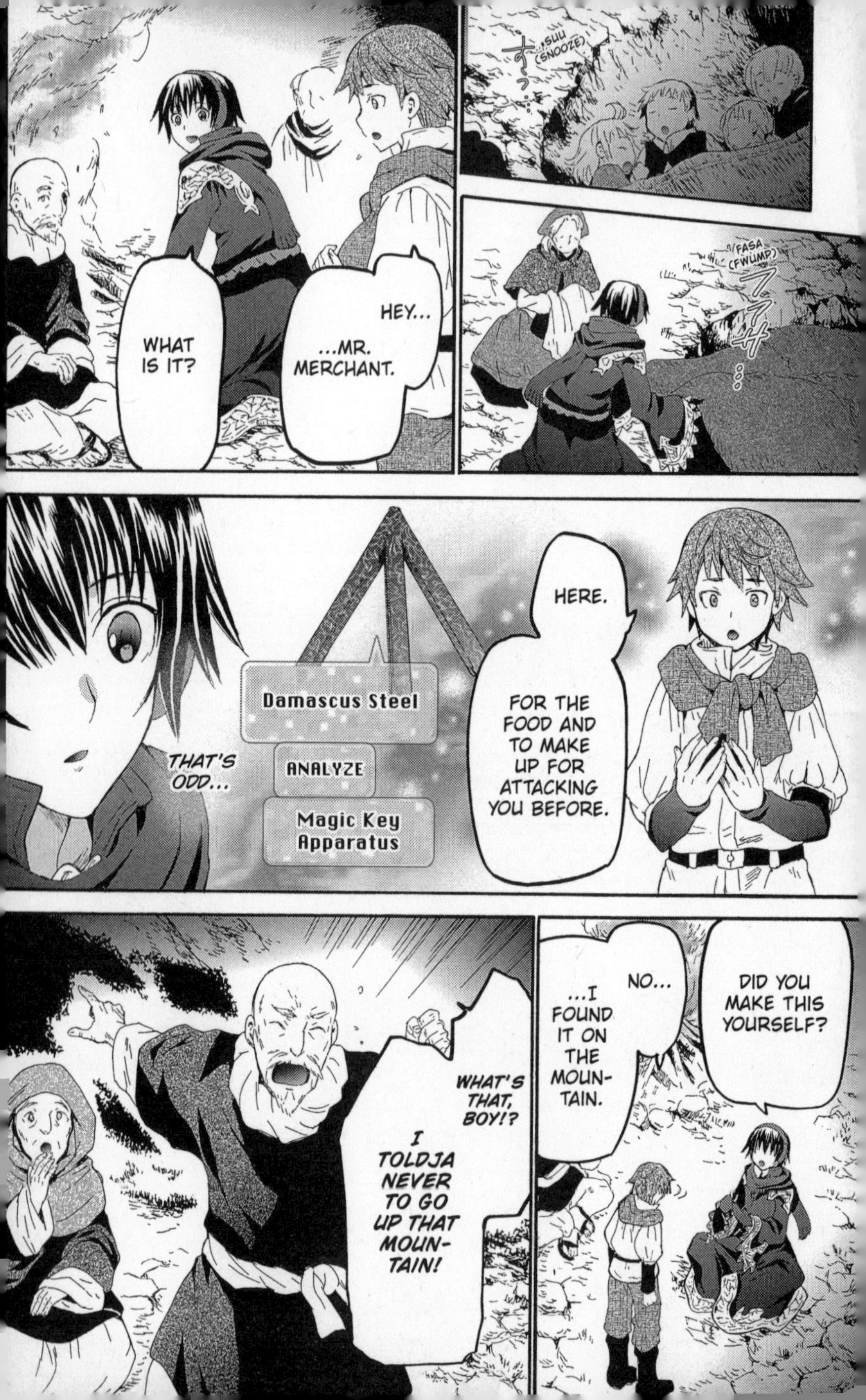
SUU (SNOOZE)
FASA (FWUMP)
HEY... ...MR. MERCHANT.
WHAT IS IT?
HERE.
FOR THE FOOD AND TO MAKE UP FOR ATTACKING YOU BEFORE.
Damascus Steel
ANALYZE
Magic Key Apparatus
THAT'S ODD...
DID YOU MAKE THIS YOURSELF?
NO...
...I FOUND IT ON THE MOUN-TAIN.
WHAT'S THAT, BOY!?
I TOLDJA NEVER TO GO UP THAT MOUN-TAIN!

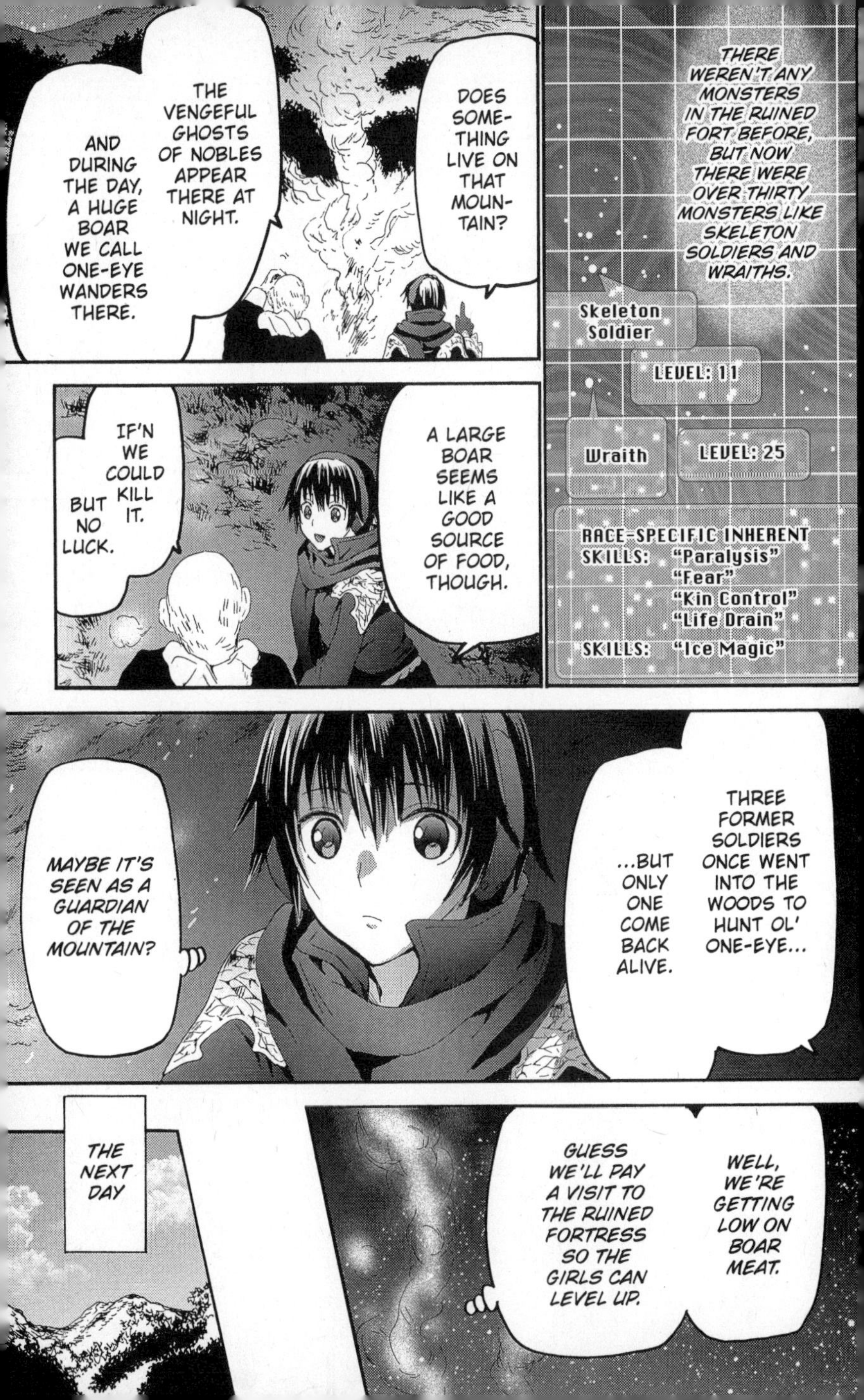
THERE WEREN'T ANY MONSTERS IN THE RUINED FORT BEFORE, BUT NOW THERE WERE OVER THIRTY MONSTERS LIKE SKELETON SOLDIERS AND WRAITHS.
Skeleton Soldier
LEVEL: 11
Wraith
LEVEL: 25
RACE-SPECIFIC INHERENT SKILLS: "Paralysis" "Fear" "Kin Control" "Life Drain"
SKILLS: "Ice Magic"
DOES SOMETHING LIVE ON THAT MOUNTAIN?
THE VENGEFUL GHOSTS OF NOBLES APPEAR THERE AT NIGHT.
AND DURING THE DAY, A HUGE BOAR WE CALL ONE-EYE WANDERS THERE.
A LARGE BOAR SEEMS LIKE A GOOD SOURCE OF FOOD, THOUGH.
IF'N WE COULD KILL IT.
BUT NO LUCK.
THREE FORMER SOLDIERS ONCE WENT INTO THE WOODS TO HUNT OL' ONE-EYE...
...BUT ONLY ONE COME BACK ALIVE.
MAYBE IT'S SEEN AS A GUARDIAN OF THE MOUNTAIN?
WELL, WE'RE GETTING LOW ON BOAR MEAT.
GUESS WE'LL PAY A VISIT TO THE RUINED FORTRESS SO THE GIRLS CAN LEVEL UP.
THE NEXT DAY

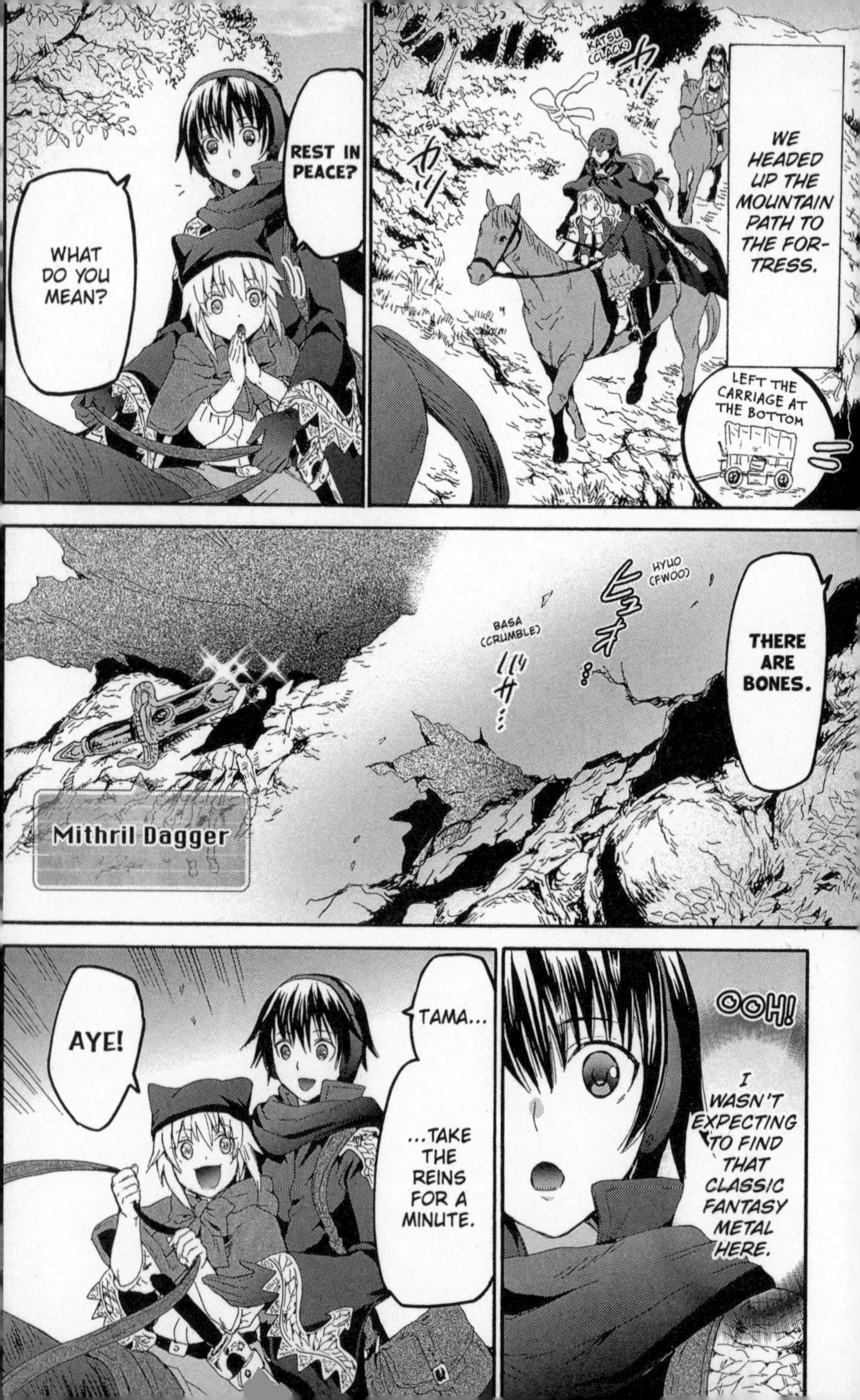
KATSU (CLACK)
KATSU
WE HEADED UP THE MOUNTAIN PATH TO THE FORTRESS.
LEFT THE CARRIAGE AT THE BOTTOM
REST IN PEACE?
WHAT DO YOU MEAN?
HYUO (FWOO)
BASA (CRUMBLE)
THERE ARE BONES.
Mithril Dagger
OOH!
I WASN'T EXPECTING TO FIND THAT CLASSIC FANTASY METAL HERE.
TAMA...
...TAKE THE REINS FOR A MINUTE.
AYE!

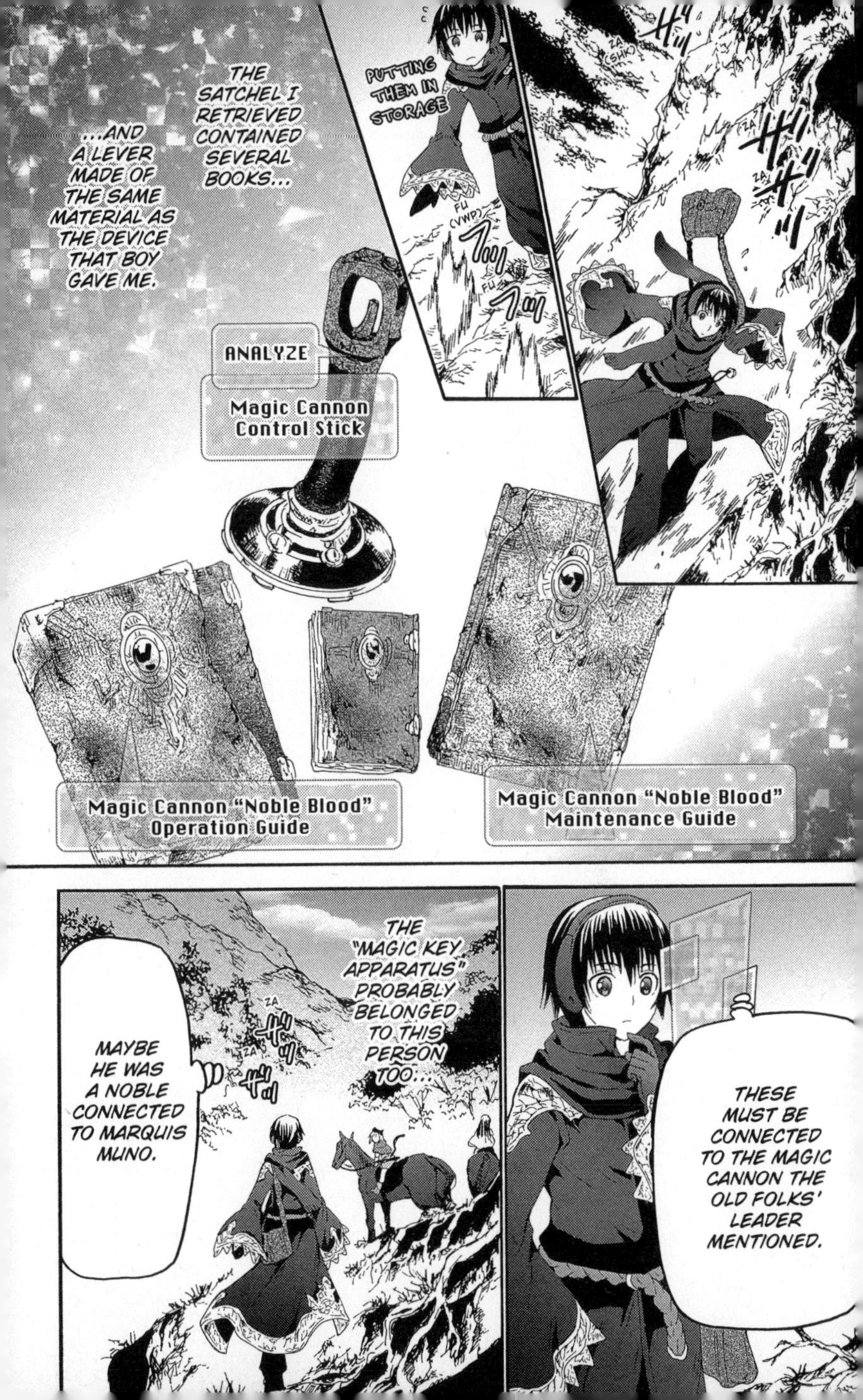
ZA (SHK)
ZA
ZA
PUTTING THEM IN STORAGE
FU (VWP)
FU
THE SATCHEL I RETRIEVED CONTAINED SEVERAL BOOKS...
...AND A LEVER MADE OF THE SAME MATERIAL AS THE DEVICE THAT BOY GAVE ME.
ANALYZE
Magic Cannon Control Stick
Magic Cannon "Noble Blood" Maintenance Guide
Magic Cannon "Noble Blood" Operation Guide
THESE MUST BE CONNECTED TO THE MAGIC CANNON THE OLD FOLKS' LEADER MENTIONED.
THE "MAGIC KEY APPARATUS" PROBABLY BELONGED TO THIS PERSON TOO...
ZA
ZA
MAYBE HE WAS A NOBLE CONNECTED TO MARQUIS MUNO.

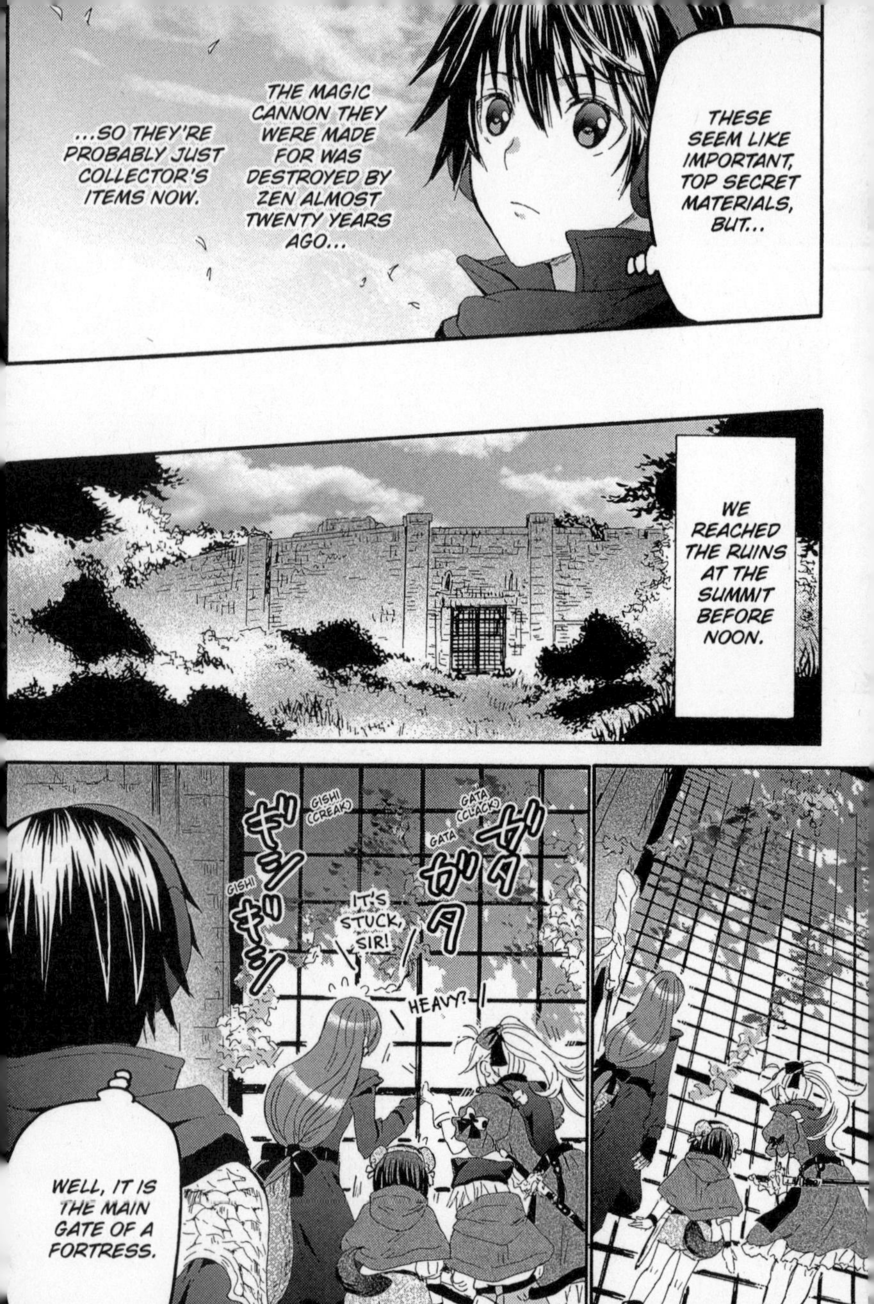

THESE SEEM LIKE IMPORTANT, TOP SECRET MATERIALS, BUT...
THE MAGIC CANNON THEY WERE MADE FOR WAS DESTROYED BY ZEN ALMOST TWENTY YEARS AGO...
...SO THEY'RE PROBABLY JUST COLLECTOR'S ITEMS NOW.
WE REACHED THE RUINS AT THE SUMMIT BEFORE NOON.
GATA (CLACK)
GATA
GISHI (CREAK)
GISHI
IT'S STUCK, SIR!
HEAVY?!
WELL, IT IS THE MAIN GATE OF A FORTRESS.

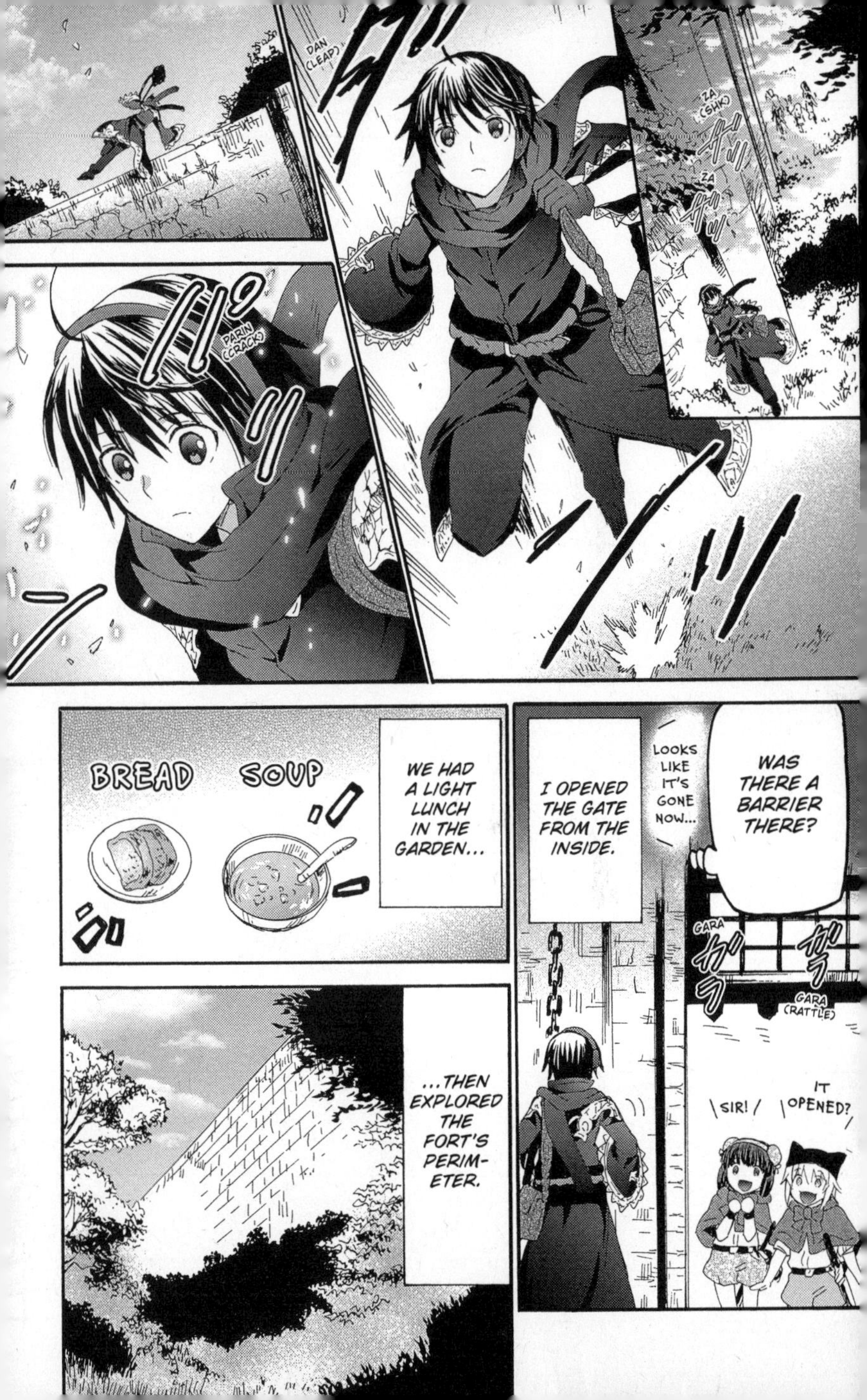

ZA (SHK)
ZA
DAN (LEAP)
PARIN (CRACK)
WAS THERE A BARRIER THERE?
LOOKS LIKE IT'S GONE NOW...
I OPENED THE GATE FROM THE INSIDE.
GARA
GARA (RATTLE)
IT OPENED?
SIR!
WE HAD A LIGHT LUNCH IN THE GARDEN...
BREAD
SOUP
...THEN EXPLORED THE FORT'S PERIMETER.

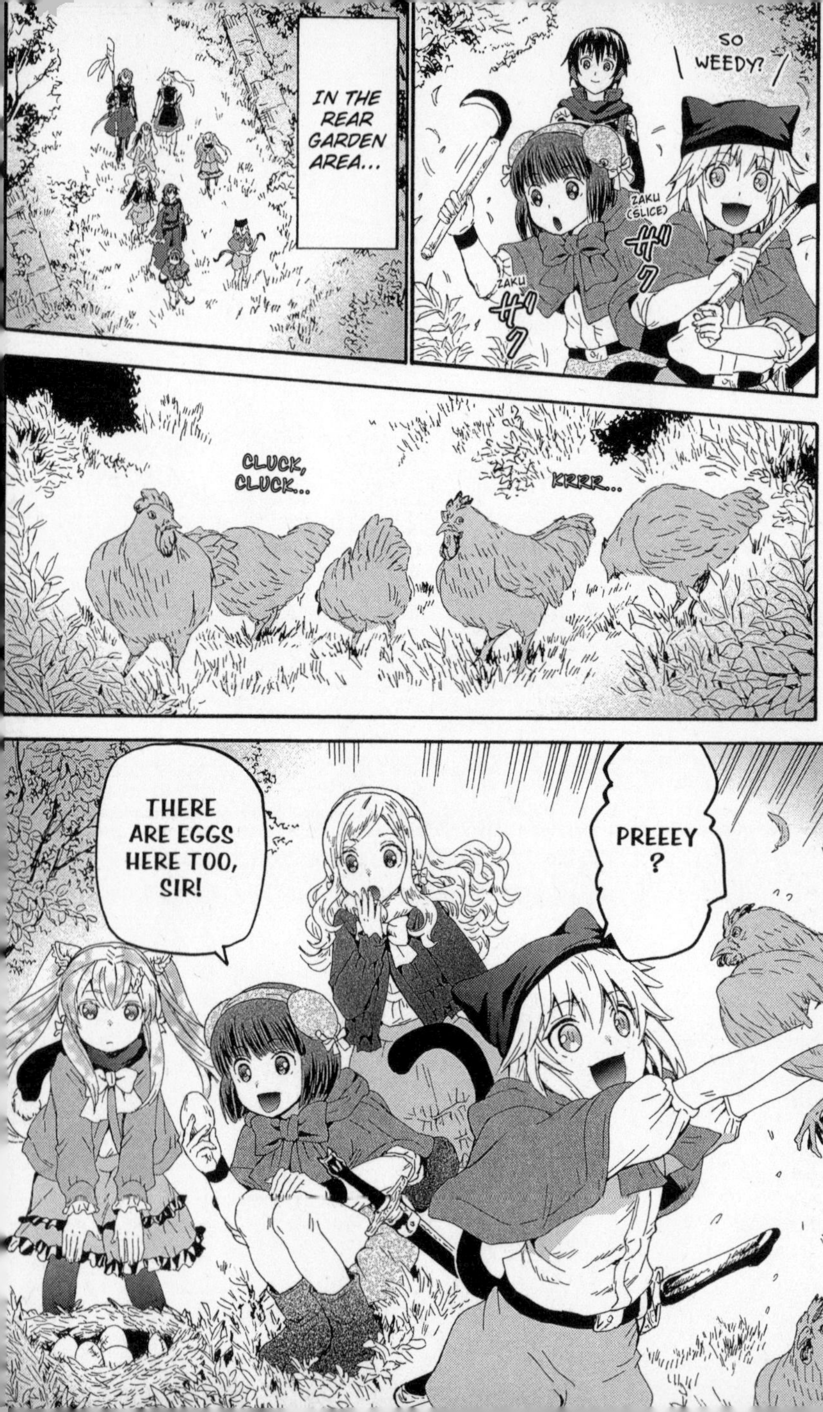
SO WEEDY?
ZAKU (SLICE)
ザク
ZAKU
ザク
IN THE REAR GARDEN AREA...
KRRR...
CLUCK, CLUCK...
PREEEY ?
THERE ARE EGGS HERE TOO, SIR!

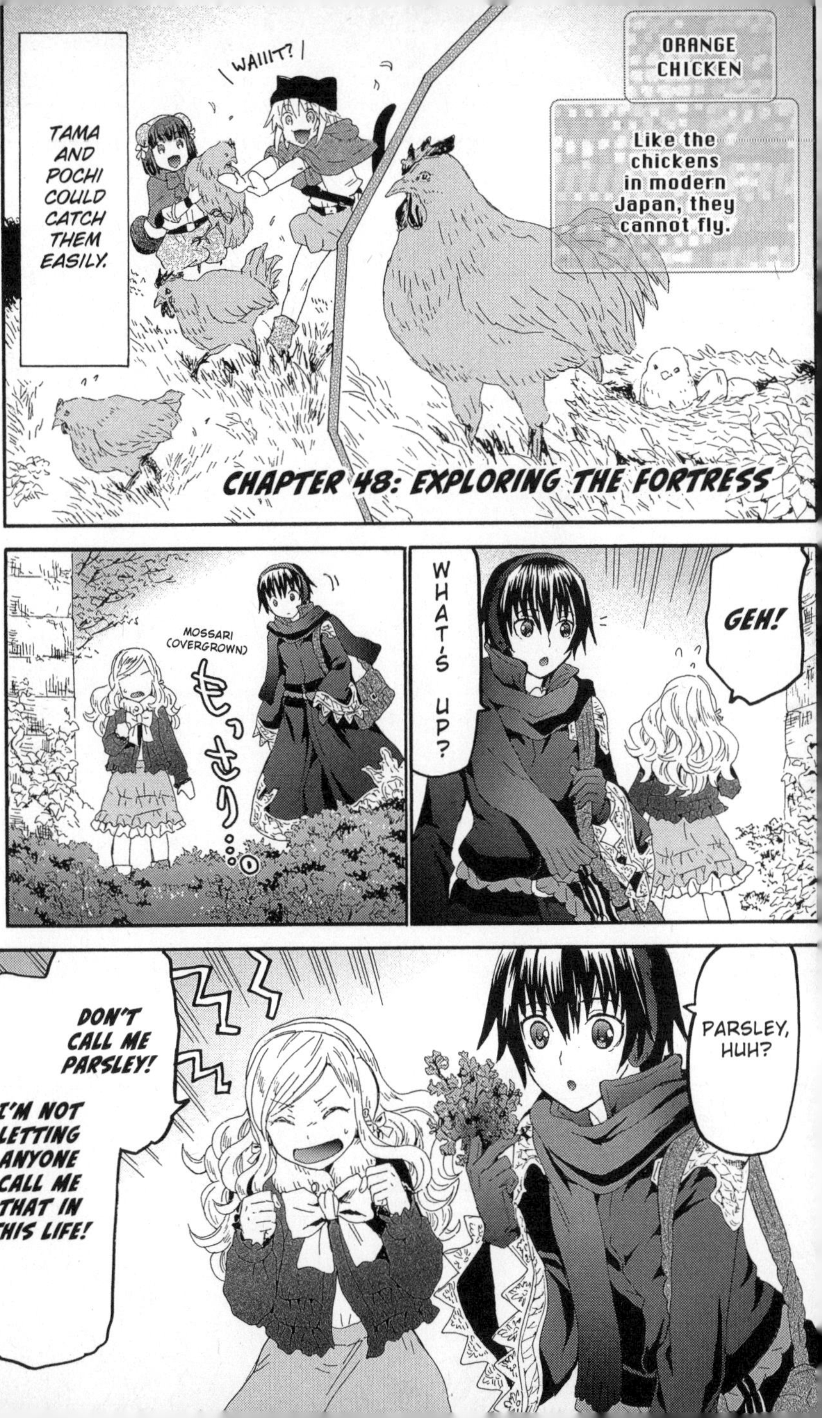
ORANGE CHICKEN
Like the chickens in modern Japan, they cannot fly.
WAIIIT?!
TAMA AND POCHI COULD CATCH THEM EASILY.
CHAPTER 48: EXPLORING THE FORTRESS
GEH!
WHAT'S UP?
MOSSARI (OVERGROWN)
もっさり…
PARSLEY, HUH?
DON'T CALL ME PARSLEY!
I'M NOT LETTING ANYONE CALL ME THAT IN THIS LIFE!

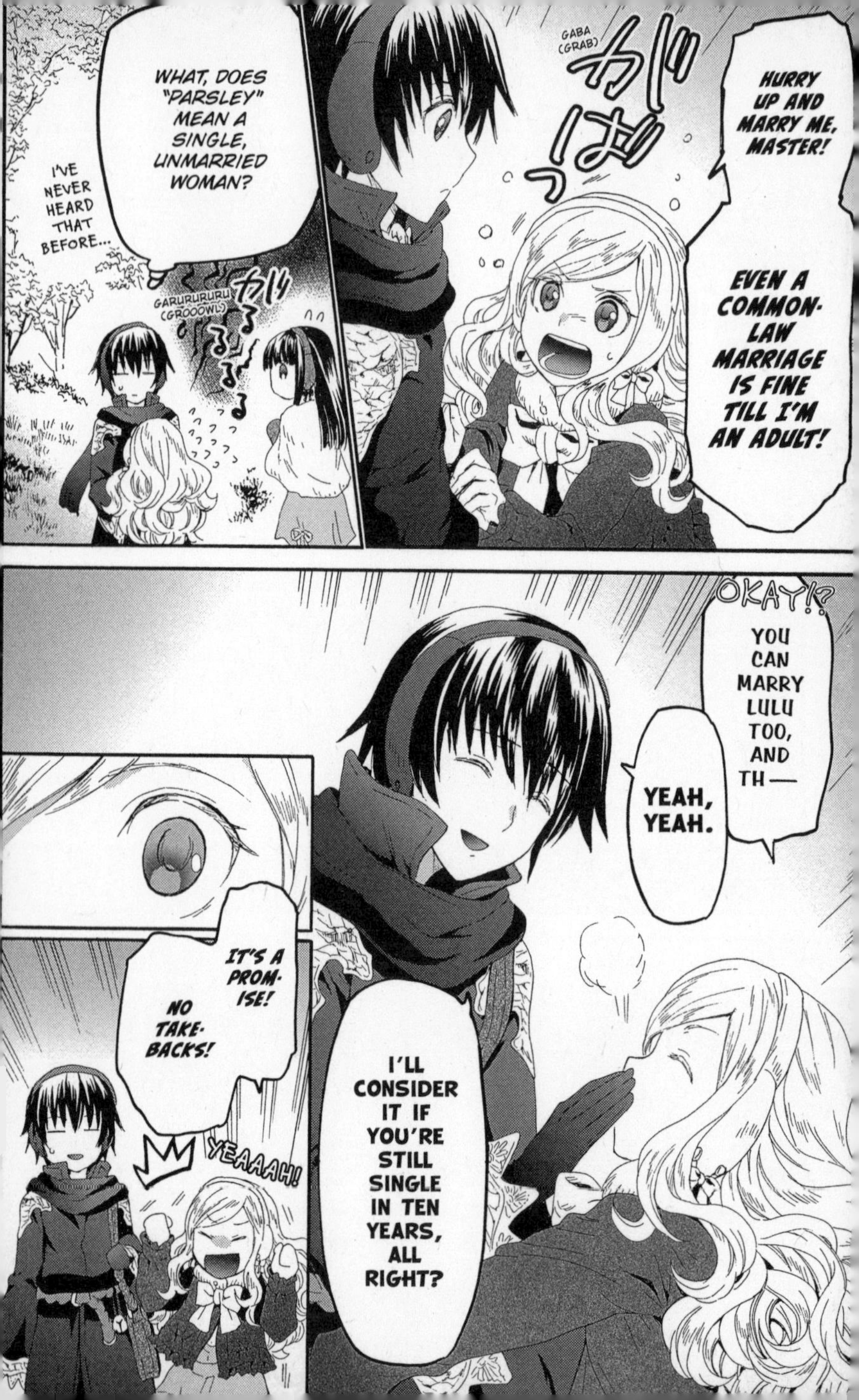
GABA (GRAB)
HURRY UP AND MARRY ME, MASTER!
EVEN A COMMON-LAW MARRIAGE IS FINE TILL I'M AN ADULT!
WHAT, DOES "PARSLEY" MEAN A SINGLE, UNMARRIED WOMAN?
I'VE NEVER HEARD THAT BEFORE...
GARURURURU (GROOOWL)
OKAY!?
YOU CAN MARRY LULU TOO, AND TH—
YEAH, YEAH.
I'LL CONSIDER IT IF YOU'RE STILL SINGLE IN TEN YEARS, ALL RIGHT?
IT'S A PROMISE!
NO TAKE-BACKS!
YEAAAAH!

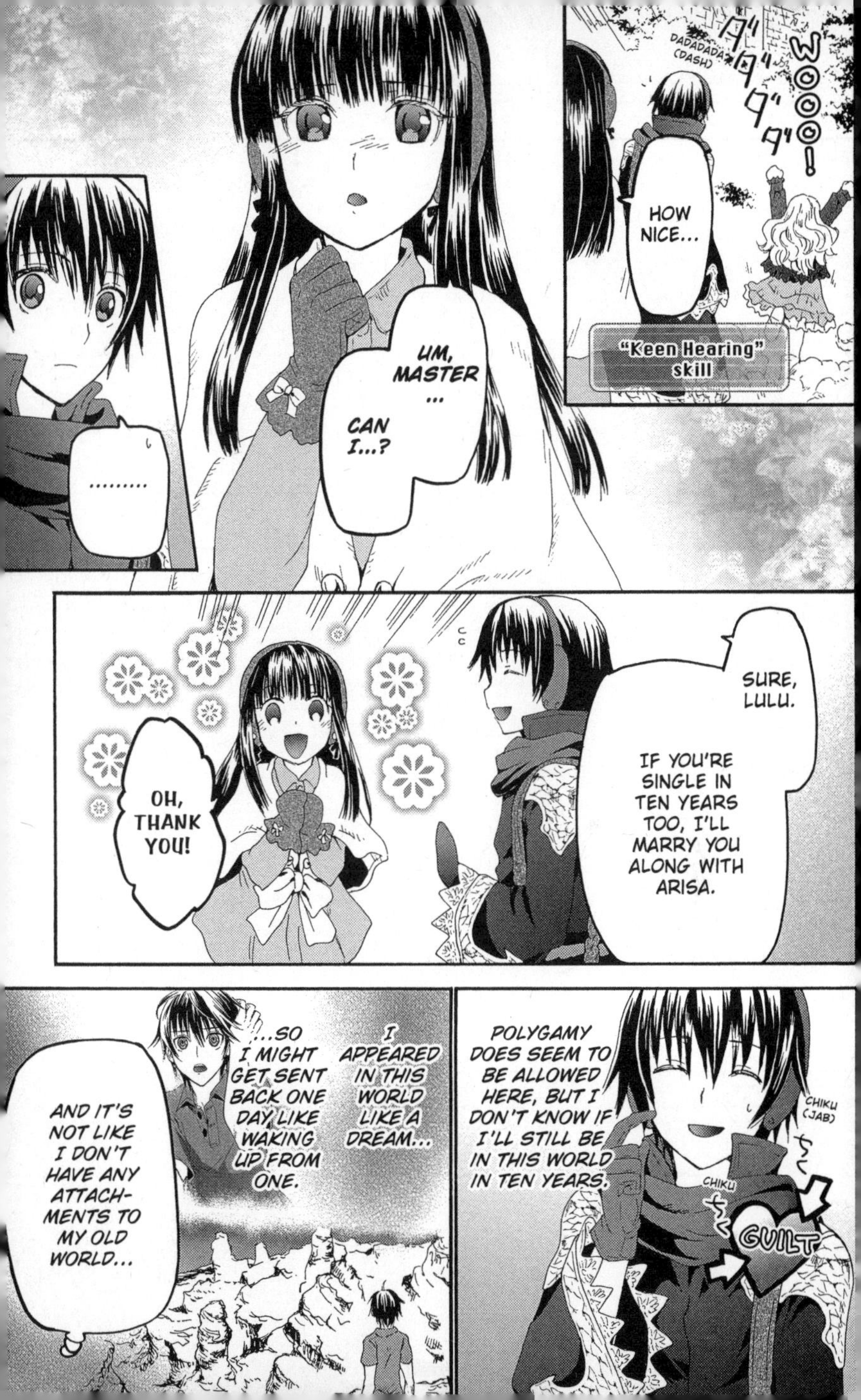
WOOOO!
DADADADA (DASH)
HOW NICE...
"Keen Hearing" skill
UM, MASTER...
CAN I...?
....
SURE, LULU.
IF YOU'RE SINGLE IN TEN YEARS TOO, I'LL MARRY YOU ALONG WITH ARISA.
OH, THANK YOU!
POLYGAMY DOES SEEM TO BE ALLOWED HERE, BUT I DON'T KNOW IF I'LL STILL BE IN THIS WORLD IN TEN YEARS.
CHIKU (JAB)
CHIKU
GUILT
I APPEARED IN THIS WORLD LIKE A DREAM...
...SO I MIGHT GET SENT BACK ONE DAY LIKE WAKING UP FROM ONE.
AND IT'S NOT LIKE I DON'T HAVE ANY ATTACHMENTS TO MY OLD WORLD...

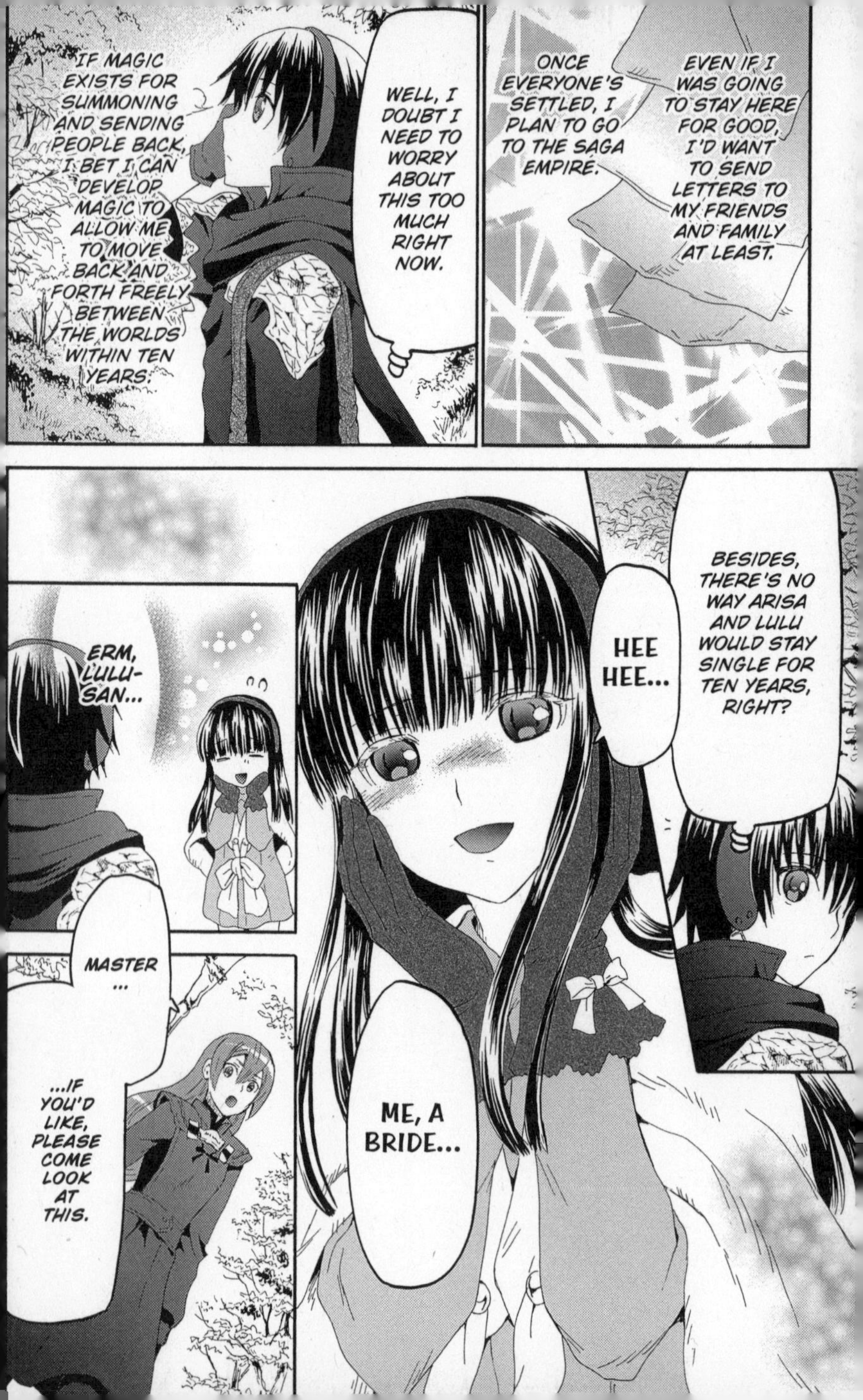
EVEN IF I WAS GOING TO STAY HERE FOR GOOD, I'D WANT TO SEND LETTERS TO MY FRIENDS AND FAMILY AT LEAST.
ONCE EVERYONE'S SETTLED, I PLAN TO GO TO THE SAGA EMPIRE.
WELL, I DOUBT I NEED TO WORRY ABOUT THIS TOO MUCH RIGHT NOW.
IF MAGIC EXISTS FOR SUMMONING AND SENDING PEOPLE BACK, I BET I CAN DEVELOP MAGIC TO ALLOW ME TO MOVE BACK AND FORTH FREELY BETWEEN THE WORLDS WITHIN TEN YEARS.
BESIDES, THERE'S NO WAY ARISA AND LULU WOULD STAY SINGLE FOR TEN YEARS, RIGHT?
HEE HEE...
ME, A BRIDE...
ERM, LULU-SAN...
MASTER...
...IF YOU'D LIKE, PLEASE COME LOOK AT THIS.

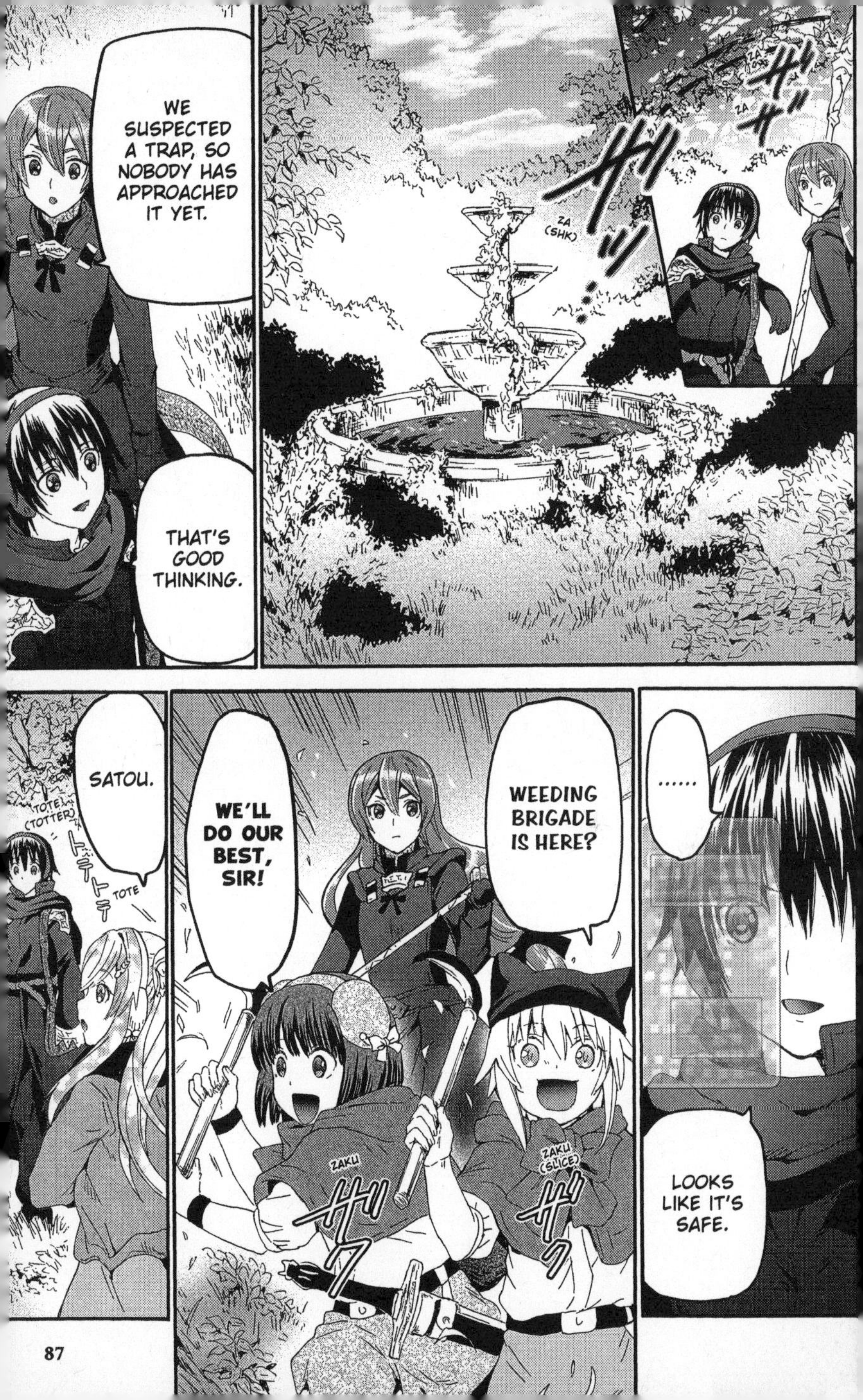
ZA
ZA
ZA (SHK)
WE SUSPECTED A TRAP, SO NOBODY HAS APPROACHED IT YET.
THAT'S GOOD THINKING.
......
LOOKS LIKE IT'S SAFE.
WEEDING BRIGADE IS HERE?
WE'LL DO OUR BEST, SIR!
ZAKU (SLICE)
ZAKU
SATOU.
TOTE (TOTTER)
TOTE

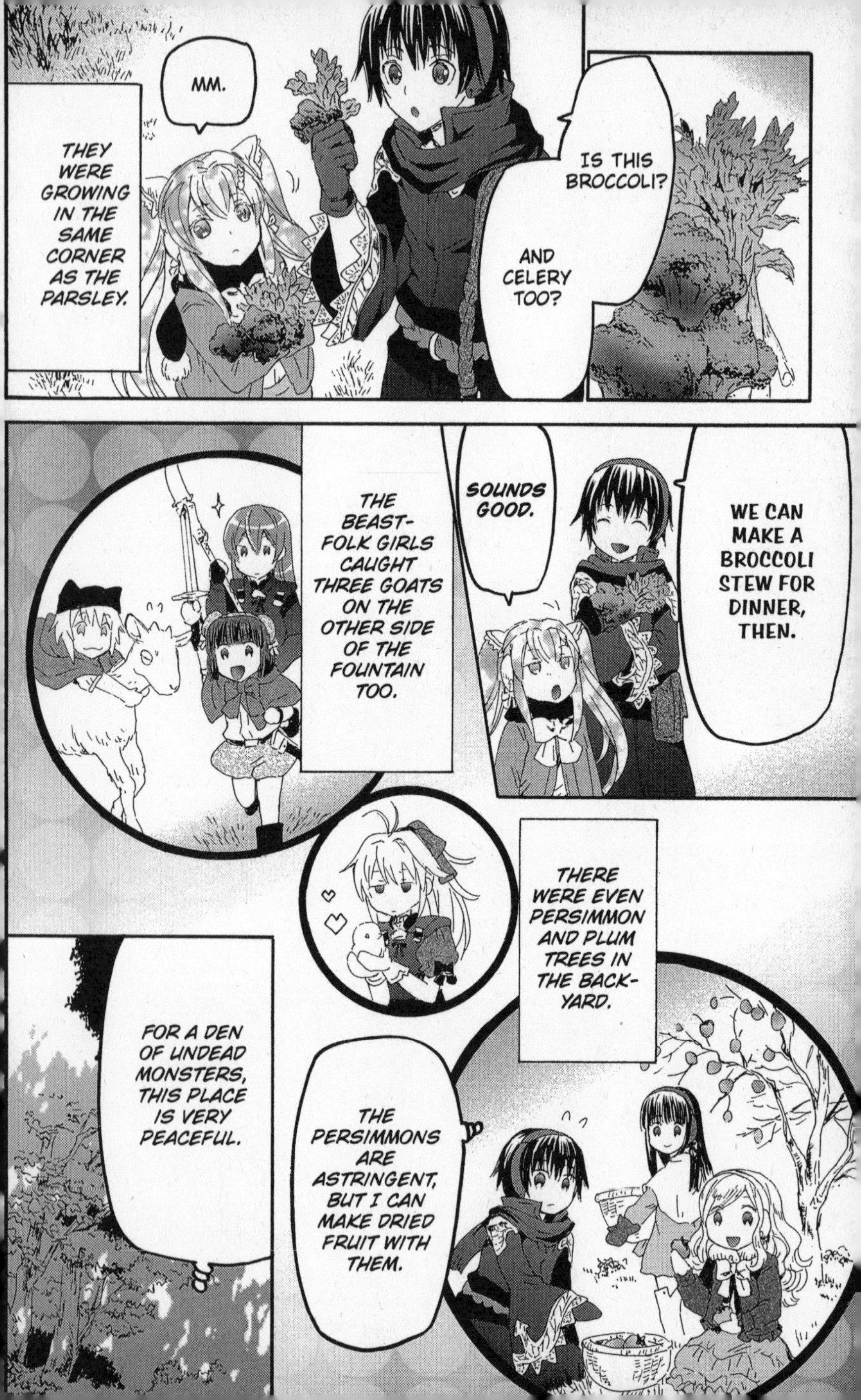
IS THIS BROCCOLI?
AND CELERY TOO?
MM.
THEY WERE GROWING IN THE SAME CORNER AS THE PARSLEY.
WE CAN MAKE A BROCCOLI STEW FOR DINNER, THEN.
SOUNDS GOOD.
THE BEAST-FOLK GIRLS CAUGHT THREE GOATS ON THE OTHER SIDE OF THE FOUNTAIN TOO.
THERE WERE EVEN PERSIMMON AND PLUM TREES IN THE BACK-YARD.
THE PERSIMMONS ARE ASTRINGENT, BUT I CAN MAKE DRIED FRUIT WITH THEM.
FOR A DEN OF UNDEAD MONSTERS, THIS PLACE IS VERY PEACEFUL.

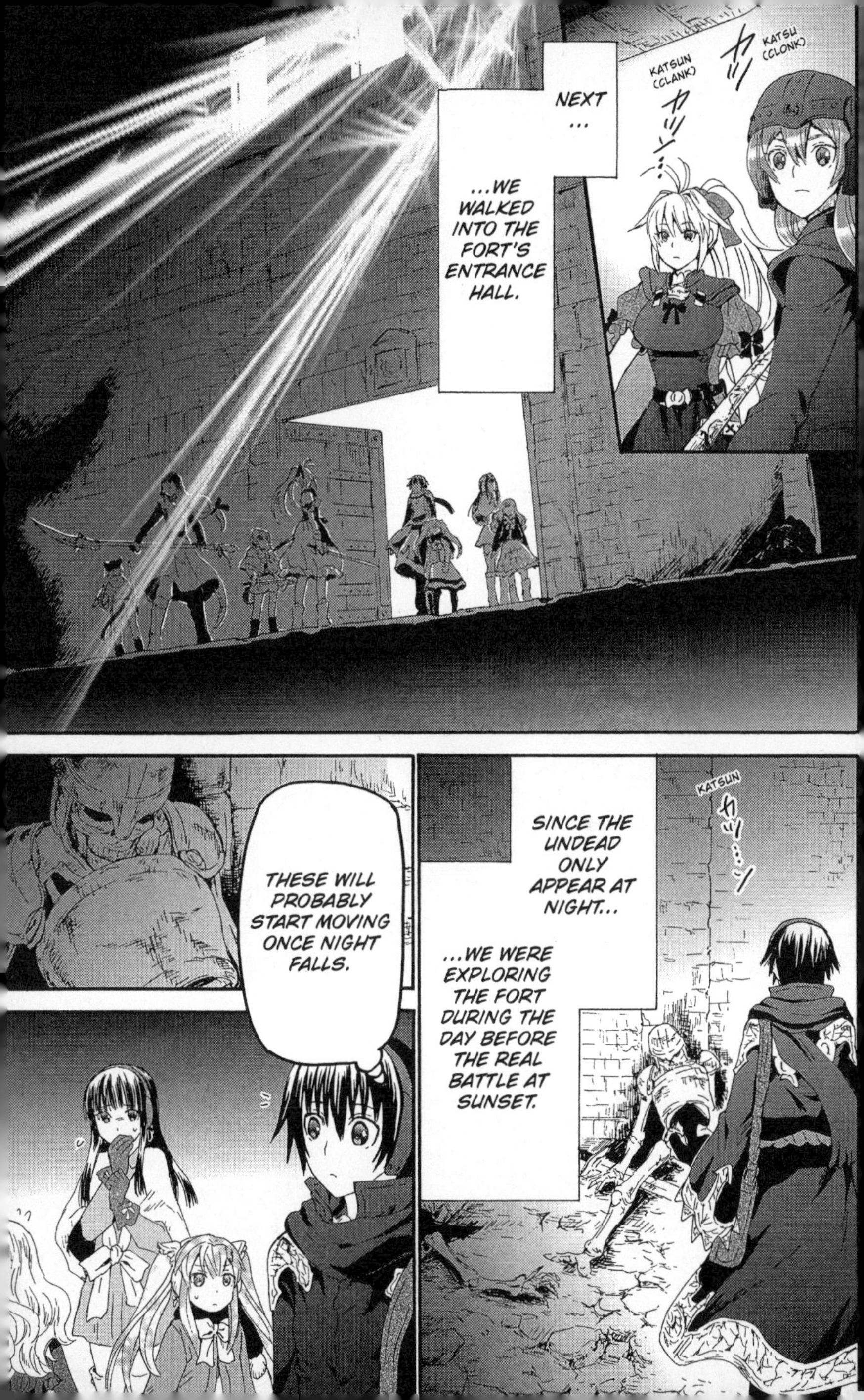
KATSU (CLONK)
KATSUN (CLANK)
NEXT ...
...WE WALKED INTO THE FORT'S ENTRANCE HALL.
KATSUN
SINCE THE UNDEAD ONLY APPEAR AT NIGHT...
...WE WERE EXPLORING THE FORT DURING THE DAY BEFORE THE REAL BATTLE AT SUNSET.
THESE WILL PROBABLY START MOVING ONCE NIGHT FALLS.

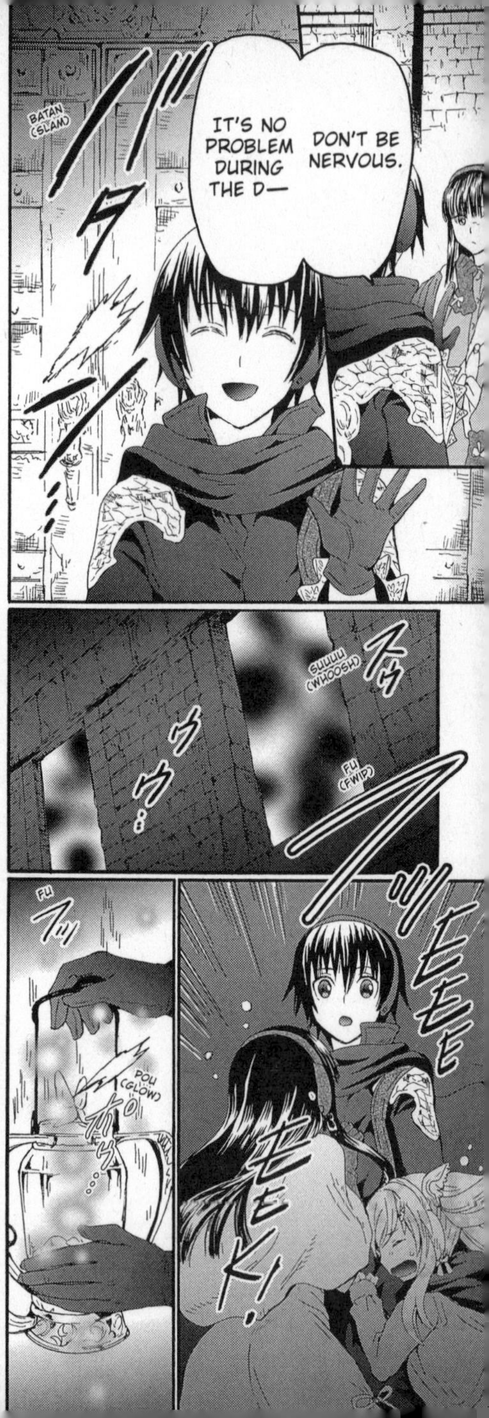
BATAN (SLAM)
DON'T BE NERVOUS.
IT'S NO PROBLEM DURING THE D—
SUUUN (WHOOSH)
FU (FWIP)
EEEE
EEEK!
FU
POU (GLOW)

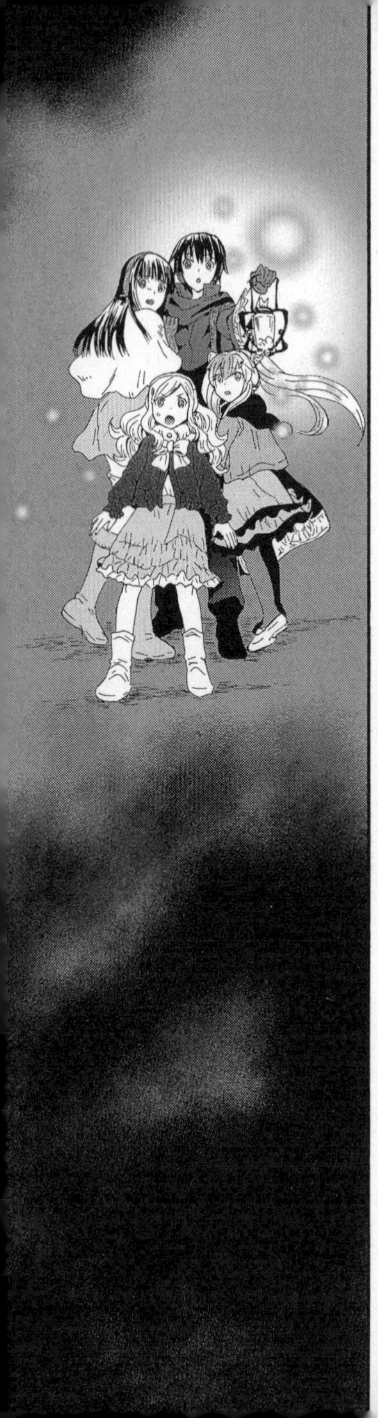

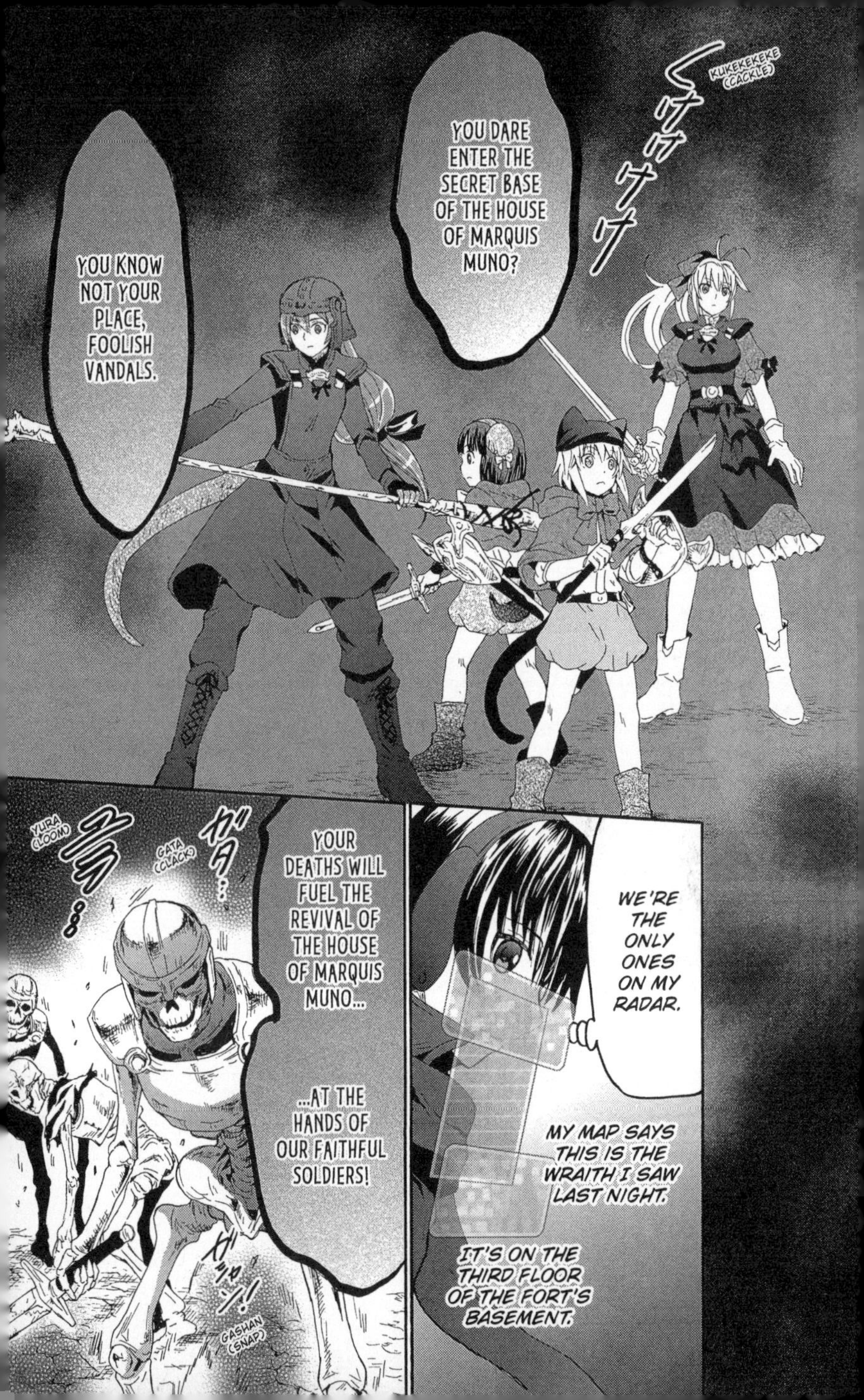
KUKEKEKEKE (CACKLE)
YOU DARE ENTER THE SECRET BASE OF THE HOUSE OF MARQUIS MUNO?
YOU KNOW NOT YOUR PLACE, FOOLISH VANDALS.
WE'RE THE ONLY ONES ON MY RADAR.
MY MAP SAYS THIS IS THE WRAITH I SAW LAST NIGHT.
IT'S ON THE THIRD FLOOR OF THE FORT'S BASEMENT.
GATA (CLACK)
YURA (LOOM)
YOUR DEATHS WILL FUEL THE REVIVAL OF THE HOUSE OF MARQUIS MUNO...
...AT THE HANDS OF OUR FAITHFUL SOLDIERS!
GASHAN (SNAP)

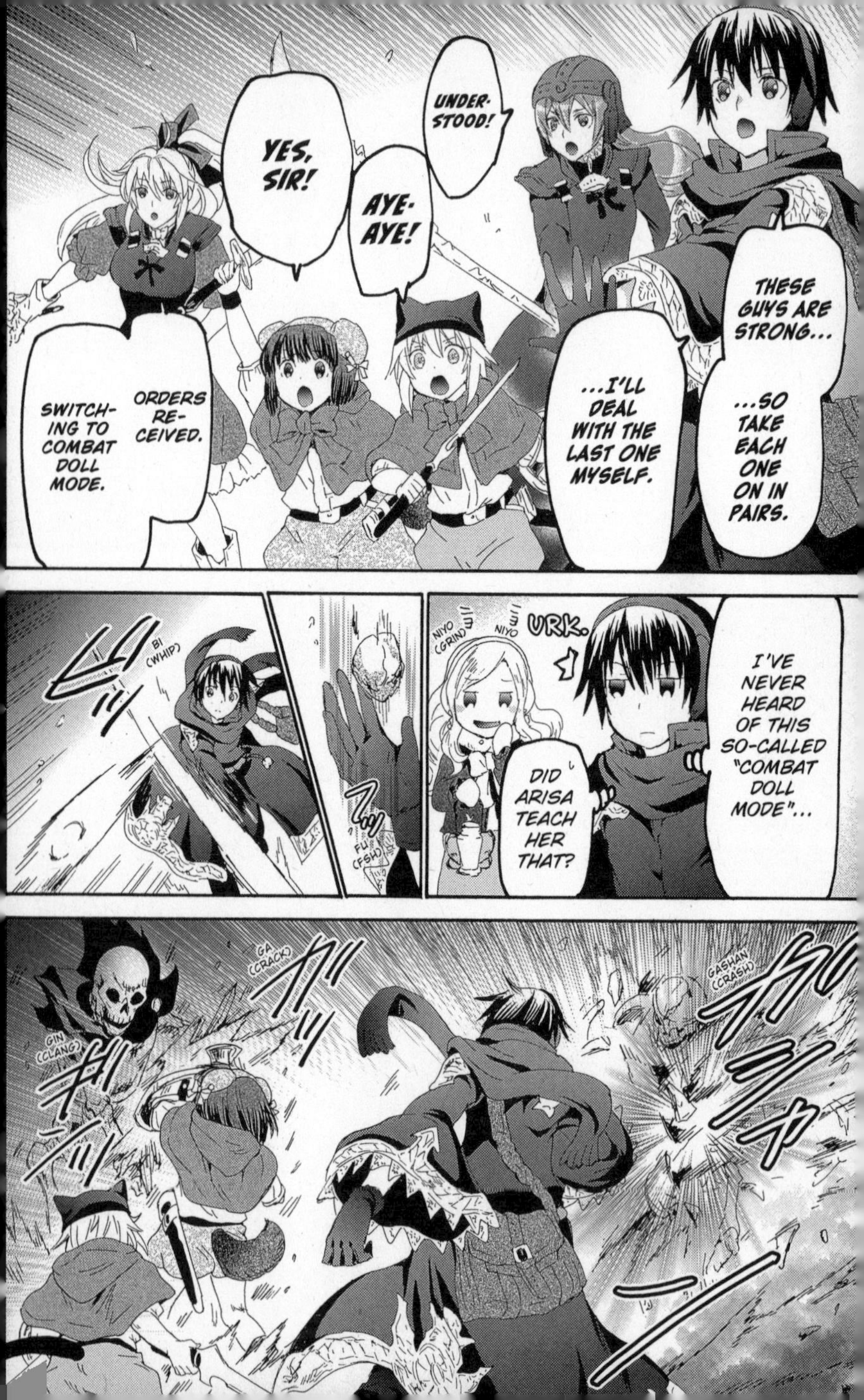
THESE GUYS ARE STRONG...
...SO TAKE EACH ONE ON IN PAIRS.
...I'LL DEAL WITH THE LAST ONE MYSELF.
UNDER-STOOD!
AYE-AYE!
YES, SIR!
ORDERS RE-CEIVED.
SWITCH-ING TO COMBAT DOLL MODE.
I'VE NEVER HEARD OF THIS SO-CALLED "COMBAT DOLL MODE"...
URK.
NIYO
NIYO (GRIN)
DID ARISA TEACH HER THAT?
FU (FSH)
BI (WHIP)
GASHAN (CRASH)
GA (CRACK)
GIN (CLANG)

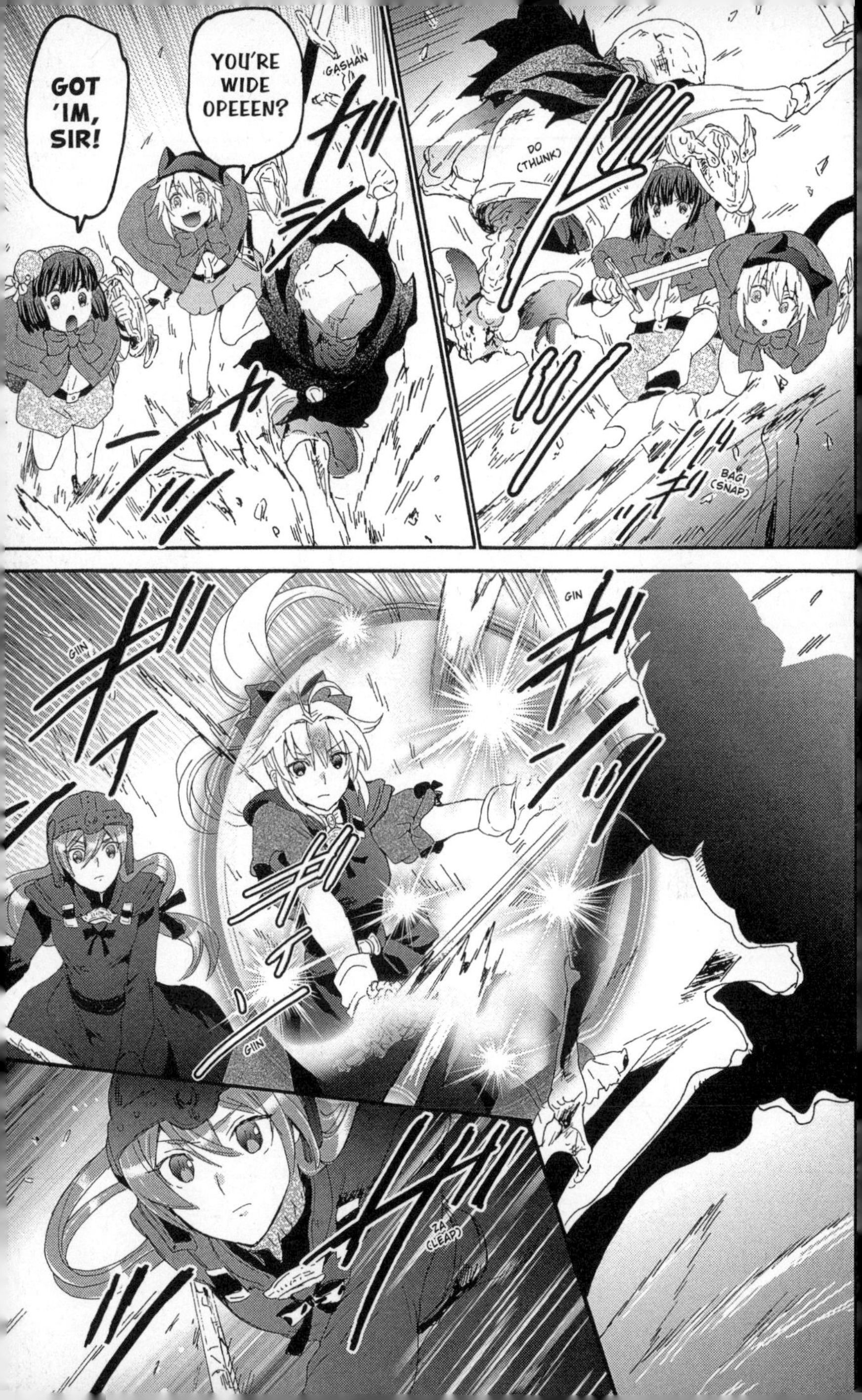
DO (THUNK)
BAGI (SNAP)
GASHAN
YOU'RE WIDE OPEEEN?
GOT 'IM, SIR!
GIN
GIIN
GIIN
ZA (LEAP)

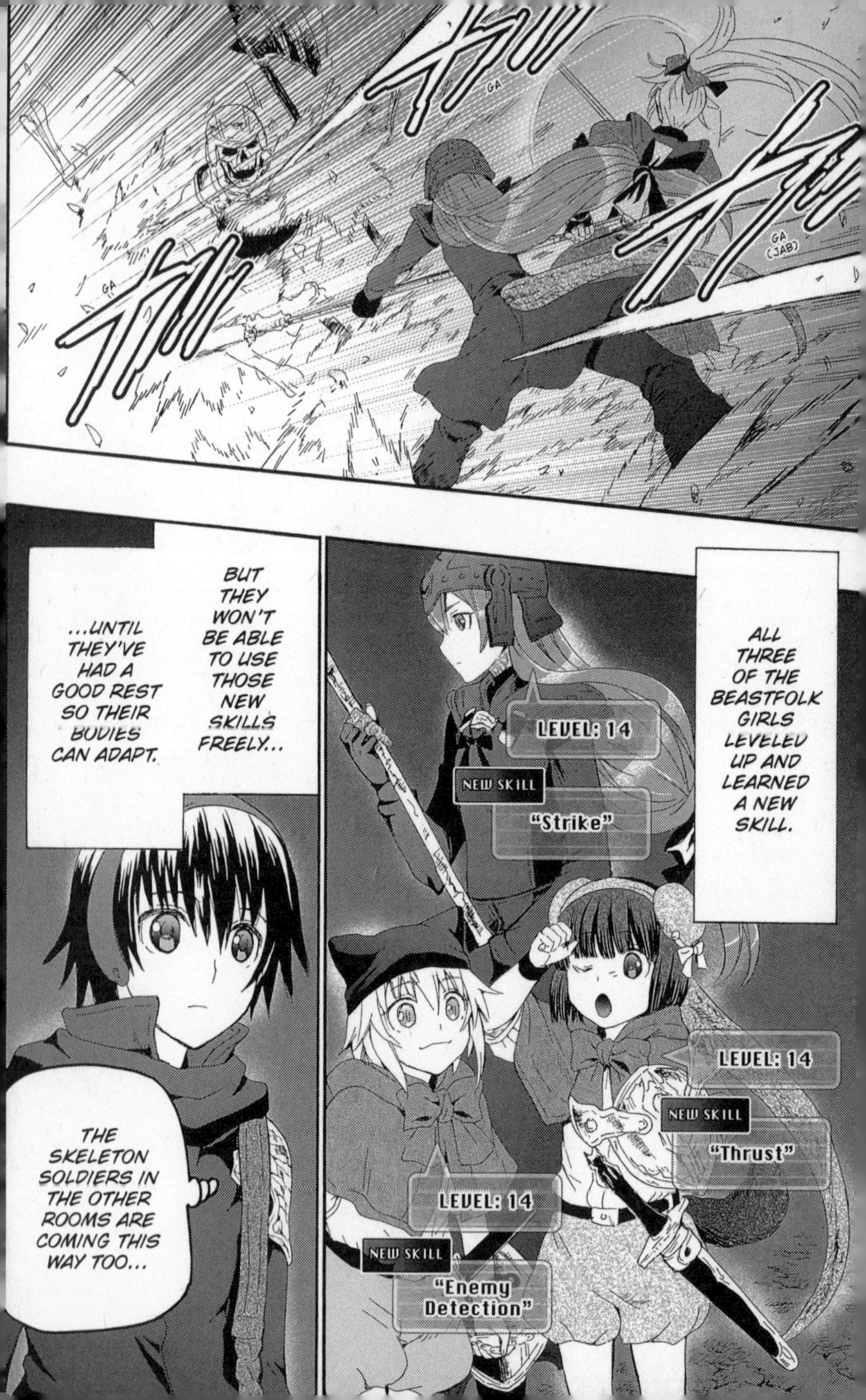
GA
(JAB)
GA
GA
ALL THREE OF THE BEASTFOLK GIRLS LEVELED UP AND LEARNED A NEW SKILL.
LEVEL: 14
NEW SKILL
"Strike"
LEVEL: 14
NEW SKILL
"Thrust"
LEVEL: 14
NEW SKILL
"Enemy Detection"
BUT THEY WON'T BE ABLE TO USE THOSE NEW SKILLS FREELY...
...UNTIL THEY'VE HAD A GOOD REST SO THEIR BODIES CAN ADAPT.
THE SKELETON SOLDIERS IN THE OTHER ROOMS ARE COMING THIS WAY TOO...

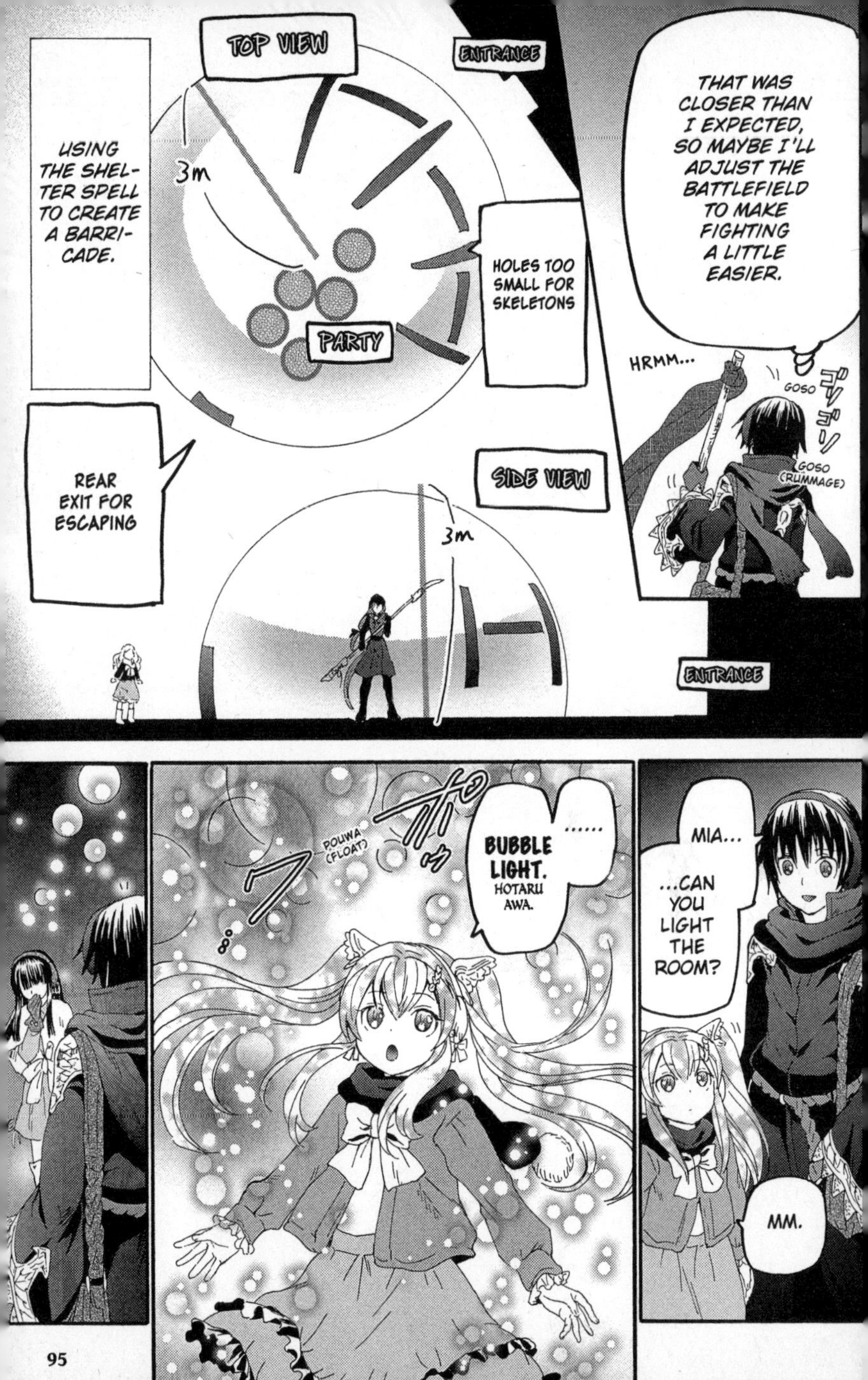
THAT WAS CLOSER THAN I EXPECTED, SO MAYBE I'LL ADJUST THE BATTLEFIELD TO MAKE FIGHTING A LITTLE EASIER.
HRMM...
ゴソゴソ
GOSO
GOSO (RUMMAGE)
TOP VIEW
ENTRANCE
USING THE SHELTER SPELL TO CREATE A BARRICADE.
3m
HOLES TOO SMALL FOR SKELETONS
PARTY
REAR EXIT FOR ESCAPING
SIDE VIEW
3m
ENTRANCE
MIA...
...CAN YOU LIGHT THE ROOM?
MM.
......
BUBBLE LIGHT. HOTARU AWA.
ポワ
POUWA (FLOAT)

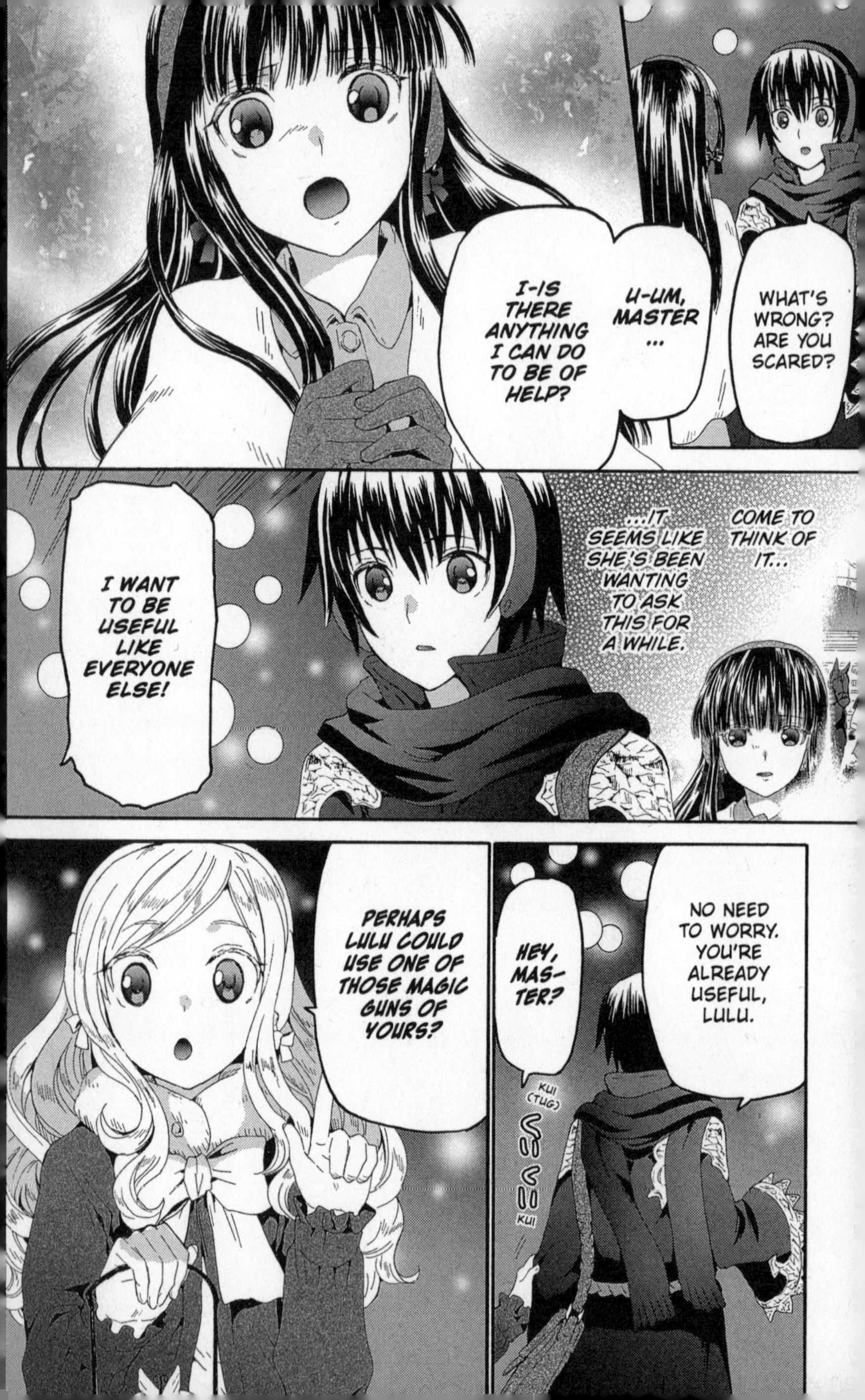
WHAT'S WRONG? ARE YOU SCARED?
U-UM, MASTER...
I-IS THERE ANYTHING I CAN DO TO BE OF HELP?
COME TO THINK OF IT...
...IT SEEMS LIKE SHE'S BEEN WANTING TO ASK THIS FOR A WHILE.
I WANT TO BE USEFUL LIKE EVERYONE ELSE!
NO NEED TO WORRY. YOU'RE ALREADY USEFUL, LULU.
KUI (TUG)
KUI
HEY, MAS-TER?
PERHAPS LULU COULD USE ONE OF THOSE MAGIC GUNS OF YOURS?

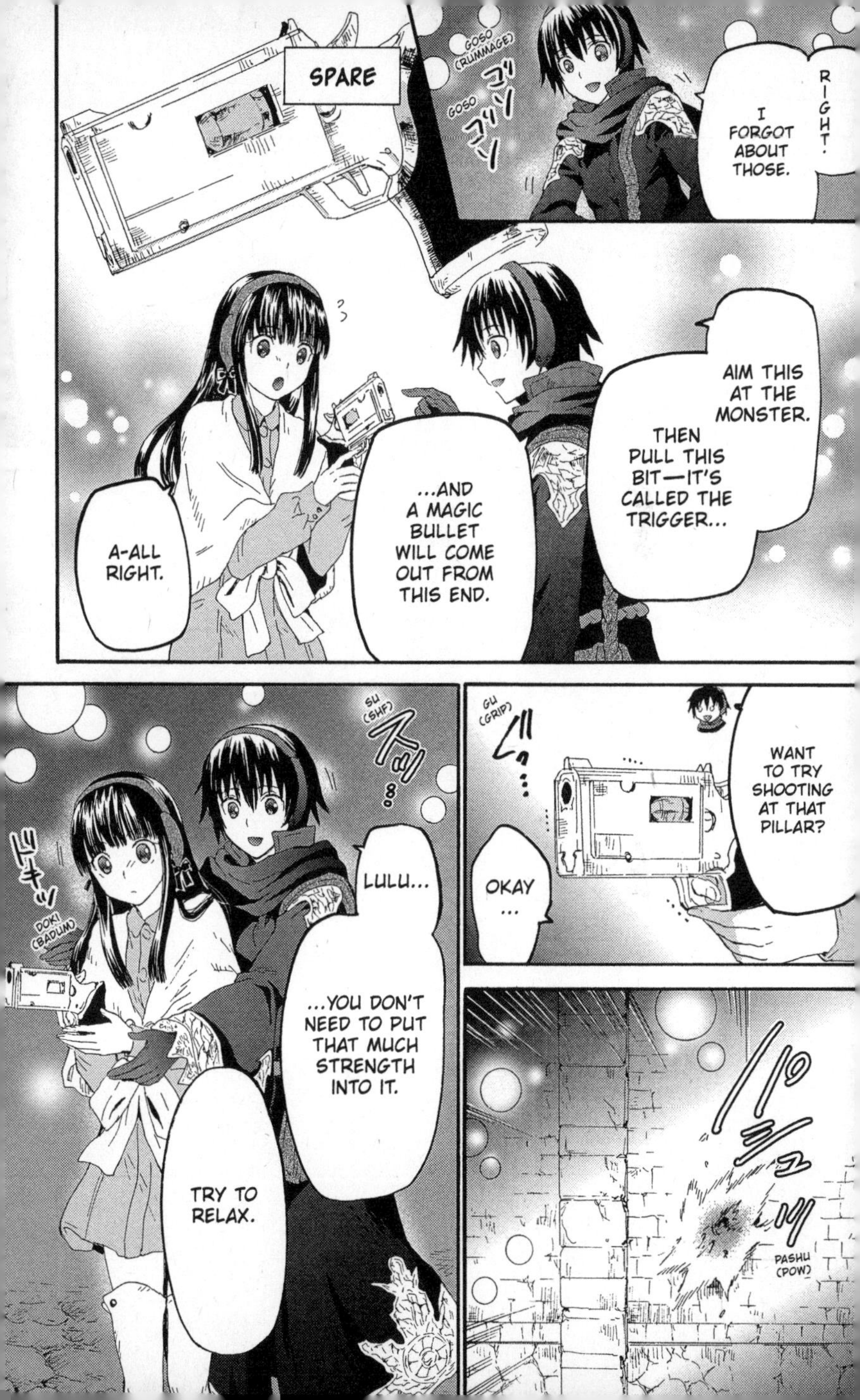
GOSO GOSO (RUMMAGE)
RIGHT.
I FORGOT ABOUT THOSE.
SPARE
AIM THIS AT THE MONSTER.
THEN PULL THIS BIT—IT'S CALLED THE TRIGGER...
...AND A MAGIC BULLET WILL COME OUT FROM THIS END.
A-ALL RIGHT.
GU (GRIP)
WANT TO TRY SHOOTING AT THAT PILLAR?
OKAY...
PASHU (POW)
SU (SHF)
LULU...
DOKI (BADUM)
...YOU DON'T NEED TO PUT THAT MUCH STRENGTH INTO IT.
TRY TO RELAX.

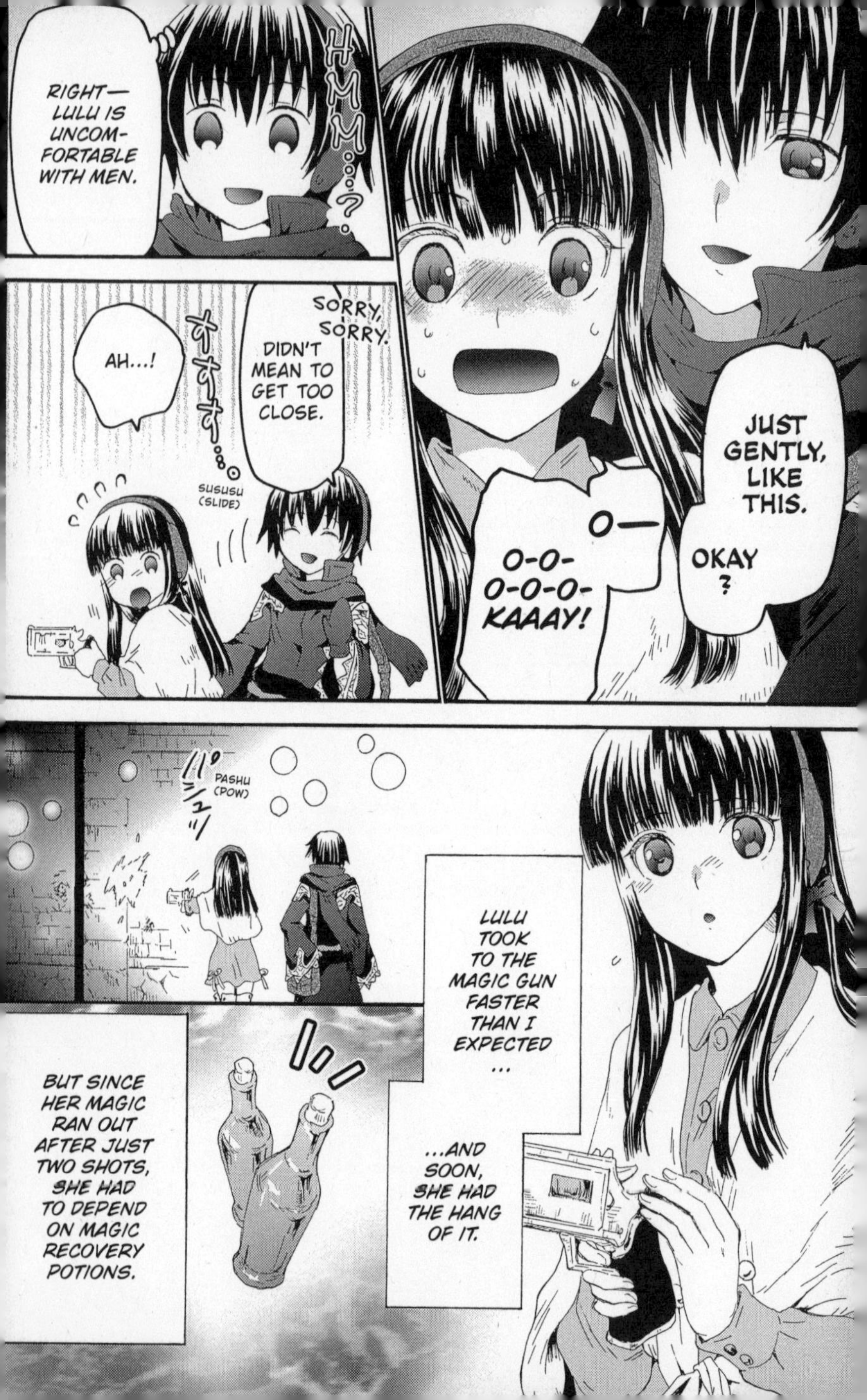
JUST GENTLY, LIKE THIS.
OKAY?
O—
O-O-O-O-O-KAAAY!
HMMM...?
RIGHT— LULU IS UNCOM-FORTABLE WITH MEN.
SORRY, SORRY.
DIDN'T MEAN TO GET TOO CLOSE.
SUSUSU (SLIDE)
AH...!
LULU TOOK TO THE MAGIC GUN FASTER THAN I EXPECTED...
...AND SOON, SHE HAD THE HANG OF IT.
PASHU (POW)
BUT SINCE HER MAGIC RAN OUT AFTER JUST TWO SHOTS, SHE HAD TO DEPEND ON MAGIC RECOVERY POTIONS.

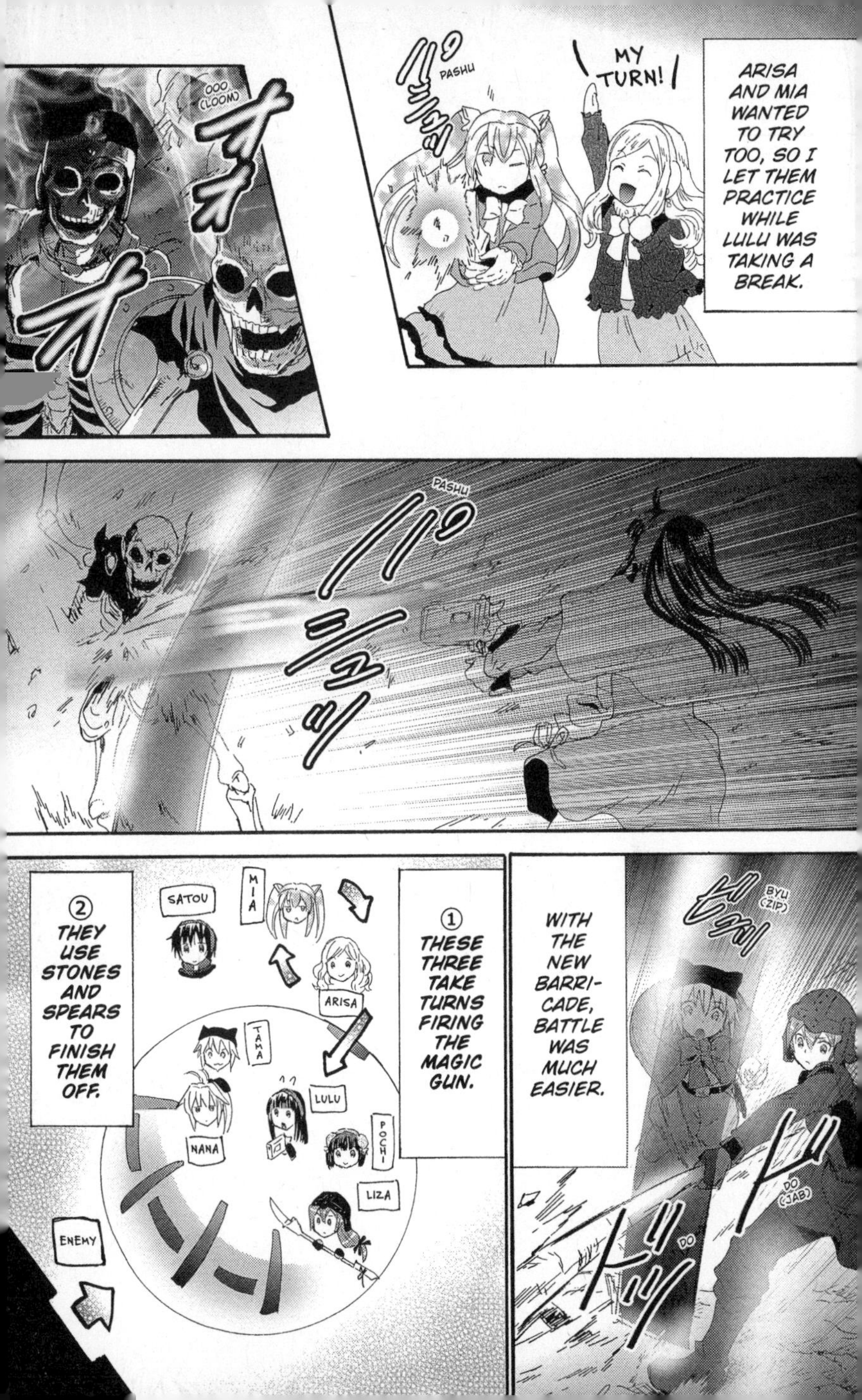
ARISA AND MIA WANTED TO TRY TOO, SO I LET THEM PRACTICE WHILE LULU WAS TAKING A BREAK.
MY TURN!
PASHU
OOO (LOOM)
PASHU
WITH THE NEW BARRICADE, BATTLE WAS MUCH EASIER.
BYU (ZIP)
DO (JAB)
DO
① THESE THREE TAKE TURNS FIRING THE MAGIC GUN.
MIA
SATOU
ARISA
TAMA
LULU
NANA
POCHI
LIZA
ENEMY
② THEY USE STONES AND SPEARS TO FINISH THEM OFF.

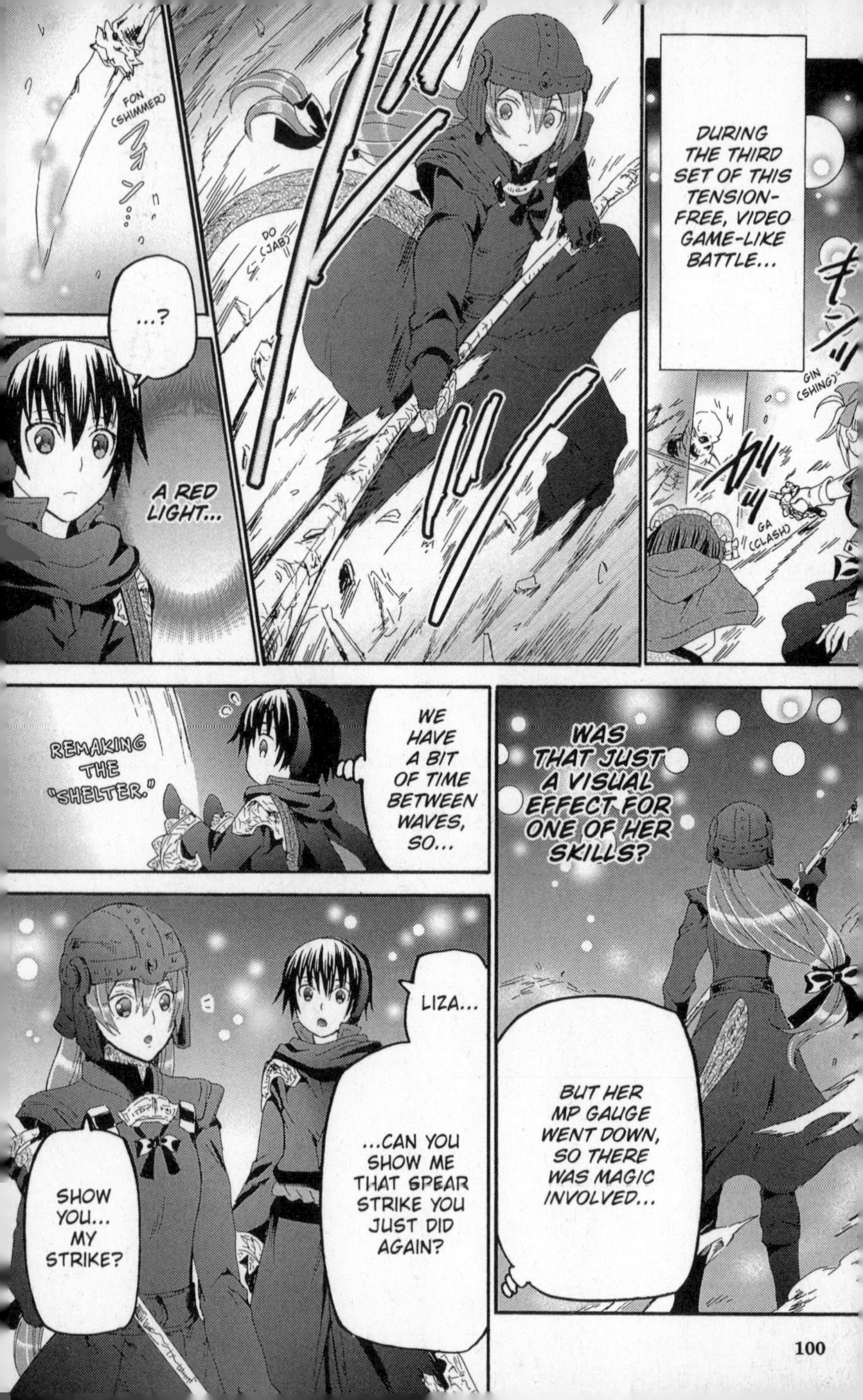
DURING THE THIRD SET OF THIS TENSION-FREE, VIDEO GAME-LIKE BATTLE...
GIN (SHING)
GA (CLASH)
DO (JAB)
FON (SHIMMER)
...?
A RED LIGHT...
WAS THAT JUST A VISUAL EFFECT FOR ONE OF HER SKILLS?
BUT HER MP GAUGE WENT DOWN, SO THERE WAS MAGIC INVOLVED...
WE HAVE A BIT OF TIME BETWEEN WAVES, SO...
REMAKING THE "SHELTER."
LIZA...
...CAN YOU SHOW ME THAT SPEAR STRIKE YOU JUST DID AGAIN?
SHOW YOU... MY STRIKE?

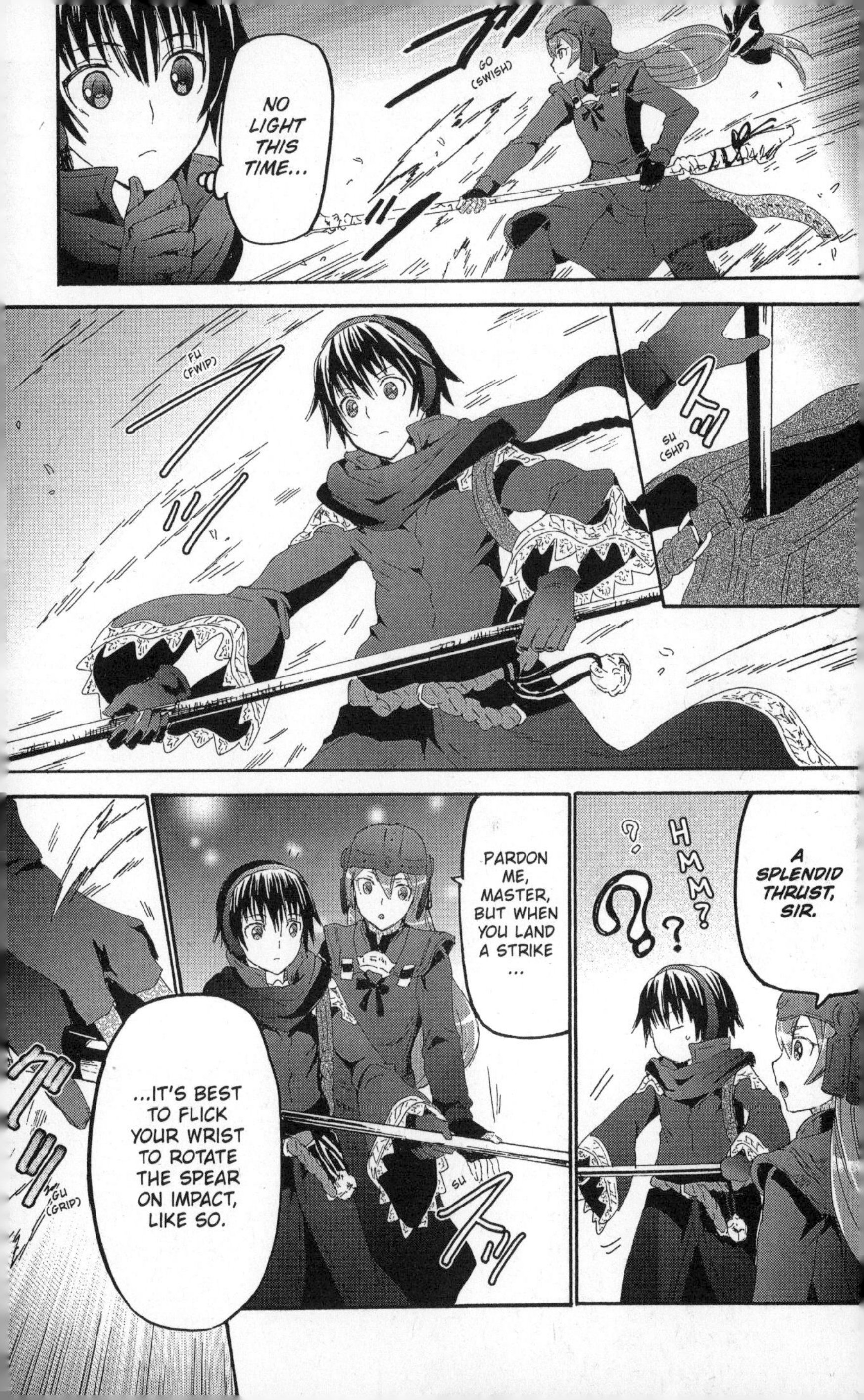
GO (SWISH)
NO LIGHT THIS TIME...
SU (SHP)
FU (FWIP)
A SPLENDID THRUST, SIR.
HMM??
PARDON ME, MASTER, BUT WHEN YOU LAND A STRIKE...
...IT'S BEST TO FLICK YOUR WRIST TO ROTATE THE SPEAR ON IMPACT, LIKE SO.
SU
GU (GRIP)

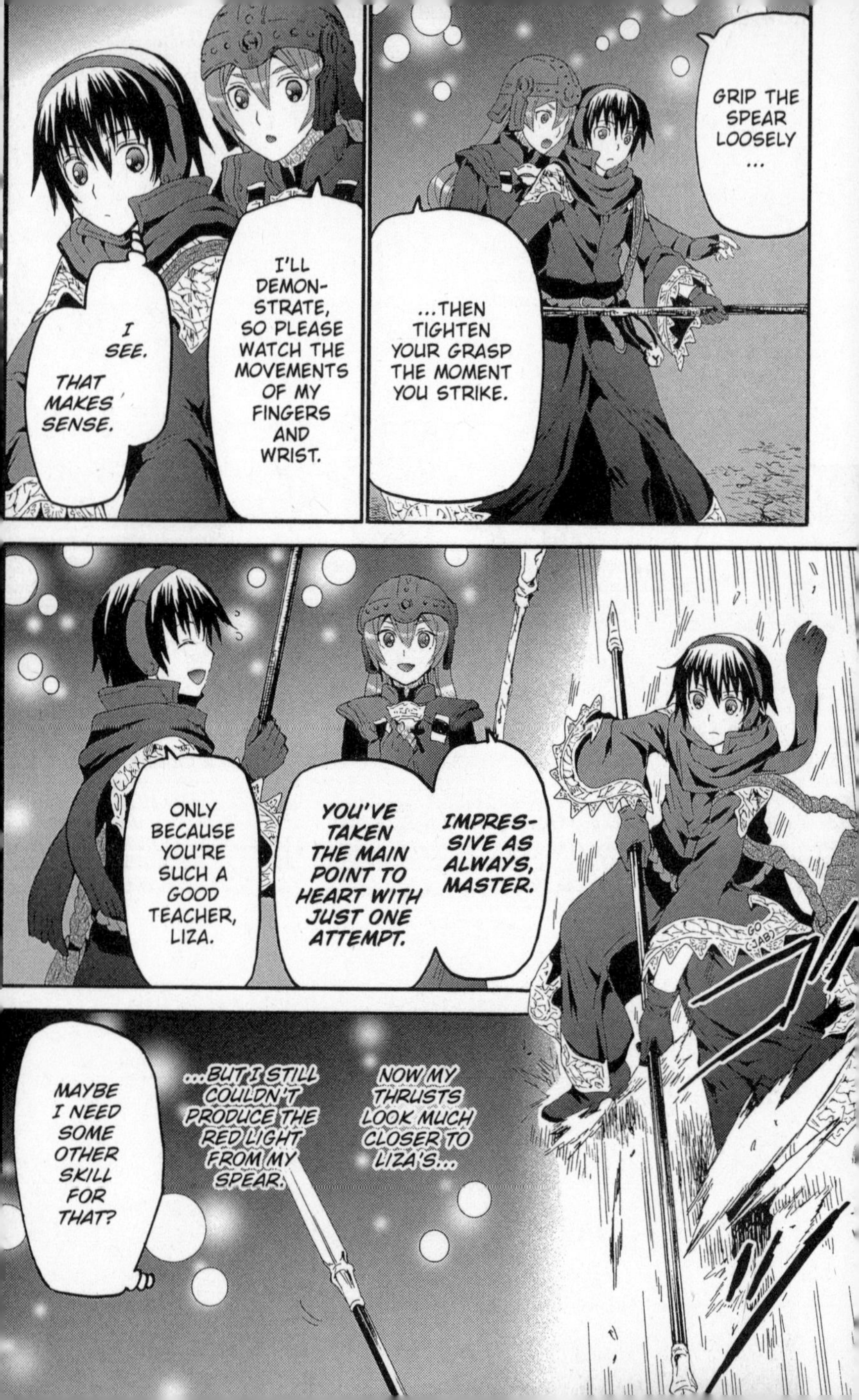
GRIP THE SPEAR LOOSELY ...
...THEN TIGHTEN YOUR GRASP THE MOMENT YOU STRIKE.
I'LL DEMON-STRATE, SO PLEASE WATCH THE MOVEMENTS OF MY FINGERS AND WRIST.
I SEE. THAT MAKES SENSE.
GO (JAB)
IMPRES-SIVE AS ALWAYS, MASTER.
YOU'VE TAKEN THE MAIN POINT TO HEART WITH JUST ONE ATTEMPT.
ONLY BECAUSE YOU'RE SUCH A GOOD TEACHER, LIZA.
NOW MY THRUSTS LOOK MUCH CLOSER TO LIZA'S...
...BUT I STILL COULDN'T PRODUCE THE RED LIGHT FROM MY SPEAR.
MAYBE I NEED SOME OTHER SKILL FOR THAT?

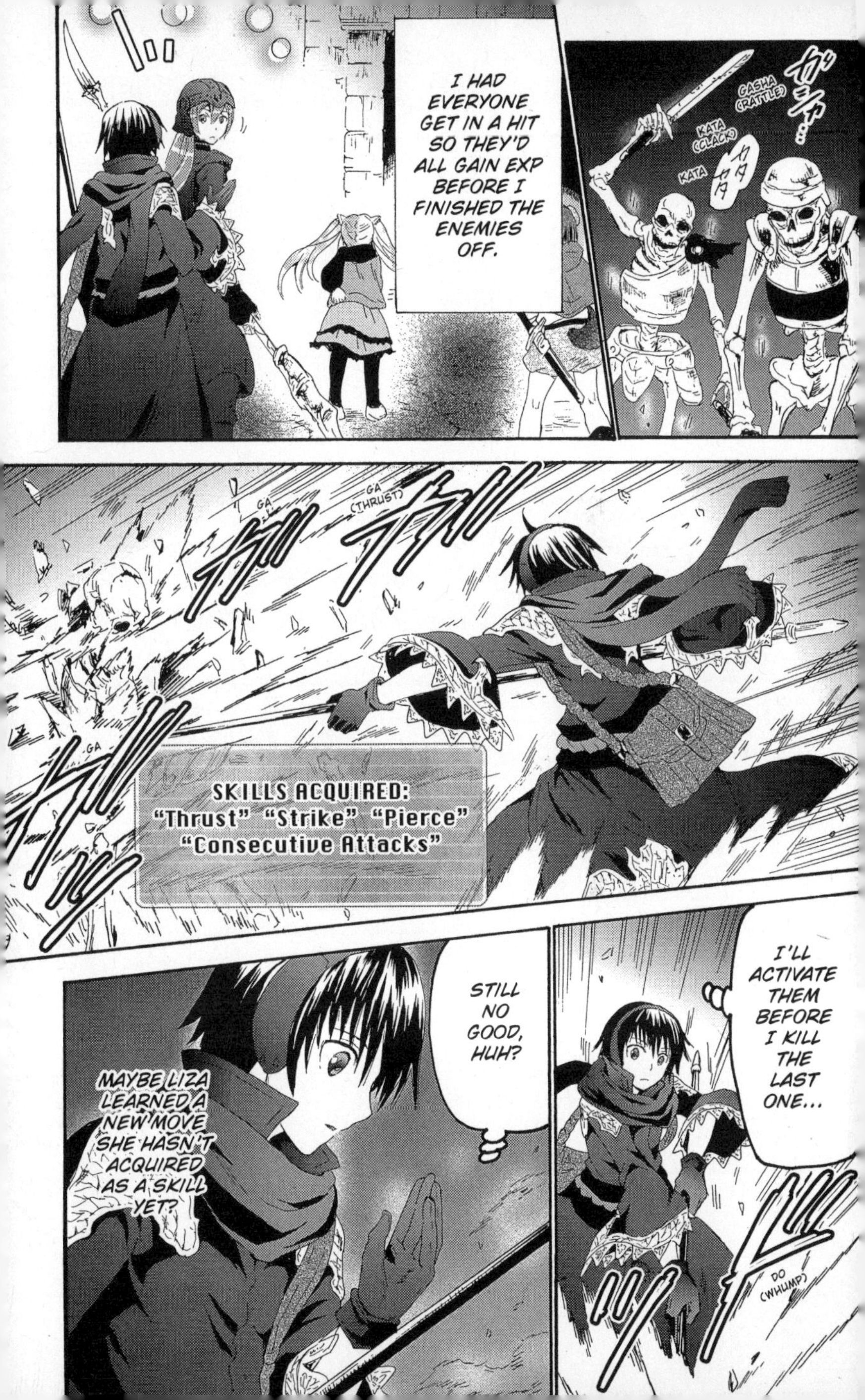
GASHA (RATTLE)
KATA (CLACK)
KATA
I HAD EVERYONE GET IN A HIT SO THEY'D ALL GAIN EXP BEFORE I FINISHED THE ENEMIES OFF.
GA (THRUST)
GA
GA
SKILLS ACQUIRED: "Thrust" "Strike" "Pierce" "Consecutive Attacks"
I'LL ACTIVATE THEM BEFORE I KILL THE LAST ONE...
DO (WHUMP)
STILL NO GOOD, HUH?
MAYBE LIZA LEARNED A NEW MOVE SHE HASN'T ACQUIRED AS A SKILL YET?

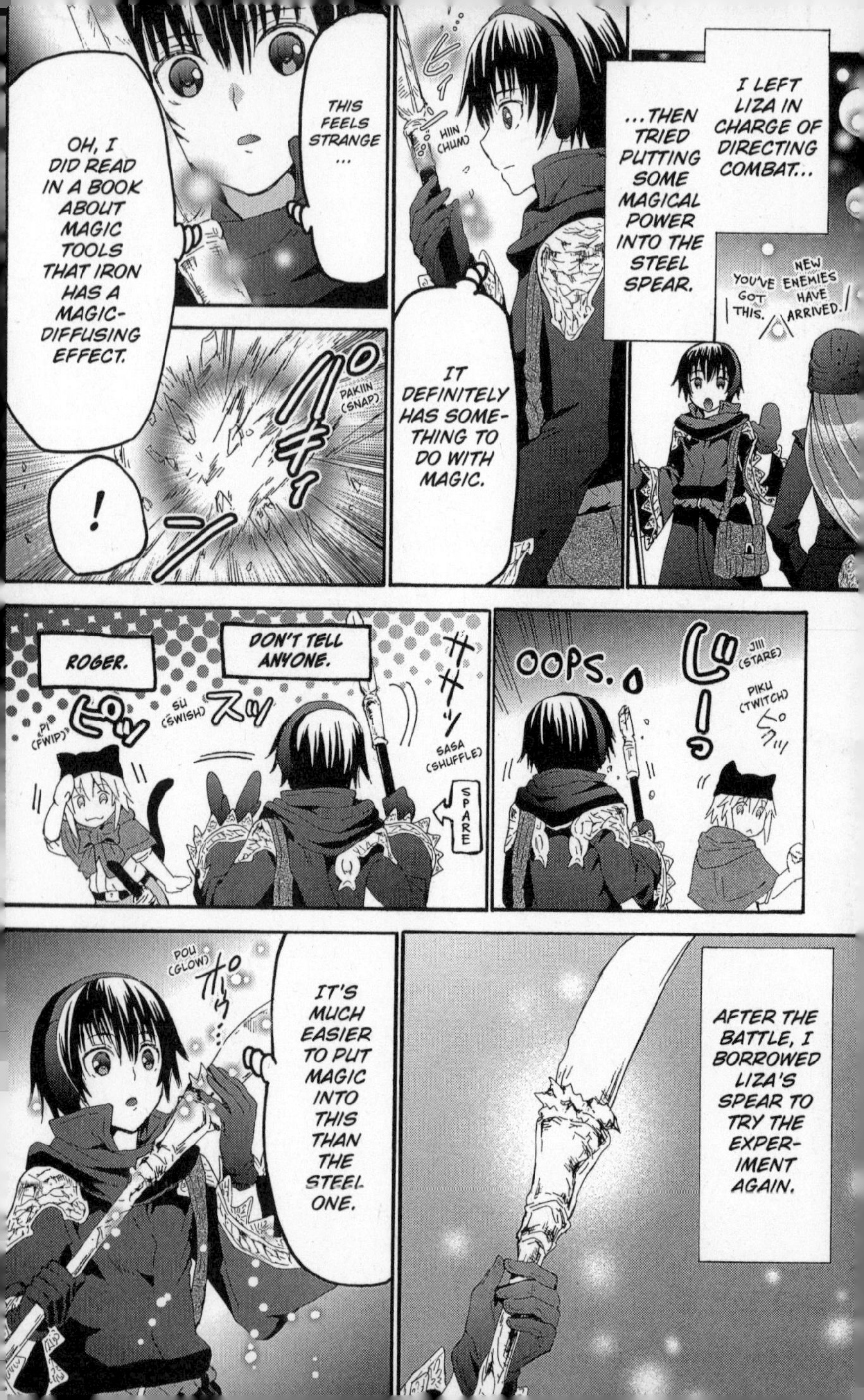
I LEFT LIZA IN CHARGE OF DIRECTING COMBAT...
NEW ENEMIES HAVE ARRIVED.
YOU'VE GOT THIS.
...THEN TRIED PUTTING SOME MAGICAL POWER INTO THE STEEL SPEAR.
HIIN (HUM)
IT DEFINITELY HAS SOMETHING TO DO WITH MAGIC.
THIS FEELS STRANGE...
OH, I DID READ IN A BOOK ABOUT MAGIC TOOLS THAT IRON HAS A MAGIC-DIFFUSING EFFECT.
PAKIIN (SNAP)
!
JIII (STARE)
OOPS.
PIKU (TWITCH)
DON'T TELL ANYONE.
ROGER.
SASA (SHUFFLE)
SPARE
SU (SWISH)
PI (FWIP)
AFTER THE BATTLE, I BORROWED LIZA'S SPEAR TO TRY THE EXPERIMENT AGAIN.
POU (GLOW)
IT'S MUCH EASIER TO PUT MAGIC INTO THIS THAN THE STEEL ONE.

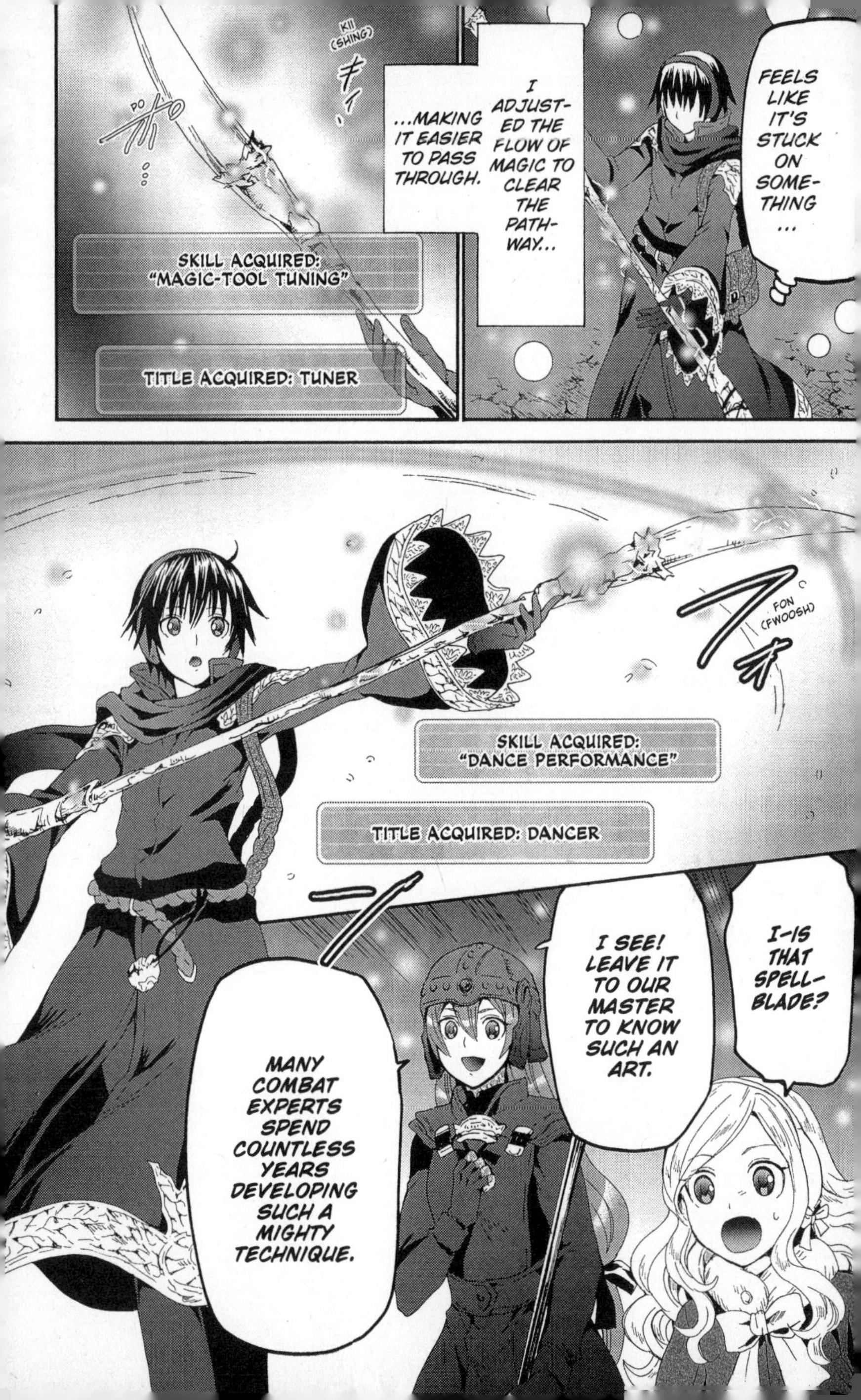
FEELS LIKE IT'S STUCK ON SOMETHING...
I ADJUSTED THE FLOW OF MAGIC TO CLEAR THE PATHWAY...
...MAKING IT EASIER TO PASS THROUGH.
KII (SHING)
SKILL ACQUIRED: "MAGIC-TOOL TUNING"
TITLE ACQUIRED: TUNER
FON (FWOOSH)
SKILL ACQUIRED: "DANCE PERFORMANCE"
TITLE ACQUIRED: DANCER
I-IS THAT SPELLBLADE?
I SEE! LEAVE IT TO OUR MASTER TO KNOW SUCH AN ART.
MANY COMBAT EXPERTS SPEND COUNTLESS YEARS DEVELOPING SUCH A MIGHTY TECHNIQUE.

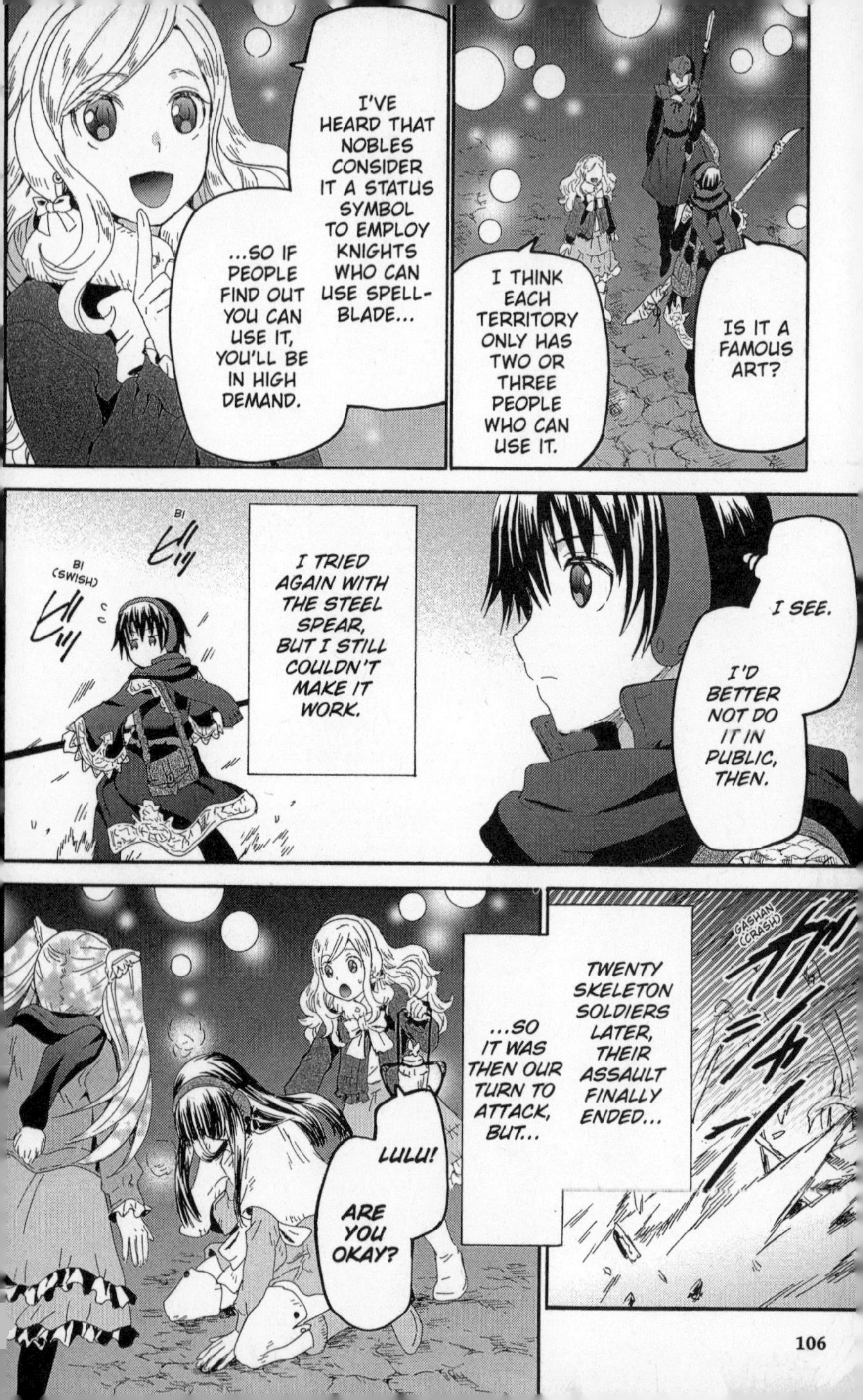
IS IT A FAMOUS ART?
I THINK EACH TERRITORY ONLY HAS TWO OR THREE PEOPLE WHO CAN USE IT.
I'VE HEARD THAT NOBLES CONSIDER IT A STATUS SYMBOL TO EMPLOY KNIGHTS WHO CAN USE SPELL-BLADE...
...SO IF PEOPLE FIND OUT YOU CAN USE IT, YOU'LL BE IN HIGH DEMAND.
I SEE.
I'D BETTER NOT DO IT IN PUBLIC, THEN.
I TRIED AGAIN WITH THE STEEL SPEAR, BUT I STILL COULDN'T MAKE IT WORK.
BI
BI (SWISH)
GASHAN (CRASH)
TWENTY SKELETON SOLDIERS LATER, THEIR ASSAULT FINALLY ENDED...
...SO IT WAS THEN OUR TURN TO ATTACK, BUT...
LULU!
ARE YOU OKAY?

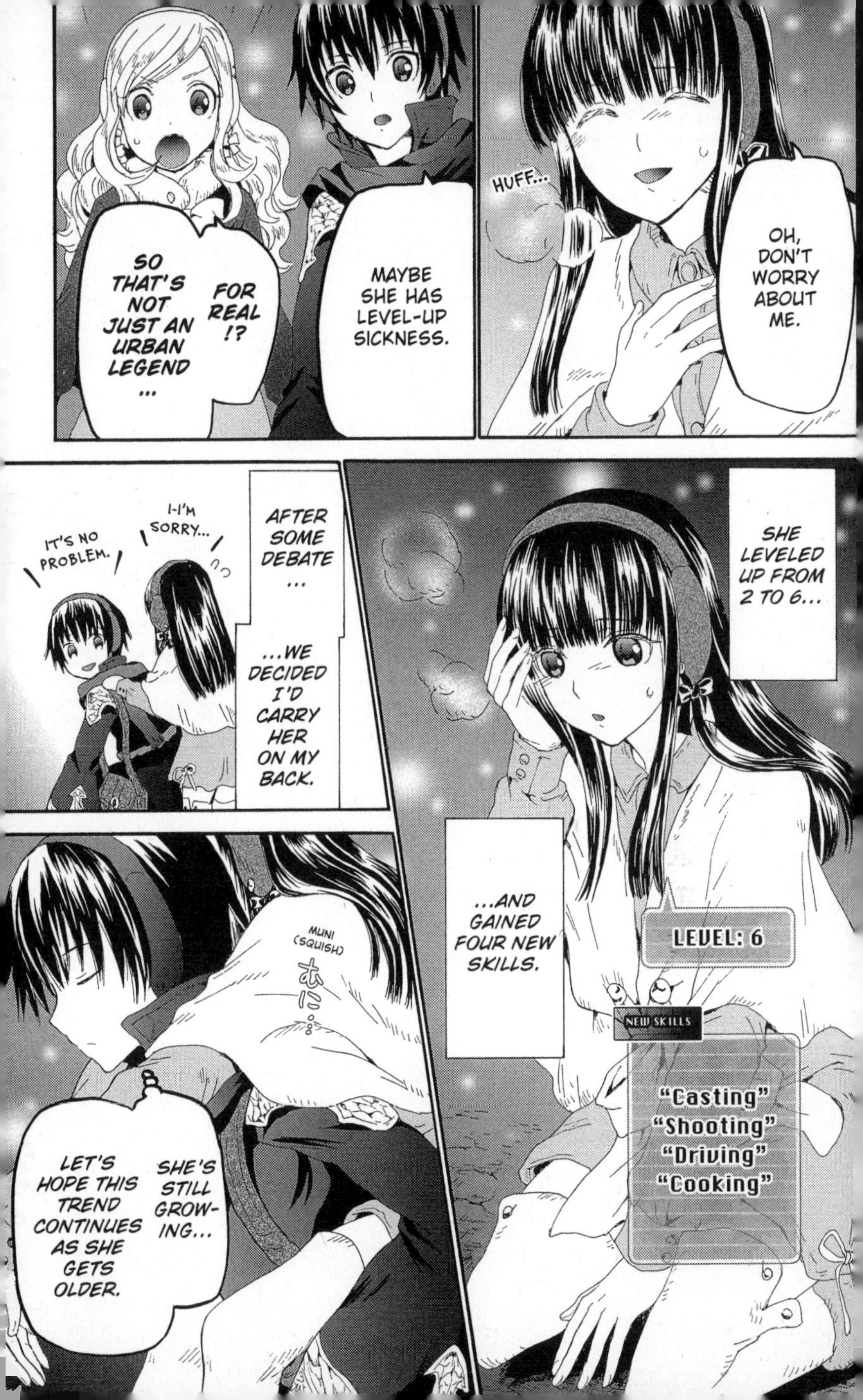
HUFF...
OH, DON'T WORRY ABOUT ME.
MAYBE SHE HAS LEVEL-UP SICKNESS.
FOR REAL!?
SO THAT'S NOT JUST AN URBAN LEGEND...
SHE LEVELED UP FROM 2 TO 6...
...AND GAINED FOUR NEW SKILLS.
LEVEL: 6
NEW SKILLS
"Casting" "Shooting" "Driving" "Cooking"
AFTER SOME DEBATE...
...WE DECIDED I'D CARRY HER ON MY BACK.
I-I'M SORRY...
IT'S NO PROBLEM.
MUNI (SQUISH)
むに…
SHE'S STILL GROWING...
LET'S HOPE THIS TREND CONTINUES AS SHE GETS OLDER.

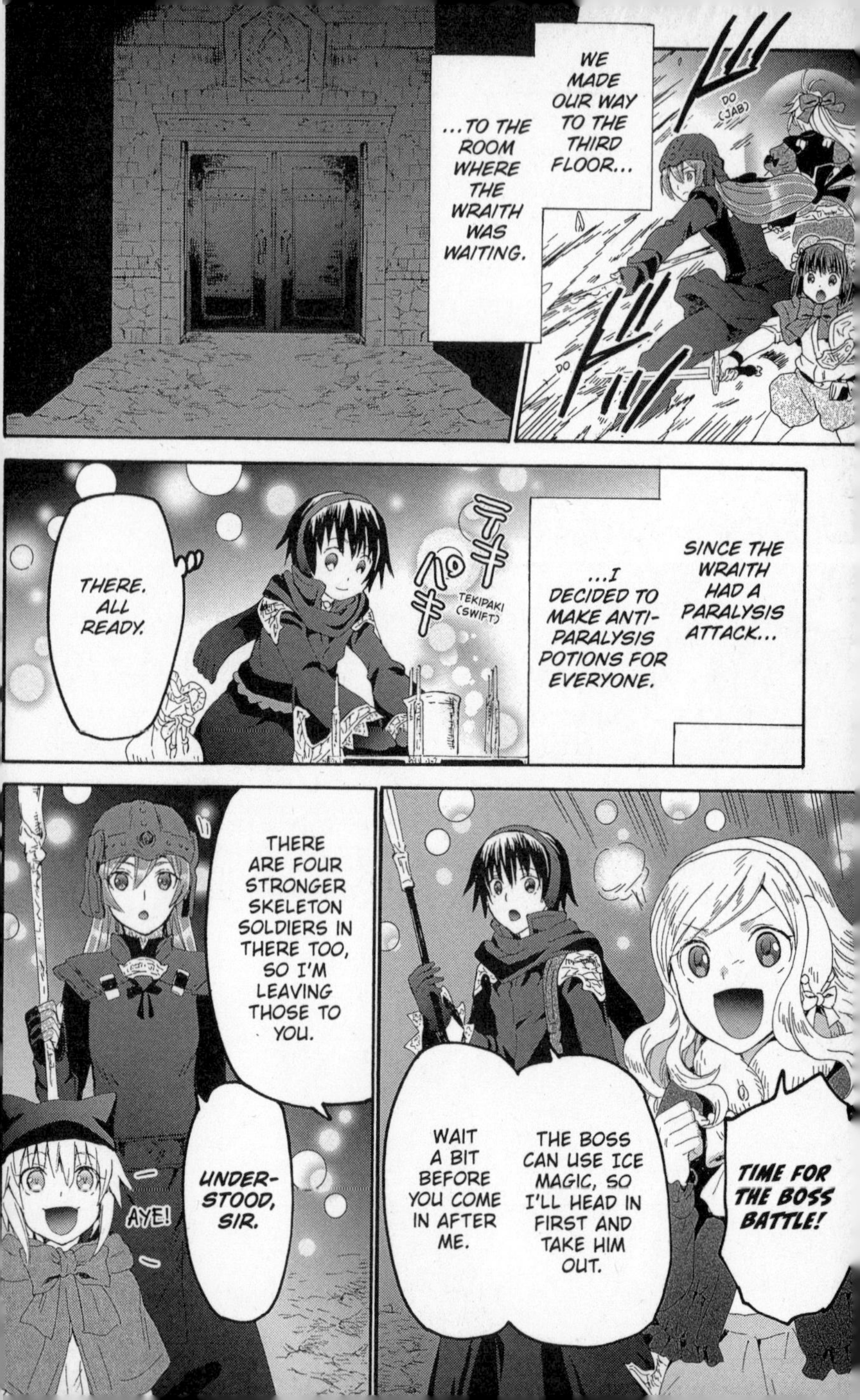
WE MADE OUR WAY TO THE THIRD FLOOR...
...TO THE ROOM WHERE THE WRAITH WAS WAITING.
DO (JAB)
DO
SINCE THE WRAITH HAD A PARALYSIS ATTACK...
...I DECIDED TO MAKE ANTI-PARALYSIS POTIONS FOR EVERYONE.
TEKIPAKI (SWIFT)
THERE. ALL READY.
TIME FOR THE BOSS BATTLE!
THE BOSS CAN USE ICE MAGIC, SO I'LL HEAD IN FIRST AND TAKE HIM OUT.
WAIT A BIT BEFORE YOU COME IN AFTER ME.
THERE ARE FOUR STRONGER SKELETON SOLDIERS IN THERE TOO, SO I'M LEAVING THOSE TO YOU.
UNDER-STOOD, SIR.
AYE!

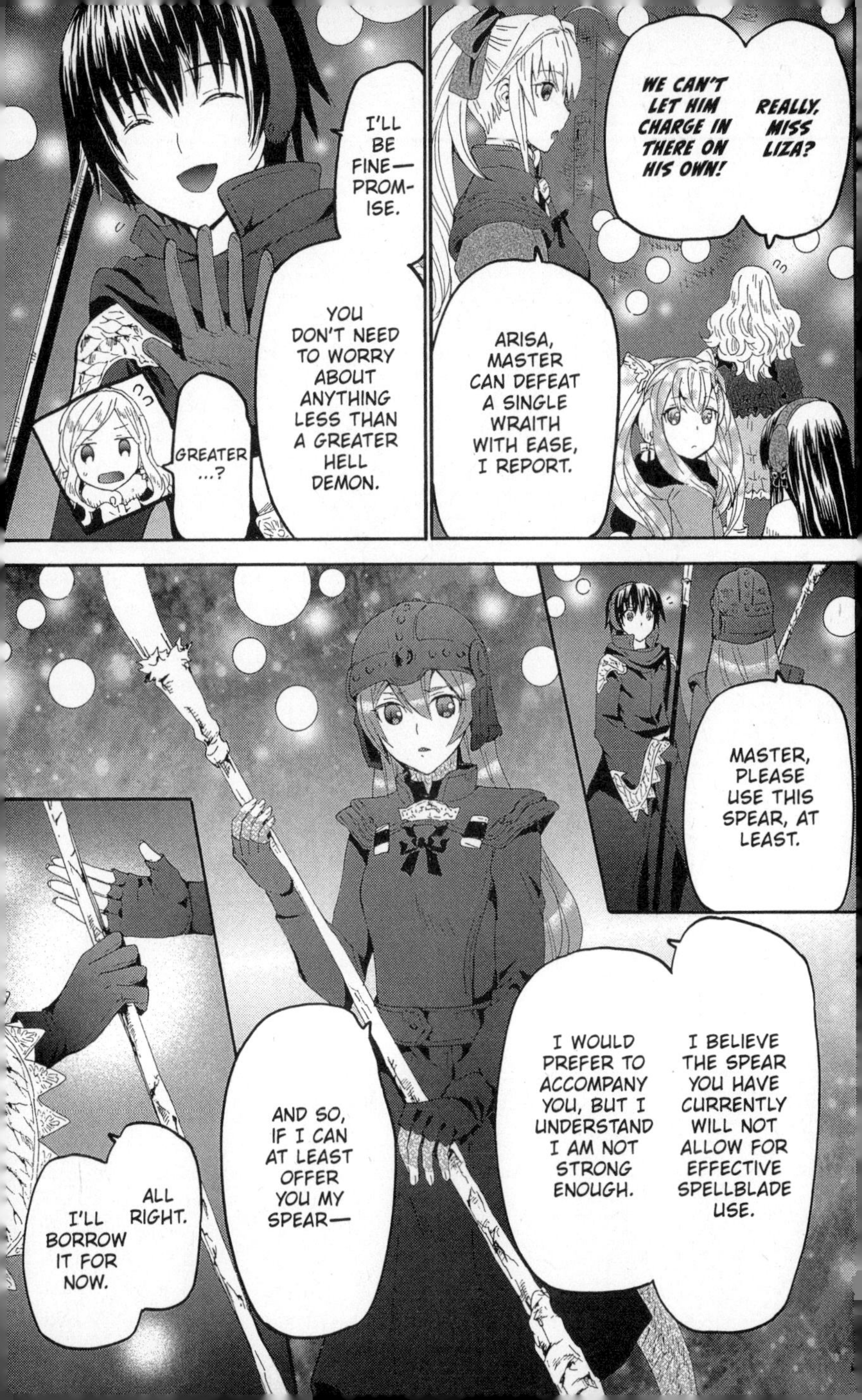

WE CAN'T LET HIM CHARGE IN THERE ON HIS OWN!
REALLY, MISS LIZA?
ARISA, MASTER CAN DEFEAT A SINGLE WRAITH WITH EASE, I REPORT.
I'LL BE FINE—PROMISE.
YOU DON'T NEED TO WORRY ABOUT ANYTHING LESS THAN A GREATER HELL DEMON.
GREATER...?
MASTER, PLEASE USE THIS SPEAR, AT LEAST.
I BELIEVE THE SPEAR YOU HAVE CURRENTLY WILL NOT ALLOW FOR EFFECTIVE SPELLBLADE USE.
I WOULD PREFER TO ACCOMPANY YOU, BUT I UNDERSTAND I AM NOT STRONG ENOUGH.
AND SO, IF I CAN AT LEAST OFFER YOU MY SPEAR—
ALL RIGHT.
I'LL BORROW IT FOR NOW.

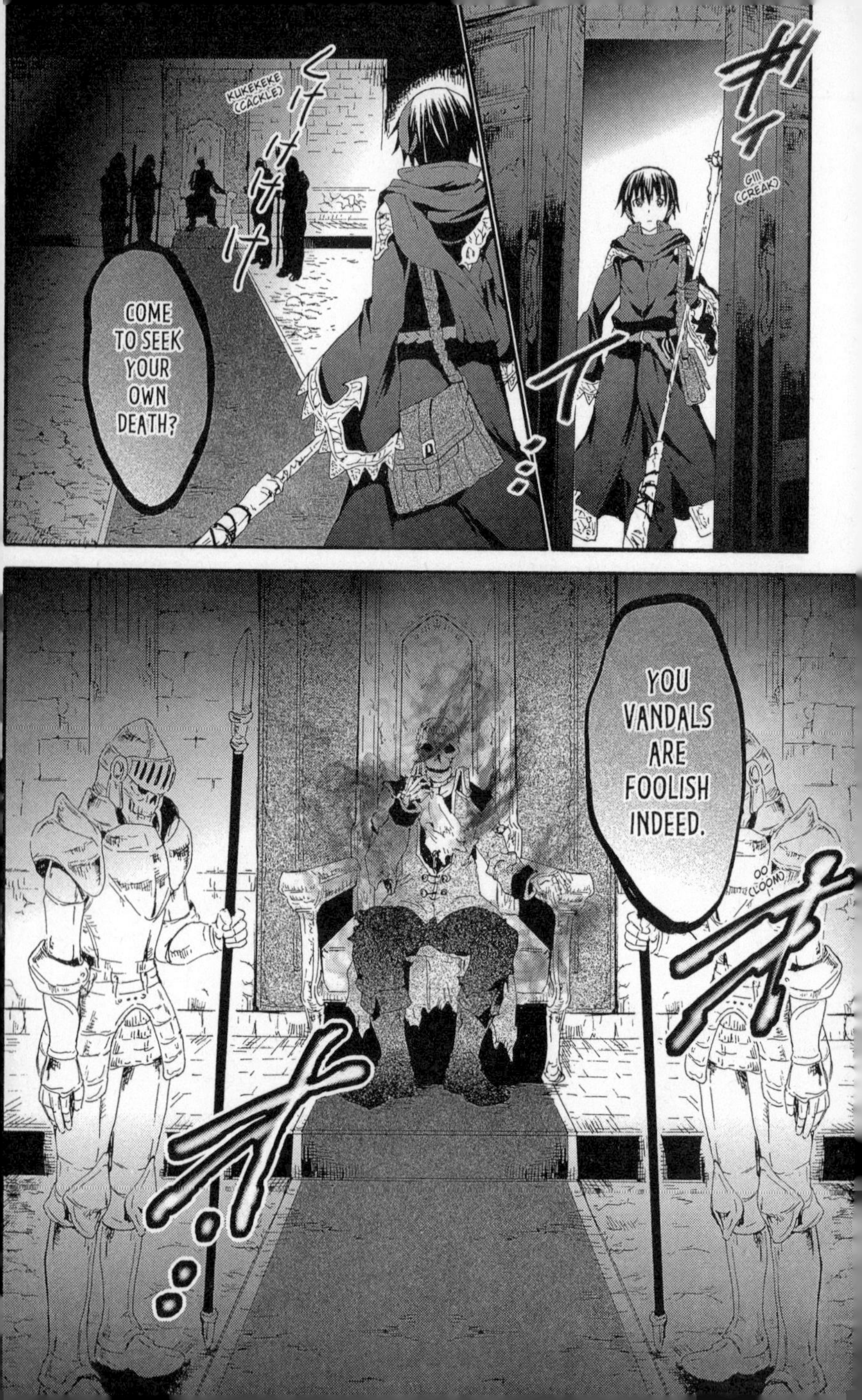
ギィ
GIII (CREAK)
KUKEKEKE (CACKLE)
くけけけけけ
COME TO SEEK YOUR OWN DEATH?
YOU VANDALS ARE FOOLISH INDEED.
OO (LOOM)

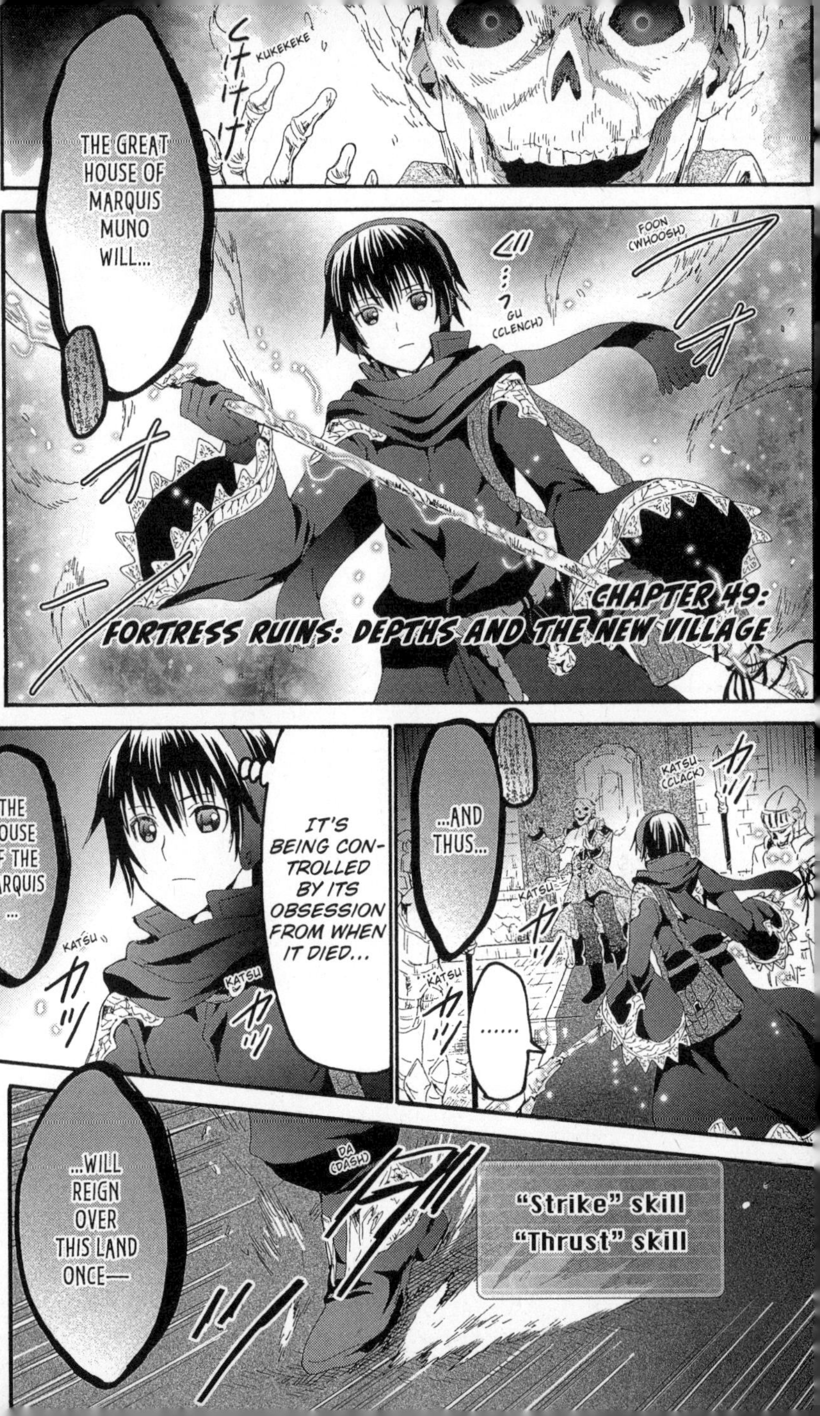
KUKEKEKE
THE GREAT HOUSE OF MARQUIS MUNO WILL...
FOON (WHOOSH)
GU (CLENCH)
CHAPTER 49:
FORTRESS RUINS: DEPTHS AND THE NEW VILLAGE
KATSU (CLACK)
...AND THUS...
KATSU
KATSU
......
IT'S BEING CONTROLLED BY ITS OBSESSION FROM WHEN IT DIED...
THE HOUSE OF THE MARQUIS ...
KATSU
KATSU
...WILL REIGN OVER THIS LAND ONCE—
DA (DASH)
"Strike" skill
"Thrust" skill

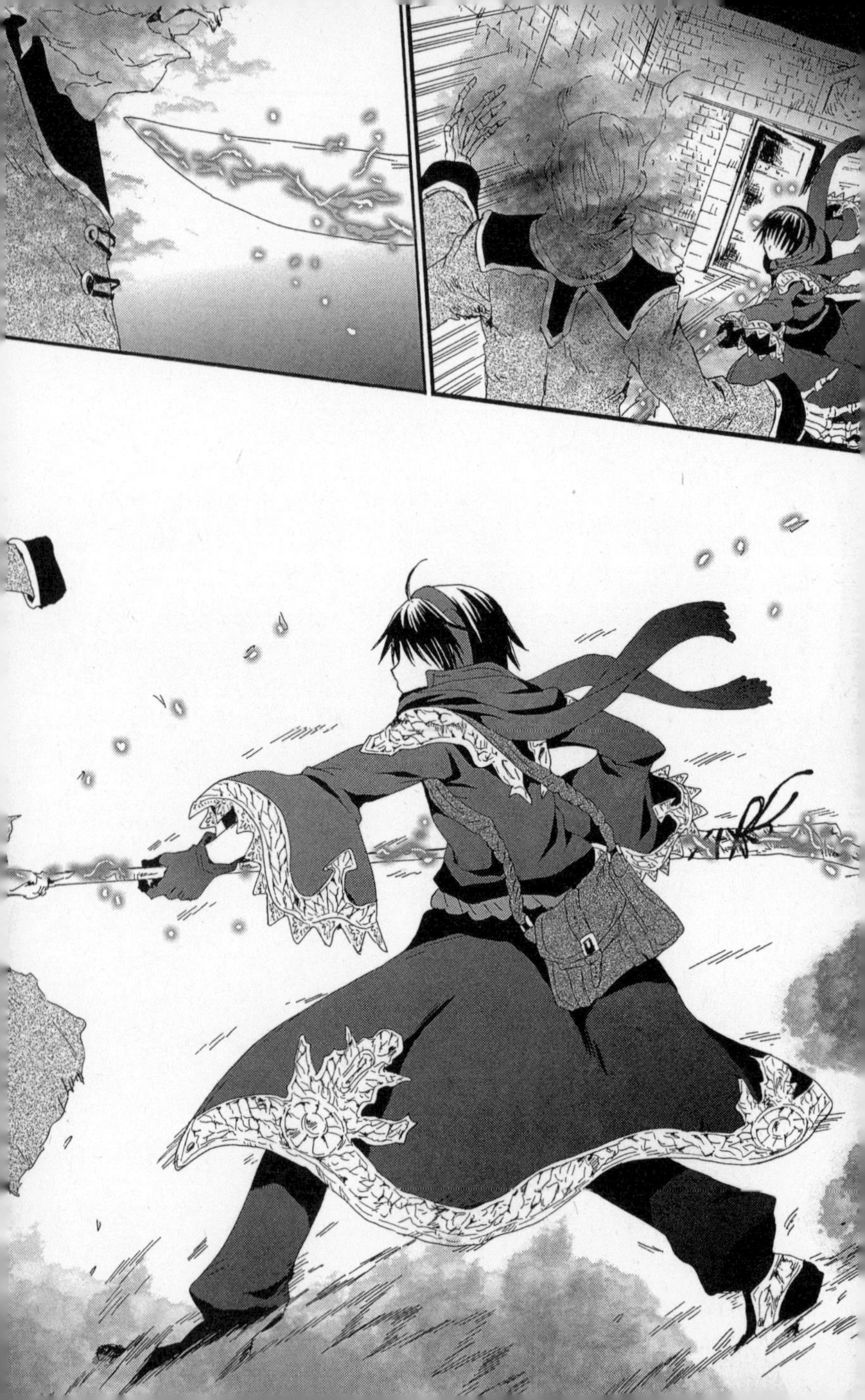

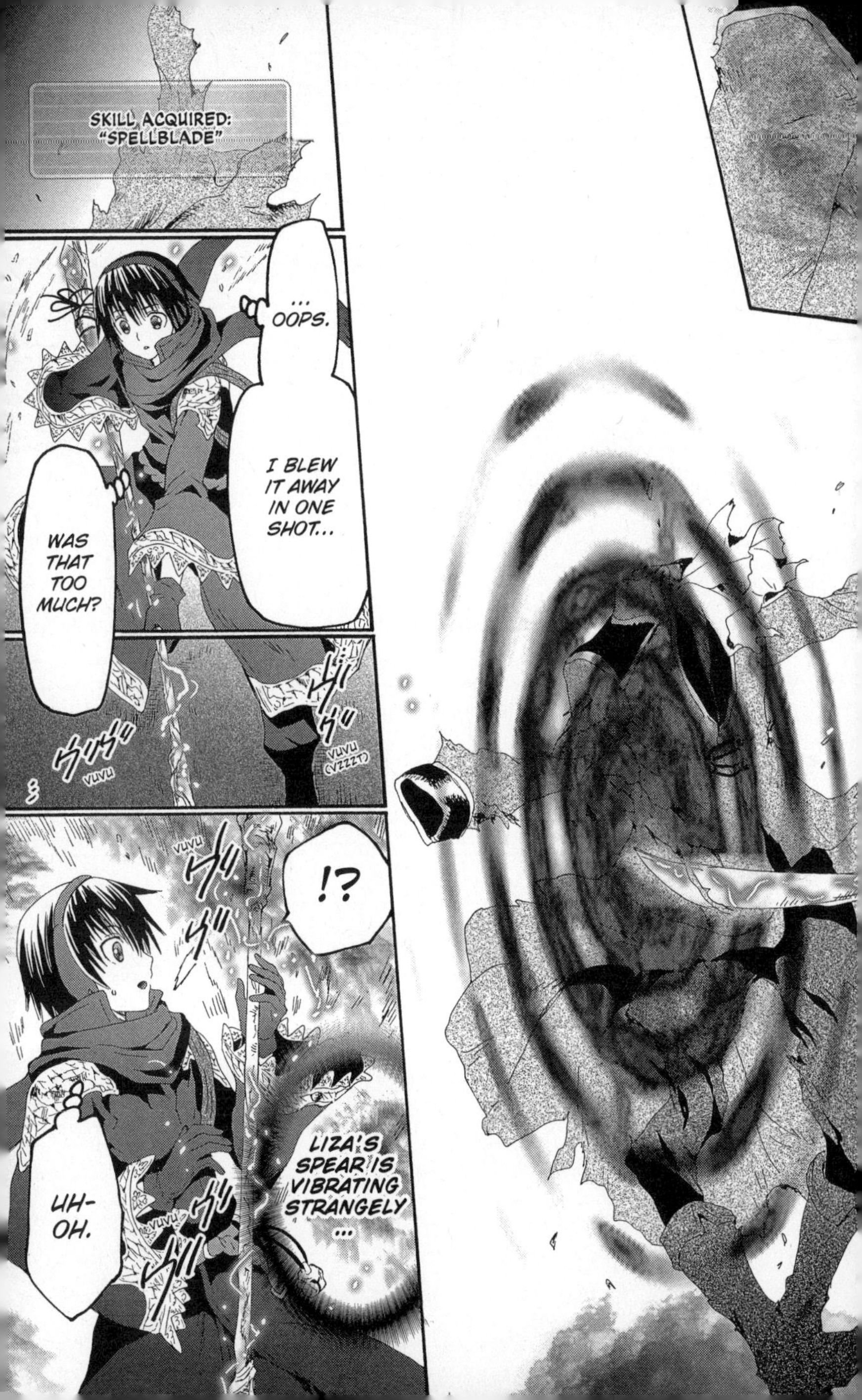
SKILL ACQUIRED: "SPELLBLADE"
... OOPS.
I BLEW IT AWAY IN ONE SHOT...
WAS THAT TOO MUCH?
VUVU (VZZZT)
VUVU
VUVU
!?
LIZA'S SPEAR IS VIBRATING STRANGELY...
VUVU
UH-OH.

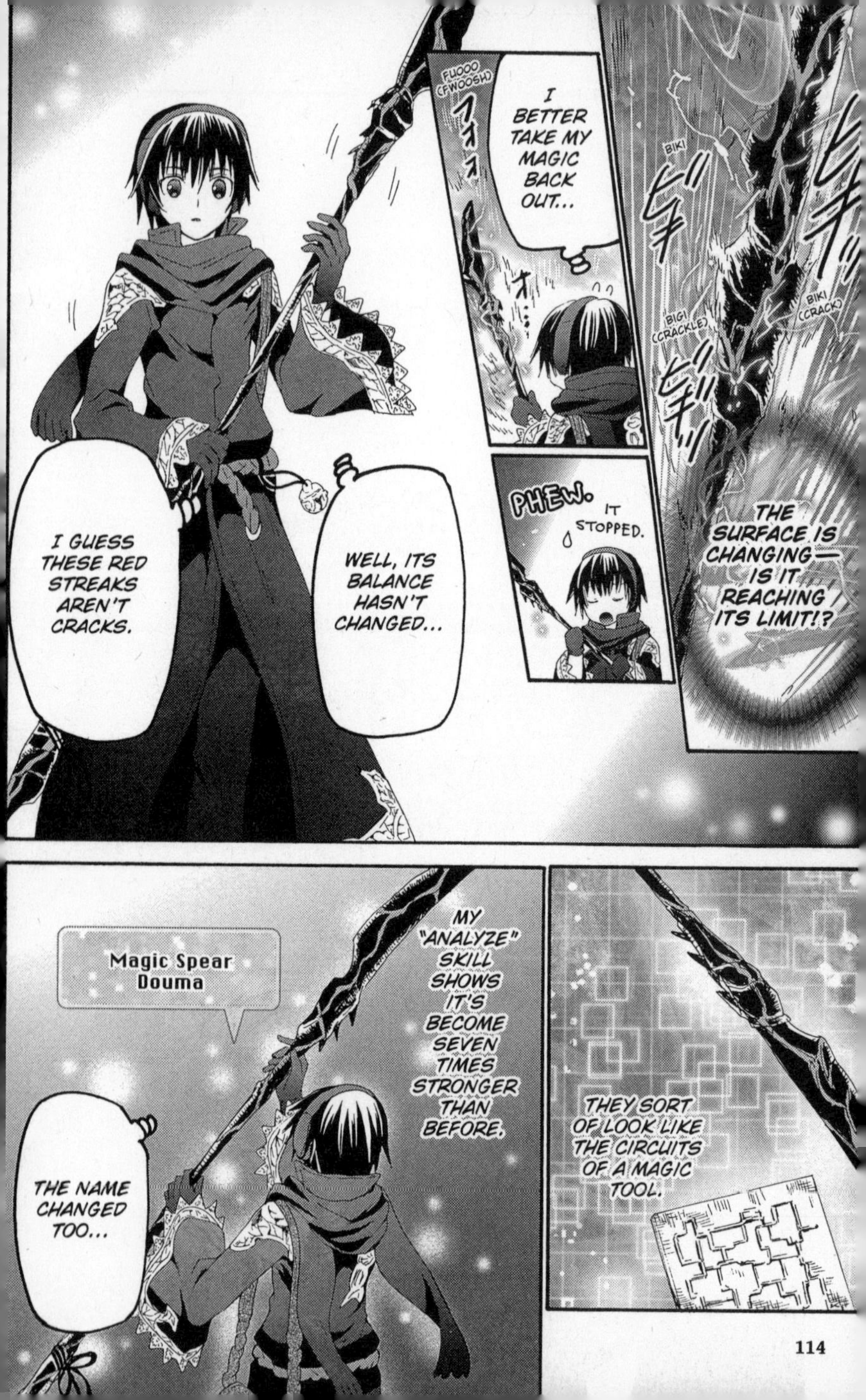
BIKI
BIKI (CRACK)
BIGI (CRACKLE)
THE SURFACE IS CHANGING—IS IT REACHING ITS LIMIT!?
FUOOO (FWOOSH)
I BETTER TAKE MY MAGIC BACK OUT...
PHEW.
IT STOPPED.
WELL, ITS BALANCE HASN'T CHANGED...
I GUESS THESE RED STREAKS AREN'T CRACKS.
THEY SORT OF LOOK LIKE THE CIRCUITS OF A MAGIC TOOL.
MY "ANALYZE" SKILL SHOWS IT'S BECOME SEVEN TIMES STRONGER THAN BEFORE.
Magic Spear Douma
THE NAME CHANGED TOO...

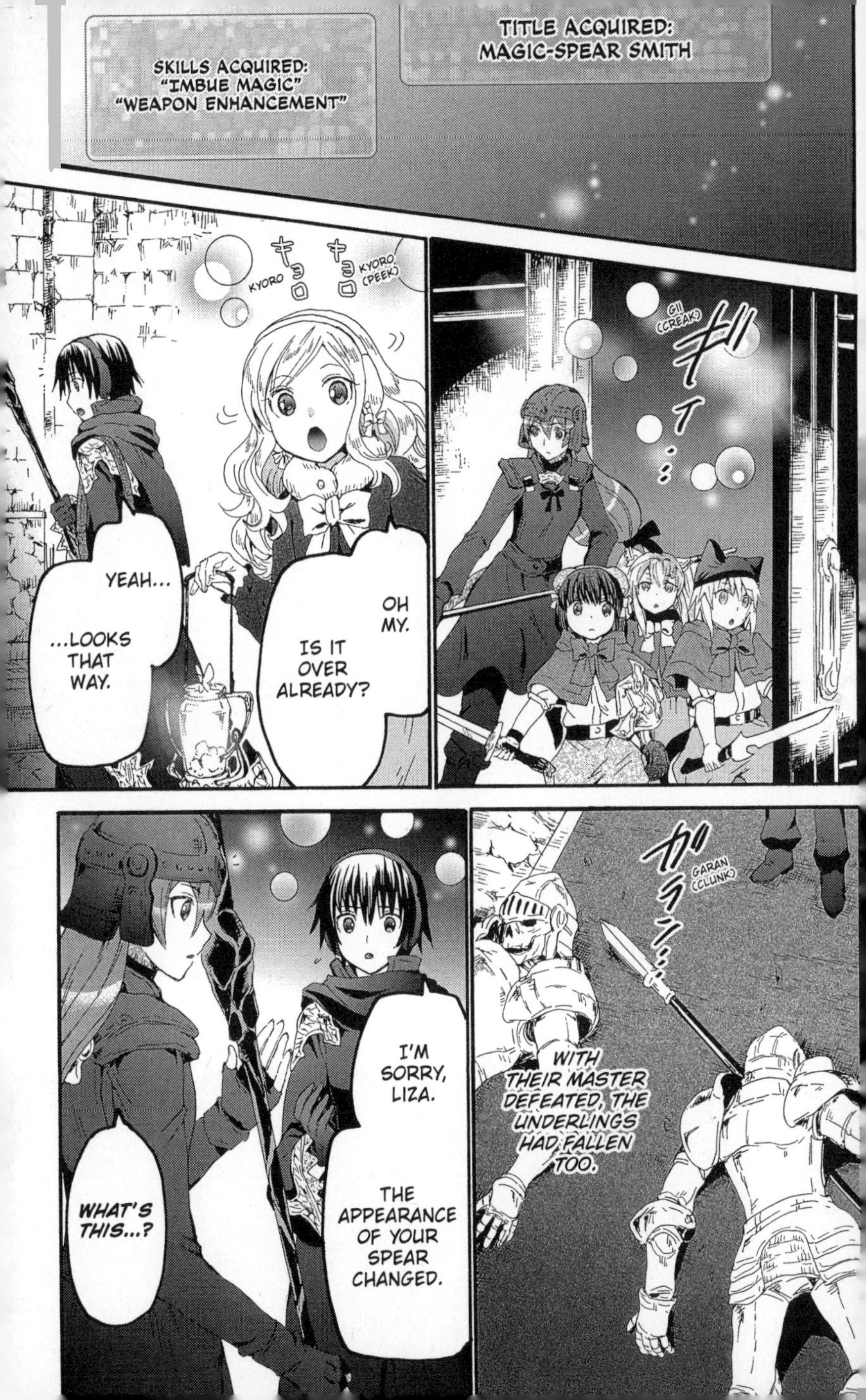
TITLE ACQUIRED: MAGIC-SPEAR SMITH
SKILLS ACQUIRED: "IMBUE MAGIC" "WEAPON ENHANCEMENT"
GII (CREAK)
KYORO (PEEK)
KYORO
OH MY.
IS IT OVER ALREADY?
YEAH...
...LOOKS THAT WAY.
GARAN (CLUNK)
WITH THEIR MASTER DEFEATED, THE UNDERLINGS HAD FALLEN TOO.
I'M SORRY, LIZA.
THE APPEARANCE OF YOUR SPEAR CHANGED.
WHAT'S THIS...?

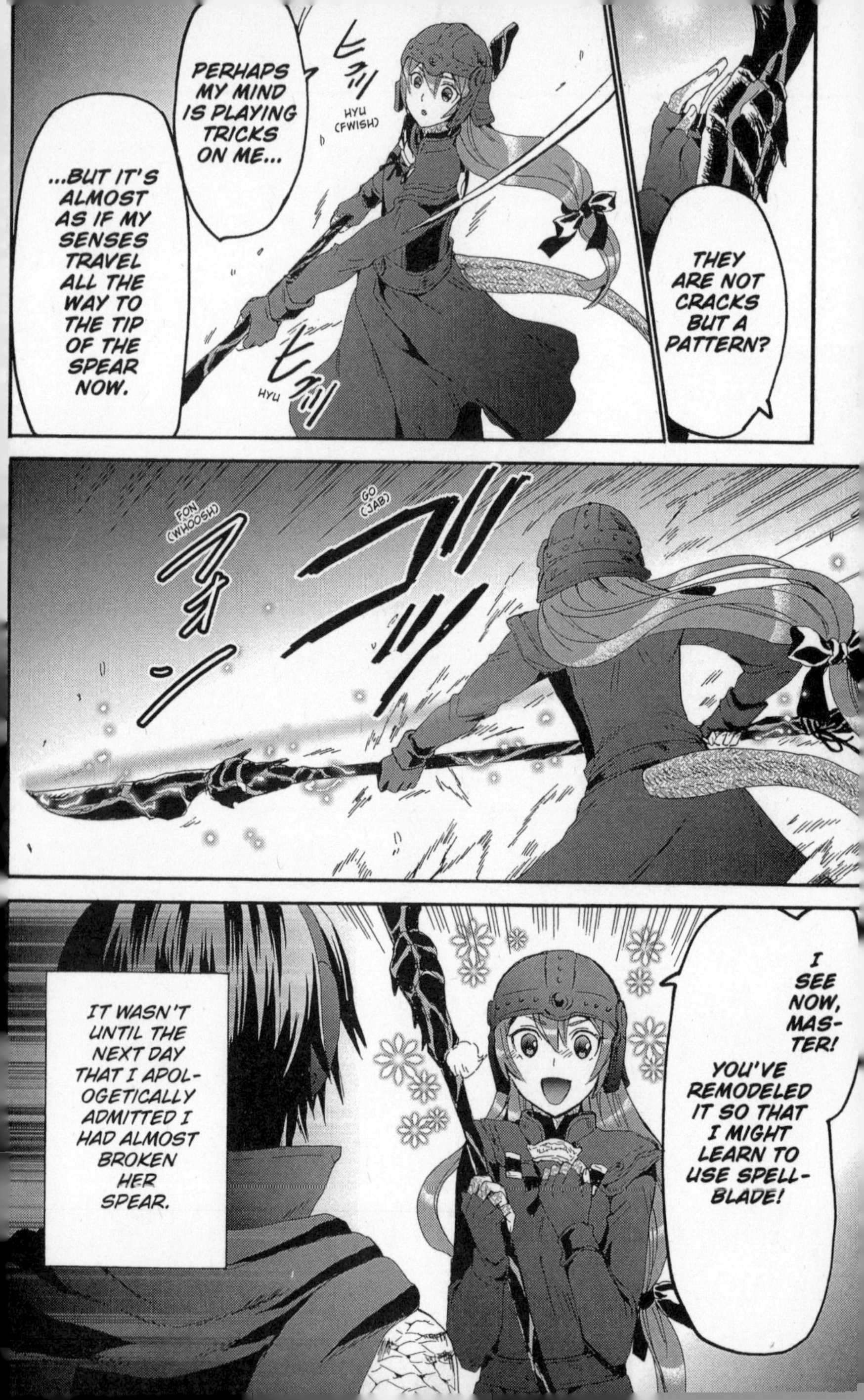

THEY ARE NOT CRACKS BUT A PATTERN?
PERHAPS MY MIND IS PLAYING TRICKS ON ME...
HYU (FWISH)
...BUT IT'S ALMOST AS IF MY SENSES TRAVEL ALL THE WAY TO THE TIP OF THE SPEAR NOW.
HYU
GO (JAB)
FON (WHOOSH)
I SEE NOW, MASTER!
YOU'VE REMODELED IT SO THAT I MIGHT LEARN TO USE SPELL-BLADE!
IT WASN'T UNTIL THE NEXT DAY THAT I APOLOGETICALLY ADMITTED I HAD ALMOST BROKEN HER SPEAR.

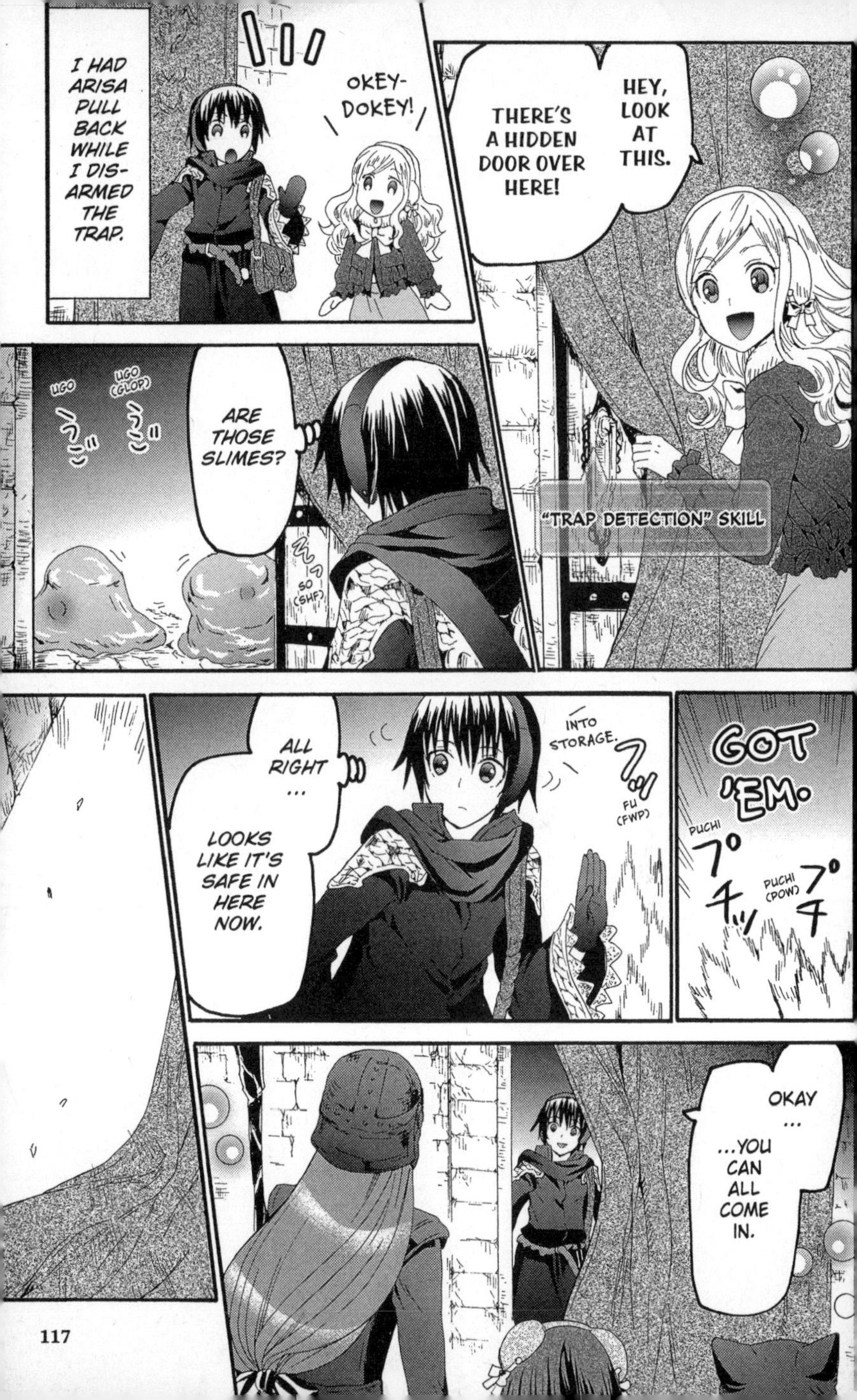
HEY, LOOK AT THIS.
THERE'S A HIDDEN DOOR OVER HERE!
"TRAP DETECTION" SKILL
OKEY-DOKEY!
I HAD ARISA PULL BACK WHILE I DIS-ARMED THE TRAP.
ARE THOSE SLIMES?
SO (SHF)
UGO (GLOP)
UGO
GOT 'EM.
PUCHI
PUCHI (POW)
INTO STORAGE.
FU (FWP)
ALL RIGHT...
LOOKS LIKE IT'S SAFE IN HERE NOW.
OKAY...
...YOU CAN ALL COME IN.

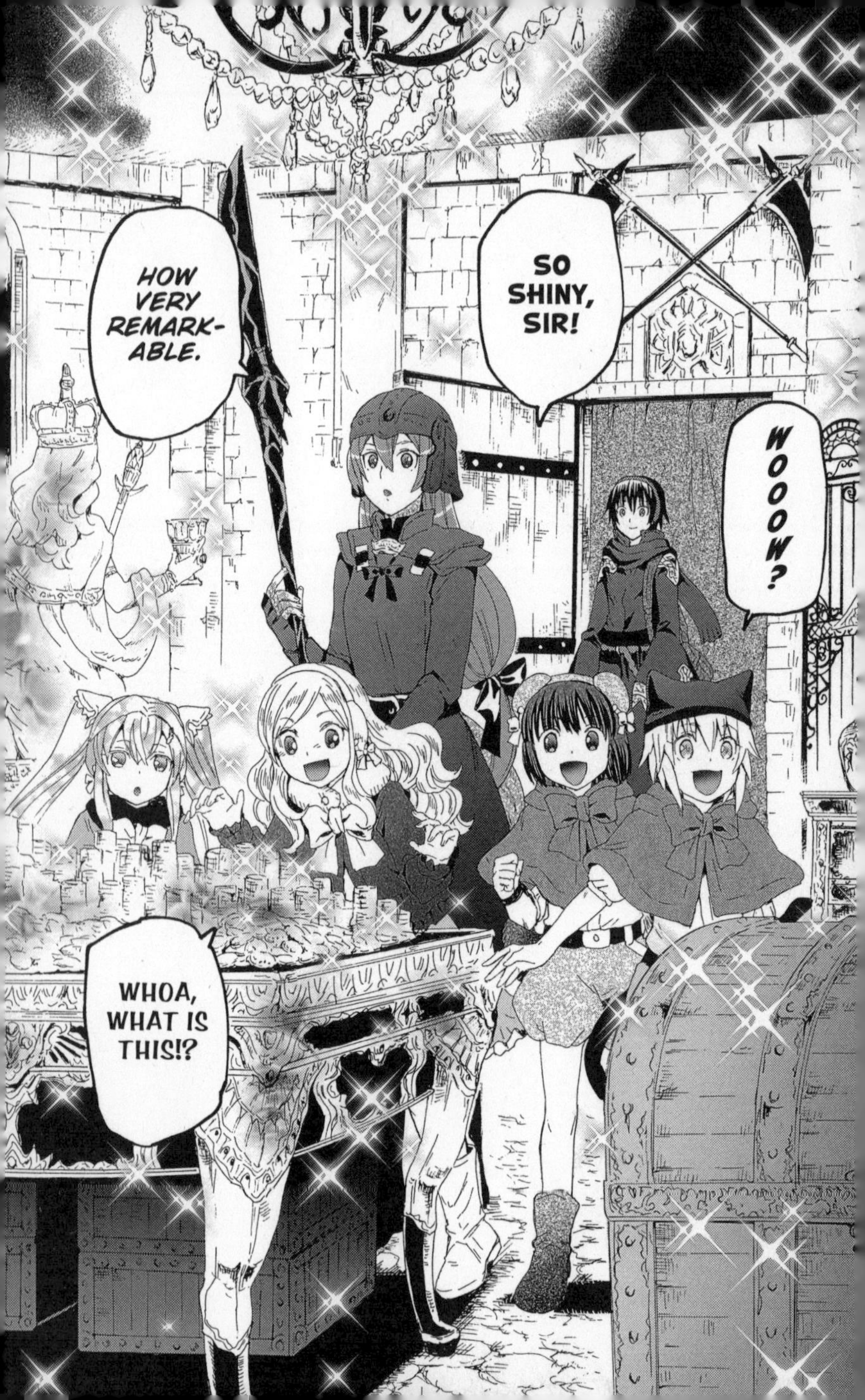
WOOOOW?
SO SHINY, SIR!
HOW VERY REMARK-ABLE.
WHOA, WHAT IS THIS!?

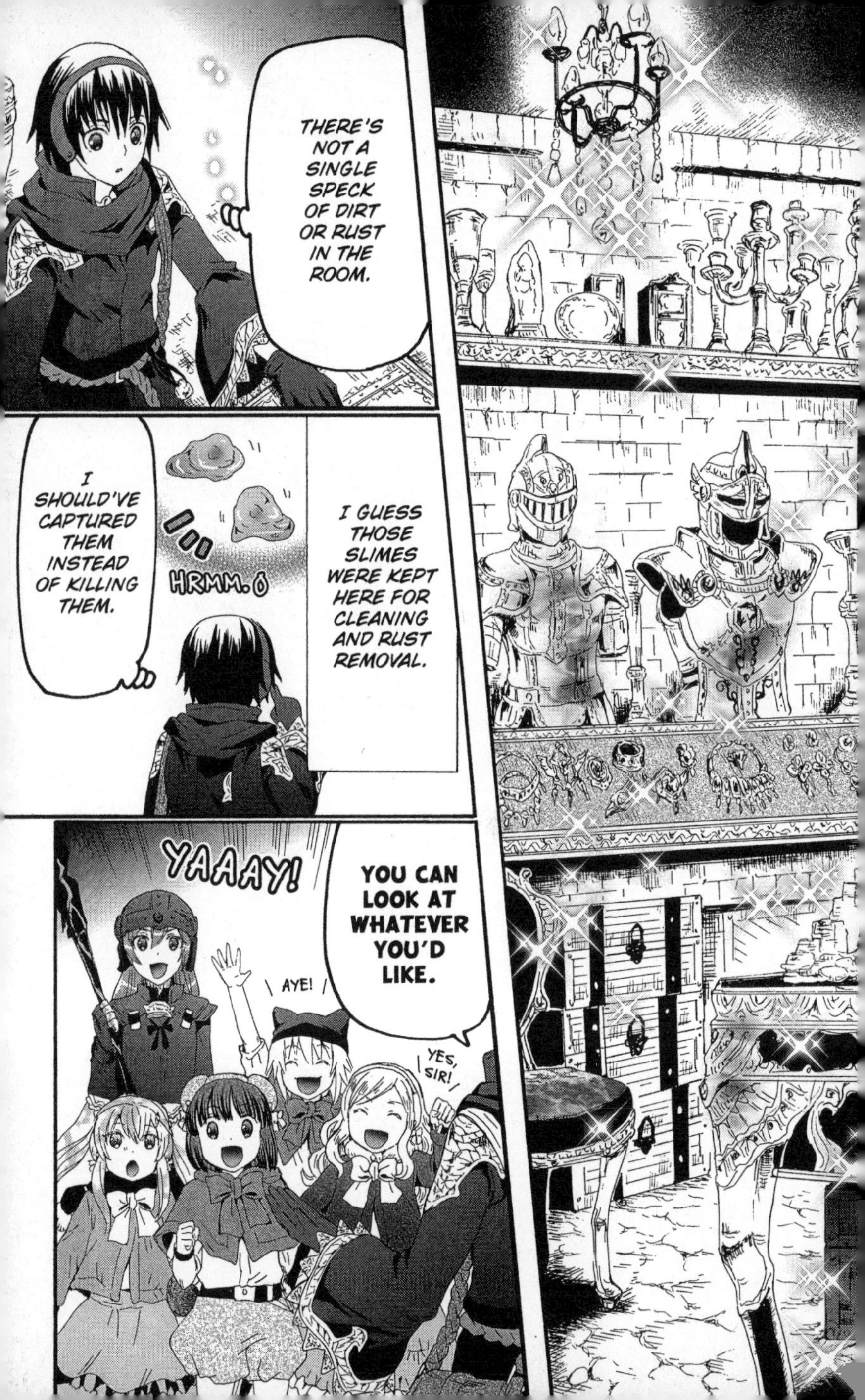
THERE'S NOT A SINGLE SPECK OF DIRT OR RUST IN THE ROOM.
I GUESS THOSE SLIMES WERE KEPT HERE FOR CLEANING AND RUST REMOVAL.
HRMM.
I SHOULD'VE CAPTURED THEM INSTEAD OF KILLING THEM.
YOU CAN LOOK AT WHATEVER YOU'D LIKE.
YAAAY!
AYE!
YES, SIR!

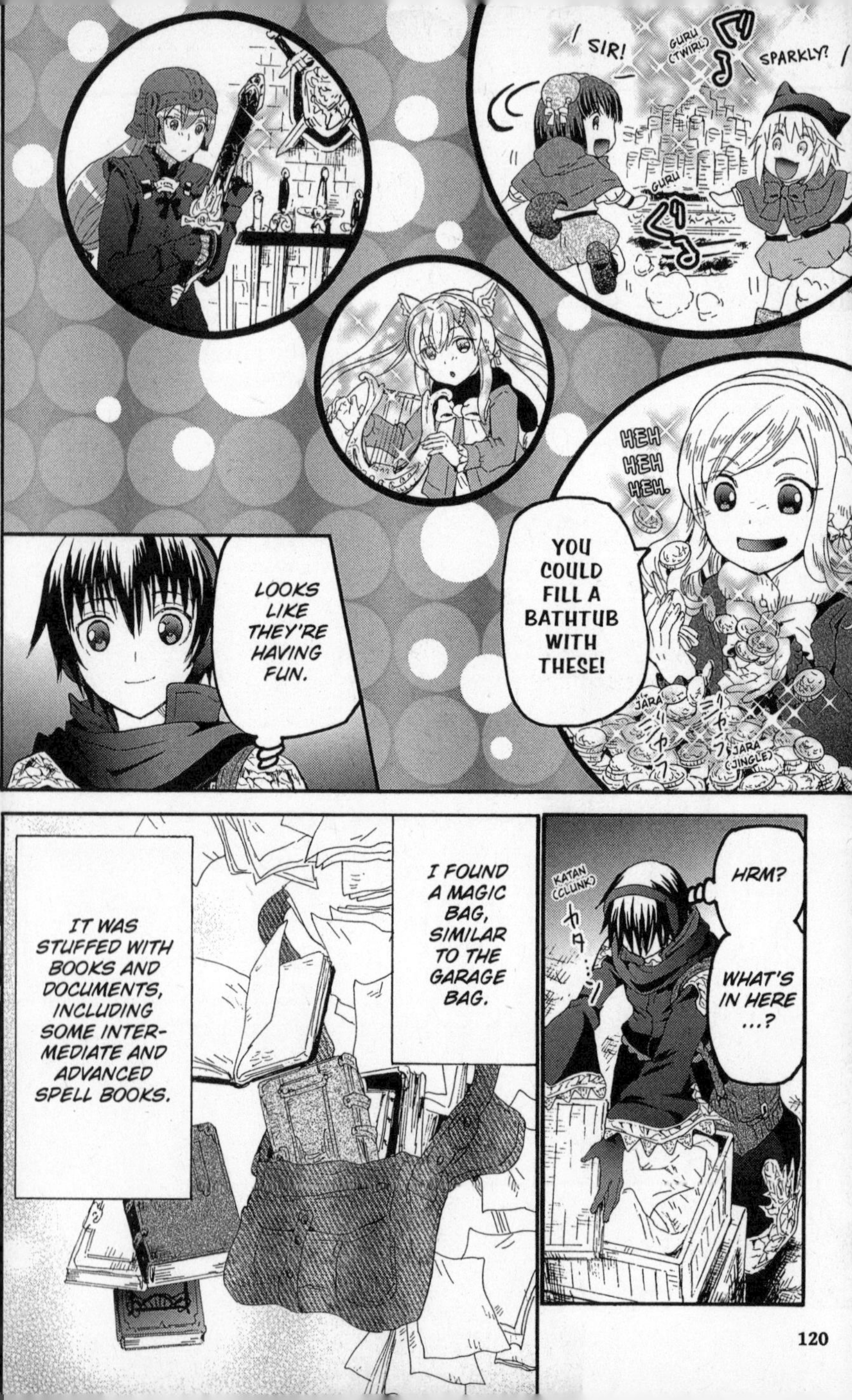
SIR!
GURU (TWIRL)
SPARKLY!?
GURU
HEH HEH HEH.
YOU COULD FILL A BATHTUB WITH THESE!
JARA
JARA (JINGLE)
LOOKS LIKE THEY'RE HAVING FUN.
KATAN (CLUNK)
HRM?
WHAT'S IN HERE ...?
I FOUND A MAGIC BAG, SIMILAR TO THE GARAGE BAG.
IT WAS STUFFED WITH BOOKS AND DOCUMENTS, INCLUDING SOME INTERMEDIATE AND ADVANCED SPELL BOOKS.

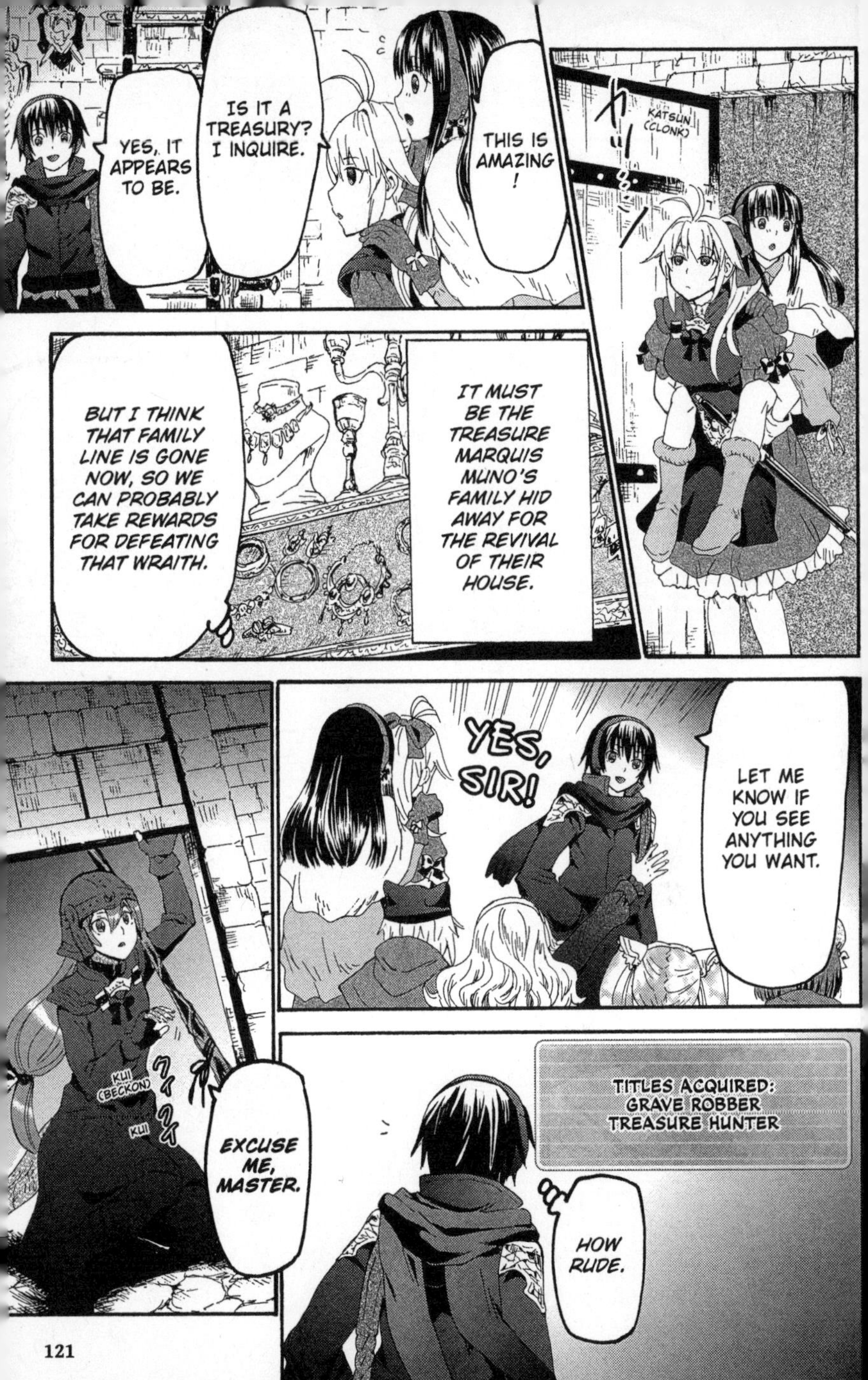
KATSUN (CLONK)
THIS IS AMAZING!
IS IT A TREASURY? I INQUIRE.
YES, IT APPEARS TO BE.
IT MUST BE THE TREASURE MARQUIS MUNO'S FAMILY HID AWAY FOR THE REVIVAL OF THEIR HOUSE.
BUT I THINK THAT FAMILY LINE IS GONE NOW, SO WE CAN PROBABLY TAKE REWARDS FOR DEFEATING THAT WRAITH.
LET ME KNOW IF YOU SEE ANYTHING YOU WANT.
YES, SIR!
TITLES ACQUIRED:
GRAVE ROBBER
TREASURE HUNTER
HOW RUDE.
KUI (BECKON)
KUI
EXCUSE ME, MASTER.

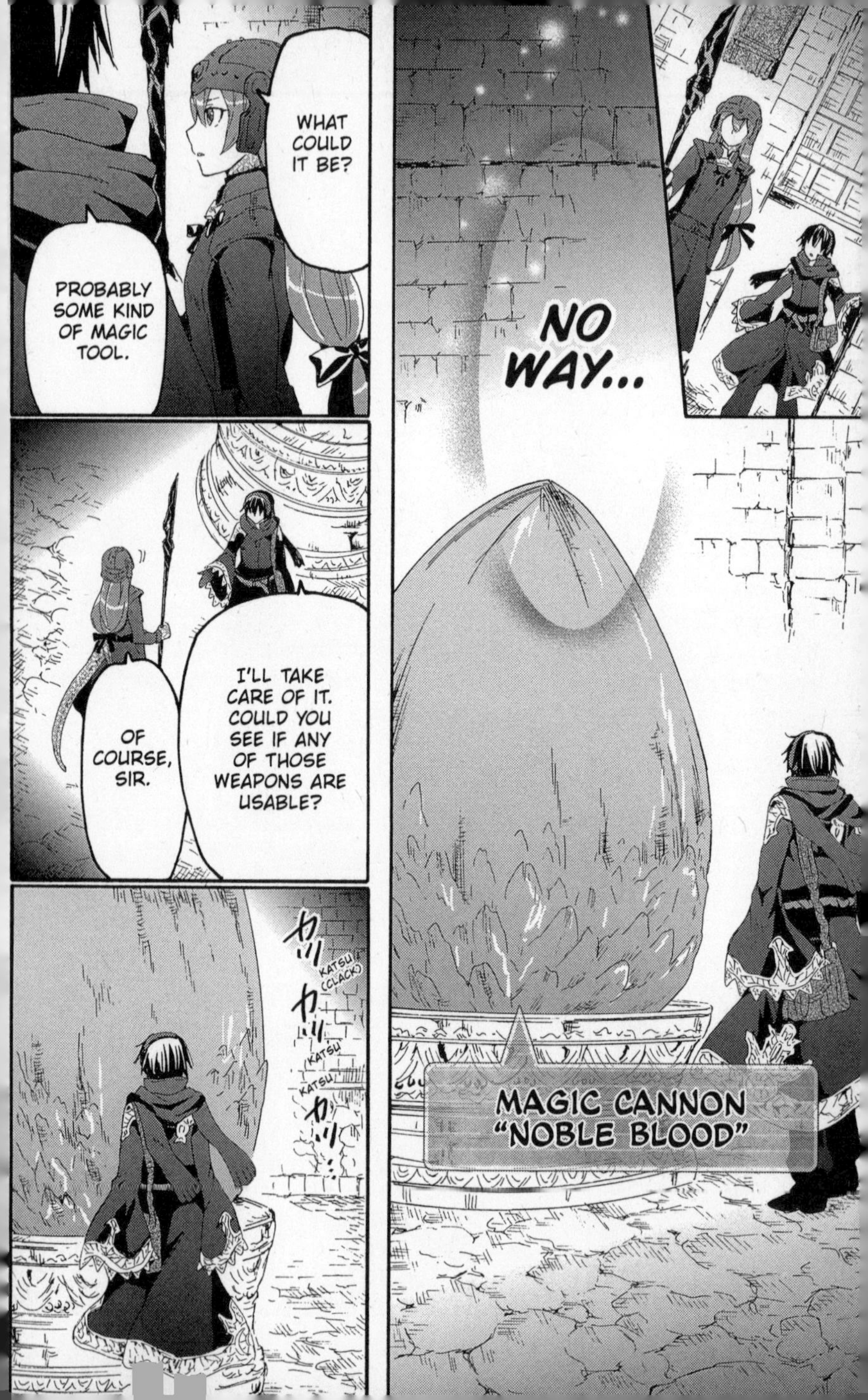
NO WAY...
MAGIC CANNON "NOBLE BLOOD"
WHAT COULD IT BE?
PROBABLY SOME KIND OF MAGIC TOOL.
I'LL TAKE CARE OF IT. COULD YOU SEE IF ANY OF THOSE WEAPONS ARE USABLE?
OF COURSE, SIR.
カッ
KATSU (CLACK)
カッ
KATSU
KATSU
カッ

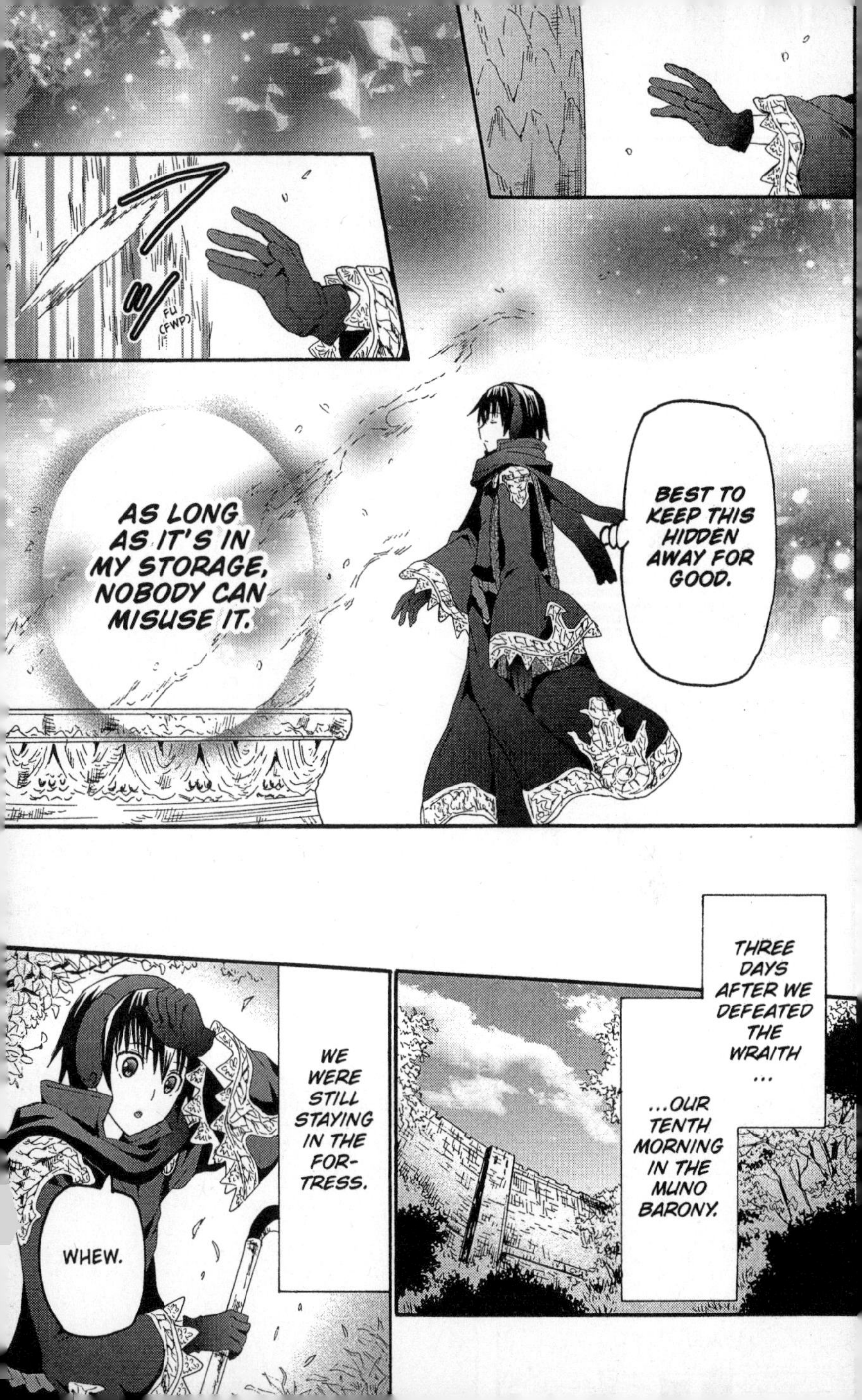
FU (FWP)
BEST TO KEEP THIS HIDDEN AWAY FOR GOOD.
AS LONG AS IT'S IN MY STORAGE, NOBODY CAN MISUSE IT.
THREE DAYS AFTER WE DEFEATED THE WRAITH...
...OUR TENTH MORNING IN THE MUNO BARONY.
WE WERE STILL STAYING IN THE FOR-TRESS.
WHEW.

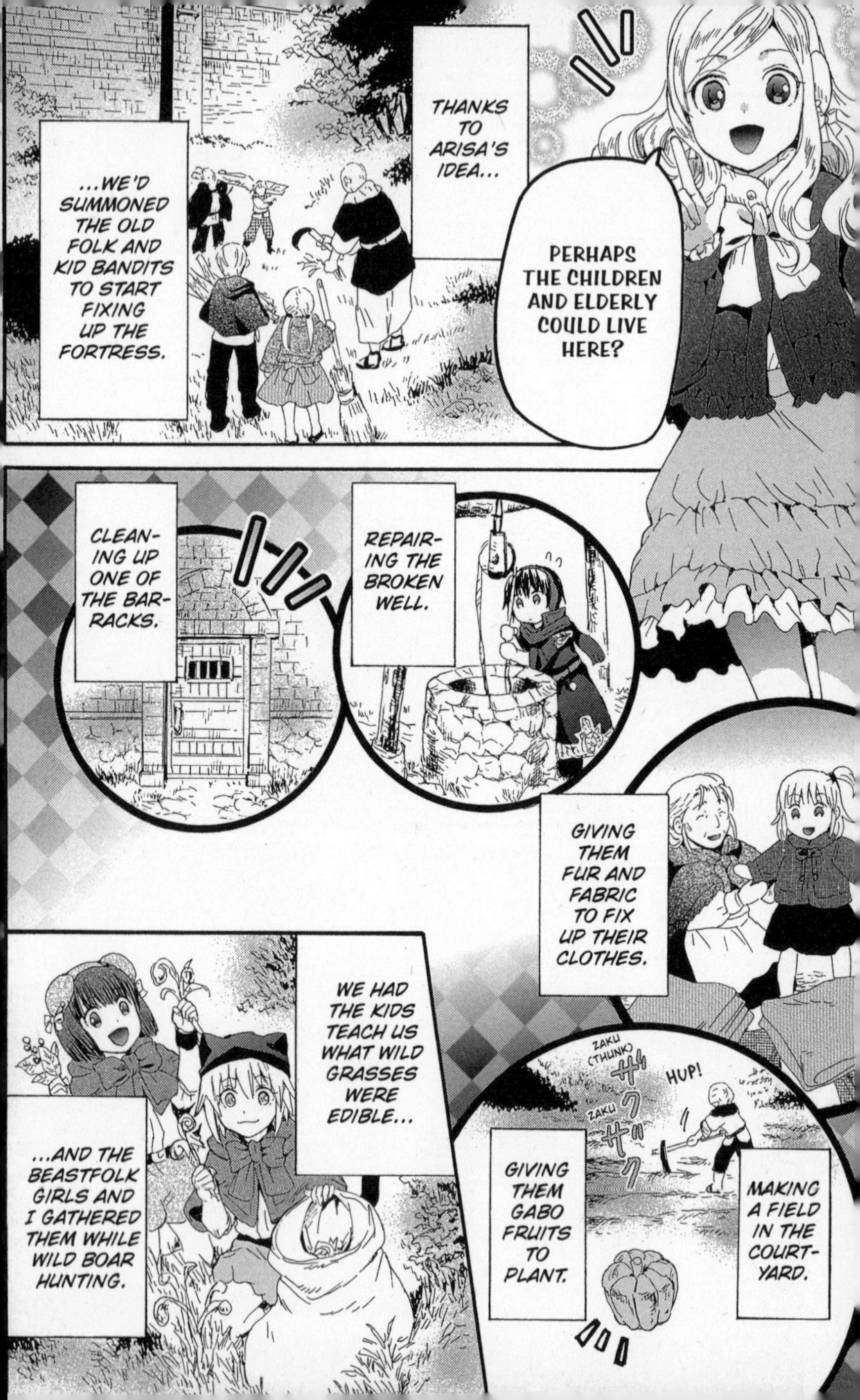
PERHAPS THE CHILDREN AND ELDERLY COULD LIVE HERE?
THANKS TO ARISA'S IDEA...
...WE'D SUMMONED THE OLD FOLK AND KID BANDITS TO START FIXING UP THE FORTRESS.
REPAIRING THE BROKEN WELL.
CLEANING UP ONE OF THE BARRACKS.
GIVING THEM FUR AND FABRIC TO FIX UP THEIR CLOTHES.
MAKING A FIELD IN THE COURTYARD.
HUP!
ZAKU (THUNK)
ZAKU
GIVING THEM GABO FRUITS TO PLANT.
WE HAD THE KIDS TEACH US WHAT WILD GRASSES WERE EDIBLE...
...AND THE BEASTFOLK GIRLS AND I GATHERED THEM WHILE WILD BOAR HUNTING.

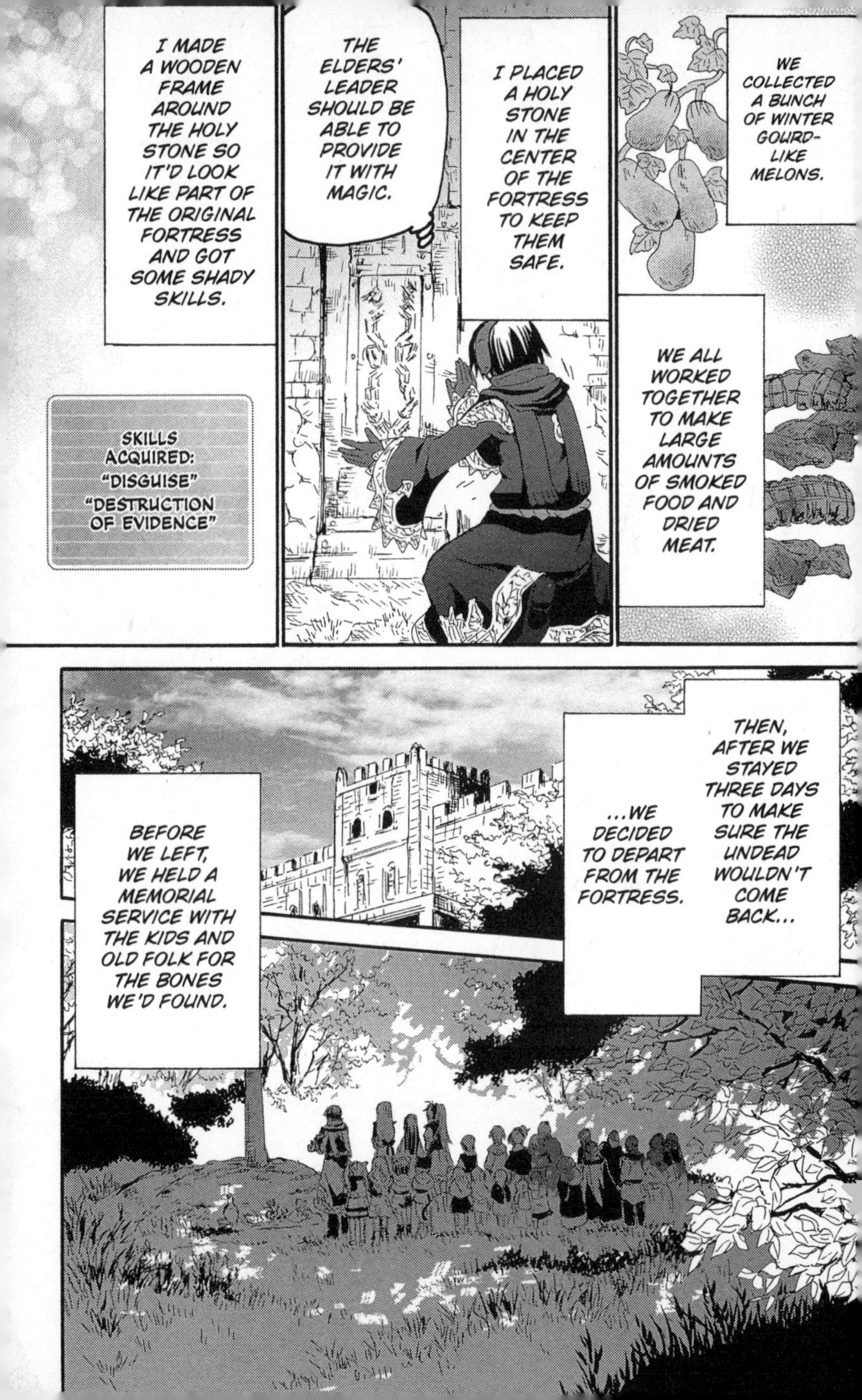
WE COLLECTED A BUNCH OF WINTER GOURD-LIKE MELONS.
WE ALL WORKED TOGETHER TO MAKE LARGE AMOUNTS OF SMOKED FOOD AND DRIED MEAT.
I PLACED A HOLY STONE IN THE CENTER OF THE FORTRESS TO KEEP THEM SAFE.
THE ELDERS' LEADER SHOULD BE ABLE TO PROVIDE IT WITH MAGIC.
I MADE A WOODEN FRAME AROUND THE HOLY STONE SO IT'D LOOK LIKE PART OF THE ORIGINAL FORTRESS AND GOT SOME SHADY SKILLS.
SKILLS ACQUIRED: "DISGUISE" "DESTRUCTION OF EVIDENCE"
THEN, AFTER WE STAYED THREE DAYS TO MAKE SURE THE UNDEAD WOULDN'T COME BACK...
...WE DECIDED TO DEPART FROM THE FORTRESS.
BEFORE WE LEFT, WE HELD A MEMORIAL SERVICE WITH THE KIDS AND OLD FOLK FOR THE BONES WE'D FOUND.

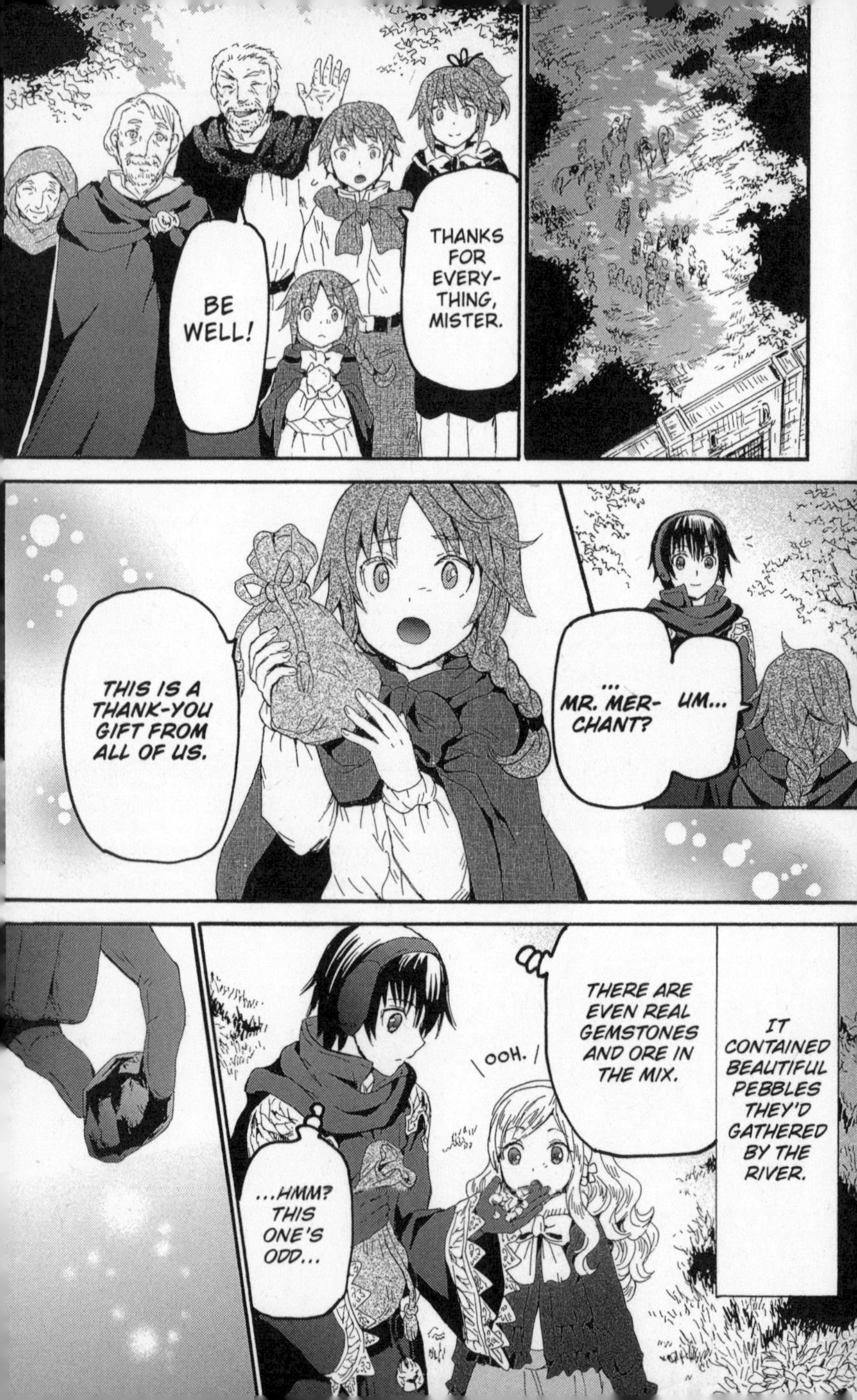
THANKS FOR EVERY-THING, MISTER.
BE WELL!
UM...
...MR. MER-CHANT?
THIS IS A THANK-YOU GIFT FROM ALL OF US.
IT CONTAINED BEAUTIFUL PEBBLES THEY'D GATHERED BY THE RIVER.
THERE ARE EVEN REAL GEMSTONES AND ORE IN THE MIX.
OOH.
...HMM? THIS ONE'S ODD...

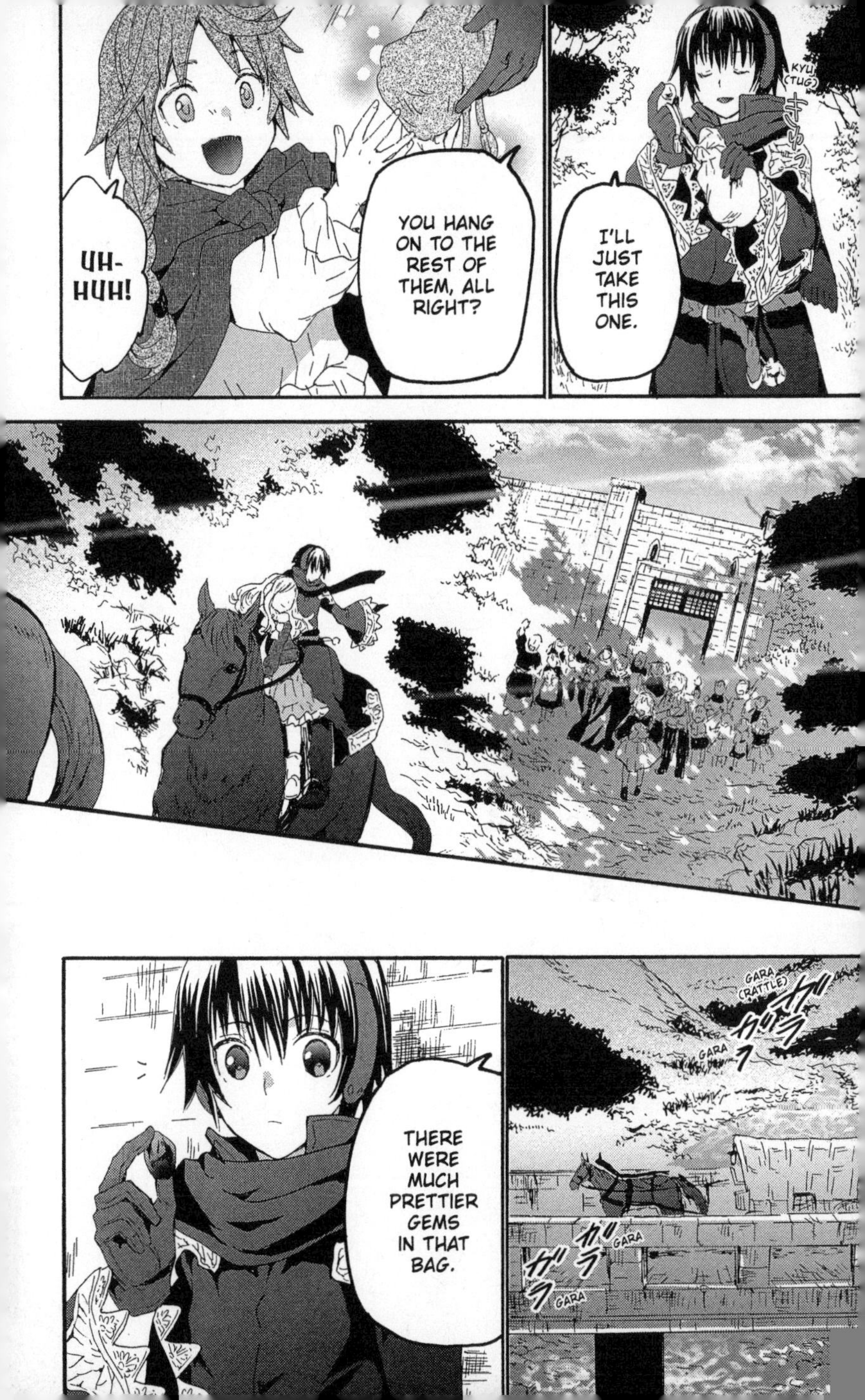
KYU (TUG)
きゅっ
I'LL JUST TAKE THIS ONE.
YOU HANG ON TO THE REST OF THEM, ALL RIGHT?
UH-HUH!
GARA (RATTLE)
GARA
GARA
GARA
THERE WERE MUCH PRETTIER GEMS IN THAT BAG.

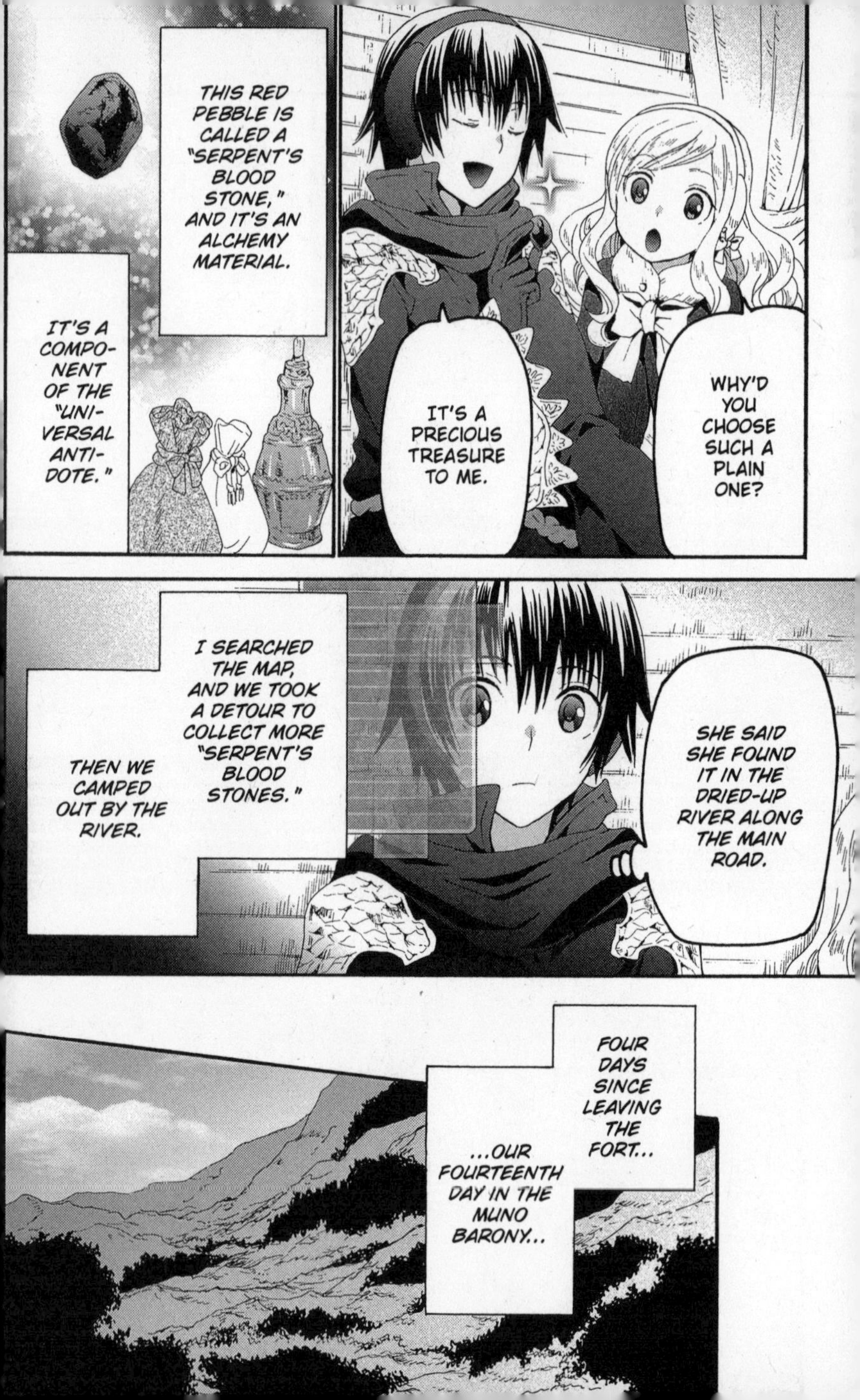
WHY'D YOU CHOOSE SUCH A PLAIN ONE?
IT'S A PRECIOUS TREASURE TO ME.
THIS RED PEBBLE IS CALLED A "SERPENT'S BLOOD STONE," AND IT'S AN ALCHEMY MATERIAL.
IT'S A COMPONENT OF THE "UNIVERSAL ANTIDOTE."
SHE SAID SHE FOUND IT IN THE DRIED-UP RIVER ALONG THE MAIN ROAD.
I SEARCHED THE MAP, AND WE TOOK A DETOUR TO COLLECT MORE "SERPENT'S BLOOD STONES."
THEN WE CAMPED OUT BY THE RIVER.
FOUR DAYS SINCE LEAVING THE FORT...
...OUR FOURTEENTH DAY IN THE MUNO BARONY...

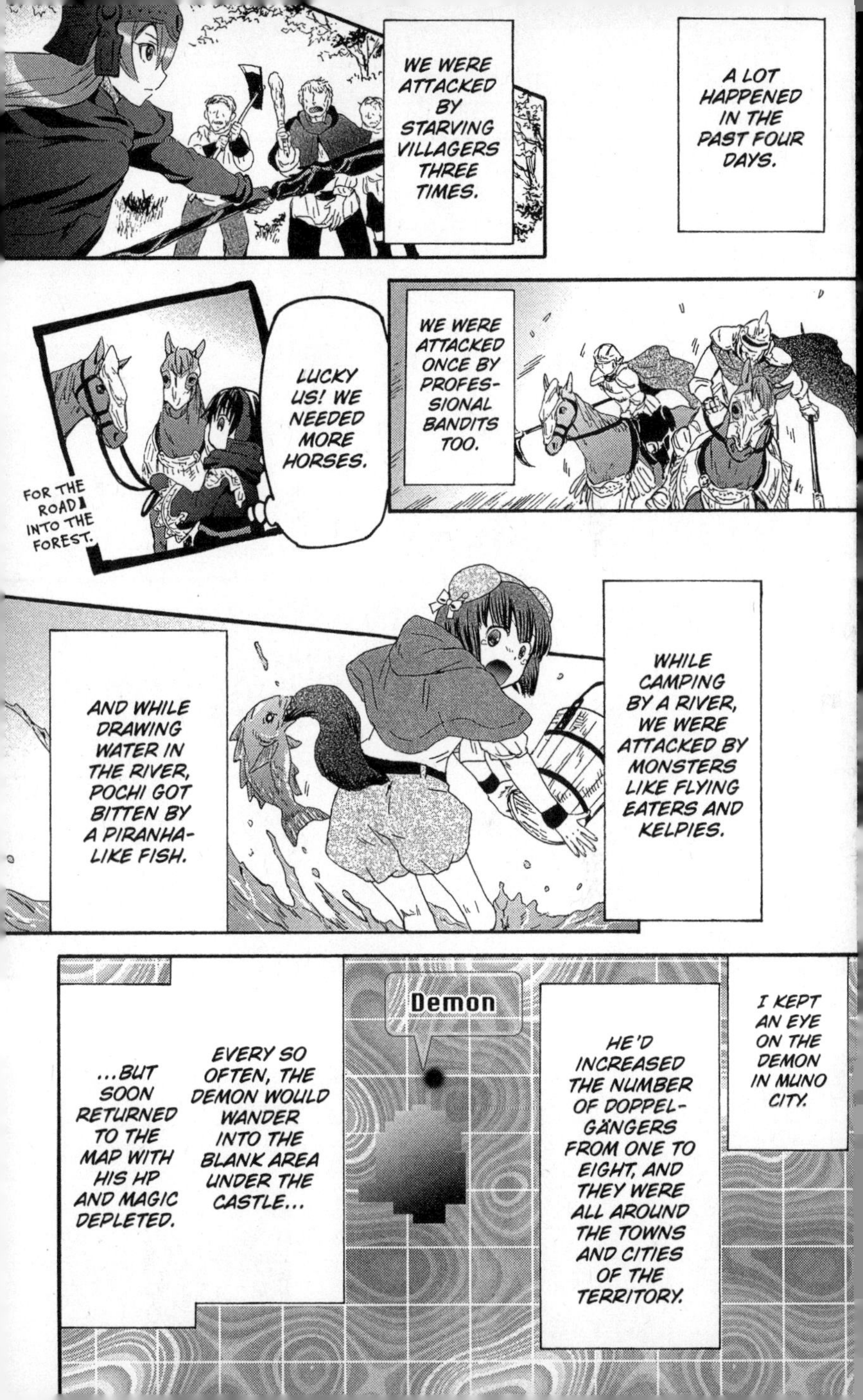
A LOT HAPPENED IN THE PAST FOUR DAYS.
WE WERE ATTACKED BY STARVING VILLAGERS THREE TIMES.
WE WERE ATTACKED ONCE BY PROFES-SIONAL BANDITS TOO.
LUCKY US! WE NEEDED MORE HORSES.
FOR THE ROAD INTO THE FOREST.
WHILE CAMPING BY A RIVER, WE WERE ATTACKED BY MONSTERS LIKE FLYING EATERS AND KELPIES.
AND WHILE DRAWING WATER IN THE RIVER, POCHI GOT BITTEN BY A PIRANHA-LIKE FISH.
I KEPT AN EYE ON THE DEMON IN MUNO CITY.
HE'D INCREASED THE NUMBER OF DOPPEL-GÄNGERS FROM ONE TO EIGHT, AND THEY WERE ALL AROUND THE TOWNS AND CITIES OF THE TERRITORY.
Demon
EVERY SO OFTEN, THE DEMON WOULD WANDER INTO THE BLANK AREA UNDER THE CASTLE...
...BUT SOON RETURNED TO THE MAP WITH HIS HP AND MAGIC DEPLETED.

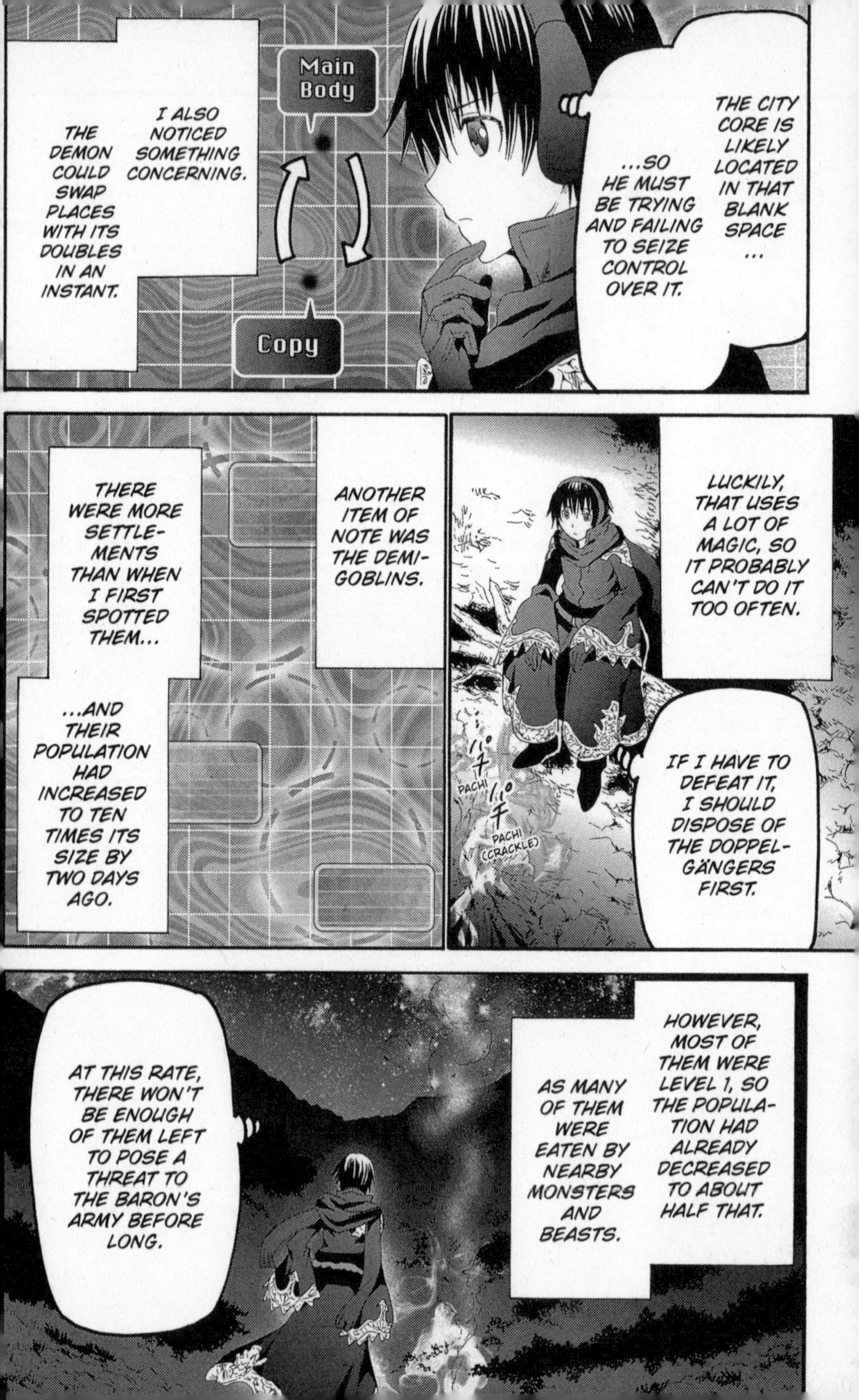
THE CITY CORE IS LIKELY LOCATED IN THAT BLANK SPACE...
...SO HE MUST BE TRYING AND FAILING TO SEIZE CONTROL OVER IT.
Main Body
Copy
I ALSO NOTICED SOMETHING CONCERNING.
THE DEMON COULD SWAP PLACES WITH ITS DOUBLES IN AN INSTANT.
LUCKILY, THAT USES A LOT OF MAGIC, SO IT PROBABLY CAN'T DO IT TOO OFTEN.
IF I HAVE TO DEFEAT IT, I SHOULD DISPOSE OF THE DOPPELGÄNGERS FIRST.
パチ
PACHI
パチ
PACHI (CRACKLE)
ANOTHER ITEM OF NOTE WAS THE DEMI-GOBLINS.
THERE WERE MORE SETTLEMENTS THAN WHEN I FIRST SPOTTED THEM...
...AND THEIR POPULATION HAD INCREASED TO TEN TIMES ITS SIZE BY TWO DAYS AGO.
HOWEVER, MOST OF THEM WERE LEVEL 1, SO THE POPULATION HAD ALREADY DECREASED TO ABOUT HALF THAT.
AS MANY OF THEM WERE EATEN BY NEARBY MONSTERS AND BEASTS.
AT THIS RATE, THERE WON'T BE ENOUGH OF THEM LEFT TO POSE A THREAT TO THE BARON'S ARMY BEFORE LONG.

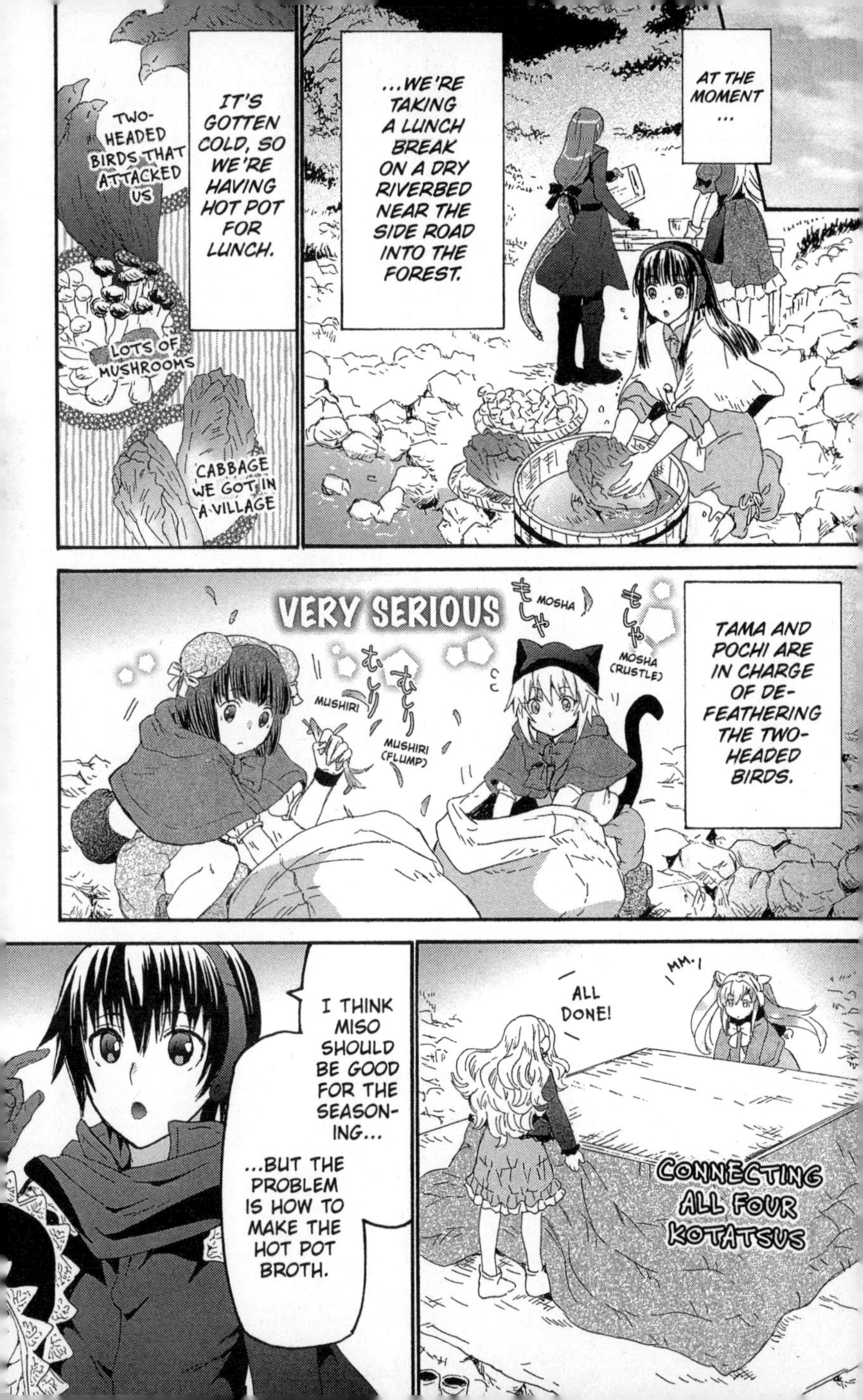
AT THE MOMENT...
...WE'RE TAKING A LUNCH BREAK ON A DRY RIVERBED NEAR THE SIDE ROAD INTO THE FOREST.
IT'S GOTTEN COLD, SO WE'RE HAVING HOT POT FOR LUNCH.
TWO-HEADED BIRDS THAT ATTACKED US
LOTS OF MUSHROOMS
CABBAGE WE GOT IN A VILLAGE
TAMA AND POCHI ARE IN CHARGE OF DE-FEATHERING THE TWO-HEADED BIRDS.
もしゃ
MOSHA (RUSTLE)
もしゃ
MOSHA
むしり
MUSHIRI (FLUMP)
むしり
MUSHIRI
VERY SERIOUS
MM.
ALL DONE!
CONNECTING ALL FOUR KOTATSUS
I THINK MISO SHOULD BE GOOD FOR THE SEASON-ING...
...BUT THE PROBLEM IS HOW TO MAKE THE HOT POT BROTH.

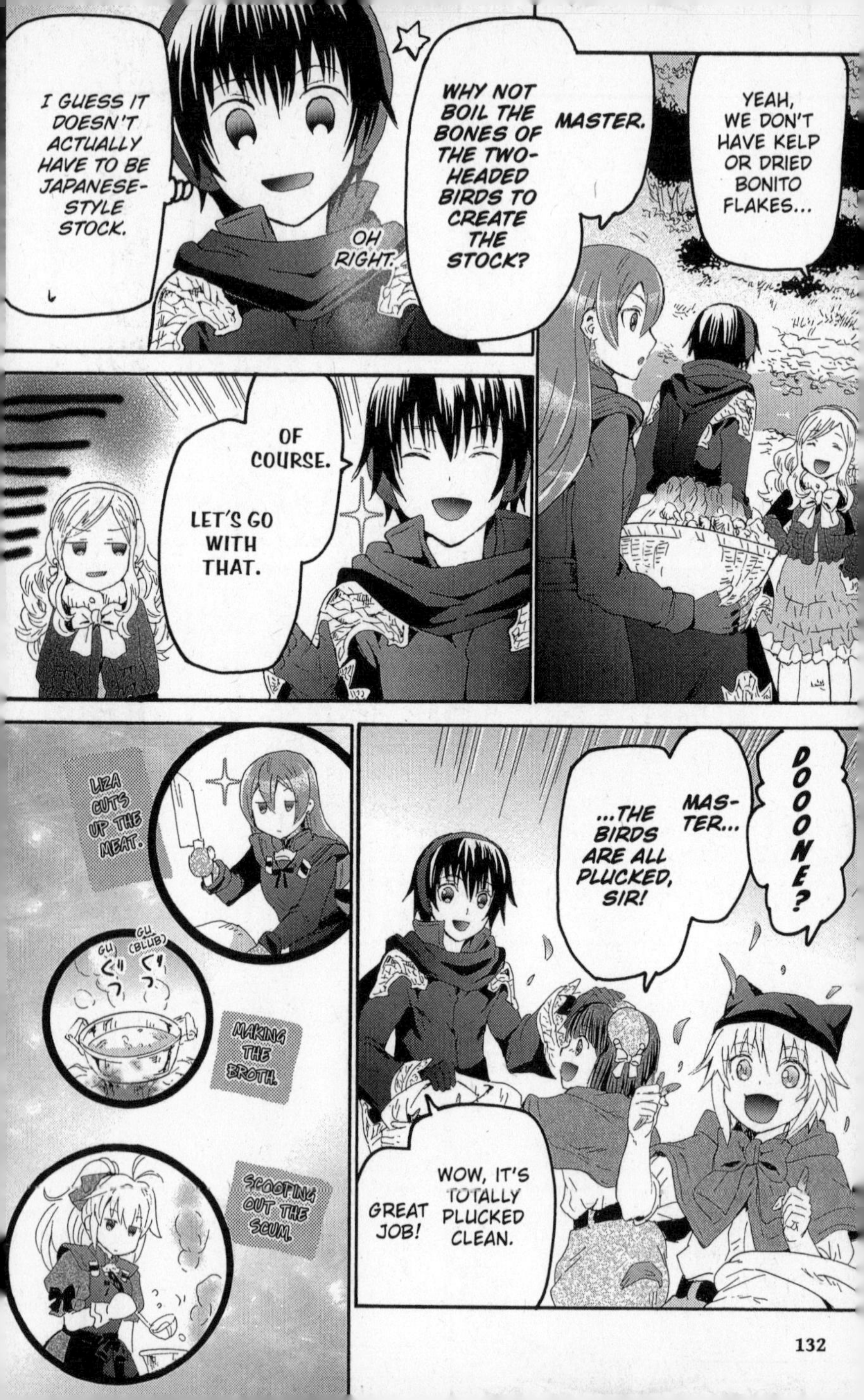

YEAH, WE DON'T HAVE KELP OR DRIED BONITO FLAKES...
MASTER.
WHY NOT BOIL THE BONES OF THE TWO-HEADED BIRDS TO CREATE THE STOCK?
OH RIGHT.
I GUESS IT DOESN'T ACTUALLY HAVE TO BE JAPANESE-STYLE STOCK.
OF COURSE.
LET'S GO WITH THAT.
DOOOONE?
MASTER...
...THE BIRDS ARE ALL PLUCKED, SIR!
WOW, IT'S TOTALLY PLUCKED CLEAN.
GREAT JOB!
LIZA CUTS UP THE MEAT.
GU GU (BLUB)
MAKING THE BROTH.
SCOOPING OUT THE SCUM.

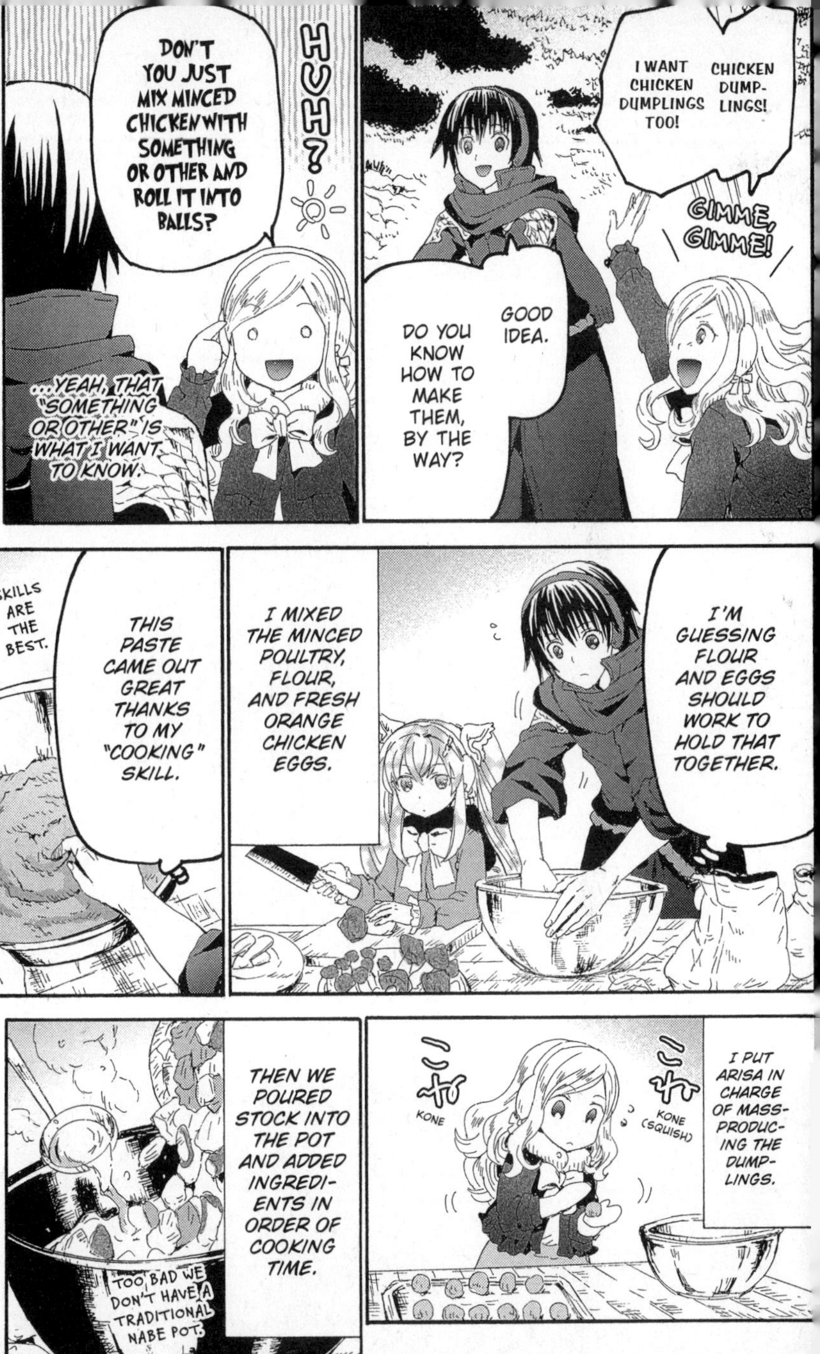
CHICKEN DUMPLINGS!
I WANT CHICKEN DUMPLINGS TOO!
GIMME, GIMME!
GOOD IDEA.
DO YOU KNOW HOW TO MAKE THEM, BY THE WAY?
HUH?
DON'T YOU JUST MIX MINCED CHICKEN WITH SOMETHING OR OTHER AND ROLL IT INTO BALLS?
...YEAH, THAT "SOMETHING OR OTHER" IS WHAT I WANT TO KNOW.
I'M GUESSING FLOUR AND EGGS SHOULD WORK TO HOLD THAT TOGETHER.
I MIXED THE MINCED POULTRY, FLOUR, AND FRESH ORANGE CHICKEN EGGS.
THIS PASTE CAME OUT GREAT THANKS TO MY "COOKING" SKILL.
SKILLS ARE THE BEST.
I PUT ARISA IN CHARGE OF MASS-PRODUCING THE DUMPLINGS.
こね
KONE (SQUISH)
こね
KONE
THEN WE POURED STOCK INTO THE POT AND ADDED INGREDIENTS IN ORDER OF COOKING TIME.
TOO BAD WE DON'T HAVE A TRADITIONAL NABE POT.

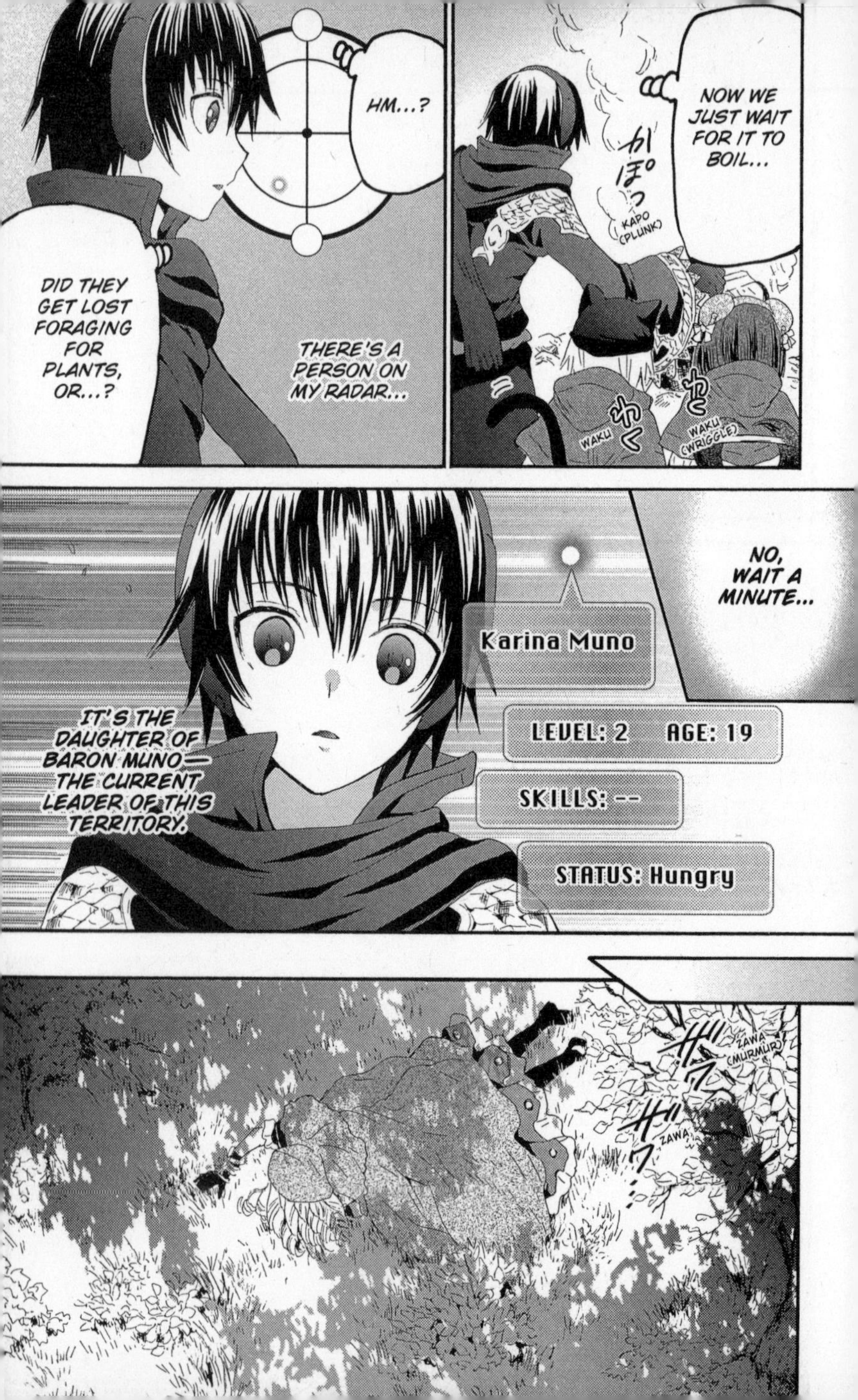
NOW WE JUST WAIT FOR IT TO BOIL...
かぽっ
KAPO (PLUNK)
わく
WAKU
わく
WAKU (WRIGGLE)
HM...?
THERE'S A PERSON ON MY RADAR...
DID THEY GET LOST FORAGING FOR PLANTS, OR...?
NO, WAIT A MINUTE...
Karina Muno
LEVEL: 2 AGE: 19
SKILLS: --
STATUS: Hungry
IT'S THE DAUGHTER OF BARON MUNO—THE CURRENT LEADER OF THIS TERRITORY.
ZAWA (MURMUR)
ZAWA

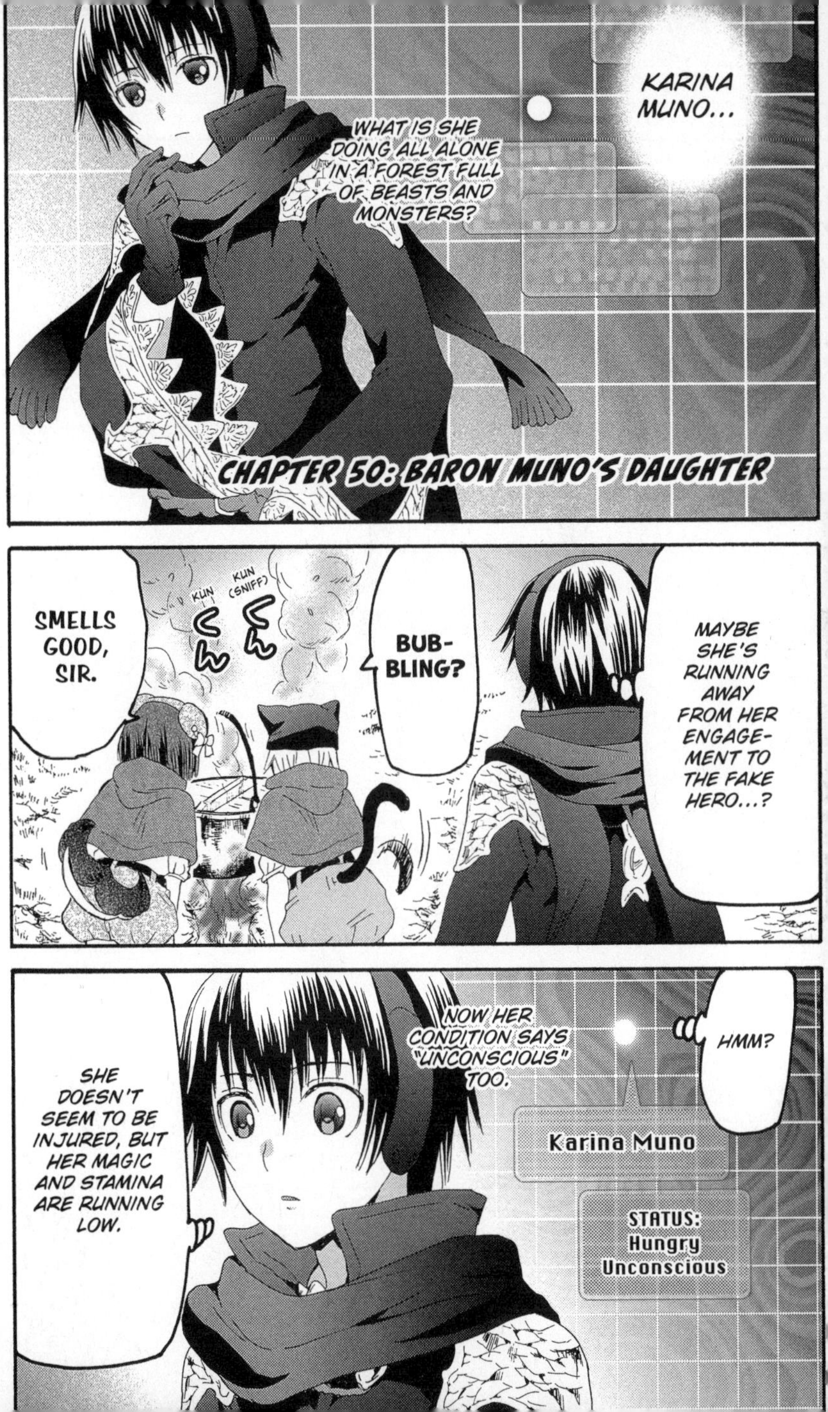
KARINA MUNO...
WHAT IS SHE DOING ALL ALONE IN A FOREST FULL OF BEASTS AND MONSTERS?
CHAPTER 50: BARON MUNO'S DAUGHTER
MAYBE SHE'S RUNNING AWAY FROM HER ENGAGE-MENT TO THE FAKE HERO...?
BUB-BLING?
KUN (SNIFF)
KUN
SMELLS GOOD, SIR.
HMM?
NOW HER CONDITION SAYS "UNCONSCIOUS" TOO.
Karina Muno
STATUS: Hungry Unconscious
SHE DOESN'T SEEM TO BE INJURED, BUT HER MAGIC AND STAMINA ARE RUNNING LOW.

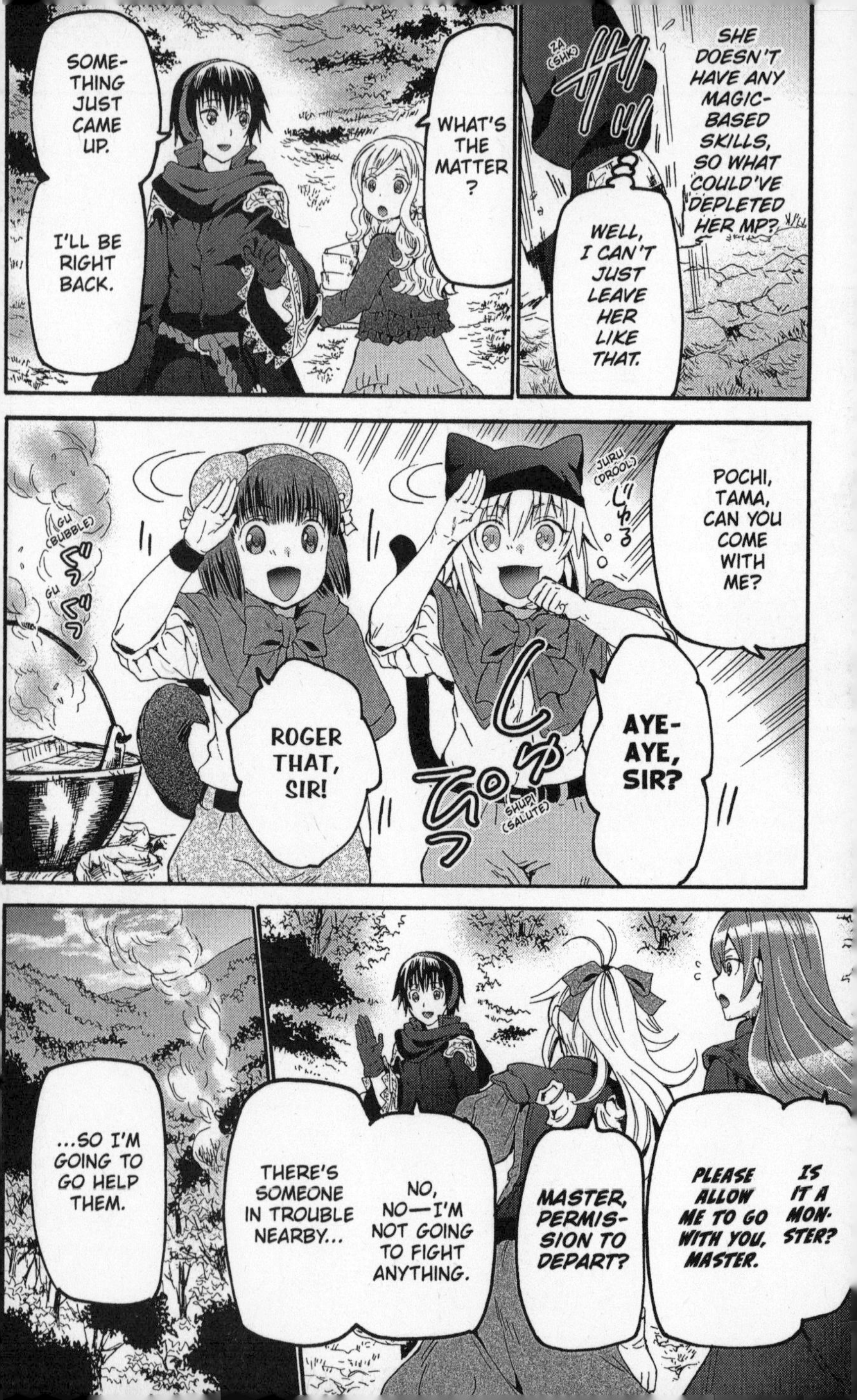
ZA (SHK)
SHE DOESN'T HAVE ANY MAGIC-BASED SKILLS, SO WHAT COULD'VE DEPLETED HER MP?
WELL, I CAN'T JUST LEAVE HER LIKE THAT.
WHAT'S THE MATTER?
SOME-THING JUST CAME UP.
I'LL BE RIGHT BACK.
POCHI, TAMA, CAN YOU COME WITH ME?
JURU (DROOL)
AYE-AYE, SIR?
SHUP! (SALUTE)
ROGER THAT, SIR!
GU (BUBBLE) GU
IS IT A MON-STER?
PLEASE ALLOW ME TO GO WITH YOU, MASTER.
MASTER, PERMIS-SION TO DEPART?
NO, NO—I'M NOT GOING TO FIGHT ANYTHING.
THERE'S SOMEONE IN TROUBLE NEARBY...
...SO I'M GOING TO GO HELP THEM.

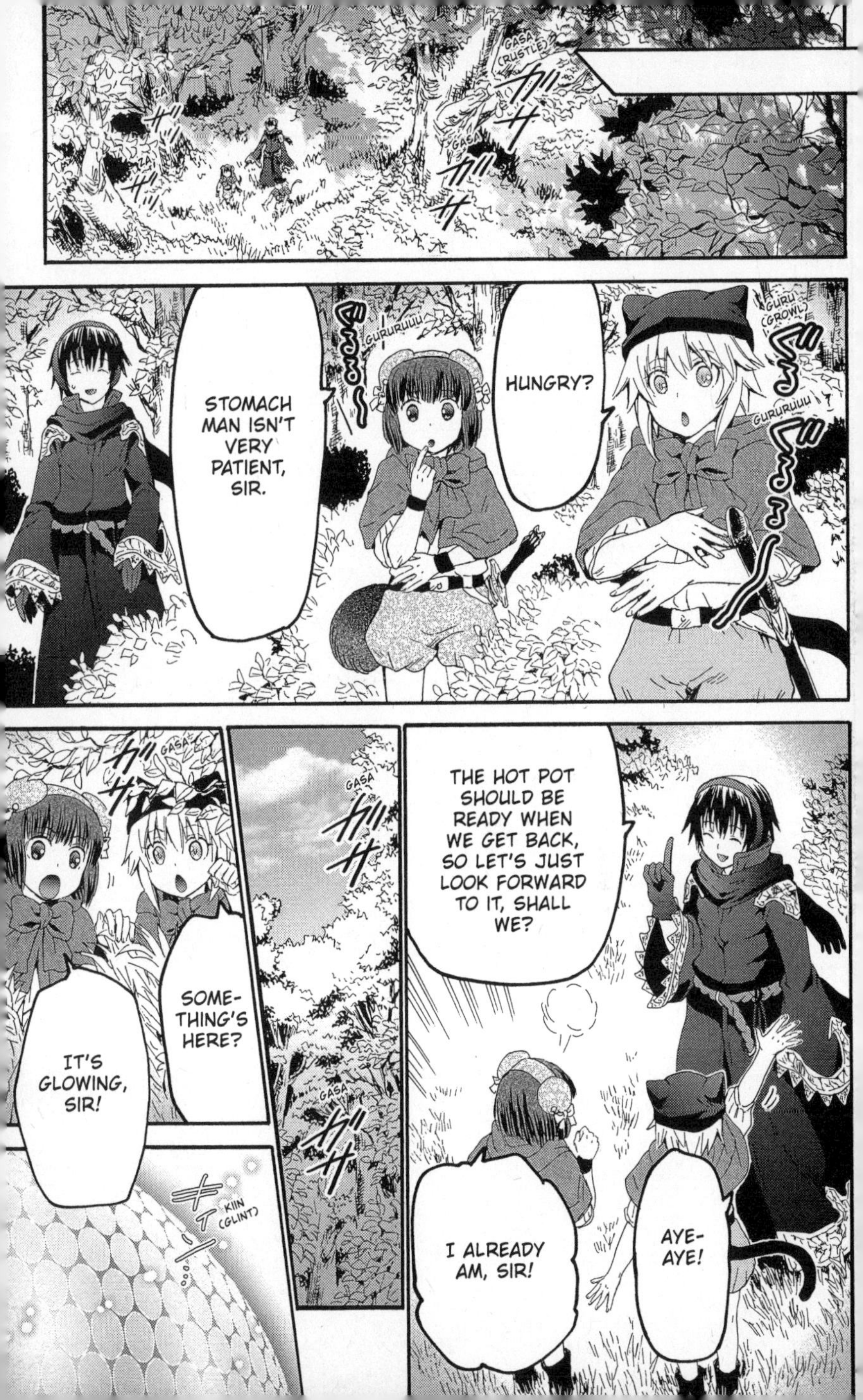
GASA (RUSTLE)
GASA
ZA
ZA
GURU (GROWL)
GURURUUU
HUNGRY?
GURURUUU
STOMACH MAN ISN'T VERY PATIENT, SIR.
THE HOT POT SHOULD BE READY WHEN WE GET BACK, SO LET'S JUST LOOK FORWARD TO IT, SHALL WE?
AYE-AYE!
I ALREADY AM, SIR!
GASA
GASA
GASA
SOME-THING'S HERE?
IT'S GLOWING, SIR!
KIIN (GLINT)

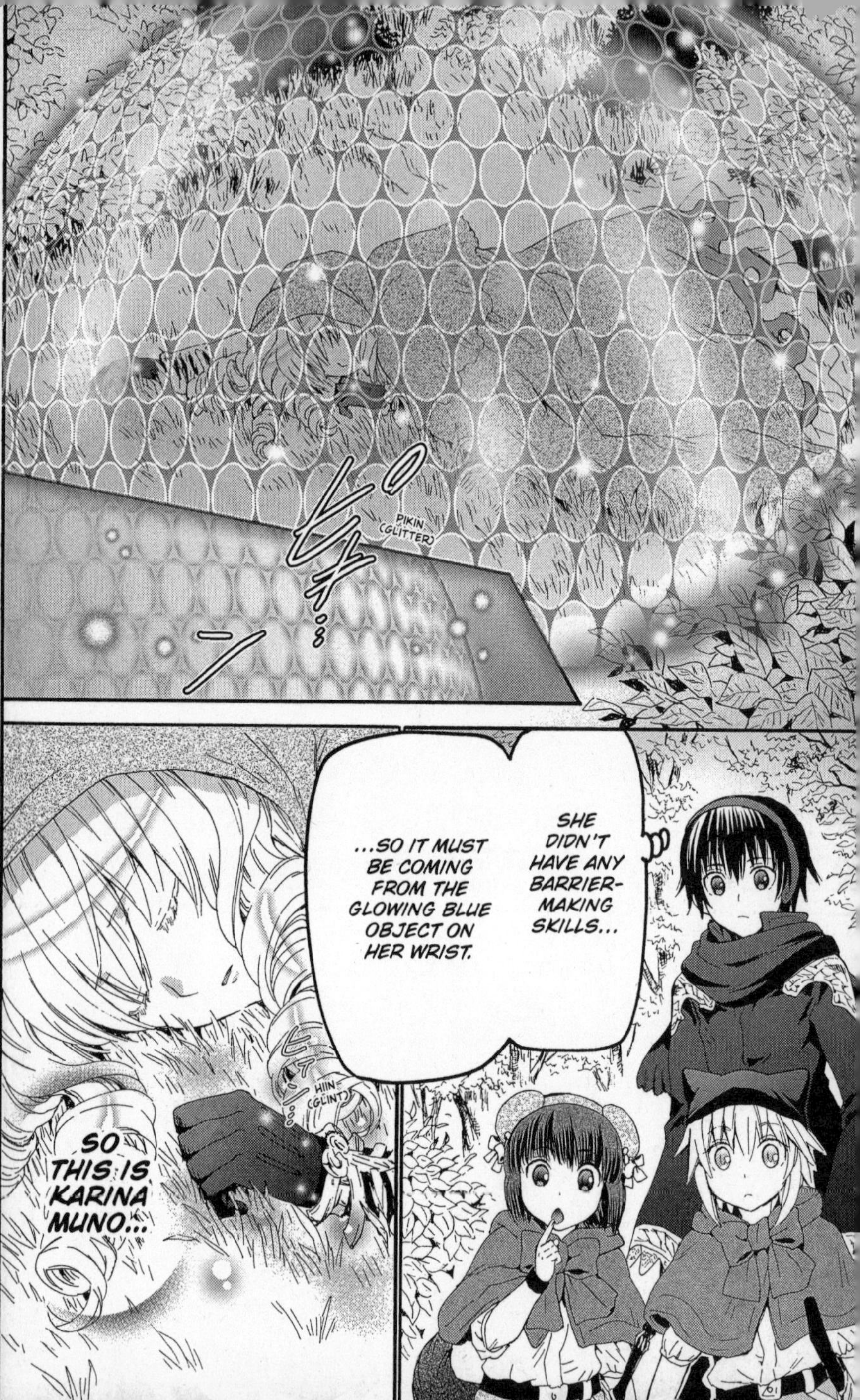
PIKIN (GLITTER)
SHE DIDN'T HAVE ANY BARRIER-MAKING SKILLS...
...SO IT MUST BE COMING FROM THE GLOWING BLUE OBJECT ON HER WRIST.
HIIN (GLINT)
SO THIS IS KARINA MUNO...

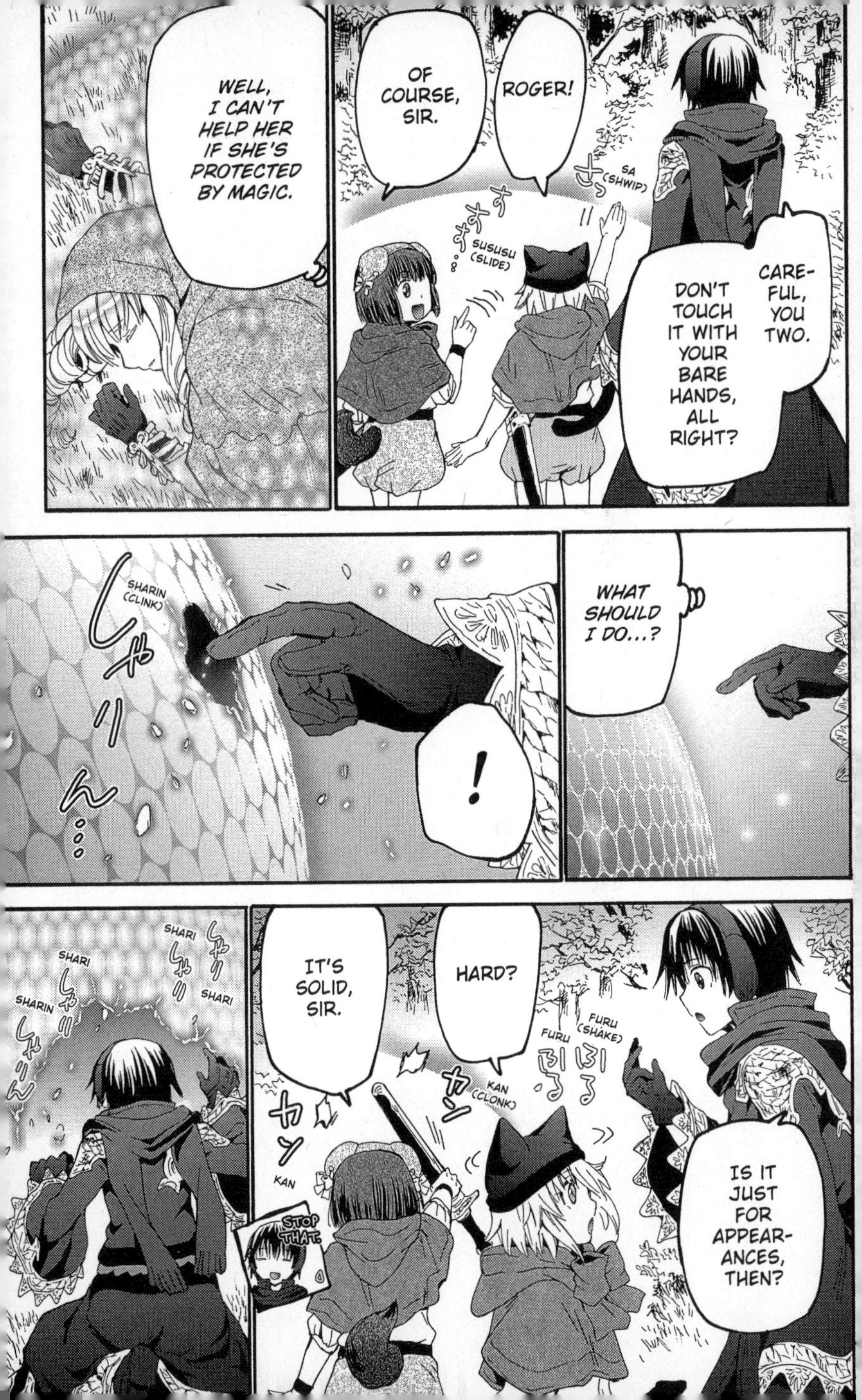
CARE-FUL, YOU TWO.
DON'T TOUCH IT WITH YOUR BARE HANDS, ALL RIGHT?
SA (SHWIP)
ROGER!
OF COURSE, SIR.
SUSUSU (SLIDE)
WELL, I CAN'T HELP HER IF SHE'S PROTECTED BY MAGIC.
WHAT SHOULD I DO...?
!
SHARIN (CLINK)
IS IT JUST FOR APPEAR-ANCES, THEN?
FURU (SHAKE)
FURU
HARD?
IT'S SOLID, SIR.
KAN (CLONK)
KAN
STOP THAT.
SHARI
SHARI
SHARIN

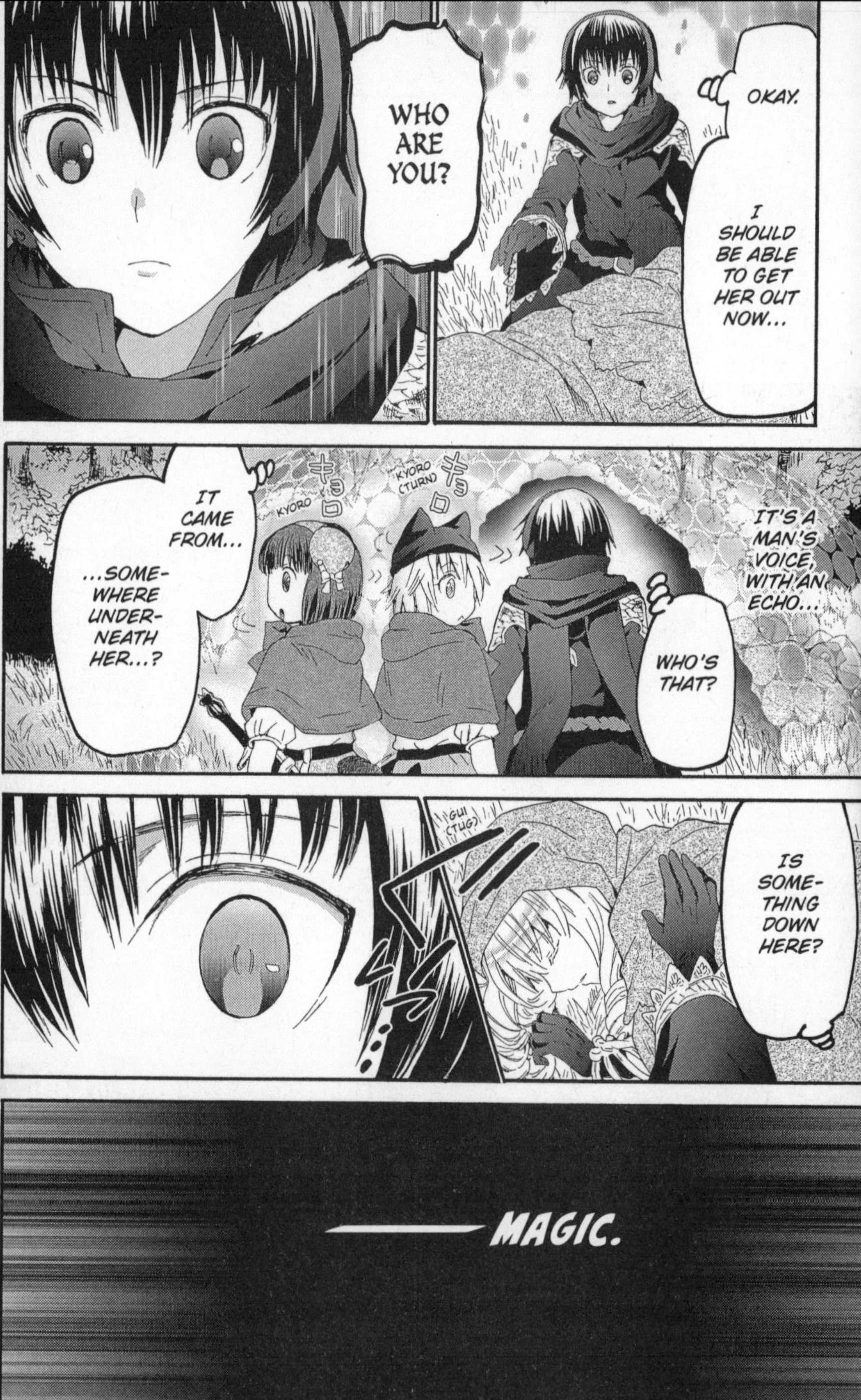
OKAY.
I SHOULD BE ABLE TO GET HER OUT NOW...
WHO ARE YOU?
IT'S A MAN'S VOICE, WITH AN ECHO...
WHO'S THAT?
KYORO (TURN)
KYORO
IT CAME FROM...
...SOME-WHERE UNDER-NEATH HER...?
GUI (TUG)
IS SOME-THING DOWN HERE?
——MAGIC.

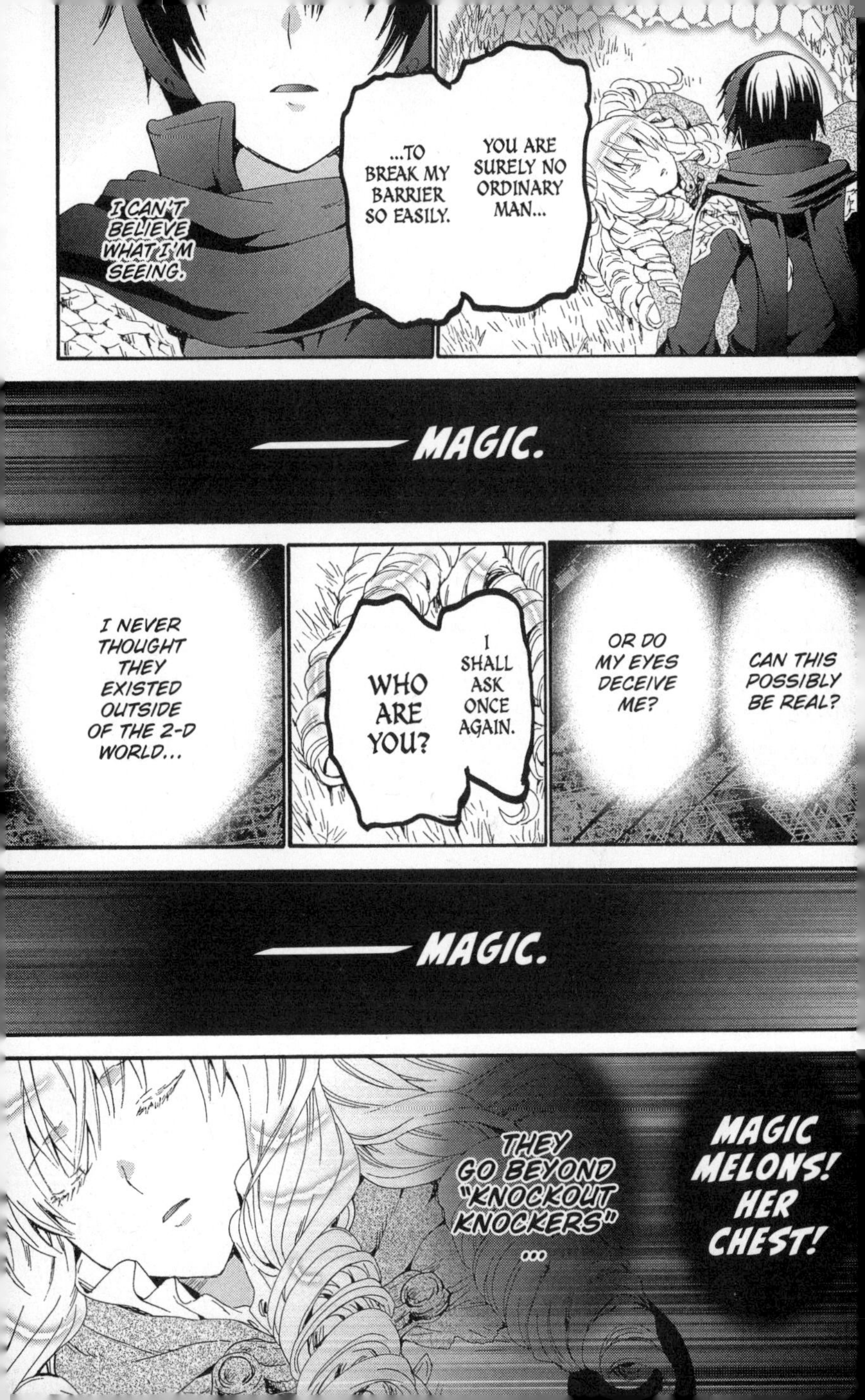
YOU ARE SURELY NO ORDINARY MAN...
...TO BREAK MY BARRIER SO EASILY.
I CAN'T BELIEVE WHAT I'M SEEING.
——MAGIC.
CAN THIS POSSIBLY BE REAL?
OR DO MY EYES DECEIVE ME?
I SHALL ASK ONCE AGAIN.
WHO ARE YOU?
I NEVER THOUGHT THEY EXISTED OUTSIDE OF THE 2-D WORLD...
——MAGIC.
MAGIC MELONS! HER CHEST!
THEY GO BEYOND "KNOCKOUT KNOCKERS"...

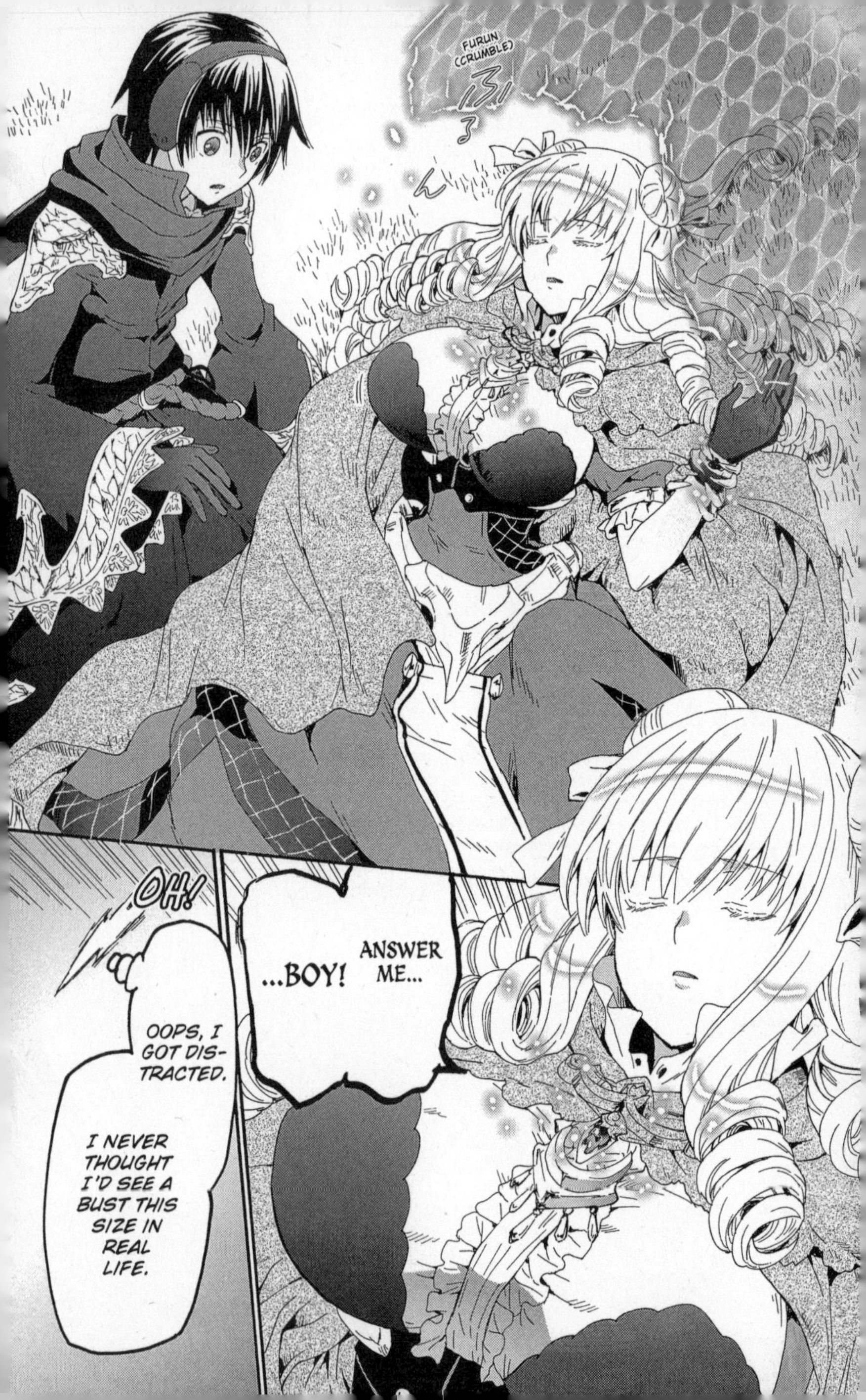
FURUN (CRUMBLE)
ふるん
ANSWER ME...
...BOY!
OH!
OOPS, I GOT DIS-TRACTED.
I NEVER THOUGHT I'D SEE A BUST THIS SIZE IN REAL LIFE.

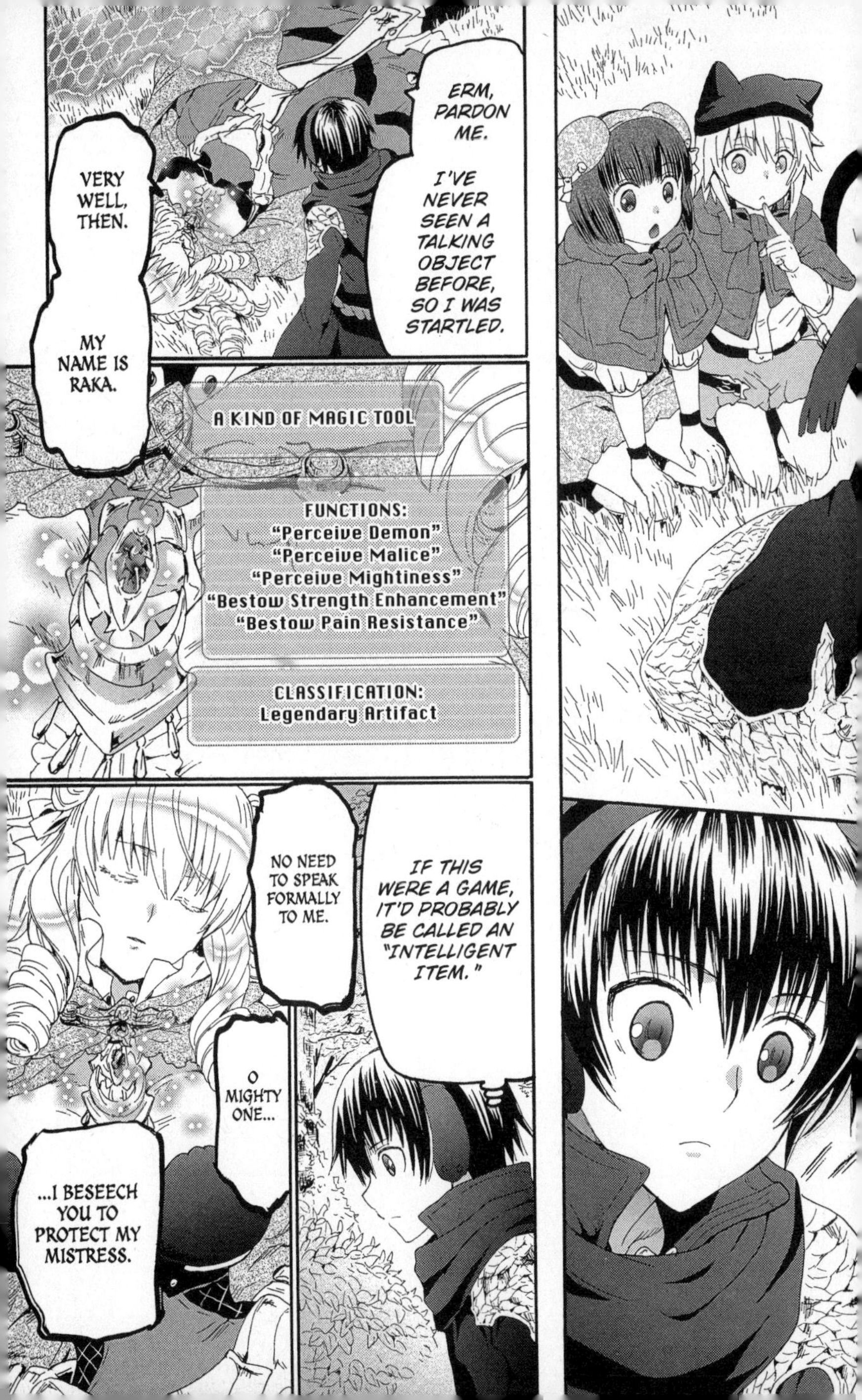
ERM, PARDON ME.
I'VE NEVER SEEN A TALKING OBJECT BEFORE, SO I WAS STARTLED.
VERY WELL, THEN.
MY NAME IS RAKA.
A KIND OF MAGIC TOOL
FUNCTIONS: "Perceive Demon" "Perceive Malice" "Perceive Mightiness" "Bestow Strength Enhancement" "Bestow Pain Resistance"
CLASSIFICATION: Legendary Artifact
IF THIS WERE A GAME, IT'D PROBABLY BE CALLED AN "INTELLIGENT ITEM."
NO NEED TO SPEAK FORMALLY TO ME.
O MIGHTY ONE...
...I BESEECH YOU TO PROTECT MY MISTRESS.

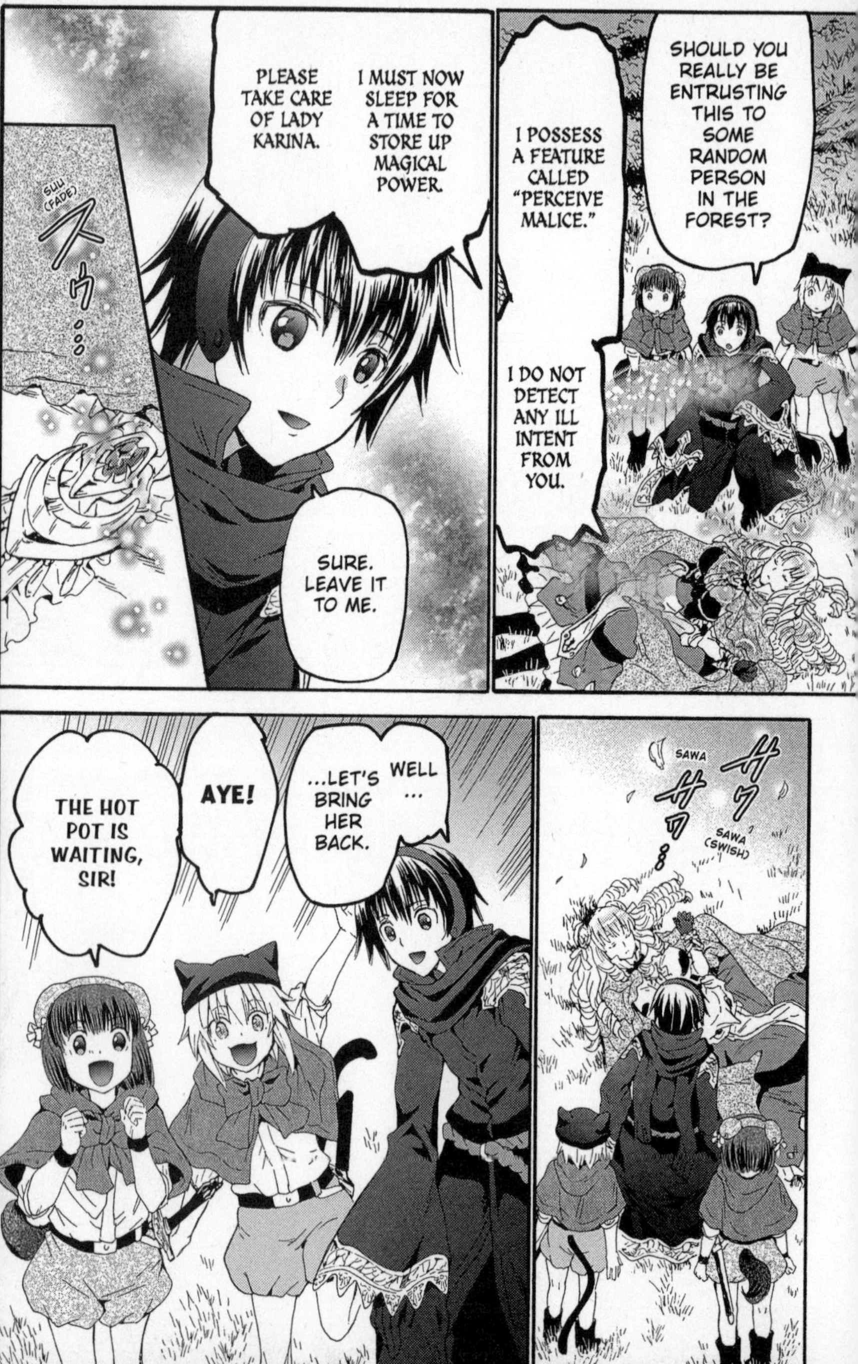
SHOULD YOU REALLY BE ENTRUSTING THIS TO SOME RANDOM PERSON IN THE FOREST?
I POSSESS A FEATURE CALLED "PERCEIVE MALICE."
I DO NOT DETECT ANY ILL INTENT FROM YOU.
I MUST NOW SLEEP FOR A TIME TO STORE UP MAGICAL POWER.
PLEASE TAKE CARE OF LADY KARINA.
SUU (FADE)
スゥ…
SURE. LEAVE IT TO ME.
サワ
SAWA
サワ…
SAWA (SWISH)
WELL…
…LET'S BRING HER BACK.
AYE!
THE HOT POT IS WAITING, SIR!

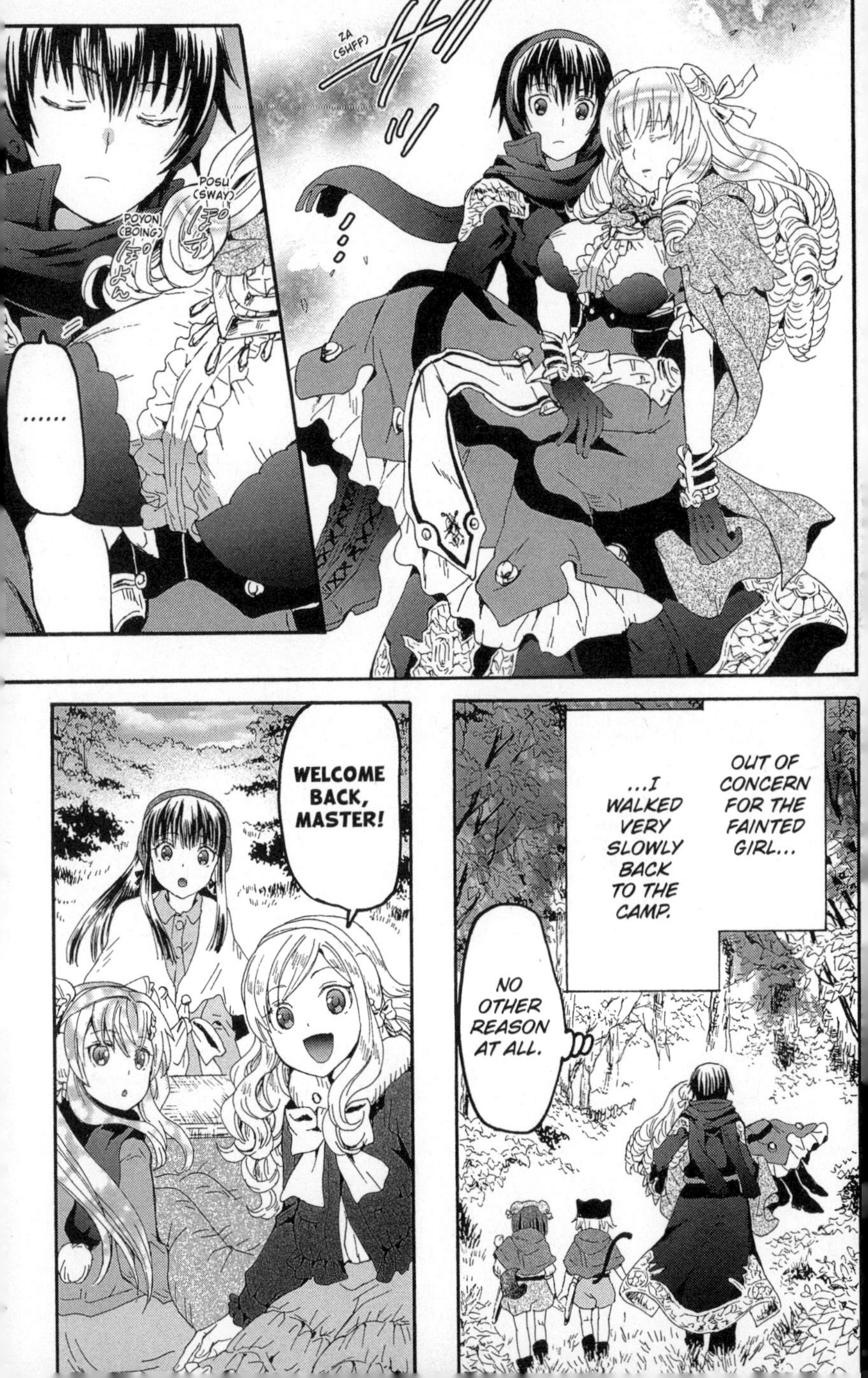
ZA (SHFF)
POSU (SWAY)
POYON (BOING)
......
OUT OF CONCERN FOR THE FAINTED GIRL...
...I WALKED VERY SLOWLY BACK TO THE CAMP.
NO OTHER REASON AT ALL.
WELCOME BACK, MASTER!

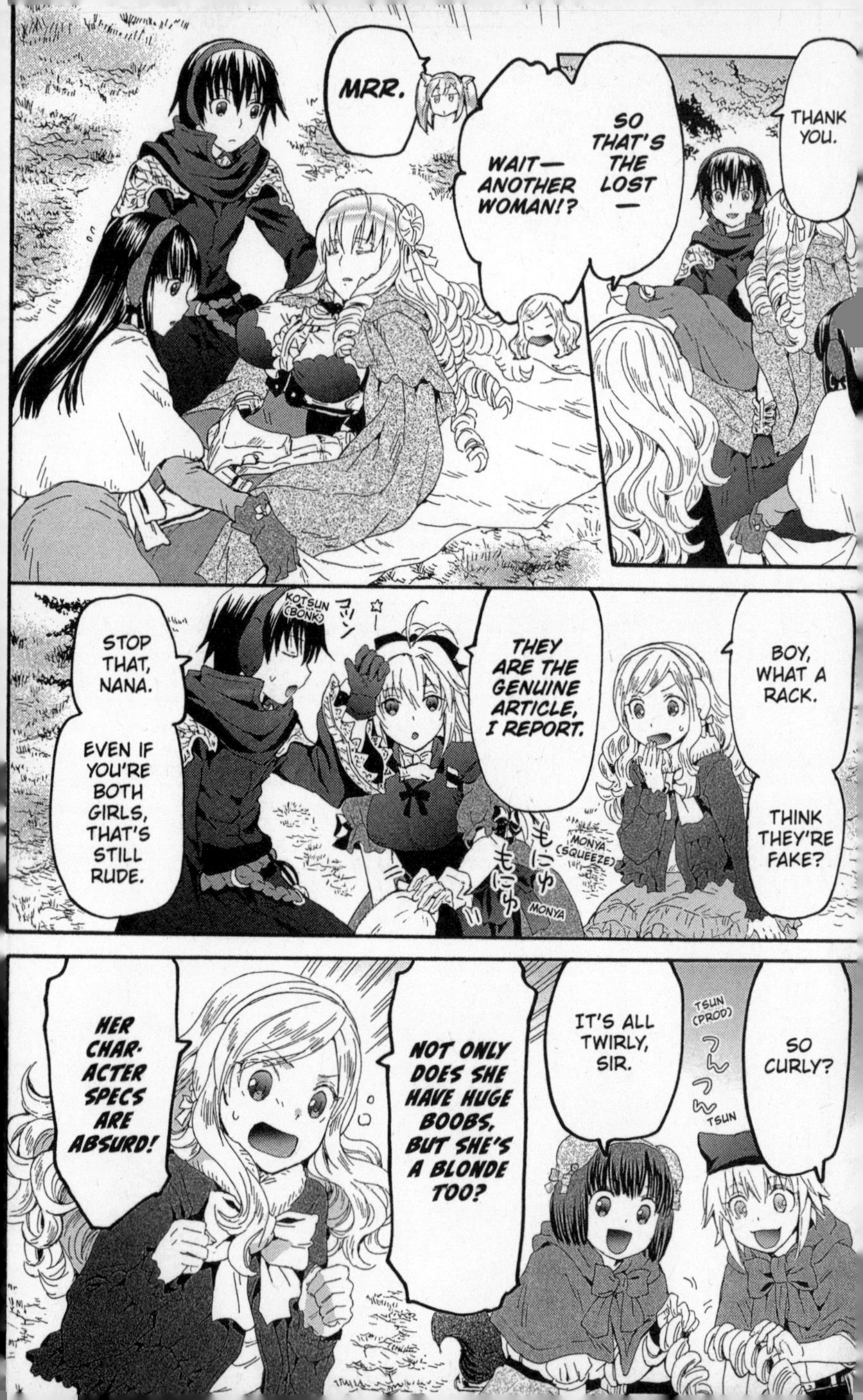
THANK YOU.
SO THAT'S THE LOST—
WAIT—ANOTHER WOMAN!?
MRR.
BOY, WHAT A RACK.
THINK THEY'RE FAKE?
THEY ARE THE GENUINE ARTICLE, I REPORT.
もにゅ もにゅ
MONYA (SQUEEZE)
MONYA
コツン
KOTSUN (BONK)
STOP THAT, NANA.
EVEN IF YOU'RE BOTH GIRLS, THAT'S STILL RUDE.
SO CURLY?
つん つん
TSUN (PROD)
TSUN
IT'S ALL TWIRLY, SIR.
NOT ONLY DOES SHE HAVE HUGE BOOBS, BUT SHE'S A BLONDE TOO?
HER CHARACTER SPECS ARE ABSURD!

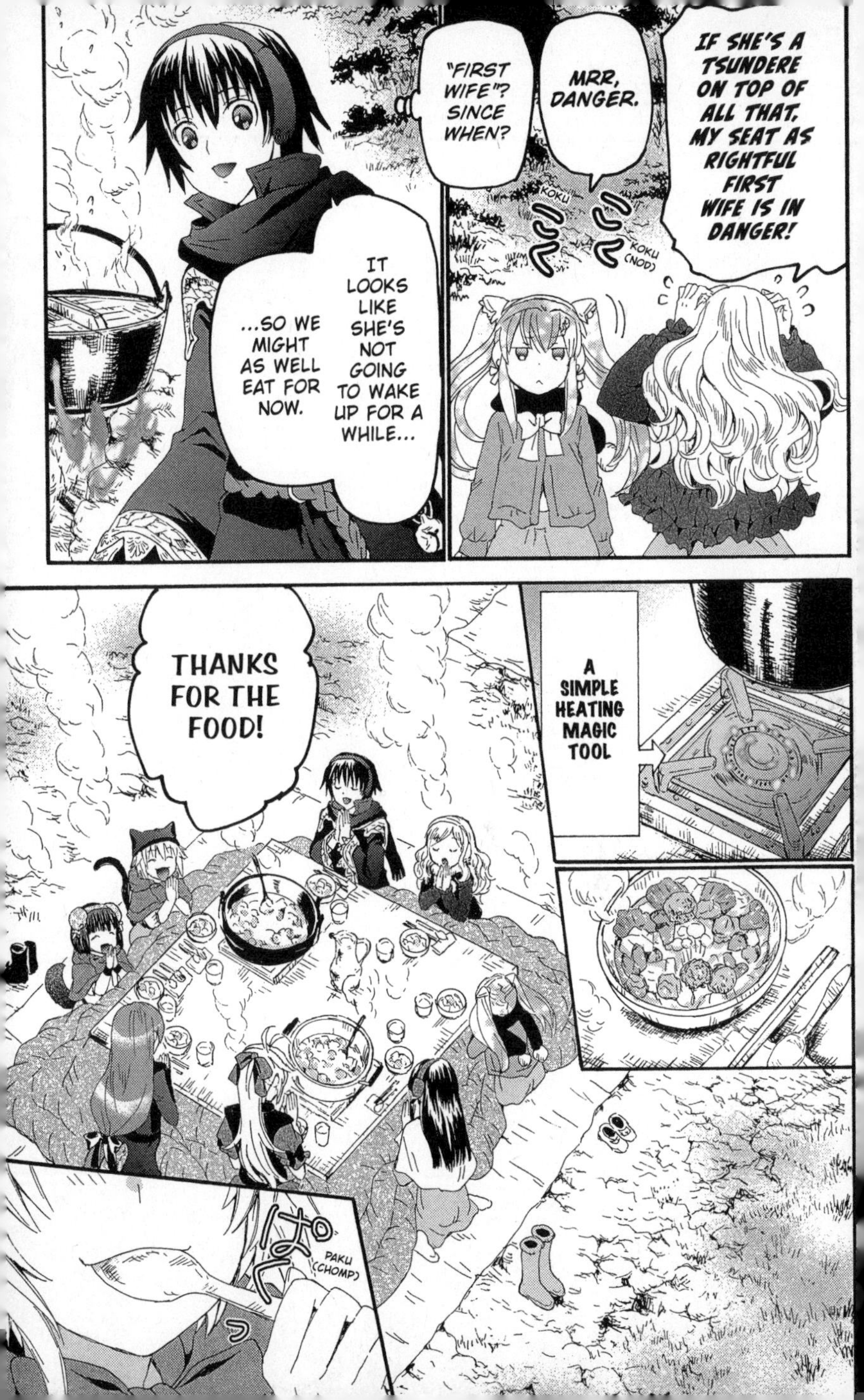
IF SHE'S A TSUNDERE ON TOP OF ALL THAT, MY SEAT AS RIGHTFUL FIRST WIFE IS IN DANGER!
MRR, DANGER.
KOKU
KOKU (NOD)
"FIRST WIFE"? SINCE WHEN?
IT LOOKS LIKE SHE'S NOT GOING TO WAKE UP FOR A WHILE...
...SO WE MIGHT AS WELL EAT FOR NOW.
A SIMPLE HEATING MAGIC TOOL
THANKS FOR THE FOOD!
PAKU (CHOMP)

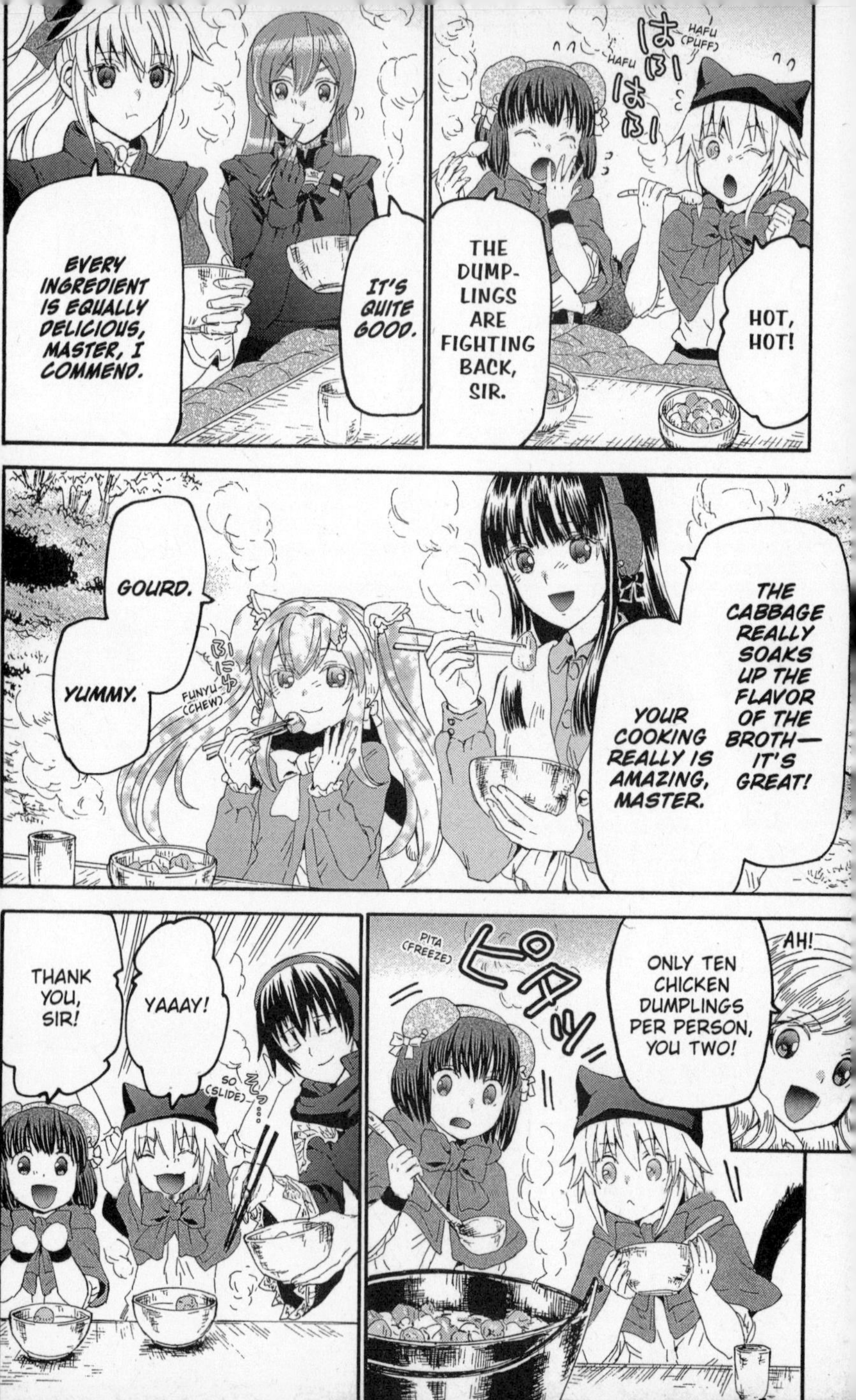
はふはふ
HAFU (PUFF)
HAFU
HOT, HOT!
THE DUMPLINGS ARE FIGHTING BACK, SIR.
IT'S QUITE GOOD.
EVERY INGREDIENT IS EQUALLY DELICIOUS, MASTER, I COMMEND.
THE CABBAGE REALLY SOAKS UP THE FLAVOR OF THE BROTH—IT'S GREAT!
YOUR COOKING REALLY IS AMAZING, MASTER.
ふにゅ
FUNYU (CHEW)
GOURD.
YUMMY.
AH!
ONLY TEN CHICKEN DUMPLINGS PER PERSON, YOU TWO!
ピタッ
PITA (FREEZE)
YAAAY!
THANK YOU, SIR!
そっ
SO (SLIDE)

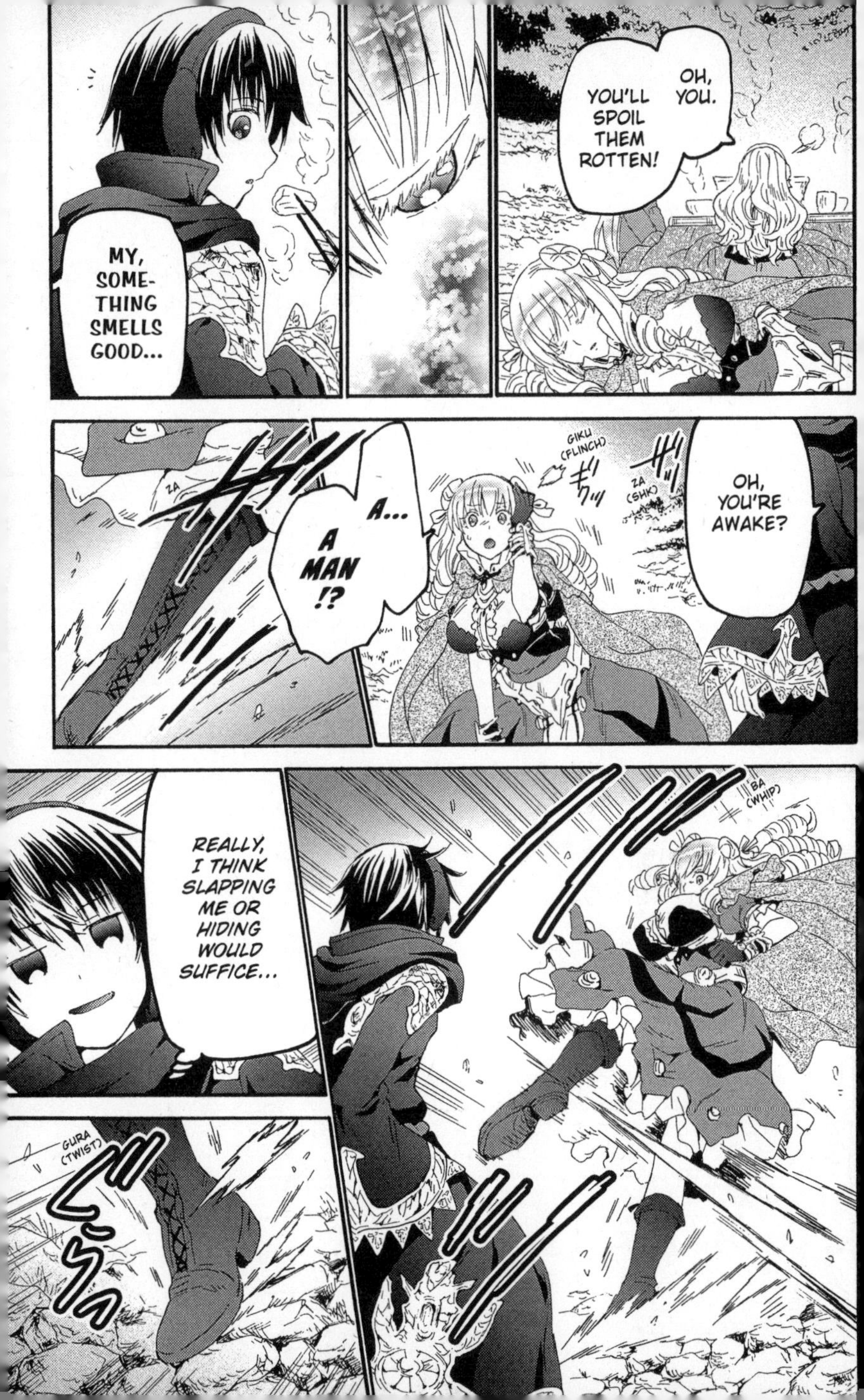
OH, YOU. YOU'LL SPOIL THEM ROTTEN!
MY, SOMETHING SMELLS GOOD...
OH, YOU'RE AWAKE?
ZA (SHK)
GIKU (FLINCH)
A... A MAN!?
ZA
BA (WHIP)
REALLY, I THINK SLAPPING ME OR HIDING WOULD SUFFICE...
GURA (TWIST)

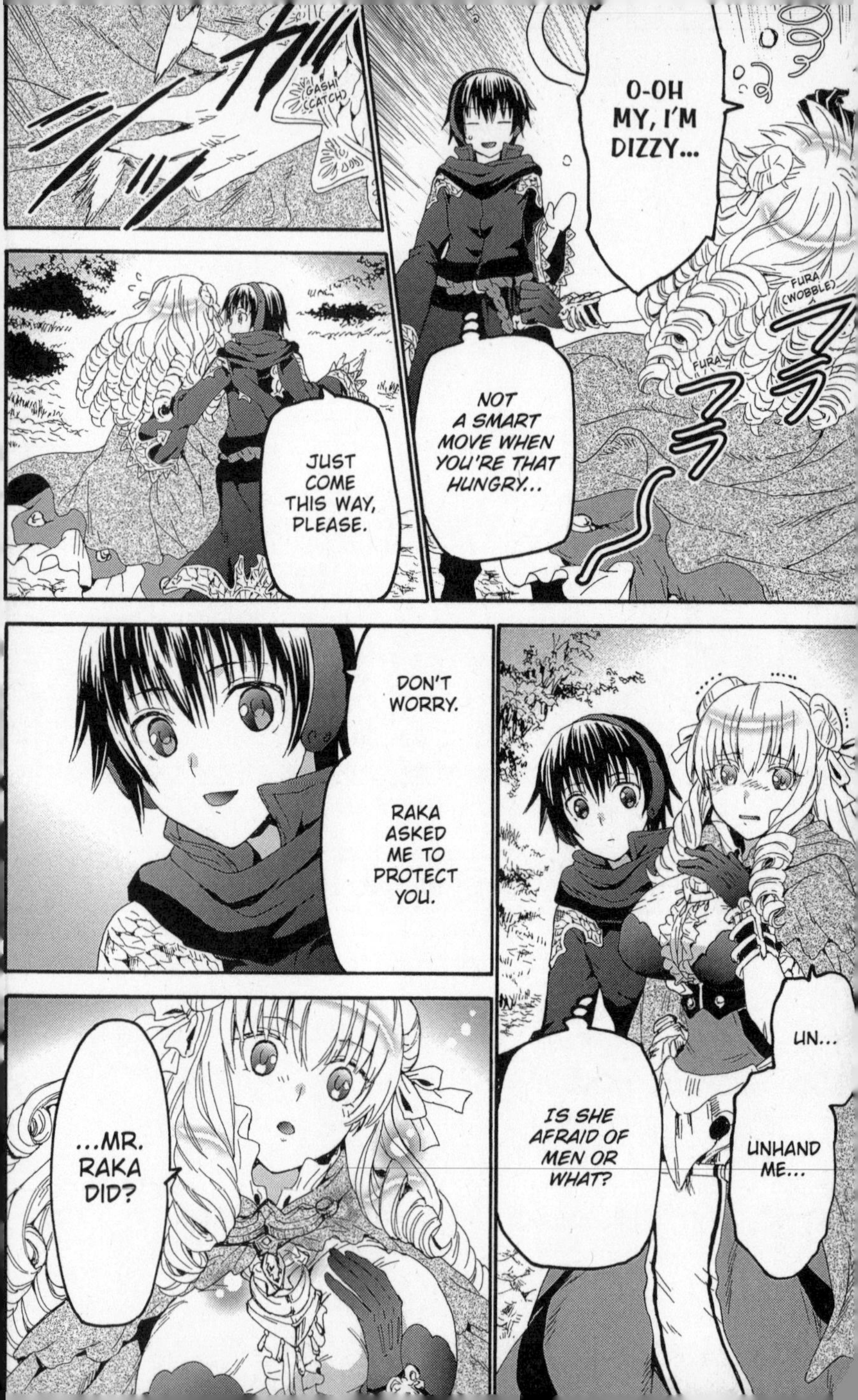
O-OH MY, I'M DIZZY...
FURA (WOBBLE)
FURA
NOT A SMART MOVE WHEN YOU'RE THAT HUNGRY...
GASHI (CATCH)
JUST COME THIS WAY, PLEASE.
UN...
UNHAND ME...
IS SHE AFRAID OF MEN OR WHAT?
DON'T WORRY.
RAKA ASKED ME TO PROTECT YOU.
...MR. RAKA DID?

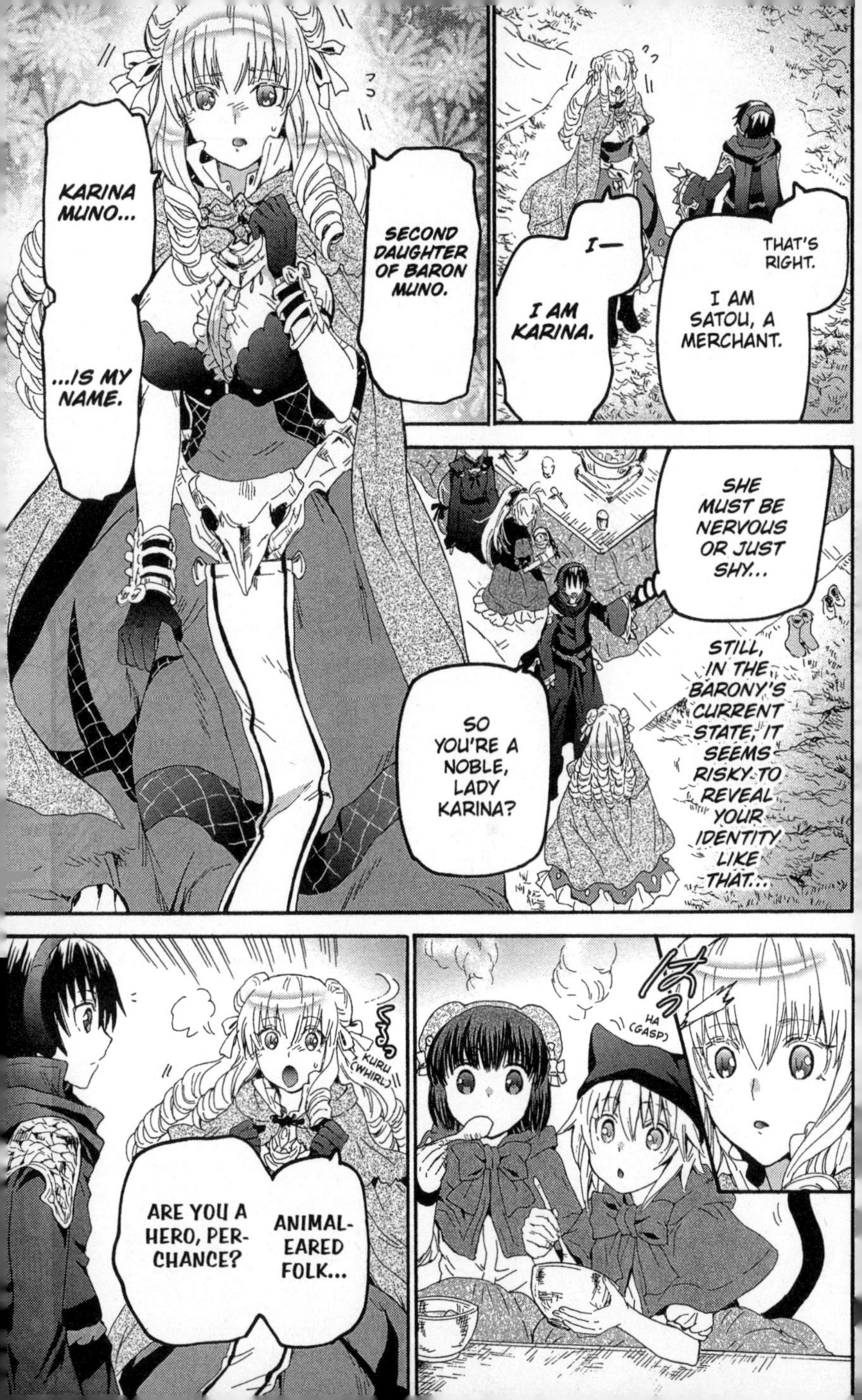
THAT'S RIGHT.
I AM SATOU, A MERCHANT.
I—
I AM KARINA.
SHE MUST BE NERVOUS OR JUST SHY...
STILL, IN THE BARONY'S CURRENT STATE, IT SEEMS RISKY TO REVEAL YOUR IDENTITY LIKE THAT...
SO YOU'RE A NOBLE, LADY KARINA?
SECOND DAUGHTER OF BARON MUNO.
KARINA MUNO...
...IS MY NAME.
HA (GASP)
KURU (WHIRL)
ANIMAL-EARED FOLK...
ARE YOU A HERO, PER-CHANCE?

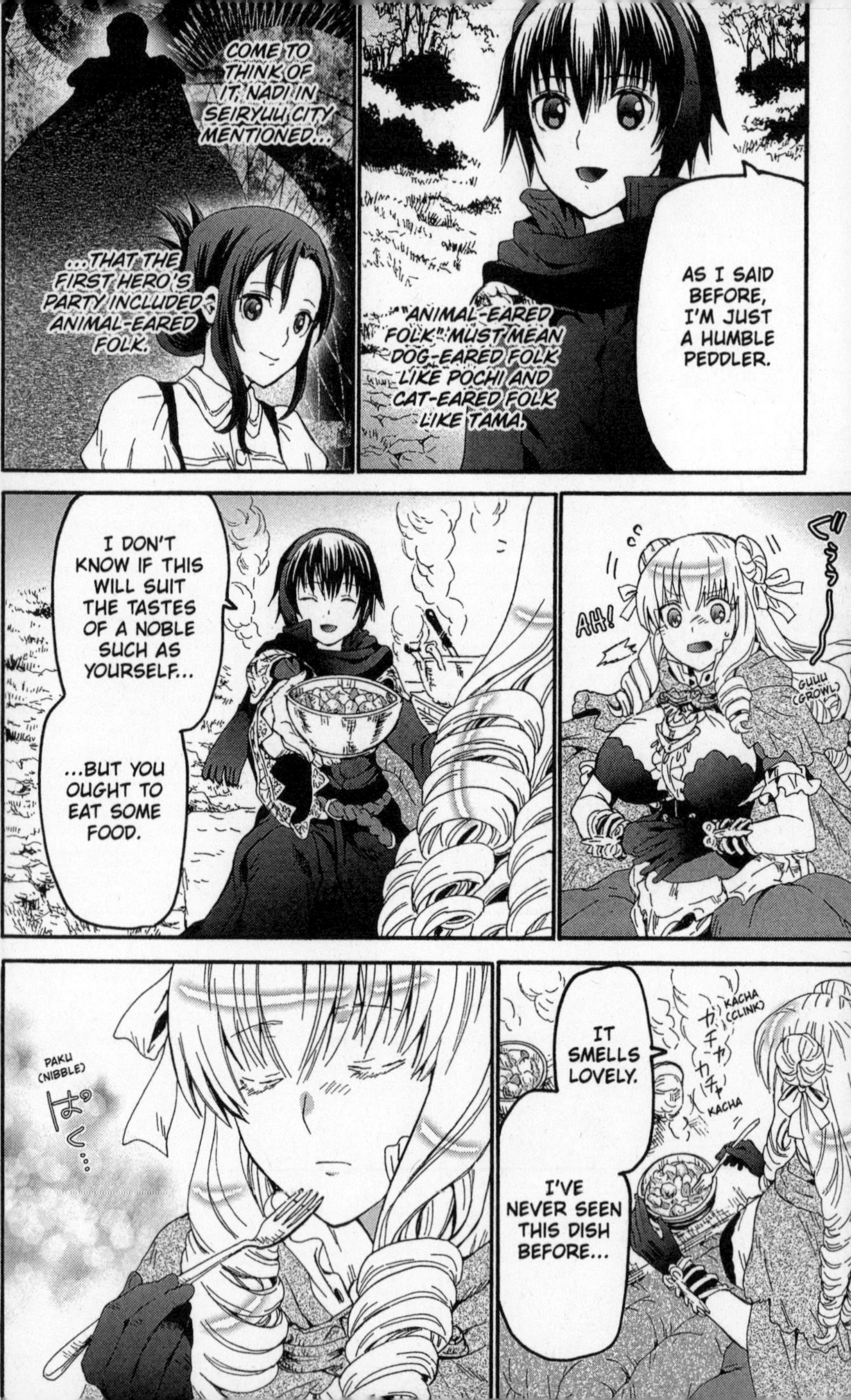
AS I SAID BEFORE, I'M JUST A HUMBLE PEDDLER.
"ANIMAL-EARED FOLK" MUST MEAN DOG-EARED FOLK LIKE POCHI AND CAT-EARED FOLK LIKE TAMA.
COME TO THINK OF IT, NADI IN SEIRYUU CITY MENTIONED...
...THAT THE FIRST HERO'S PARTY INCLUDED ANIMAL-EARED FOLK.
GUUU (GROWL)
AH!
I DON'T KNOW IF THIS WILL SUIT THE TASTES OF A NOBLE SUCH AS YOURSELF...
...BUT YOU OUGHT TO EAT SOME FOOD.
KACHA (CLINK)
カチャ
IT SMELLS LOVELY.
カチャ
KACHA
I'VE NEVER SEEN THIS DISH BEFORE...
PAKU (NIBBLE)
ぱく...

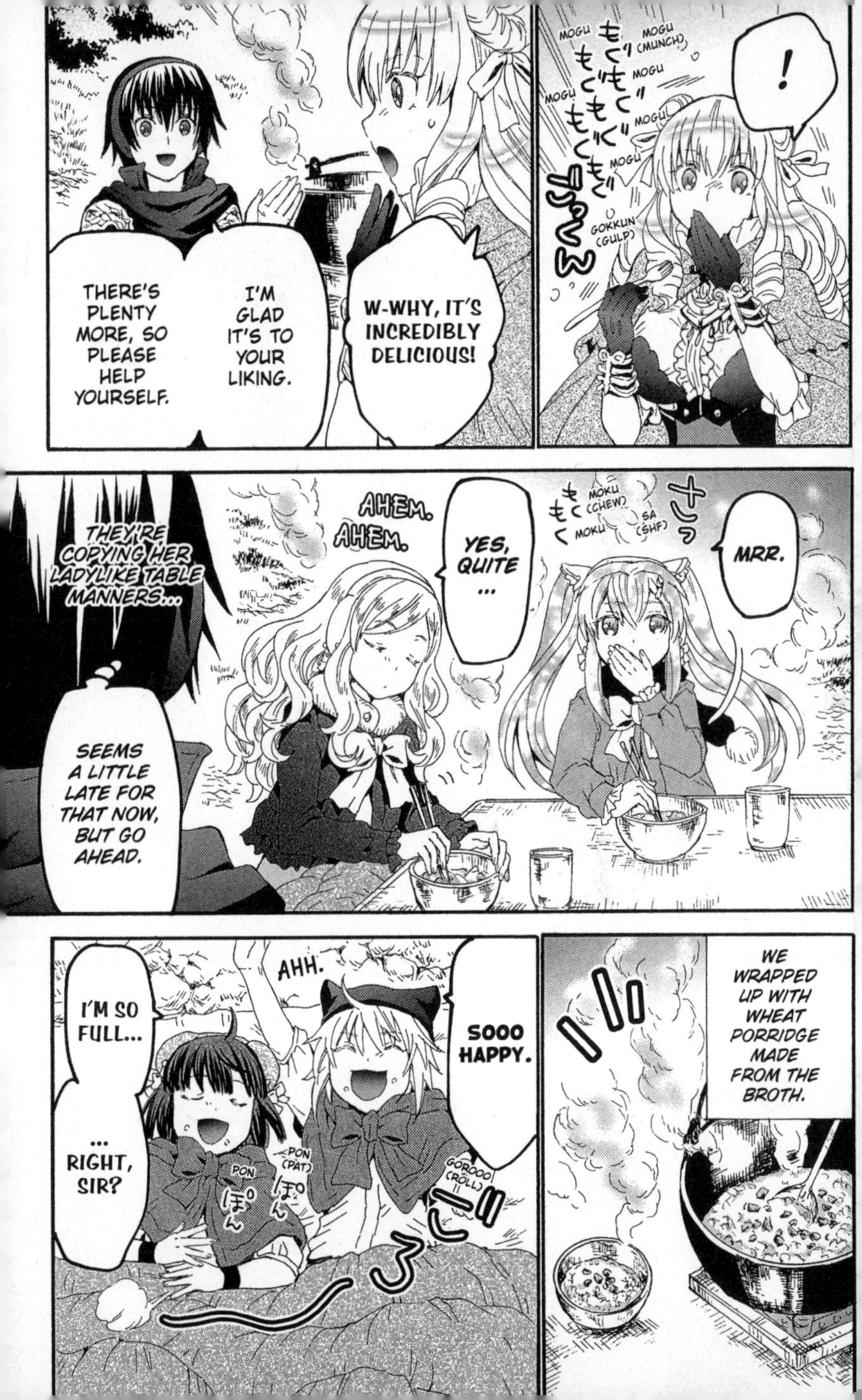

MOGU MOGU (MUNCH)
MOGU
MOGU
MOGU
MOGU
!
GOKKUN (GULP)
W-WHY, IT'S INCREDIBLY DELICIOUS!
I'M GLAD IT'S TO YOUR LIKING.
THERE'S PLENTY MORE, SO PLEASE HELP YOURSELF.
MRR.
SA (SHF)
MOKU (CHEW) MOKU
YES, QUITE ...
AHEM. AHEM.
THEY'RE COPYING HER LADYLIKE TABLE MANNERS...
SEEMS A LITTLE LATE FOR THAT NOW, BUT GO AHEAD.
WE WRAPPED UP WITH WHEAT PORRIDGE MADE FROM THE BROTH.
SOOO HAPPY.
AHH.
GOROOO (ROLL)
PON (PAT)
PON
I'M SO FULL...
... RIGHT, SIR?

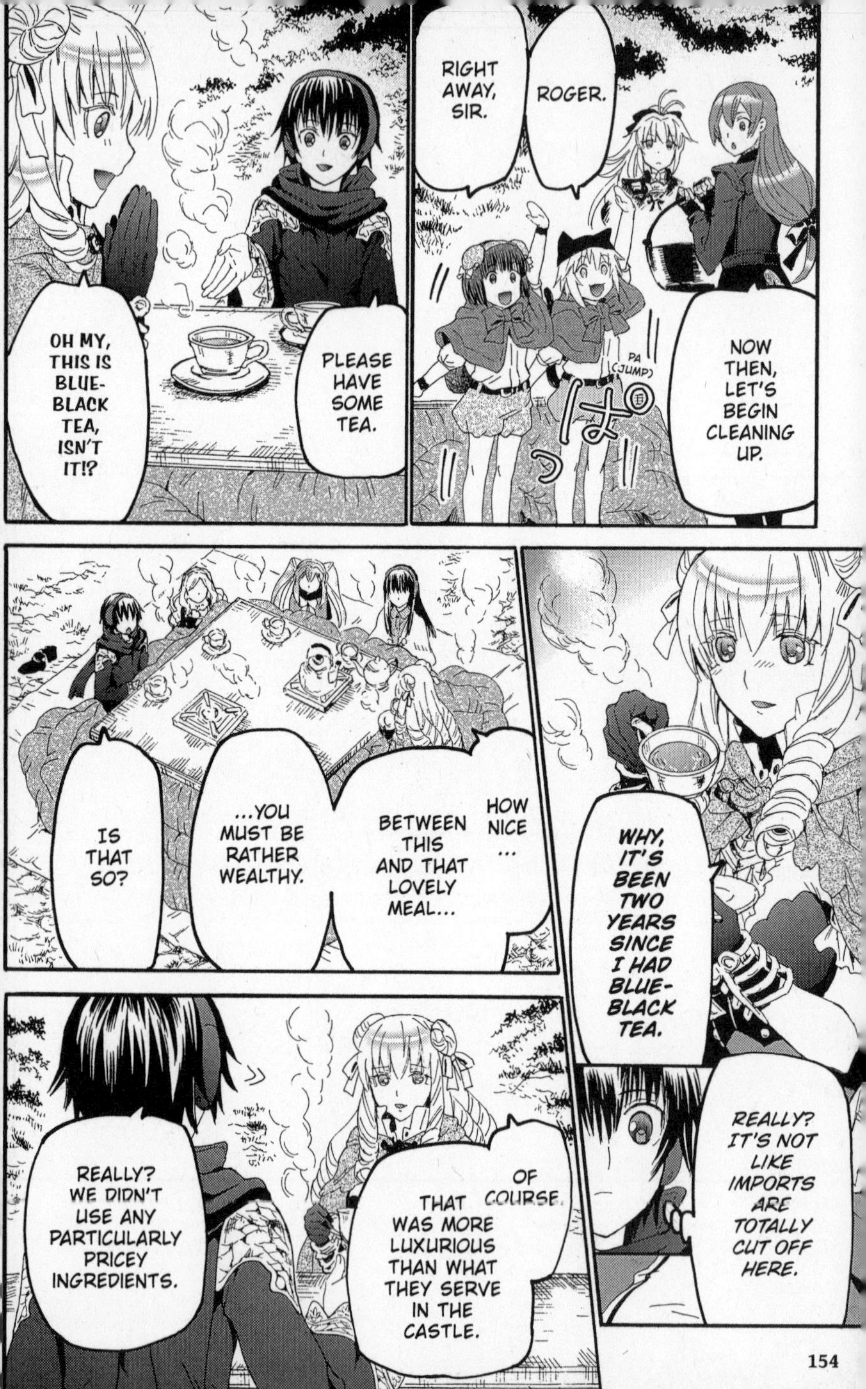
ROGER.
RIGHT AWAY, SIR.
NOW THEN, LET'S BEGIN CLEANING UP.
PA (JUMP)
ぱっ
PLEASE HAVE SOME TEA.
OH MY, THIS IS BLUE-BLACK TEA, ISN'T IT!?
WHY, IT'S BEEN TWO YEARS SINCE I HAD BLUE-BLACK TEA.
HOW NICE...
BETWEEN THIS AND THAT LOVELY MEAL...
...YOU MUST BE RATHER WEALTHY.
IS THAT SO?
REALLY? IT'S NOT LIKE IMPORTS ARE TOTALLY CUT OFF HERE.
OF COURSE.
THAT WAS MORE LUXURIOUS THAN WHAT THEY SERVE IN THE CASTLE.
REALLY? WE DIDN'T USE ANY PARTICULARLY PRICEY INGREDIENTS.

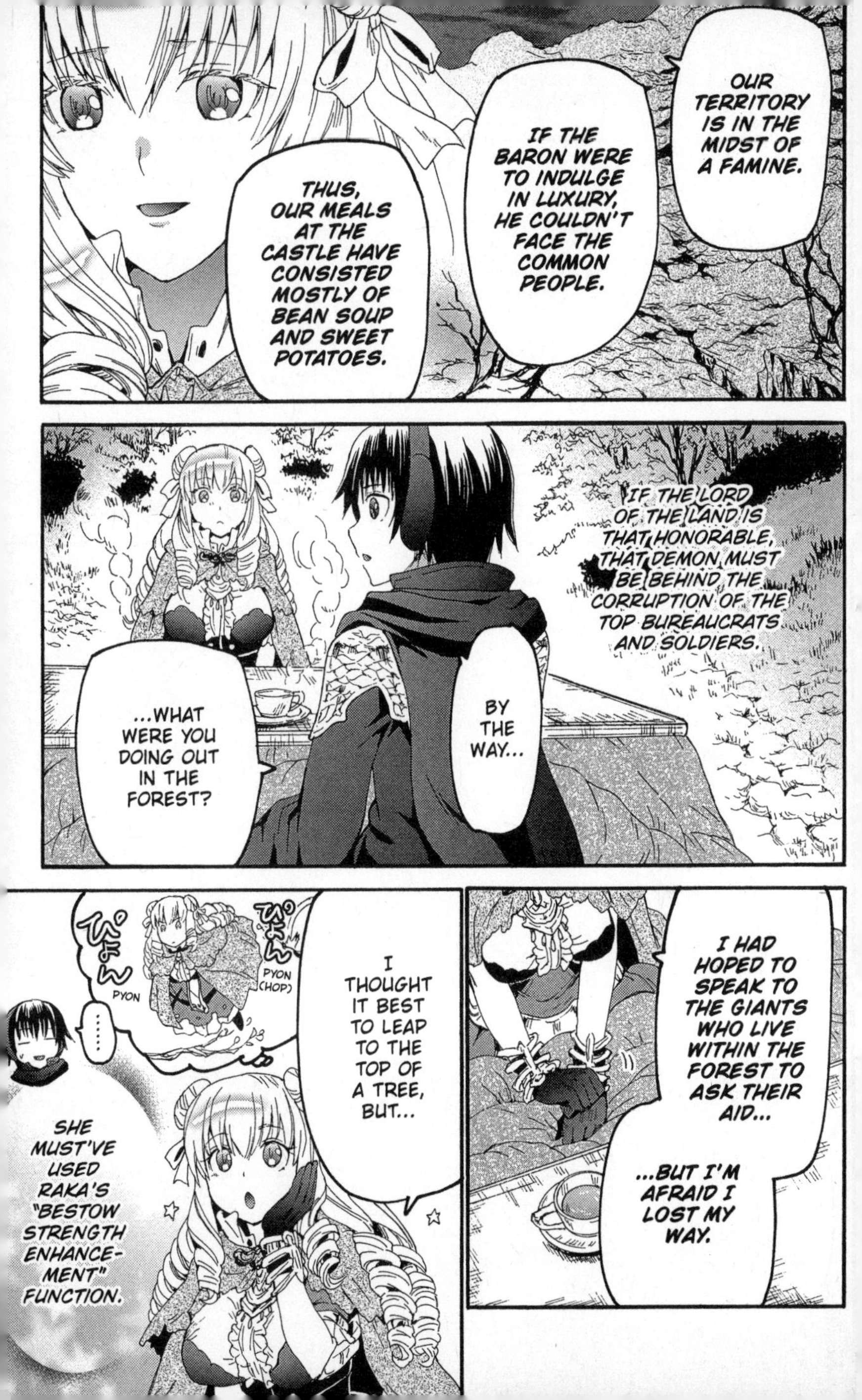
OUR TERRITORY IS IN THE MIDST OF A FAMINE.
IF THE BARON WERE TO INDULGE IN LUXURY, HE COULDN'T FACE THE COMMON PEOPLE.
THUS, OUR MEALS AT THE CASTLE HAVE CONSISTED MOSTLY OF BEAN SOUP AND SWEET POTATOES.
IF THE LORD OF THE LAND IS THAT HONORABLE, THAT DEMON MUST BE BEHIND THE CORRUPTION OF THE TOP BUREAUCRATS AND SOLDIERS.
BY THE WAY...
...WHAT WERE YOU DOING OUT IN THE FOREST?
I HAD HOPED TO SPEAK TO THE GIANTS WHO LIVE WITHIN THE FOREST TO ASK THEIR AID...
...BUT I'M AFRAID I LOST MY WAY.
I THOUGHT IT BEST TO LEAP TO THE TOP OF A TREE, BUT...
ぴょん
PYON (HOP)
ぴょん
PYON
......
SHE MUST'VE USED RAKA'S "BESTOW STRENGTH ENHANCEMENT" FUNCTION.

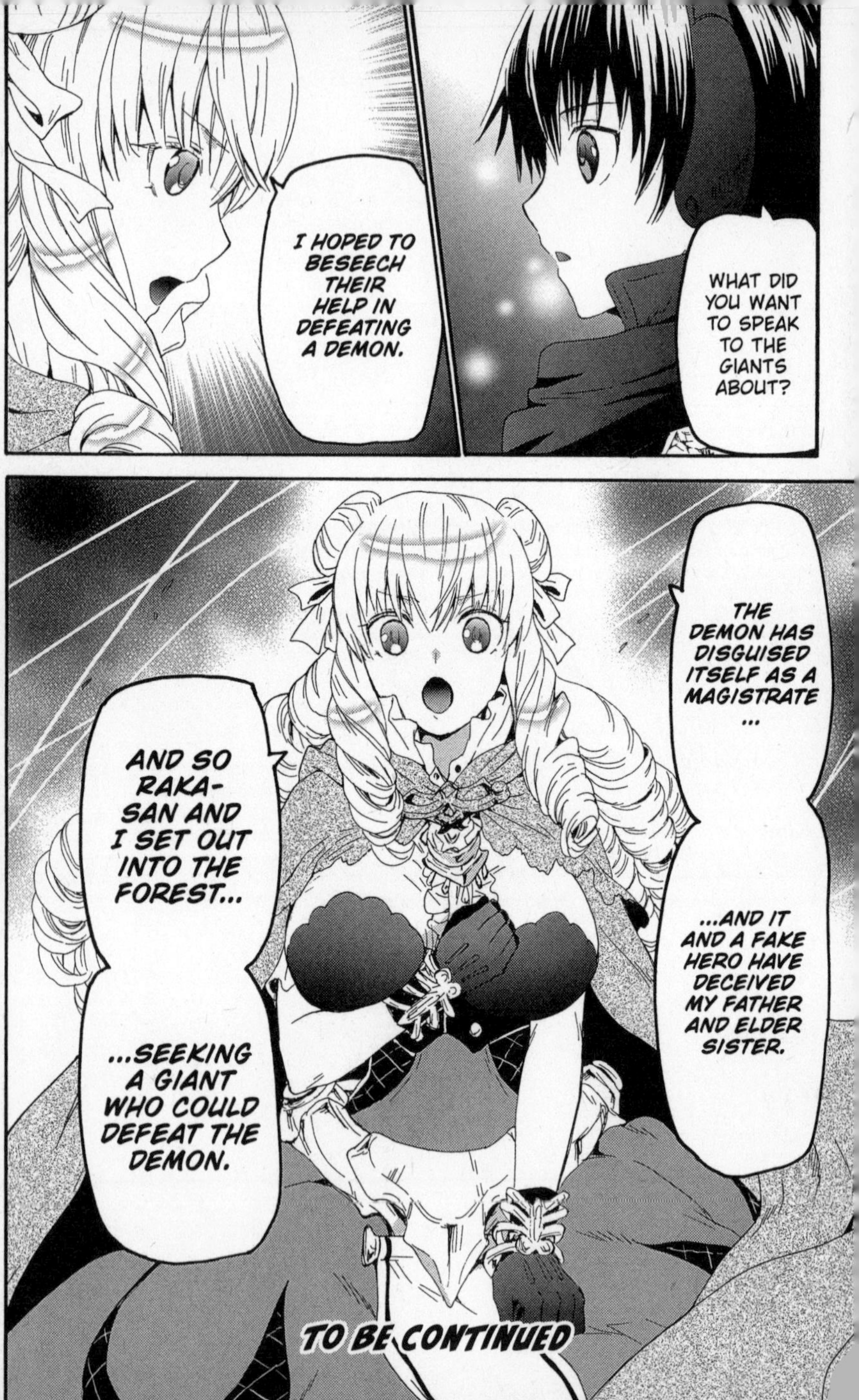
WHAT DID YOU WANT TO SPEAK TO THE GIANTS ABOUT?
I HOPED TO BESEECH THEIR HELP IN DEFEATING A DEMON.
THE DEMON HAS DISGUISED ITSELF AS A MAGISTRATE ...
...AND IT AND A FAKE HERO HAVE DECEIVED MY FATHER AND ELDER SISTER.
AND SO RAKA-SAN AND I SET OUT INTO THE FOREST...
...SEEKING A GIANT WHO COULD DEFEAT THE DEMON.
TO BE CONTINUED

This is Volume 8.

Miss Karina of the Muno Barony finally makes her appearance. I'm sure you've all been looking forward to this.

I took the utmost care to draw the "magic melons" just right.

I hope we can meet again in the next volume. Thank you very much.

-Ayamegumu

...Special Thanks

● Manuscript production collaborators
Kaname Yukishiro-sama

Satoru Ezaki-sama
Yuna Kobayashi-sama

Hacchan-sama

● Editors
Toyohara-sama
Hagiwara-sama
Kuwazuru-sama
Arakawa-sama
Ishiguro-sama

● Binding
coil-sama

● Supervision
Hiro Ainana-sama
shri-sama

● Everyone who helped with the production and publication of this book

And you!

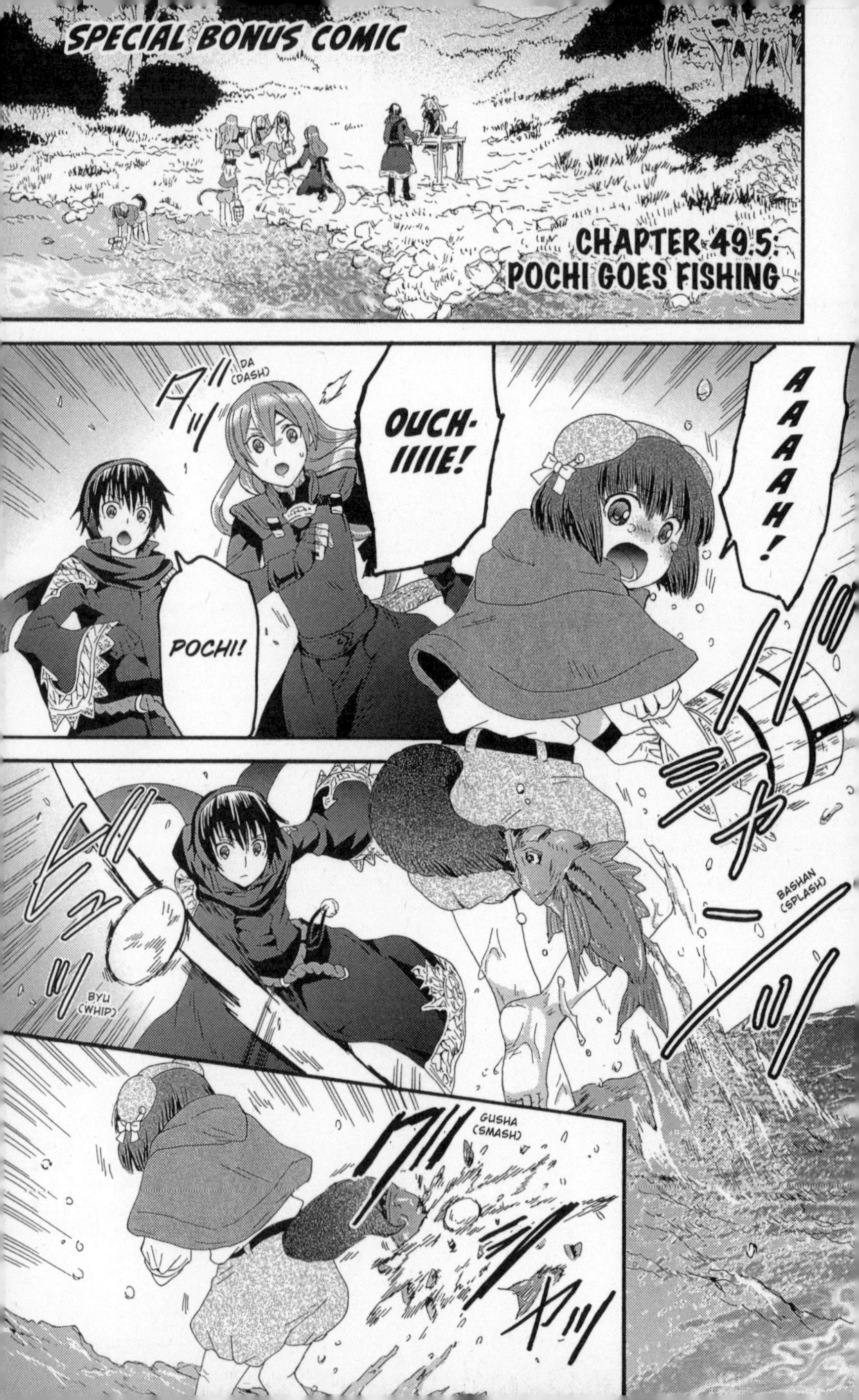
SPECIAL BONUS COMIC
CHAPTER 49.5: POCHI GOES FISHING
AAAAAH!
OUCH-IIIIE!
DA (DASH)
POCHI!
BASHAN (SPLASH)
BYU (WHIP)
GUSHA (SMASH)

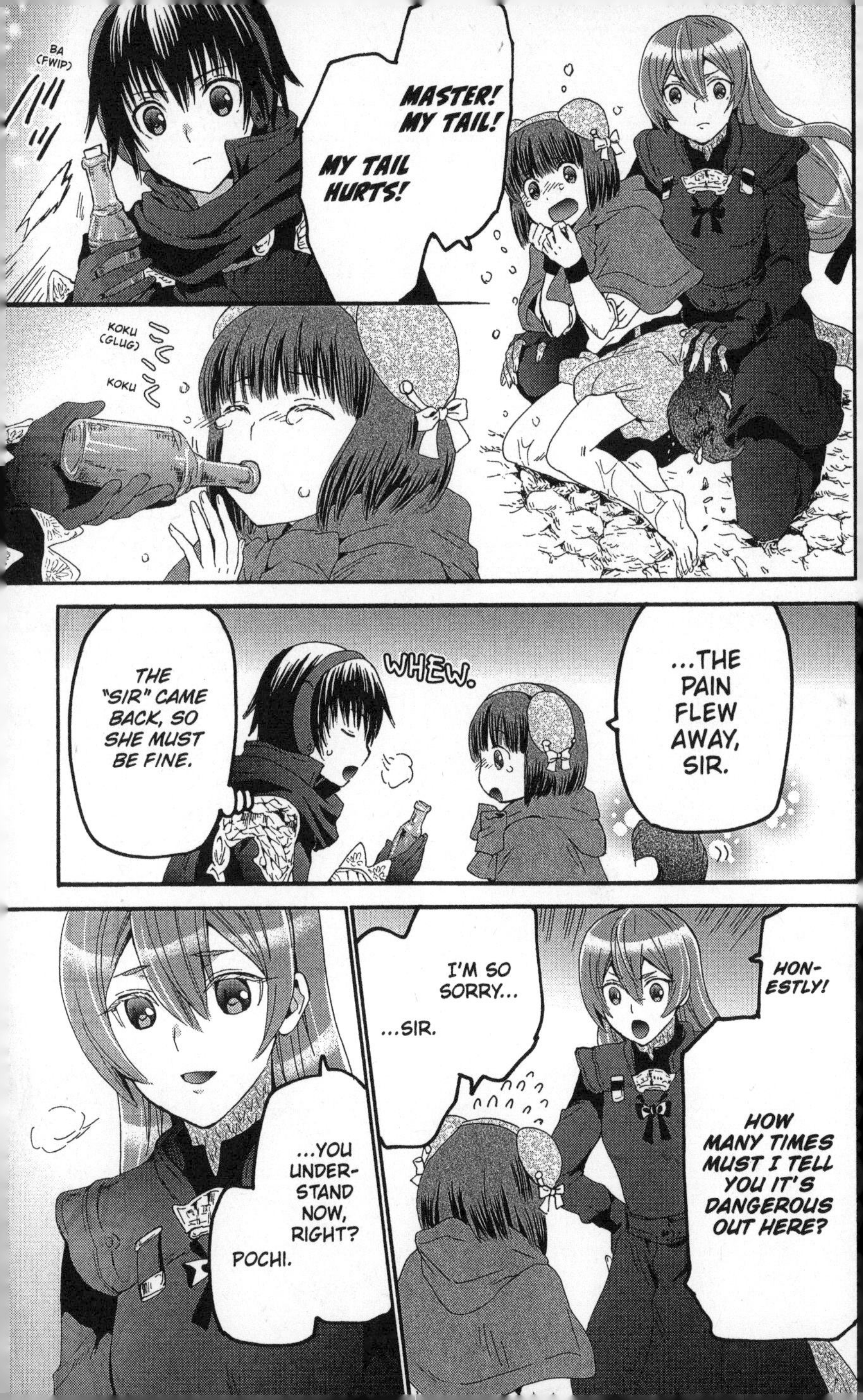
MASTER! MY TAIL!
MY TAIL HURTS!
BA (FWIP)
KOKU (GLUG)
KOKU
...THE PAIN FLEW AWAY, SIR.
WHEW.
THE "SIR" CAME BACK, SO SHE MUST BE FINE.
HON-ESTLY!
HOW MANY TIMES MUST I TELL YOU IT'S DANGEROUS OUT HERE?
I'M SO SORRY...
...SIR.
...YOU UNDER-STAND NOW, RIGHT?
POCHI.

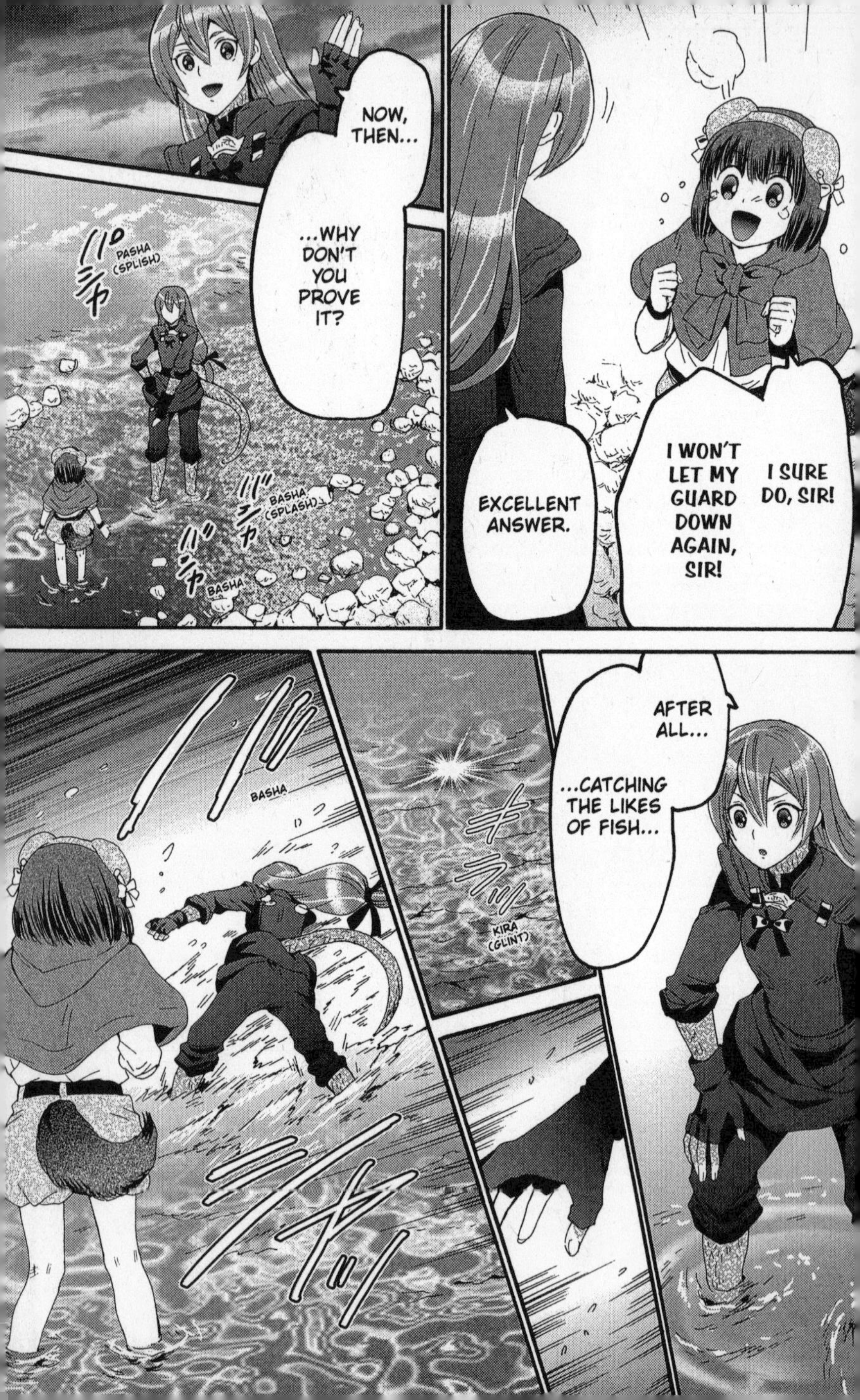
I SURE DO, SIR!
I WON'T LET MY GUARD DOWN AGAIN, SIR!
EXCELLENT ANSWER.
NOW, THEN...
...WHY DON'T YOU PROVE IT?
PASHA (SPLISH)
BASHA (SPLASH)
BASHA
AFTER ALL...
...CATCHING THE LIKES OF FISH...
KIRA (GLINT)
BASHA

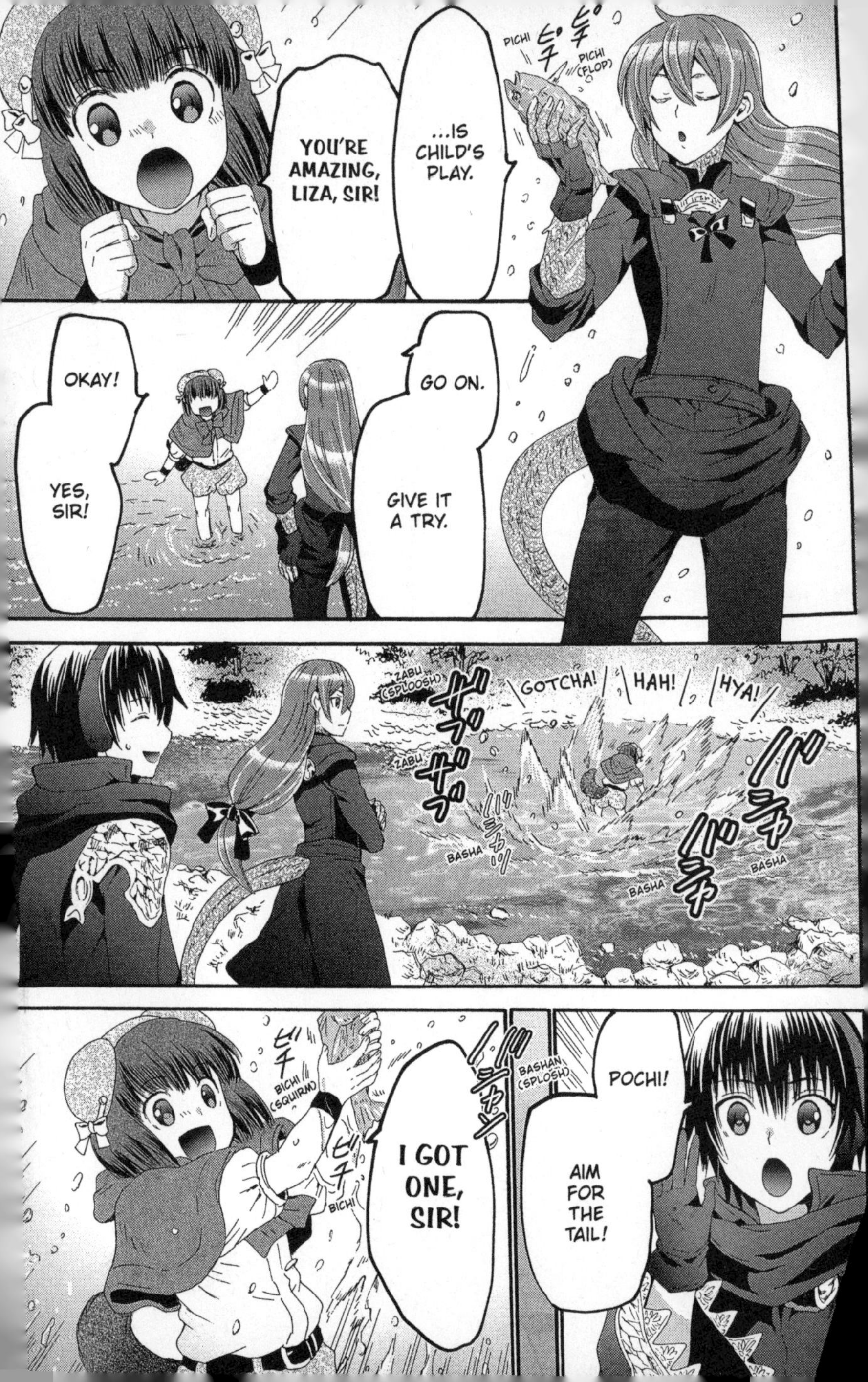
PICHI
PICHI (FLOP)
...IS CHILD'S PLAY.
YOU'RE AMAZING, LIZA, SIR!
GO ON.
GIVE IT A TRY.
OKAY!
YES, SIR!
HYA!
HAH!
GOTCHA!
ZABU (SPLOOSH)
ZABU
BASHA
BASHA
BASHA
POCHI!
AIM FOR THE TAIL!
BASHAN (SPLOSH)
I GOT ONE, SIR!
BICHI (SQUIRM)
BICHI

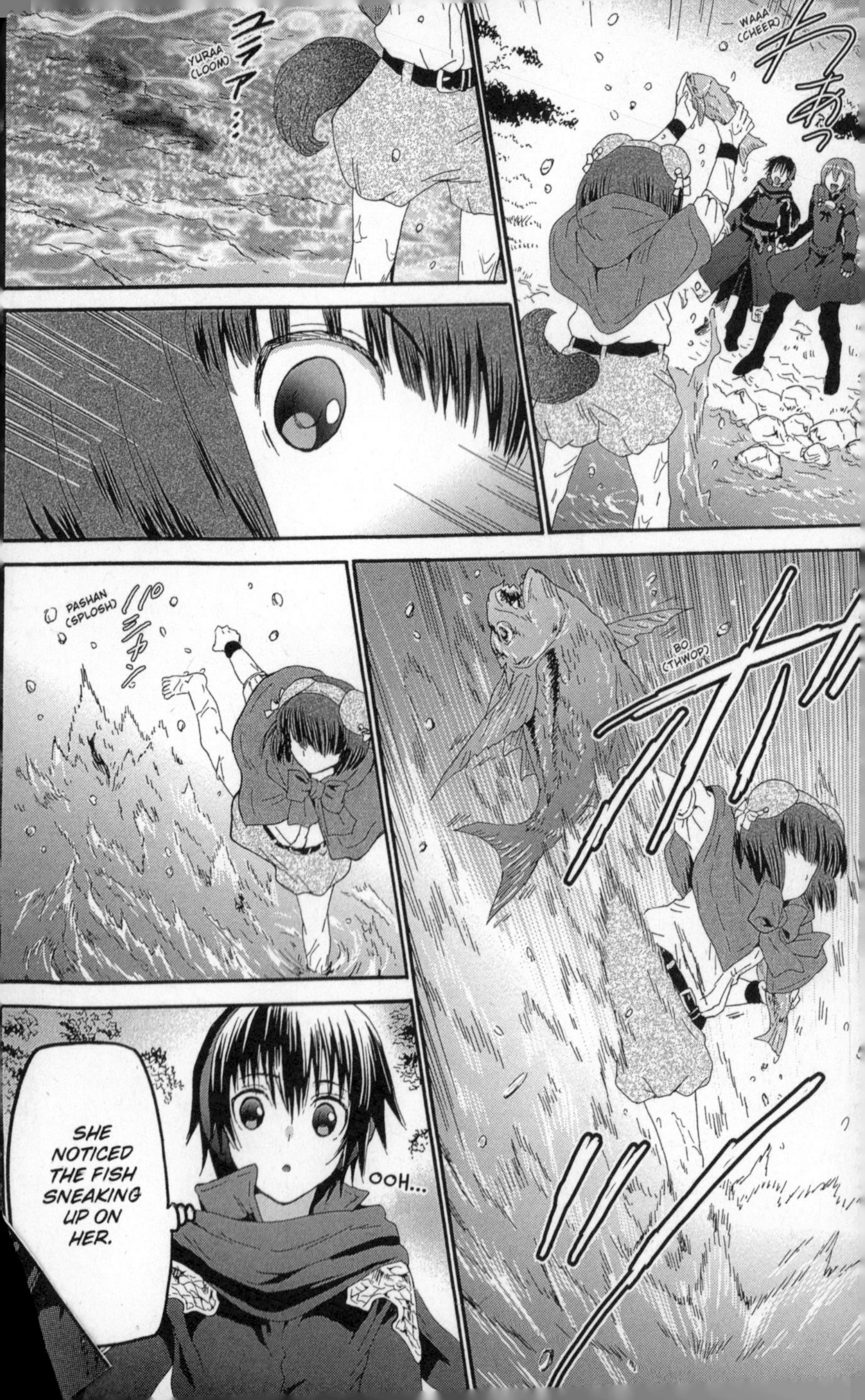
わあっ
WAAA (CHEER)
ユラア…
YURAA (LOOM)
BO (THWOP)
パシャン
PASHAN (SPLOSH)
SHE NOTICED THE FISH SNEAKING UP ON HER.
OOH...

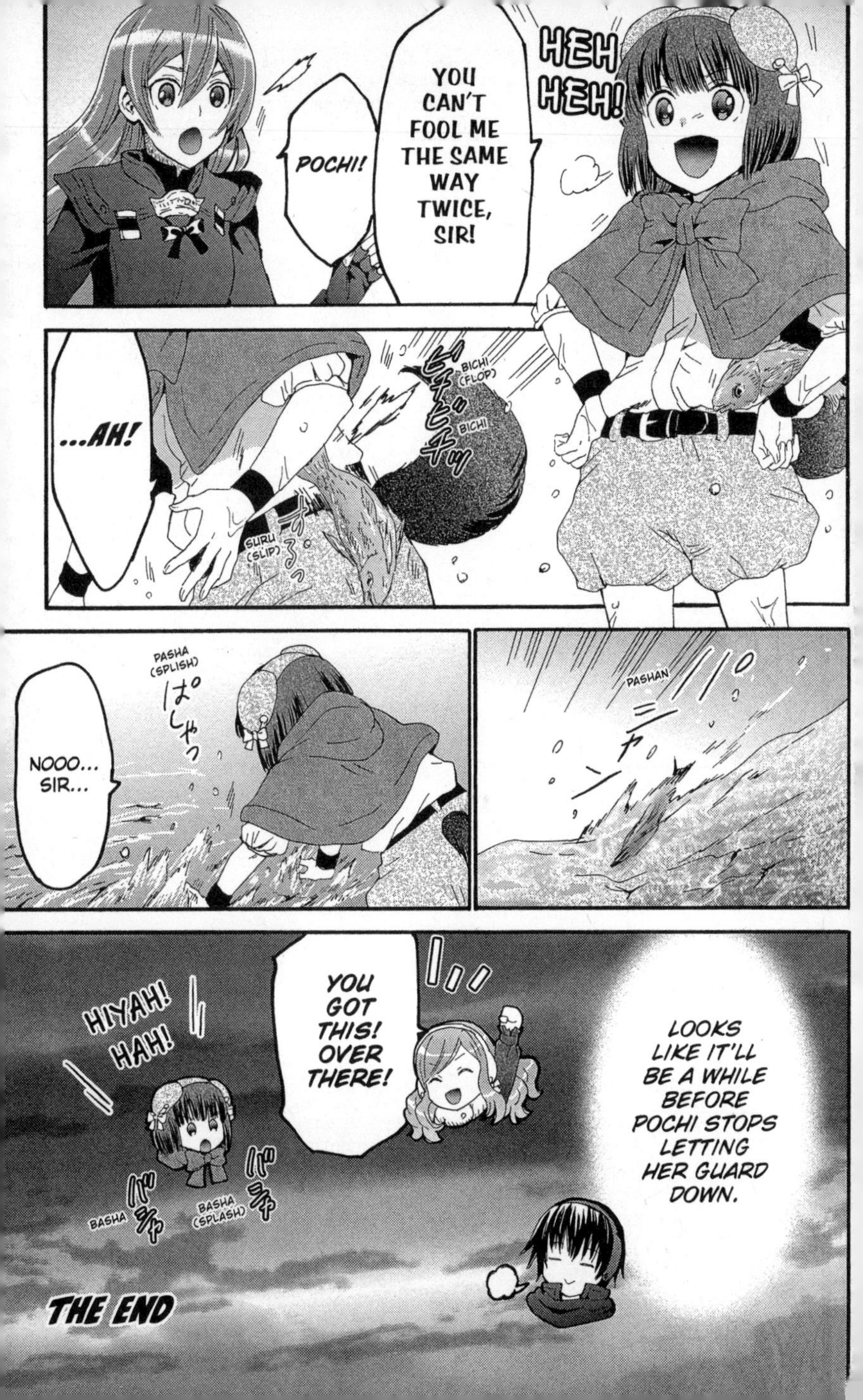
HEH HEH!
YOU CAN'T FOOL ME THE SAME WAY TWICE, SIR!
POCHI!
BICHI (FLOP)
BICHI
SURU (SLIP)
...AH!
PASHAN
PASHA (SPLISH)
NOOO... SIR...
LOOKS LIKE IT'LL BE A WHILE BEFORE POCHI STOPS LETTING HER GUARD DOWN.
YOU GOT THIS! OVER THERE!
HIYAH! HAH!
BASHA (SPLASH)
BASHA
THE END

DEATH M~~ TO THE~~ PARALLEL WORLD RHAPSO~~

Original Story: Hiro Ainana
Art: AYAMEGUMU
Character Design: shri

Translation: Jenny McKeon ◆ Lettering: Rochelle Gancio

DEATH MARCHING TO THE PARALLEL WORLD RHAPSODY Vol. 8
©AYAMEGUMU 2019
©HIRO AINANA, shri 2019
First published in Japan in 2019 by KADOKAWA CORPORATION, Tokyo. English translation rights arranged with KADOKAWA CORPORATION, Tokyo through TUTTLE-MORI AGENCY, INC., Tokyo.

English translation © 2019 by Yen Press, LLC

Yen Press
150 West 30th Street, 19th Floor
New York, NY 10001

Visit us at yenpress.com
facebook.com/yenpress
twitter.com/yenpress
yenpress.tumblr.com
instagram.com/yenpress

First Yen Press Edition: November 2019

Yen Press is an imprint of Yen Press, LLC.
The Yen Press name and logo are trademarks of Yen Press, LLC.

Printed in the United States of America